YOUTH CRIME

VARIETIES, THEORIES, AND PREVENTION

Russell C. Smandych

University of Manitoba

Harcourt Canada

Harcourt Canada

Toronto Montreal Fort Worth New York Orlando
Philadelphia San Diego London Sydney Tokyo

Canadian Cataloguing in Publication Data

Main entry under title:
Youth crime: varieties, theories, and prevention

Includes bibliographical references.
ISBN 0-7747-3693-3

1. Juvenile delinquency — Canada. 2. Juvenile delinquency — Canada – Prevention. 3. Juvenile justice, Administration of — Canada. I. Smandych, Russell Charles.

HV9108.Y68 2000 364.36'0971 C99-932137-4

Senior Acquisitions Editor: Heather McWhinney
Developmental Editor: Jutta Brendemühl
Production Editor: Linh Vu
Production Coordinator: Cheryl Tiongson

Copy Editor: James Leahy
Permissions Editor: Cindy Howard
Cover Design: Rivet Art + Design
Interior Design: Sonya V. Thursby, Opus House Incorporated
Typesetting and Assembly: Carolyn Hutchings Sebestyen
Printing and Binding: Tri-Graphic Printing

Cover Art: *Walking in the Night* by Karl Baumann. Reproduced courtesy of Maxwell Galleries Ltd., San Francisco, from the collection of Mr. and Mrs. Jay Rosen.

Harcourt Canada
55 Horner Avenue, Toronto, ON, Canada M8Z 4X6
Customer Service
Toll-Free Tel.: 1-800-387-7278
Toll-Free Fax: 1-800-665-7307

This book was printed in Canada.
1 2 3 4 5 04 03 02 01 00

To Simon Verdun-Jones for helping me get started in my career as a criminologist, and to Richard Ericson, for helping to motivate my insatiable curiosity about crime control.

PREFACE

This book is designed to fill the need for a collection of readings of research materials that focuses specifically on the topic of youth crime. Despite the recent publication of various readers on youth crime and the youth justice system in Canada, a strong argument can be made for a separate book that deals primarily with youth crime. Previous collections of readings have tended to adopt an inclusive approach, with editors trying to cover all of the wide-ranging aspects of youth justice systems, legislation, and youth crime in Canada. This has tended to result in overly long and uneven collections that are difficult to use in one-semester courses. Also, because of this inclusive approach, previously published collections have tended to quickly become outdated. For example, with the recent introduction of a new federal Youth Criminal Justice Act, all Canadian textbooks and readers that adopt this inclusive approach now need to be revised. Most recent updates on new legislation and trends in youth crime and justice to bridge those gaps can be found on Harcourt Canada's criminology Web site at www.crim canada.com, including links and book recommendations.*

Another problem I have experienced in trying to select the best readings for students taking my "Youth, Crime, and Society" course at the University of Manitoba is that most books deal almost exclusively with Canadian research on youth crime and the youth justice system. As a result, a great deal of relevant cross-national research tends to be ignored. My hope, reflected in this book and its companion reader on youth justice, is that by treating youth crime and youth justice more as distinct topics in the classroom and

* Russell C. Smandych also addresses current questions of youth justice in the reader *Youth Justice: History, Legislation, and Reform* (Harcourt Canada, 2001, in press), incorporating the new YCJA.

in prescribed course-related readings, one can also make more use of important theoretical perspectives and research on youth crime and youth justice that have been produced in other countries.

The present volume of Canadian and cross-national research materials on youth crime fills a large void in reading materials that are available for teaching introductory-level undergraduate college and university courses on youth, crime, and society.

Step by step, students learn

- to interpret and evaluate data and methodological approaches used to study youth crime.
- to become familiar with recent integrative theories of youth crime including life-course and social-psychological strain theories.
- to become familiar with the latest research on specific types of youth crime including youth street crimes and youth gang-related crimes.
- to assess the effectiveness of different youth crime prevention measures ranging from primary and secondary prevention programs to incarceration and boot camps.

This book can be used as a supplement to a core textbook or together with its companion reader *Youth Justice: History, Legislation, and Reform.* It will be equally valuable in more advanced undergraduate and graduate courses in which the instructor wants to focus in more detail on topics and issues surrounding youth crime trends and patterns, theoretical perspectives, street kids and youth gangs, and youth crime prevention. While written especially for Canadian college and university criminology programs, the book's broad international research base will make it attractive in any course dealing with the widely recognized issues surrounding youth and crime that are discussed in the following chapters.

ACKNOWLEDGEMENTS

The timely completion of this book is due mainly to my wife, Kathryn, and my children, Timothy, Amelia, and Alissa, who graciously gave me the time and support I needed to finish the book during our summer in Vancouver. I would also like to thank our parents and grandparents, Barb and Arne Torresen, for giving an itinerant academic and his family a place to stay, and for their many years of parental love and support. At Harcourt Canada, I would like to thank Heather McWhinney for supporting my book proposals, and Jutta Brendemühl for her greatly appreciated work as developmental editor. In addition, I would like to thank Rod Kueneman, Rick Linden, Ray Corrado, and the manuscript reviewers Chris McNaught and William Rowberry for their helpful suggestions and advice.

A Note from the Publisher

Thank you for selecting *Youth Crime: Varieties, Theories, and Prevention,* edited by Russell C. Smandych. The editor and publisher have devoted considerable time to the careful development of this book. We appreciate your recognition of this effort and accomplishment.

We want to hear what you think about *Youth Crime.* Please take a few minutes to fill in the stamped reader reply card at the end of the book. Your comments and suggestions will be valuable to us as we prepare new editions and other books.

CONTENTS

INTRODUCTION

The organization and operation of youth justice systems is strongly influenced by the current extent of youth crime and by prevailing theories of its causes and possible prevention. It is partly because of this that youth crime has become a major concern of criminologists and criminal justice policy-makers in many countries, including Canada. One of the problems associated with teaching a course on youth crime in Canada is finding appropriate reading materials. The Canadian youth justice system is constantly changing, and, as a result, books that attempt to merge the topics of youth crime and youth justice often quickly become outdated. In addition, research on youth crime and youth crime prevention is growing at an incredibly fast pace, which also makes it difficult to meet the demand for up-to-date books that can be used in teaching college and university courses. This book ventures to bring together readings that highlight the range and significance of recent research on the causes and prevention of youth crime.

While this text has been designed primarily for Canadian students, a basic premise underlying the approach adopted in this book is that, regardless of the country one lives in, one cannot develop an adequate understanding of issues surrounding youth crime without adopting a critical comparative approach. A key element of this approach is that it recognizes the value of reviewing existing information on youth crime and youth crime prevention from a number of countries. For example, one could argue that a much better appreciation of the problems involved in defining and carrying out research on youth crime can be gained by looking at the way in which leading researchers from different countries have approached the task of attempting to make sense of youth crime trends and patterns captured in official crime statistics. Similarly, many useful ideas on youth crime prevention, which we would otherwise not have been exposed to, can be gained from looking at the development and outcome of youth crime prevention efforts in other comparable countries. This, of course, does not mean that societal and national differences can be ignored. Indeed, as we will see in specific chapter readings, it is mainly by recognizing the significant differences in the approaches to dealing with youth crime in different countries that we can learn to better appreciate the strengths and weaknesses of Canadian approaches.

The aim of this book is to provide students with a collection of current readings and study questions that cover a wide range of topics relating to youth crime. Toward this end, the book is divided into five parts. An introduction to each part outlines the following three chapters and puts them into a context. Part One presents trends and patterns of officially recorded youth crime in Britain, the United States, and Canada, with particular attention to how leading researchers in each country have approached interpreting and explaining official data on youth crime. Part Two gathers the most important current theoretical perspectives on youth crime that can help us develop a better understanding of the causal factors associated with youth crime. Parts Three and Four examine recent Canadian and cross-national research on youth street crime and youth gang-related crime in order to achieve a deeper insight into the causes and consequences of youth involvement in these specific kinds of criminal activity. Subsequently, in Part Five, attention is turned to highlighting the findings of recent research on the implementation and evaluation of different types of primary, secondary, and tertiary youth crime–prevention efforts, including community-based early intervention programs, mentoring programs, and boot camps for young offenders. A recurrent theme, returned to in each part of the book, is that an understanding of this type of theory and research is essential for developing more adequate national and international as well as local community initiatives in the areas of youth crime prevention and youth justice system reform.

Every book that is written for teaching purposes reflects, to a certain extent, the experiences and biases of the author/instructor. This book is no different in that, organizationally, it compliments the way I have structured the course on "Youth, Crime, and Society" that I have taught to undergraduate criminology students for a number of years. Yet, at the same time, in deciding on the chapters to be included in the book, I have tried to keep in mind the need for a more "generic" book on youth crime that other criminology instructors may find useful in teaching their own, also probably quite unique, courses on youth crime and youth justice. The development of knowledge about youth crime and justice is arguably a collective and cooperative enterprise, and it is my hope that this book contributes, at least in a small way, to this important collective effort.

PART ONE
Youth Crime: Cross-National Trends and Patterns

INTRODUCTION

In recent years, youth crime has become a major concern of criminologists and criminal justice policymakers in many countries. This cross-national concern is reflected in the rapid growth of youth crime–related research in a number of Western countries, including Canada, the United States, Britain, France, Germany, Australia, and New Zealand (Terrill 1999; Winterdyck 1996, 1997). Research on youth crime is also now being carried out in other non-Western countries including Japan, India, and China (Fields and Moore 1996; Heiland, Shelley, and Katoh, 1992). While it is not possible here to deal with the wide, and rather complex, array of research on youth crime in these many different countries, it is nonetheless important to have some exposure to comparable cross-national research.

One of the advantages of looking at research on youth crime from different countries is that it helps us develop a better sense of the general methodological problems and issues associated with carrying out research on youth crime. In Part One, the three chapters by David Farrington, Franklin Zimring, and Peter Carrington offer a comparative look at youth crime in Britain, the United States, and Canada. In addition to providing information on youth crime trends and patterns, these chapters highlight some of the methodological challenges criminologists have faced in attempting to determine the nature and extent of youth crime from official statistics and other data sources, such as self-report or hidden-delinquency studies.

The study of youth crime poses many of the same challenges as the study of crime in general. For example, in the same way that the definition of crime can be ambiguous and open to dispute, the chapters in Part One address the issues surrounding the definition of "youth crime" and the need to differentiate it from other concepts like "juvenile delinquency" and youth "antisocial behaviour." Similarly, in each of the chapters, attention is given to issues surrounding the interpretation of official statistics and other types of data on youth crime.

In Chapter One, Farrington reviews evidence about youth crime and antisocial behaviour by drawing mainly on British and North American research. Farrington begins by looking at the advantages and disadvantages of different data sources on youth crime and antisocial behaviour, focusing specifically on official statistics and self-report studies. He then turns to a critical examination of official statistics for England and Wales, which indicate a significant decline in youth crime in the decade from 1983 to 1993. Farrington sorts through a range of factors that may have contributed to this reported decrease in youth crime. In addition, he surveys a number of recognized correlates of youth crime and identifies specific patterns of youth crime and antisocial behaviour. In the end, Farrington concludes that, rather than reflecting any real decline in the level of youth crime, the reported decrease from 1983 to 1993 resulted primarily from changes in official youth crime reporting practices that stemmed from changes in criminal-procedural law and new youth crime policies. Based on his analysis of self-report data, including data he collected in his famous Cambridge Study in Delinquent Development, which tracked the extent of criminal involvement of more than 400 London boys over a twenty-year period, Farrington suggests that the real level of youth crime in Britain has probably increased over the last fifteen years. Farrington uses existing British and North American data on youth crime as an empirical base for his own theory of youth offending which is briefly described in the chapter. As we will see in Part Two which looks at current theories of youth crime, Farrington's theory, which he has developed in more detail in other publications written over the past decade, has had a significant influence on the development of other current theoretical perspectives on youth crime.

In Chapter Two, Zimring challenges the argument made by other researchers that violent youth crime is increasing in epidemic proportions in the United States. Despite both media reports and arrest statistics, which give the impression that violent youth crime increased in the 1990s, Zimring questions the extent to which this alleged increase is actually supported by official youth crime statistics. In other words, while Farrington points to problems with British crime statistics that show a decline in the level of youth crime, Zimring shows that U.S. crime statistics have been used to falsely argue that "violent" youth crime has increased dramatically in recent years. In order to understand Zimring's argument, it is important to understand how national-level data on youth crime are gathered in the United States. The major source of official data on violent youth crime in the United States are the youth arrest rates for Part I, or Index, offences — including homicide, rape, robbery, and aggravated assault — collected by the Federal Bureau of Investigation. Previous researchers maintained that the data for these Part I offences provided proof of substantial increases in violence attributable to young offenders. This interpretation of the data in turn led to predictions about inevitable future increases in violent youth crime and provided justification for harsher laws to punish young offenders. Zimring's chapter is important in that it provides a counterargument to those widely accepted beliefs. As you will see from reading the chapter, Zimring challenges this viewpoint of the development of youth crime by taking a more careful look at data on youth crime index offences for the period from 1990 to 1996. In essence, by disaggregating and looking separately at the data on the four major index offences, Zimring shows that there is no single trend that can be identified for youth homicide, rape, robbery, and aggravated assault, and that therefore criminal justice officials and policymakers have been misled by previous research.

In his study of Canadian youth crime trends from 1977 to 1996, Carrington, in Chapter Three, offers a similar insightful discussion of the challenges involved in attempting to interpret Canadian youth crime statistics. Like Zimring, Carrington questions previous research that has concluded that youth crime has increased in Canada over the past two decades, and especially since the enactment of the Young Offenders Act (YOA) in 1984. Carrington counters this argument by undertaking a careful re-examination of Uniform Crime Report (UCR) data on youth crime collected by the Canadian Centre for Justice Statistics. Carrington's research points to a number of important findings, including significant interprovincial variation in levels of reported youth crime — with the Maritimes and Western Canada showing opposite low and high extremes — as well as notable fluctuations in the rate of young persons apprehended and charged for committing criminal offences, two statistics which peaked in 1991 and then began to decline. Carrington concludes that contrary to previous research and popular public opinion, "there is no basis in fact for public concern about increased levels of youth crime or the supposed failure of the YOA to control youth crime."

The chapters in Part One are good examples of the critical research that is now being conducted on youth crime by researchers in Canada and in other countries. Most importantly, they show that we can only begin to adequately explain youth crime after we have developed a solid understanding of changes in patterns and levels of youth crime across a number of societies. The following readings also provide the basic foundation for the discussion of the causes and prevention of different types of youth crime that will take place in later parts of the book.

REFERENCES

Fields, C., and R. Moore, eds. 1996. *Comparative Criminal Justice: Traditional and Non-Traditional Systems of Law and Social Control*. Prospect Heights: Waveland Press.

Heiland, H., L. Shelley, and H. Katoh, eds. 1992. *Crime and Control in Comparative Perspectives*. Berlin and New York: Walter de Gruyter.

Terrill, R., ed. 1999. *World Criminal Justice Systems: A Survey,* 4th ed. Cincinnati: Anderson Publishing.

Winterdyck, J., ed. 1996. *Issues and Perspectives on Young Offenders in Canada*. Toronto: Harcourt Brace.

———. 1997. *Juvenile Justice Systems: International Perspectives*. Toronto: Canadian Scholars Press.

CHAPTER ONE
The Nature and Extent of Youth Crime

DAVID P. FARRINGTON
Cambridge University, UK

The major aim of this chapter is to review evidence about youth crime and antisocial behaviour. The main focus is on research in Great Britain and North America. I will review the natural history of offending and antisocial behaviour, the most crucial risk factors, and a plausible theory that explains many of the most important results.

Fortunately or unfortunately, there is no shortage of factors that are significantly correlated with youth crime and antisocial behaviour; indeed, literally thousands of variables differentiate significantly between official offenders and nonoffenders and correlate significantly with reports of antisocial behaviour by teenagers, peers, parents, and teachers. In this chapter, it is only possible to review briefly some of the most important risk factors for offending and antisocial behaviour.

Offending is a type of behaviour, similar in many respects to other types of antisocial or deviant behaviour. Hence, the theories, methods, and knowledge of other types of antisocial behaviour can be applied to the study of youth crime. It is plausible to suggest that, like other types of behaviour, criminal behaviour results from the interaction between a person (with a certain degree of criminal potential or antisocial tendency) and the environment (which provides criminal opportunities). Some people will be consistently more likely to commit offences than others in different environments, and conversely the same person will be more likely to commit offences in some environments than in others.

Source: David P. Farrington, "The Nature and Extent of Youth Crime," excerpt from D.P. Farrington, "Youth Crime and Antisocial Behaviour." In A. Campbell and S. Muncer, eds., *The Social Child: Studies in Developmental Psychology* (1998): 353–91 (to be published under a new title). Reprinted by permission of Psychology Press Ltd.

This chapter has a developmental focus. In order to understand the causes of offending, it is important to study influences on developmental processes such as onset, persistence, escalation, and desistance. The focus is not only on offending when it is in full flow in the teenage years, but also the childhood precursors and adult results. Because of the chapter's focus on human development, unchanging variables such as gender and ethnicity are not reviewed. Most criminological research has concentrated on offending by males, since this is generally more frequent and serious than offending by females (e.g., Farrington 1987). Hence, this chapter is primarily concerned with male offending.

In this short chapter, it is obviously impossible to review everything that is known about predictors and possible causes of delinquency (for more detailed reviews of risk factors, see Blackburn 1993; Rutter and Giller 1983; Wilson and Herrnstein 1985). I will be very selective in focusing on some of the more important and replicable findings obtained in some of the more methodologically adequate studies, especially prospective longitudinal follow-up studies of large community samples, with information from several data sources (e.g., the child, the parent, the teacher, official records) to maximize validity. I will refer especially to knowledge gained in the Cambridge Study in Delinquent Development, which is a prospective longitudinal survey of over 400 London males from age 8 to age 32 (e.g., Farrington and West 1990; Farrington 1995). Fortunately, results obtained in British longitudinal surveys of delinquency (e.g., Kolvin et al. 1990; Wadsworth 1979) are highly concordant with those obtained in comparable surveys in North America (e.g., McCord 1979; Robins 1979), the Scandinavian countries (e.g., Pulkkinen 1988; Wikström 1987), and New Zealand (e.g., Fergusson, Horwood, and Lynskey 1993; Moffitt and Silva 1988), and indeed with results obtained in British cross-sectional surveys (e.g., Boswell 1995; Graham and Bowling 1995; Hagell and Newburn 1994).

DEFINITION AND MEASUREMENT OF YOUTH CRIME

Antisocial behaviour covers a multitude of sins. It includes acts prohibited by the criminal law, such as theft, burglary, robbery, violence, vandalism, and drug use; the definition of youth crime in this chapter focuses on these types of acts. It also includes other clearly deviant acts, such as bullying, reckless driving, heavy drinking, and sexual promiscuity, and more marginally or arguably deviant acts, such as heavy smoking, heavy gambling, employment instability, and conflict with parents. All of these acts tend to be interrelated, in the sense that people who commit any one of them have a considerably increased risk of committing any of the others (West and Farrington 1977).

Certain types of antisocial behaviour are used as diagnostic criteria for the psychiatric category of "conduct disorder" in the International Classification of Diseases of the World Health Organisation and in the Diagnostic and Statistical Manual of the American Psychiatric Association (see, for example, Robins 1991). The major types are stealing, running away from home, lying, arson, truancy, burglary, vandalism, forced sex, fighting, robbery, and cruelty to people and animals. Conduct disorder is diagnosed when the disturbed behaviour includes at least two or three of the specified symptoms displayed in the previous year. Although this is usually termed "childhood conduct disorder," the diagnosis can be made up to age 17, and hence often reflects teenage antisocial behaviour.

Offending is commonly measured using either official records of arrests or convictions or self-reports of offending. The advantages and disadvantages of official records and self-reports are to some extent complementary. In general, official records include the worst offenders and the worst offences, whereas self-reports include more of the normal range of delinquent activity. Self-reports have the advantage of including undetected offences, but the disadvantages of concealment and forgetting. The key issue is whether the same results are obtained with both methods. For example, if official records and self-reports both show a link between parental supervision and delinquency, it is likely that supervision is related to delinquent behaviour (rather than to any biases in measurement).

In reviewing knowledge about youth crime in England and Wales, the focus is on the more serious "indictable" offences rather than the less serious "summary" offences (Barclay 1995). The most important indictable offences are theft, burglary, robbery, violence, vandalism, fraud, and drug use, while the most important summary offences are motoring and drunkenness. Since October 1, 1992, youth crime in England and Wales (dealt with in the Youth Court) covers the years 10 to 17 inclusive; prior to that date, the maximum age for Juvenile Court processing was 16. Officially recorded juvenile offenders are either found guilty in court or cautioned. Although the minimum age of criminal responsibility is 10, few offenders under the age of 14 are found guilty in the Youth Court. In the United States, the focus is on arrests of juveniles (in most states, those under 18) for the "index" offences of homicide, rape, robbery, aggravated assault, burglary, motor vehicle theft, larceny, and arson.

Self-reports of offending reveal many more offences than official records, but not necessarily many more offenders. In the Cambridge Study, only 13 percent of burglaries committed between ages 15 and 18 led to convictions, and only 6 percent of vehicle thefts. However, 62 percent of burglars were convicted of burglary at least once, and 38 percent of vehicle thieves were convicted of this offence (West and Farrington 1977: 28). Between ages 15 and 18, 11 percent of boys admitted to burglary and 7 percent were convicted of burglary; 15 percent admitted to vehicle theft and 6 percent were convicted of this offence. Hence, although self-reports revealed many more offences than official records of convictions, self-reports and official records agreed fairly well in estimating the prevalence of serious offenders.

Self-reports and official records agreed less well in estimating the prevalence of less serious offenders. In the Cambridge Study, 39 percent of boys admitted to shoplifting between ages 10 and 14 and 16 percent between ages 15 and 18, but the corresponding proportions convicted of shoplifting were 3 percent and 2 percent, respectively (Farrington 1989; this was before the widespread use of police cautioning in London). As many as 89 percent of boys admitted to at least one indictable offence between ages 10 and 14, and 67 percent between ages 15 and 18; but the corresponding proportions convicted were 11 percent and 20 percent, respectively. Generally, minor offending is very common, serious offending (such as burglary) is uncommon, and the most frequent and serious offenders are the ones who tend to get convicted (Farrington 1973). To a considerable extent, the convicted boys are the worst self-reported offenders, and conclusions about characteristics of offenders based on convictions are very similar to those based on self-reports of offending (Farrington 1992b).

CHANGES IN YOUTH CRIME OVER TIME

Recorded male juvenile offending has decreased markedly in England and Wales in the last 15 years. The number of boys per 100 aged 10 to 13 found guilty or cautioned decreased by 42 percent between 1983 and 1993, and the decrease for 14- to 17-year-olds was 15 percent. The number of girls per 100 aged 10 to 13 found guilty or cautioned decreased by 34 percent, but the number aged 14 to 17 increased by 25 percent (Home Office 1994, Table 5.24). The biggest decreases in recorded juvenile offenders were between 1985 and 1989. During these years, 10- to 13-year-old boys decreased by 40 percent, 14- to 16-year-old boys by 31 percent, 10- to 13-year-old girls by 60 percent, and 14- to 16-year-old girls by 36 percent (Home Office 1990, Table 5.22). Combining all 10- to 16-year-olds (the juvenile ages at that time), there was a 32 percent decrease in recorded male juvenile offenders and a 44 percent decrease in recorded female juvenile offenders between 1985 and 1989 — remarkable decreases in a very short time period (Farrington 1992c).

In the United States in the last 15 years, recorded juvenile violent crimes have increased, but recorded juvenile property crimes have not (Snyder and Sickmund 1995; Snyder, Sickmund, and Poe-Yamagata 1996). The biggest increase in violence was between 1988 and 1991, when there was a 38 percent increase in the arrest rate. The juvenile arrest rate for homicide increased by an amazing 84 percent between 1987 and 1991, but then remained constant up to 1994. In contrast, the juvenile arrest rate for burglary (like the number of recorded burglaries in the United States) has steadily decreased (e.g., by 44 percent between 1975 and 1992).

Did the decrease in recorded juvenile offenders in English and Wales reflect a real decrease in juvenile offending? This seems highly unlikely. For example, burglary and vehicle theft are crimes typically committed by young people. Between 1981 and 1991, the rate of domestic burglary per household in England and Wales increased by 66 percent according to the British Crime Survey (BCS) and by 63 percent according to police-recorded offences

(Farrington, Langan, and Wikström 1994). The corresponding increases for the rate of vehicle theft were 65 percent according to the BCS and 70 percent according to the police. And yet, recorded juvenile offending (findings of guilt and cautions per 100 population) decreased by 22 percent between 1981 and 1991 (Home Office 1993, Table 5.22). As another example, between 1985 and 1989, the number of recorded juvenile shoplifters decreased by 59 percent, but the number of juvenile shoplifters apprehended by major stores and reported to the police did not change significantly (Farrington and Burrows 1993).

In the light of the large increases in crimes reported by victims and crimes recorded by the police, it seems likely that the true prevalence of youth crime in England and Wales has increased in the last 15 years. Why, then, has there been a decrease in recorded juvenile offenders? Since 1985, police forces have increasingly begun to use informal (unrecorded) warnings and to take no further action with apprehended juveniles whom they believe to be guilty (Barclay 1990), thereby eliminating them from the official records. Also, the introduction in 1986 of the Police and Criminal Evidence Act 1984, which provided increased safeguards for accused persons, caused a marked decrease in the number of detected offenders (Irving and MacKenzie 1989).

The introduction in 1985 of the Crown Prosecution Service, which transferred responsibility of the prosecution of offenders from the police to lawyers, caused a decrease in the number of persons prosecuted; the number of discontinued or withdrawn cases increased from 21 300 in 1981 to 108 300 in 1991 (Home Office 1993, Table 6.2). The Criminal Justice Act 1988 downgraded the offence of unauthorized taking of a motor vehicle from the indictable to the summary category, thereby eliminating about 25 000 (mostly young) offenders from the statistics of recorded offenders. Consequently, the decrease in recorded juvenile offenders between 1985 and 1989 is attributable to procedural changes and is almost certainly illusory.

The Home Affairs Committee of the House of Commons (1993) tried to reconcile the increase in recorded crime with the decrease in recorded juvenile offenders by suggesting that there was an increasing number of persistent juvenile offenders. However, there is little hard evidence either about true changes in juvenile delinquency in England and Wales or about the most likely explanations for any such changes. In order to advance knowledge in the future, repeated surveys of nationally representative samples of juveniles are needed, which measure both self-reported offending and possible causal influences on offending. Repeated surveys of this kind have been carried out in the United States. For example, in the "Monitoring the Future" project, a nationally representative sample of American high school students is interviewed each year and asked about their delinquency and drug use (Johnson, O'Malley, and Bachman 1987).

Setting aside a few questions in the British Crime Survey (Mayhew and Elliott 1990), the first large-scale national self-reported delinquency survey was completed in England in 1993 (Bowling, Graham, and Ross 1994). The first large-scale drugs survey was carried out in four areas: Bradford, Glasgow, Lewisham (London), and Nottingham, in 1992 (Leitner, Shapland, and Wiles 1993). These kinds of surveys need to be repeated at intervals. It is very important that validity checks on the accuracy of the self-report data are carried out (e.g., by comparing them with official records of offending by the same people).

NATURAL HISTORY OF OFFENDING

The prevalence of offending increases to a peak in the teenage years and then decreases in the twenties. This pattern is seen both cross-sectionally and longitudinally (Farrington 1986a). The peak age of official offending (convictions plus cautions) for English males was 15 until 1987, but it increased to 18 in 1988 as a result of the decrease in detected juvenile shoplifting offenders (Barclay 1990) and it remained at 18 until 1994 (Home Office 1995). The peak age for females is 14. In England and Wales in 1994, the rate of findings of guilt or cautions of males for indictable offences increased from 0.5 per 100 at age 10 to 6.2 at age 15 and a peak of 8.9 at age 18, then decreased to 7.0 at age 20 and 1.6 at age 30–40 (Home Office 1995, Table 5.25). The corresponding figures for females were 0.1 per 100 at age 10, a peak of 2.1 at age 14, 1.6 at age 18, 1.2 at age 20, and 0.4 at age 30–40.

The cumulative or lifetime prevalence of convictions is much greater than most people realize. On the basis of 1977 figures, it was estimated that 44 percent of males and 15 percent of females in England and Wales would be convicted of "standard list" (nontraffic) offences during their lifetimes (Farrington 1981). These estimates were later verified by a longitudinal follow-up of a 1953 birth cohort in official records (Home Office Statistical Bulletin 1995); 34 percent of males and 9 percent of females were convicted of nontraffic offences up to age 39. Because of the decrease in conviction rates during the 1980s, the conviction figures for later cohorts would be somewhat lower, although cumulative prevalence would be greater if cautions were included.

In the Cambridge Study, the rate of convictions increased to a peak at age 17 and then declined (Farrington 1992a). It was 1.7 per 100 males at age 10, 6.8 at age 13, 16.8 at age 17, 10.1 at age 22, and 4.2 at age 30. The median age for most types of offences (burglary, robbery, theft of and from vehicles, shoplifting) was 17, whereas is was 20 for violence and 21 for fraud. Using national data, Tarling (1993) found that peak ages varied from 14 for shoplifting to 17 for burglary, robbery and vehicle theft, 18 for violence, and 20 for drugs and fraud.

Although the cumulative prevalence of convictions in the Cambridge Study was high (37 percent up to age 32), it was nevertheless true that only 6 percent of the sample — the chronic offenders — accounted for nearly half of all the convictions (Farrington and West 1993). Similarly, chronic offenders were disproportionally likely to commit other types of antisocial behaviour. In numerous other projects, such as the Philadelphia cohort study of

Wolfgang, Thornberry, and Figlio (1987) and the Finnish research of Pulkkinen (1988), there was a similar concentration of offending in a small proportion of the sample.

Self-report studies also show that the most common types of offending decline from the teens to the twenties. In the Cambridge Study, the prevalence of burglary, shoplifting, theft of and from vehicles, theft from slot machines, and vandalism all decreased from the teens to the twenties, but the same decreases were not seen for theft from work, assault, drug abuse, and fraud (Farrington 1989).

Many theories have been proposed to explain why offending peaks in the teenage years (see Farrington 1986a). For example, offending has been linked to testosterone levels in males, which increase during adolescence and early adulthood and decrease thereafter, and to changes in physical abilities or opportunities for crime. The most popular explanation focuses on social influence. From birth, children are under the influence of their parents, who generally discourage offending. However, during their teenage years, young people gradually break away from the control of their parents and become influenced by their peers, who may encourage offending in many cases. After age 20, offending declines again as peer influence gives way to a new set of family influences hostile to offending, originating in spouses and cohabitees.

In the Cambridge Study, the peak age of onset (the first conviction) was at 14 (Farrington 1992a). An early age of onset foreshadows a long criminal career and many offences (Home Office Statistical Bulletin 1987). The males first convicted at the earliest ages (10–13) in the Cambridge Study tended to become the most persistent offenders, committing an average of 8.1 offences leading to convictions in an average criminal career lasting almost exactly 10 years up to age 32 (Farrington 1992a). Those first convicted at age 10–11 had an average career length of 11.5 years. Over a quarter of all convicted males had criminal careers lasting longer than 10 years. The average duration of criminal careers declined precipitously from onset at age 16 (7.9 years) to onset at age 17 (2.9 years), suggesting that those males first convicted as juveniles were much more persistent offenders than those first convicted as adults. These results agree with Moffitt's (1993) theory suggesting that offenders can be divided into "life-course-persistent" ones with an early onset and a long criminal career and "adolescence-limited" ones with a later onset and a short criminal career.

CO-OFFENDING AND MOTIVES FOR CRIME

Juveniles tend to commit their offences with others. In the Cambridge Study, about half of all offences were committed with (usually one or two) others, and the prevalence of co-offending decreased steadily from age 10 to age 32 (Reiss and Farrington 1991). This was not because co-offenders had short criminal careers but because the boys changed from co-offending in their teenage years to lone offending in their twenties. Boys who committed their first offence with others tended to have a longer criminal career than those who committed their first offence alone.

Burglary, robbery, and theft from vehicles were especially likely to involve co-offenders. Generally, co-offenders were similar in age, gender, and ethnicity, and lived close to each other and to the locations of offences. Co-offending relationships tended not to persist for very long, rarely more than one year. About one-third of the most persistent offenders continually offended with less criminally experienced co-offenders, and hence appeared to be repeatedly recruiting others into a life of crime. Recruiting was especially common for burglary offences.

In the Cambridge Study, the most common motives given for property offences (46 percent of self-reported offences, 43 percent of offences leading to convictions) were utilitarian, rational, or economic ones: offences were committed for material gain. This is concordant with the rational decision-making theory of Cornish and Clarke (1986). The next most common motives (31 percent of self-reported offences, 22 percent of conviction offences) might be termed "hedonistic": offences were committed for excitement, for enjoyment, or to relieve boredom (West and Farrington 1977). In general, utilitarian motives predominated for most types of property offences, such as burglary and theft, except that vandalism and motor vehicle theft were committed predominantly for hedonistic reasons, and shoplifting was partly utilitarian and partly hedonistic. Offences at younger ages (under 17) were relatively more likely to be committed for hedonistic reasons, whereas offences at older ages (17 or older) were relatively more likely to be committed for utilitarian reasons.

With regard to physical violence, the key dimension was whether the boy fought alone or in a group (Farrington, Berkowitz, and West 1982). In individual fights, the boy was usually provoked, became angry, and hit out in order to hurt his opponent and to discharge his own internal feelings of tension. In group fights, the boy often said that he became involved in order to help a friend or because he was attacked, and rarely said that he was angry. The group fights were more serious, occurring in pubs or streets, and they were more likely to involve weapons, produce injuries, and lead to police intervention. Fights often occurred when minor incidents escalated, because both sides wanted to demonstrate their toughness and masculinity and were unwilling to react to perceived challenges in a conciliatory way.

JUVENILE DELINQUENCY AND ANTISOCIAL BEHAVIOUR

Juvenile delinquents are predominantly versatile rather than specialized in their offending (e.g., Klein 1984; Farrington, Snyder, and Finnegan 1988). In other words, people who commit one type of offence have a significant tendency also to commit other types. For example, 86 percent of convicted violent offenders in the Cambridge Study also had convictions for nonviolent offences (Farrington 1991b).

Just as young offenders tend to be versatile in their types of offending, they also tend to be versatile in their antisocial behaviour generally. The Cambridge Study shows that delinquency is only one element of a much larger syndrome of antisocial behaviour that tends to persist over time. For example, the boys who were convicted up to age 18 (most commonly for offences of dishonesty, such as burglary and theft) were significantly more deviant than the nondelinquents on almost every factor that we investigated at that age (West and Farrington 1977). The convicted delinquents drank more beer, they got drunk more often, and they were more likely to say that drink made them violent. They smoked more cigarettes, they had started smoking at an earlier age, and they were more likely to be heavy gamblers. They were more likely to have been convicted for minor motoring offences, to have driven after drinking at least 10 units of alcohol (e.g., five pints of beer), and to have been injured in road accidents. The delinquents were more likely to have taken prohibited drugs, such as marijuana or LSD, although few of them had convictions for drug offences. Also, they were more likely to have had sexual intercourse, especially with a variety of different girls, and especially beginning at an early age, but they were less likely to use contraceptives.

The convicted delinquents at age 18 tended to hold relatively well-paid but low-status (unskilled manual) jobs, and they were more likely to have erratic work histories including periods of unemployment. They were more likely to be living away from home, and they tended not to get on well with their parents. They were more likely to be tattooed, possibly reflecting their "machismo" orientation. The delinquents were more likely to go out in the evenings, and were especially likely to spend time hanging about on the street. They tended to go around in groups of four or more, and were more likely to be involved in group violence or vandalism. They were much more likely to have been involved in fights, to have started fights, to have carried weapons, and to have used weapons in fights. They were also more likely to express aggressive and anti-establishment attitudes on a questionnaire (negative to police, school, rich people, and civil servants).

The convicted delinquents were also deviant in their schools. At age 8–10, before anyone was convicted, the future delinquents were more likely than nondelinquents to be rated as troublesome and dishonest in their primary schools; 45 percent of troublesome boys at age 8–10 were convicted as juveniles, compared with 14 percent of the remainder (Farrington 1995). At age 14, when they were in their last year of compulsory schooling, the delinquents were rated by their teachers as aggressive and frequent liars, and they tended to admit bullying. Interestingly, the bullies at age 14 tended still to be bullies at age 32 and to report that their children were bullies (Farrington 1993c).

Delinquents also tended to be truants, in both their primary and secondary schools (Farrington 1996). Troublesome boys in the primary school tended to become truants in the secondary school. Generally, truants and delinquents were similar in childhood, adolescent, and adult features, but the most important difference was that truants, unlike delinquents, tended to be nervous. This suggested that, for some children, truancy was a behavioural symptom of a nervous–withdrawn temperament rather than of an antisocial personality, in agreement with the distinction between truancy and school refusal (Bools et al. 1990).

These results are consistent with findings obtained in numerous other studies. For example, in a St. Louis survey, Robins and Ratcliff (1980) reported that juvenile delinquency tended to be associated with truancy, precocious sex, drinking, and drug use. In two American studies separated by 13 years, Donovan, Jessor, and Costa (1988) concluded that a single common factor accounted for the positive correlations among a number of adolescent antisocial behaviours, including problem drinking, marijuana use, precocious sexual intercourse, and delinquent behaviour. Hence, as R. Jessor and S.L. Jessor (1977) argued, there is a syndrome of problem behaviour in adolescence.

CONTINUITY IN OFFENDING

Despite the changes in prevalence with age, there is significant continuity between offending in one age range and offending in another. In the Cambridge Study, nearly three-quarters (73 percent) of those convicted as juveniles at age 10–16 were reconvicted at age 17–24, in comparison with only 16 percent of those not convicted as juveniles (Farrington 1992a). Nearly half (45 percent) of those convicted as juveniles were reconvicted at age 25–32, in comparison with only 8 percent of those not convicted as juveniles. Furthermore, this continuity over time did not merely reflect continuity in police reaction to crime. Farrington (1989) showed that, for 10 specified offences, the significant continuity between offending in one age range and offending in a later age range held for self-reports as well as official convictions.

Other studies (e.g., McCord 1991) show similar continuity. For example, in Sweden, Stattin and Magnusson (1991) reported that nearly 70 percent of males registered for crime before age 15 were registered again between ages 15 and 20, and nearly 60 percent were registered between ages 21 and 29. Also, the number of juvenile offences is an effective predictor of the number of adult offences (Wolfgang, Thornberry, and Figlio 1987). Farrington and Wikström (1994) showed that there was considerable continuity in offending between ages 10 and 25 in both London and Stockholm.

It is not always realized that relative continuity is quite compatible with absolute change. In other words, the relative ordering of people on some underlying construct such as criminal potential can remain significantly stable over time, even though the absolute level of criminal potential declines on average for everyone. For example, in the Cambridge Study, the prevalence of self-reported offending declined significantly between ages 18 and 32, but there was a significant tendency for the worst offenders at 18 also to be the worst offenders at 32 (Farrington 1990a).

DEVELOPMENTAL SEQUENCES

In studying development, it is important to investigate developmental sequences over time, for example, where one behaviour facilitates or acts as a kind of stepping stone to another. It is desirable to identify noncriminal behaviours that lead to criminal behaviours, and long-term developmental sequences including types of offending. For example, hyperactivity at age 2 may lead to cruelty to animals at 6, shoplifting at 10, burglary at 15, robbery at 20, and eventually spouse assault, child abuse and neglect, alcohol abuse, and employment and accommodation problems later on in life. Typically, a career of childhood antisocial behaviour leads to a criminal career, which often coincides with a career of teenage antisocial behaviour and leads to a career of adult antisocial behaviour. The criminal career is a legally defined subset of a longer-term and more wide-ranging antisocial career. A deeper understanding of the development of the criminal career requires a deeper understanding of the wider antisocial career.

It is important to investigate developmental sequences in antisocial and criminal careers. In a study of Montreal delinquents, LeBlanc and Frechette (1989) discovered that shoplifting and vandalism tended to occur before adolescence (average age of onset 11), burglary and motor vehicle theft in adolescence (average onset 14–15), and sex offences and drug trafficking in the later teenage years (average onset 17–19). With regard to other types of antisocial behaviour, Loeber et al. (1992), on the basis of retrospective reports by parents of clinic-referred boys, found that rule-breaking at home tended to occur at a median age of onset of 4.5 years, then cruelty to animals (5.0), bullying (5.5), lying, stealing, fighting (6.0), vandalism (6.5), and eventually burglary (10.0).

Loeber et al. (1993) proposed that there were three different developmental pathways for antisocial behaviour, which they labelled "overt, covert, and authority conflict." The overt pathway specified an escalation from minor aggression to fighting and violence, the covert pathway specified an escalation from lying to theft and burglary, and the authority conflict pathway specified an escalation from stubbornness to disobedience and truancy. The frequency of occurrence of any particular behaviour predicted the likelihood of transition to a more serious level. Three types of behavioural sequences can be distinguished (see Farrington et al. 1990). First of all, different acts following each other may be different behavioural manifestations of the same underlying construct (e.g., antisocial personality) at different ages. Second, different acts may be different behavioural manifestations of the same or similar underlying constructs at different ages and also part of a developmental sequence, where one act is a stepping stone to or facilitates another (e.g., where smoking cigarettes leads to marijuana use). Third, different acts may be indicators of different constructs and part of a causal sequence, where changes in an indicator of one construct cause changes in an indicator of a different construct (e.g., where school failure leads to truancy).

EXPLAINING THE DEVELOPMENT OF OFFENDING

In explaining the development of offending, a major problem is that most risk factors tend to coincide and tend to be interrelated. For example, adolescents living in physically deteriorated and socially disorganized neighbourhoods disproportionally tend also to come from families with poor parental supervision and erratic parental discipline and tend also to have high impulsivity and low intelligence. The concentration and co-occurrence of these kinds of adversities makes it difficult to establish their independent, interactive, and sequential influences on offending and antisocial behaviour.

A first step is to establish which factors predict offending independently of other factors. In the Cambridge Study, it was generally true that each of six categories of variables (impulsivity, intelligence, parenting, antisocial family, socioeconomic deprivation, child antisocial behaviour) predicted offending independently of each other category (Farrington 1990b; 1993a). Any theory needs to give priority to explaining these results.

The modern trend (e.g., Catalano and Hawkins 1996; Elliott, Huizinga, and Ageton 1985; Pearson and Weiner 1985) is to try to achieve increased explanatory power by integrating propositions derived from several earlier theories. My own theory of offending and antisocial behaviour (Farrington 1986b; 1992b; 1993b) is also integrative. It contains elements of Cohen's (1955) status frustration–delinquent subculture theory, Cloward and Ohlin's (1960) opportunity–strain theory, Trasler's (1962) social learning theory, Hirschi's (1969) control–social bonding theory, Sutherland and Cressey's (1974) differential association theory, Wilson and Herrnstein's (1985) discounting future consequences theory, Cornish and Clarke's (1986) situational decision-making theory, and Gottfredson and Hirschi's (1990) self-control theory. It distinguishes explicitly between the development of antisocial tendency and the occurrence of antisocial acts. The theory suggests that offending is the end result of a four-stage process: energizing, directing, inhibiting, and decision making.

The main long-term energizing factors that ultimately lead to variations in antisocial tendency are desires for material goods, status among intimates, and excitement. The main short-term energizing factors that lead to variations in antisocial tendency are boredom, frustration, anger, and alcohol consumption. The desire for excitement may be greater among children from poorer families, perhaps because excitement is more highly valued by lower-class people than by middle-class ones, because poorer children think they lead more boring lives, or because poorer children are less able to postpone immediate gratification in favour of long-term goals (which could be linked to the emphasis in lower-class culture on the concrete and present as opposed to the abstract and future).

In the directing stage, these motivations produce antisocial tendency if socially disapproved methods of satisfying them are habitually chosen. The methods chosen depend on maturation and behavioural skills (e.g., a 5-year-old would have difficulty stealing a car). Some people (e.g., children from poorer families) are less able to satisfy their desires for material goods, excitement, and social status by legal or socially approved methods, and so tend to choose illegal or socially disapproved methods. The relative inability of poorer children to achieve goals by legitimate methods could be because they tend to fail in school and tend to have erratic, low-status employment histories. School failure in turn may often be a consequence of the unstimulating intellectual environment that lower-class parents tend to provide for their children, and their lack of emphasis on abstract concepts.

In the inhibiting stage, antisocial tendencies can be inhibited by internalized beliefs and attitudes that have been built up in a social learning process as a result of a history of rewards and punishments. The belief that offending is wrong, or a strong conscience, tends to be built up if parents are in favour of legal norms, if they exercise close supervision over their children, and if they punish socially disapproved behaviour using love-oriented discipline. Antisocial tendency can also be inhibited by empathy, which may develop as a result of parental warmth and loving relationships. The belief that offending is legitimate, and anti-establishment attitudes generally, tend to be built up if children have been exposed to attitudes and behaviour favouring offending (e.g., in a modelling process), especially by members of their family, by their friends, and in their communities.

In the decision-making stage, which specifies the interaction between the individual and the environment, whether a person with a certain degree of antisocial tendency commits an antisocial act in a given situation depends on opportunities, costs and benefits, and on the subjective probabilities of the different outcomes. The costs and benefits include immediate situational factors such as the material goods that can be stolen and the likelihood and consequences of being caught by the police, as perceived by the individual. They also include social factors, such as likely disapproval by parents or spouses, and encouragement or reinforcement from peers. In general, people tend to make rational decisions. However, more impulsive people are less likely to consider the possible consequences of their actions, especially consequences that are likely to be long delayed.

CONCLUSION

Offending is one element of a larger syndrome of antisocial behaviour that arises in childhood and tends to persist into adulthood, with numerous different behavioural manifestations. However, although there is continuity over time in antisocial behaviour, changes are also occurring. It is commonly found that about half of a sample of antisocial children go on to become antisocial teenagers, and about half of antisocial teenagers go on to become antisocial adults. More research is needed on factors that vary within individuals and that predict these changes over time. Research is especially needed on changing behavioural manifestations and developmental sequences at different ages. More efforts should especially be made to identify factors that protect vulnerable children from developing into antisocial teenagers.

The stability of antisocial behaviour from childhood to adulthood suggests that delinquency prevention efforts should be implemented as early in a child's life as possible. Teenage pregnancy, substance use in pregnancy, and perinatal complications (including low birth weight), especially in conjunction with poverty, tend to be followed by a variety of undesirable outcomes, including low intelligence and attainment, hyperactivity and impulsivity, child conduct problems, aggression, and delinquency. It is important to mount delinquency prevention programs targeting these various risk factors, and to follow up the children into adolescence and adulthood to establish the long-term effects on delinquency and crime (Farrington 1994b).

Because of the link between offending and numerous other social problems, any measure that succeeds in reducing crime will have benefits that go far beyond this. Any measure that reduces crime will probably also reduce alcohol abuse, drunk driving, drug abuse, sexual promiscuity, family violence, truancy, school failure, unemployment, marital disharmony, and divorce. It is clear that problem children tend to grow up into problem adults, and that problem adults tend to produce more problem children. Major efforts to tackle the roots of crime are urgently needed, especially those focusing on early childhood development.

STUDY QUESTIONS

1. *What are the advantages and disadvantages of using official records and self-report studies to measure youth crime?*
2. *How does Farrington explain the decrease in recorded juvenile offenders in England and Wales between 1983 and 1993?*
3. *What were the major findings of the Cambridge Study in Delinquent Development referred to by Farrington throughout the chapter? Why are the research methodology and findings of the Cambridge Study particularly unique and important?*

REFERENCES

Barclay, G.C. 1990. "The Peak Age of Known Offending by Males." *Home Office Research Bulletin 28*: 20–23.

———. 1995. *The Criminal Justice System in England and Wales*, 3rd ed. London: Home Office.

Blackburn, R. 1993. *The Psychology of Criminal Conduct.* Chichester, UK: Wiley.

Bools, C., J. Foster, I. Brown, and I. Berg. 1990. "The Identification of Psychiatric Disorders in Children Who Fail to Attend School: A Cluster Analysis of a Non-Clinical Population." *Psychological Medicine 20*(1): 171–81.

Boswell, G. 1995. *Violent Victims: The Prevalence of Abuse and Loss in the Lives of Section 53 Offenders.* London: The Prince's Trust.

Bowling, B., J. Graham, and A. Ross. 1994. "Self-Reported Offending among Young People in England and Wales." In J. Junger-Tas, G.J. Terlouw, and M.W. Klein, eds., *Delinquent Behavior among Young People in the Western World,* 42–64. Amsterdam: Kugler.

Catalano, R.F., and J.D. Hawkins. 1996. "The Social Development Model: A Theory of Antisocial Behaviour." In J.D. Hawkins, ed., *Delinquency and Crime: Current Theories,* 149–97. Cambridge, UK: Cambridge University Press.

Cloward, R.A., and L.E. Ohlin. 1960. *Delinquency and Opportunity.* New York: Free Press.

Cohen, A.K. 1955. *Delinquent Boys.* Glencoe, IL: Free Press.

Cornish, D.B., and R.V. Clarke, eds. 1986. *The Reasoning Criminal.* New York: Springer.

Donovan, J.E., R. Jessor, and F.M. Costa. 1988. "Syndrome of Problem Behaviour in Adolescence: A Replication." *Journal of Consulting and Clinical Psychology 56*: 762–65.

Elliott, D.S., D. Huizinga, and S.S. Ageton. 1985. *Explaining Delinquency and Drug Use.* Beverly Hills, CA: Sage.

Farrington, D.P. 1973. "Self-Reports of Deviant Behaviour: Predictive and Stable?" *Journal of Criminal Law and Criminology 64*: 99–110.

———. 1981. "The Prevalence of Convictions." *British Journal of Criminology 21*: 173–75.

———. 1986a. "Age and Crime." In M. Tonry and N. Morris, eds., *Crime and Justice,* vol. 7, 189–250. Chicago, IL: University of Chicago Press.

———. 1986b. "Stepping Stones to Adult Criminal Careers." In D. Olweus, J. Block, and M.R. Yarrow, eds., *Development of Antisocial and Prosocial Behaviour,* 359–84. New York: Academic Press.

———. 1987. "Epidemiology." In H.C. Quay, ed., *Handbook of Juvenile Delinquency,* 33–61. New York: Wiley.

———. 1989. "Self-Reported and Official Offending from Adolescence to Adulthood." In M.W. Klein, ed., *Cross-National Research in Self-Reported Crime and Delinquency,* 399–423. Dordrecht, Netherlands: Kluwer.

———. 1990a. "Age, Period, Cohort, and Offending." In D.M. Gottfredson and R.V. Clarke, eds., *Policy and Theory in Criminal Justice: Contributions in Honour of Leslie T. Wilkins,* 51–75. Aldershot, UK: Avebury.

———. 1990b. "Implications of Criminal Career Research for the Prevention of Offending." *Journal of Adolescence 13*(2): 93–113.

———. 1991. "Childhood Aggression and Adult Violence: Early Precursors and Later Life Outcomes." In D.J. Pepler and K.H. Rubin, eds., *The Development and Treatment of Childhood Aggression,* 5–29. Hillsdale, NJ: Lawrence Erlbaum Associates Inc.

———. 1992a. "Criminal Career Research in the United Kingdom." *British Journal of Criminology 32*(4): 521–36.

———. 1992b. "Juvenile Delinquency." In J.C. Coleman, ed., *The School Years,* 2nd ed., 123–63. London: Routledge.

———. 1992c. "Trends in English Juvenile Delinquency and Their Explanation." *International Journal of Comparative and Applied Criminal Justice 16*: 151–63.

———. 1993a. "Childhood Origins of Teenage Antisocial Behaviour and Adult Social Dysfunction." *Journal of the Royal Society of Medicine 86*(1): 13–17.

———. 1993b. "Motivations for Conduct Disorder and Delinquency." *Development and Psychopathology 5*: 225–41.

———. 1993c. "Understanding and Preventing Bullying." In M. Tonry and N. Morris, eds., *Crime and Justice*, vol. 17, 381–458. Chicago, IL: University of Chicago Press.

———. 1994. "Early Developmental Prevention of Juvenile Delinquency." *Criminal Behaviour and Mental Health 4*: 209–27.

———. 1995. "The Development of Offending and Antisocial Behaviour from Childhood: Key Findings from the Cambridge Study in Delinquent Development." *Journal of Child Psychology and Psychiatry 36*(6): 929–64.

———. 1996. "Later Life Outcomes of Truants in the Cambridge Study." In I. Berg and J. Nursten, eds., *Unwillingly to School*, 4th ed., 96–118. London: Gaskell.

Farrington, D.P., L. Berkowitz, and D.J. West. 1982. "Differences between Individual and Group Fights." *British Journal of Social Psychology 21*: 323–33.

Farrington, D.P., and J.N. Burrows. 1993. "Did Shoplifting Really Decrease?" *British Journal of Criminology 33*(1): 57–69.

Farrington, D.P., P.A. Langan, and P.O. Wikström. 1994. "Changes in Crime and Punishment in America, England and Sweden between the 1980s and the 1990s." *Studies in Crime and Crime Prevention 3*: 104–31.

Farrington, D.P., R. Loeber, D.S. Elliott, J.D. Hawkins, D.B. Kandel, M.W. Klein, J. McCord, D.C. Rowe, and R.E. Tremblay. 1990. "Advancing Knowledge about the Onset of Delinquency and Crime." In B.B. Lahey and A.E. Kazdin, eds., *Advances in Clinical Child Psychology*, vol. 13, 283–342. New York: Plenum.

Farrington, D.P., H.N. Snyder, and T.A. Finnegan. 1988. "Specialization in Juvenile Court Careers." *Criminology 26*: 461–87.

Farrington, D.P., and D.J. West. 1990. "The Cambridge Study in Delinquent Development: A Long-Term Follow-Up of 411 London Males." In H.J. Kerner and G. Kaiser, eds., *Criminality: Personality, Behaviour, Life History*, 115–38. Berlin: Springer.

———. 1993. "Criminal, Penal and Life Histories of Chronic Offenders: Risk and Protective Factors and Early Identification." *Criminal Behaviour and Mental Health 3*: 492–523.

Farrington, D.P., and P.O. Wikström. 1994. "Criminal Careers in London and Stockholm: A Cross-National Comparative Study." In E.G.M. Weitekamp and H.J. Kerner, eds., *Cross-National Longitudinal Research on Human Development and Criminal Behaviour*, 65–89. Dordrecht, Netherlands: Kluwer.

Fergusson, D.M., L.J. Horwood, and M.T. Lynskey. 1993. "The Effects of Conduct Disorder and Attention Deficit in Middle Childhood on Offending and Scholastic Ability at Age 13." *Journal of Child Psychology and Psychiatry 34*(6): 899–916.

Gottfredson, M., and T. Hirschi. 1990. *A General Theory of Crime.* Stanford, CA: Stanford University Press.

Graham, J., and B. Bowling. 1995. *Young People and Crime.* London: Her Majesty's Stationery Office.

Hagell, A., and T. Newburn. 1994. *Persistent Young Offenders.* London: Policy Studies Institute.

Hirschi, T. 1969. *Causes of Delinquency.* Berkeley, CA: University of California Press.

Home Office. 1990. *Criminal Statistics, England and Wales, 1989.* London: HMSO.

———. 1993. *Criminal Statistics, England and Wales, 1991.* London: HMSO.

———. 1994. *Criminal Statistics, England and Wales, 1993.* London: HMSO.

———. 1995. *Criminal Statistics, England and Wales, 1994.* London: HMSO.

Home Office Statistical Bulletin. 1987. *Criminal Careers of Those Born in 1953: Persistent Offenders and Desistance.* London: Home Office.

———. 1995. *Criminal Careers of Those Born between 1953 and 1973.* London: Home Office.

House of Commons, Home Affairs Committee. 1993. *Juvenile Offenders.* London: HMSO.

Irving, B.L., and I.K MacKenzie. 1989. *Police Interrogation.* London: Police Foundation.

Jessor, R., and S.L. Jessor. 1977. *Problem Behaviour and Psychosocial Development.* New York: Academic Press.

Johnson, L.D., P.M. O'Malley, and J.G. Bachman. 1987. *National Trends in Drug Use and Related Factors among American High School Students and Young Adults, 1975–1986.* Rockville, MD: National Institute of Drug Abuse.

Klein, M.W. 1984. "Offence Specialization and Versatility among Juveniles." *British Journal of Criminology 24*: 185–94.

Kolvin, I., F.J.W. Miller, D.M. Scott, S.R.M. Gatzanis, and M. Fleeting. 1990. *Continuities of Deprivation?* Aldershot, UK: Avebury.

LeBlanc, M., and M. Frechette. 1989. *Male Criminal Activity from Childhood through Youth.* New York: Springer.

Leitner, M., J. Shapland, and P. Wiles. 1993. *Drug Usage and Drugs Prevention.* London: HMSO.

Loeber, R., S.M. Green, B.B. Lahey, M.A.G. Christ, and P.J. Frick. 1992. " Developmental Sequences in the Age of Onset of Disruptive Child Behaviours." *Journal of Child and Family Studies 1*: 21–41.

Loeber, R., P. Wung, K. Keenan, B. Giroux, M. Stouthamer-Loeber, and W.B. Van Kammen. 1993. "Developmental Pathways in Disruptive Child Behaviour." *Development and Psychopathology 5*: 101–32.

Mayhew, P., and D. Elliott. 1990. "Self-Reported Offending, Victimization, and the British Crime Survey." *Violence and Victims 5*: 83–96.

McCord, J. 1979. "Some Child-Rearing Antecedents of Criminal Behaviour in Adult Men." *Journal of Personality and Social Psychology 37*: 1477–86.

———. 1991. "Family Relationships, Juvenile Delinquency, and Adult Criminality." *Criminology 29*: 397–417.

Moffitt, T.E. 1993. "Adolescence-Limited and Life-Course-Persistent Antisocial Behaviour: A Developmental Taxonomy." *Psychological Review 100*(4): 674–701.

Moffitt, T.E., and P.A. Silva. 1988. "IQ and Delinquency: A Direct Test of the Differential Detection Hypothesis." *Journal of Abnormal Psychology 97*: 330–33.

Pearson, F.S., and N.A. Weiner. 1985. "Toward an Integration of Criminological Theories." *Journal of Criminal Law and Criminology 76*: 116–50.

Pulkkinen, L. 1988. "Delinquent Development: Theoretical and Empirical Considerations." In M. Rutter, ed., *Studies of Psychosocial Risk,* 184–99. Cambridge, UK: Cambridge University Press.

Reiss, A.J., and D.P. Farrington. 1991. "Advancing Knowledge about Co-Offending: Results from a Prospective Longitudinal Survey of London Males." *Journal of Criminal Law and Criminology 82*: 360–95.

Robins, L.N. 1979. "Sturdy Childhood Predictors of Adult Outcomes: Replications from Longitudinal Studies." In J.E. Barrett, R.M. Rose, and G.L. Klerman, eds., *Stress and Mental Disorder,* 219–35. New York: Raven.

———. 1991. "Conduct Disorder." *Journal of Child Psychology and Psychiatry 32*(1): 193–212.

Robins, L.N., and K.S. Ratcliff. 1980. "Childhood Conduct Disorders and Later Arrest." In L.N. Robins, P.J. Clayton, and J.K. Wing, eds., *The Social Consequences of Psychiatric Illness,* 248–63. New York: Brunner/Mazel.

Rutter, M., and H. Giller. 1983. *Juvenile Delinquency.* Harmondsworth, UK: Penguin.

Snyder, H.N., and M. Sickmund. 1995. *Juvenile Offenders and Victims: A National Report.* Washington, DC: Office of Juvenile Justice and Delinquency Prevention.

Snyder, H.N., M. Sickmund, and E. Poe-Yamagata. 1996. *Juvenile Offenders and Victims: 1996 Update on Violence.* Washington, DC: Office of Juvenile Justice and Delinquency Prevention.

Stattin, H., and D. Magnusson. 1991. "Stability and Change in Criminal Behaviour up to Age 30." *British Journal of Criminology 31*(4): 327–46.

Sutherland, E., and D. Cressey. 1974. *Criminology,* 9th ed. Philadelphia: Lippincott.

Tarling, R. 1993. *Analysing Offending.* London: HMSO.

Trasler, G.B. 1962. *The Explanation of Criminality.* London: Routledge & Kegan Paul.

Wadsworth, M. 1979. *Roots of Delinquency.* London: Martin Robertson.
West, D.J., and D.P. Farrington. 1977. *The Delinquent Way of Life.* London: Heinemann.
Wikström, P.O. 1987. *Patterns of Crime in a Birth Cohort.* Stockholm: Department of Sociology, University of Stockholm.
Wilson, J.Q., and R.J. Herrnstein. 1985. *Crime and Human Nature.* New York: Simon & Schuster.
Wolfgang, M.E., T.P. Thornberry, and R.M. Figlio. 1987. *From Boy to Man, from Delinquency to Crime.* Chicago, IL: University of Chicago Press.

CHAPTER TWO

A Youth Violence Epidemic: Myth or Reality?

FRANKLIN E. ZIMRING
University of California, Berkeley

Current concerns about youth violence policy in the United States have been driven by interpretations of official statistics on youth arrests. Arrest statistics have been quoted as proof of substantial increases in the violence attributable to young offenders. These statistics have then been used as evidence that a new and more vicious breed of juvenile offender is the reason for the increase in arrests. Finally, predictions about future rates of youth violence have been based on projecting recent trends many years in the future.

This chapter is a detailed analysis of recent trends in arrest statistics. The first section examines trends in the four Part I or Index offences of violence over the period 1980–1996. The second section focuses on youth arrests for homicide, concluding that the increase noted in this category is attributable to increases in gun violence. The third section shows that arrests for aggravated assault — the largest growth category since 1980 — may be the result of changes in police practices and reporting standards. A concluding section addresses the implications of the statistical patterns revealed in this chapter in projecting rates of youth crime.

A GENERAL TREND?

The only official statistics that provide age-specific patterns are police data on arrests. These are the statistics that have been the basis for predictions of a coming wave of youth violence. Figure 2.1 combines national-level data on arrests under the age of 18 with census-based data on age to present trends

Source: Franklin E. Zimring, "A Youth Violence Epidemic: Myth or Reality?" Chapter 3 in F.E. Zimring, *American Youth Violence* (New York: Oxford University Press, 1998): 31–47. Used by permission of Oxford University Press, Inc.

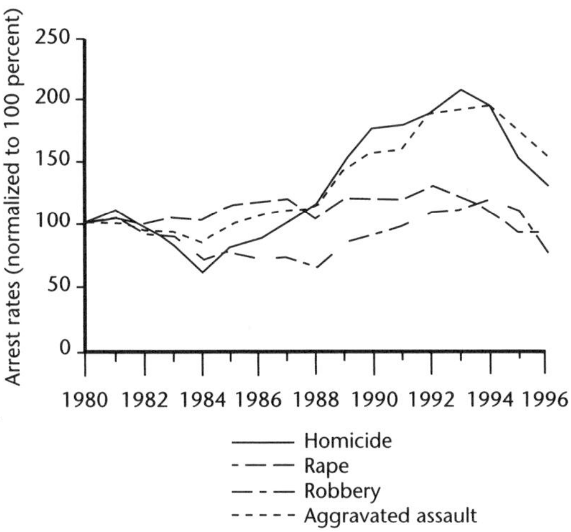

FIGURE 2.1

Arrest Rates for Offenders, Ages 13–17, for Four Violent Offences, 1980–1996

Source: U.S. Department of Justice, Federal Bureau of Investigation (1980–1993, 1994a, 1995–1996).

on arrest rates per 100 000 youth aged 13 to 17 for homicide, rape, aggravated assault, and robbery. For each offence, the arrest rate per 100 000 in 1980 is expressed as a baseline level of 100, and each succeeding year's arrest rate is expressed as a percentage of that figure. This graph shows trends in all four offence categories most directly.

The estimates generated in Figure 2.1 express the number of arrests over the entire population of 13- to 17-year-olds despite the fact that the percentage of the U.S. population in reporting agencies varies and is never 100 percent. Thus the rates derived are an index of trends rather than a precise rate.

Two of the four offences show pronounced trends over time — homicide and aggravated assault. The largest movements over time are noted for homicide, for which the arrest rate first dropped by just under 40 percent in the early 1980s and then began a sustained climb after 1984. The peak rate in 1993 was more than double the 1980 level. Then homicide arrests dropped sharply; the 1996 rate was 34 percent above that in 1980. The arrest level for aggravated assault did not drop much in the early 1980s and then increased slowly from 1985 to 1988. Large one-year jumps in 1989 and again in 1992 raised the level to nearly double the 1980 rate. The rate declined by 20 percent over the two years after its 1994 peak, but arrests for aggravated assault stayed 56 percent above the 1980 level, by far the largest increase in the four violent crimes.

Trends in rape and robbery arrests over the 1980s and early 1990s were much less pronounced. Rape arrests never dropped lower than their 1980 baseline during the years, the early 1980s, when homicide and assault declined. Rape arrest rates increased after 1988, reaching a high 32 percent above the 1980 level in 1992, but dropped back by 1996 to the lowest rate recorded at any time since 1977.

Robbery arrest trends differ from the others in two respects. While arrest rates for other violent crimes went up after 1984, robbery arrests declined in six of the first eight years of the 1980s and reached their lowest level of the 1980s in 1988. From 1988 to 1994, the arrest rates increased but were never more than 20 percent above the 1980 baseline. The 1995 rate dropped to 13 percent above the 1980 rate, and the 1996 arrest rate fell another 34 percent. By 1996, the robbery arrest rate was reported at 21 percent below the 1980 level.

There are three notable elements in the aggregate pattern reported in Figure 2.1. First, there is no common pattern for youth arrests for violent crime during the 1980–1996 period. The rate change over the sixteen-year period ranges from –21 percent for robbery to +56 percent for aggravated assault. Homicide, which had the highest increase as recently as 1993, recorded a 34 percent gain by the end of 1996. The four different offences are thus four different statistical stories.

The second major conclusion is that youth violence arrest rates usually do not run up or down in long cycles. In a period that was supposed to be noteworthy because of its sustained upward trends, only three times did the arrest rate go in the same direction for an offence for more than three consecutive years. Two of the four offences of violence were essentially trendless over the sixteen years in the aggregate.

The third important characteristic is that the arrest rate often changes substantially in a short time. Over the sixteen year-to-year transitions in Figure 2.1 homicide rates increased or decreased by over 20 percent in four years and over 15 percent a total of seven times. Aggravated assault rates recorded one-year increases of 34 percent, 19 percent, and 17 percent in the sixteen year-to-year changes. The volatility of trends in arrests means that rates of offences — which cannot be predicted — are much more important elements of future youth crime volume than population levels — which can be predicted. With large differences in rates, changes in the youth population can be expected to play a relatively minor independent role in determining the volume of youth violence. Over the fifteen years between 1995 and 2010, the youth population is expected to increase a total of 19 percent. But a large single-year increase or decrease in youth arrests will be as powerful an influence on volume as fifteen years' worth of population changes.

All of the statistical features just discussed warn us that long-range predictions above the volume of youth violence are error-prone. Offence rates are far less predictable than the size of the youth population but also much more important in determining the volume of serious violence. Assuming that any trend will continue for long is foolhardy, given the cyclical nature of youth violence. There is at least as much difference between trends in the different violent offences as there is similarity, so that projections of trends in a single aggregation of youth violence are demonstrably erroneous.

Those reviewing Figure 2.1 may notice that the increases just discussed are smaller than data reported in other studies (see, e.g., Blumstein 1995; Fox

1996; Snyder and Sickmund 1995). The reason for the discrepancy is that many analysts use the very lowest points in juvenile violence, 1984 to 1985, as their base year. Picking a low period in a cyclically fluctuating time series will generate the greatest difference between baseline rates and current rates of violence, but it also risks confusing the up-and-down movements in a cyclical pattern with trends that represent changes in the average volume of violence to be expected over time.

What Figure 2.1 shows is that rape and robbery arrests have varied substantially over the period since 1980, but there is no evidence of an underlying trend — either up or down — in the incidence of arrests over the sixteen years. This removes these two offences from further consideration in exploring the central concern of this chapter — the assessment and explanation of trends over time. Since there is no trend, there is no reason to project any trend forward.

Homicide rates in 1996 are one-third higher than in 1980. Despite the cyclical fluctuations throughout the period, this seems sufficient ground to investigate whether a change in rate has occurred and, if so, its likely explanation. This is the task of the next section. Aggravated assault levels, which increased by more than half over the period 1980–1996, are the subject of the third section. As the following two sections show, the trends in homicide and assault are quite different in origin and policy significance.

PATTERNS OF YOUTH HOMICIDE

Figure 2.2 shows trends in homicide arrest rates for offenders 13 to 17 and over 18 over the two decades from 1976 to 1995. The two arrest rates move together first up and then down in the first decade, but then the under-18

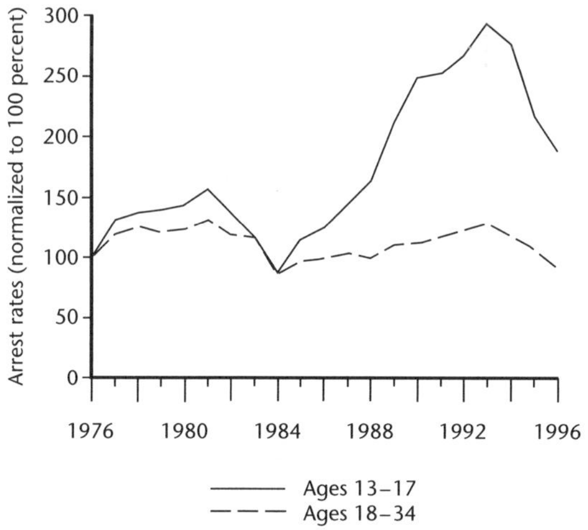

FIGURE 2.2
Trends in Arrest Rates for Homicide, 1976–1996

Source: U.S. Department of Justice, Federal Bureau of Investigation (1976–1993, 1994a, 1995–1996).

rate takes off from 1985–1993 in a pattern that diverges from the homicide arrests in the stable, older age group.

The most important reason for the sharp escalation in homicide was an escalating volume of fatal attacks with firearms, as shown in Figure 2.3. The top line is the rate of homicides by all means tied to the arrest of at least one offender under 18. The bottom line is the rate of arrests for homicides committed with all weapons other than guns, including knives, blunt objects, and personal force. The most important characteristic of the bottom line is flatness. There are minor fluctuations and no trend over time.

The middle line shows trends in arrests for homicides committed with guns, with each death that resulted in one or more arrests counted only once. Almost all of the variance during the years of the increase in total homicides was in gun cases, as was the decrease in total homicides in the early 1980s. The origins of this pattern are a puzzle. The proportion of homicides committed with guns did not increase among adults, so no general increase in handgun availability seems to explain the sharp increase in youth shootings (Zimring 1996).

That homicide increases are only gun cases has two important implications. First, it would require only a small number of attacks to change the death statistics during the 1985–1992 period. Because gunshot wounds are deadly, a relatively small number of woundings can produce a relatively large number of killings. My early studies in Chicago found a ratio of nonfatal gunshot wounds to fatalities of above seven to one, in contrast to a knife ratio of about thirty-five to one (Zimring 1968; 1972). Both numbers are undercounts because many more nonfatal woundings also go undetected. But an extra 1700 gun killings should produce only 10 000 to 15 000 extra gun-wound cases in the aggravated assault statistics, a small percentage of the total under-18 volume.

FIGURE 2.3
Number of Gun, Nongun, and Total Homicides by Offenders, Ages 10–17, 1976–1992

Source: U.S. Department of Justice, Federal Bureau of Investigation (1994b).

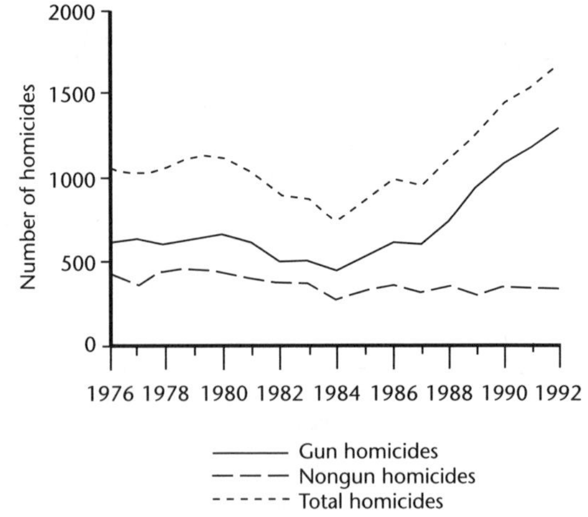

Because the homicide patterns suggest that only gun assaults increased after 1985 (there were no additional nongun killings), the number of additional assault cases one would expect would be minimal, less than a 10 percent increase in all aggravated assaults, and all of these would be gun cases. But that is not what happened. The number of aggravated assault cases grew faster even than homicides after 1985. The fact that only gun homicides increased transforms the large increase in under-18 aggravated assaults into a mystery. If the increase in homicides had been distributed across all weapons, we would have expected an increase in assaults as large as the increase in homicides.

The second implication of the guns-only pattern is that the hardware used in many attacks seems to be the major explanation for the expanding rate rather than any basic change in the youth population involved in the assaults.

Every time there is an increase in youth violence, there is worry that a new, more vicious type of juvenile offender is the cause. The guns-only pattern of Figure 2.3 is quite strong circumstantial evidence against the proposition that a violent new breed is a general phenomenon for three reasons. First, the sharp increase in gun use provides a clear alternative explanation for the higher number of killings by youth. It has long been thought that greater use of firearms in attacks can increase the death rate from violence independent of variations in intent because guns are more dangerous. This so-called instrumentality effect would explain a substantial increase in homicide without resort to changes in the motivations or scruples of young offenders if they are willing to use guns in attacks (Cook 1991). The second reason the gun-only pattern does not support a theory of a violent new breed of offender is that so few young attackers are involved in the switch to guns. At most, the shooters are 20 000 or so of the under-18 population arrested for violence. If there is a "new breed" of offender, it would have to be found only among that narrow band of firearms wounders. Third, the great majority of assaults has stayed the same over the past two decades. Knives are universally available, and the next most deadly weapon to firearms. Yet the rate of killings with knives remained stable over the eight-year expansion in total homicides. If more destructive intentions were the major cause of rate changes in homicide, some of the increase in the death rate should be found in the category of knives and other cutting instruments.

THE GROWTH OF ASSAULT ARRESTS

The task here is to restate and explore the mystery in the previous discussion. Because the growth of homicides was restricted to gun cases, there is no reason to expect a large increase in the volume of aggravated assault cases over the years when homicides increased. If all forms of homicide double, one expects all forms of aggravated assault to double as well. If only gun homicides double, only aggravated assaults with guns should double, and the total serious assault rate should increase by less than 20 percent. Instead, the aggravated assault rate nearly doubled at its peak rate in 1994 and then declined at a slower pace than homicide. Is this evidence that a broad cross section of adolescents was engaging in many types of serious assaults, not limited to the gun cases? If so, why was there no increase in homicides by other means?

From a policy and planning perspective, sorting out the meaning of the expansion in aggravated assault arrests is quite important. If only homicides have increased, the number of cases is quite small. A 20 percent increase in aggravated assaults for gun assault cases is still less than a quarter of the total case increase that occurs if the true rate of youth assault doubled to a peak and fell back only 22 percent from that peak. So if the growth in aggravated assault arrests reflects the magnitude of the true growth in the volume of serious adolescent violence, the problem is much broader than an analysis of the homicide statistics would suggest.

There have been indications for some time that observers should be cautious in taking evidence about trends in youth violence from fluctuations in aggravated assault arrest levels. Twenty years ago, I was tempted to label a section on trends in police arrests for this offence "the aggravations of aggravated assault" because increases in arrest rates for this offence did not always occur when homicide rates were increasing (Zimring 1979). How assaults are counted and classified is essentially a matter of police discretion. Changing police standards can have a huge impact on statistical trends. For the period since 1980, there is significant circumstantial evidence from many sources that changing police thresholds for when assault should be recorded and when the report should be for aggravated assault is the reason for most of the growth in arrest rates.

The first evidence that reclassification is a major factor comes from arrest rates for adults. It turns out that trends over time in assault arrests for older offenders have been strikingly similar to those noted for younger offenders. But the older group experienced declines in homicide arrests over the period, so it does not seem likely that this age group is increasing in its true rate of life-threatening violence.

Figure 2.4 shows rates of aggravated assault arrests by year from 1980 to 1995 for 13- to 17-year-olds and for those 25 to 34. The 25-to-34 age group is the youngest population group that did not have any increase in homicides. (The age group 18 to 24 had trends quite similar to the 13-to-17 group. See Cook and Laub 1998.) The trends in aggravated assault arrests for the two groups are quite similar over the whole period. There are fifteen year-to-year transitions over the period, and the two groups increased together or decreased together in thirteen. Thus an upward or downward movement in the rate for one age group predicts a move in the same direction for the other age group about 85 percent of the time. The two groups behaved over time like two peas in the same statistical pod. The similar magnitude of the year-to-year changes visible in Figure 2.4 is consistent with changing policy standards.

But is this evidence that trends in true rates of violence were quite similar for the two age groups, or is this evidence instead that changing police practices had the same impact on the two age groups at the same time? Homicide trends for the two age groups point toward the latter interpretation. The parallel trends for the two age groups do not hold for homicide arrests over time. Homicide arrests were sharply up for the younger group but down for the 25- to 34-year-olds, as shown in Figure 2.5.

Homicide arrests for the 25-to-34 age group dropped substantially after 1981 and continued a sustained decline throughout the period. There is thus no evidence that the increasing rate of serious assaults for this age group

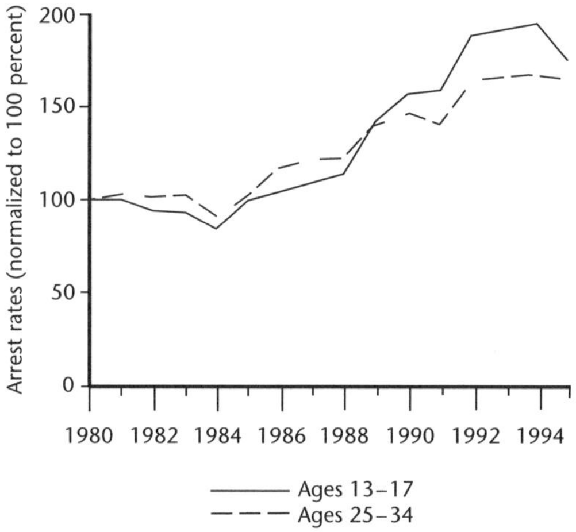

FIGURE 2.4
Trends in Arrest Rates for Aggravated Assault, 1980–1995

Source: U.S. Department of Justice, Federal Bureau of Investigation (1980–1993, 1994a, 1995).

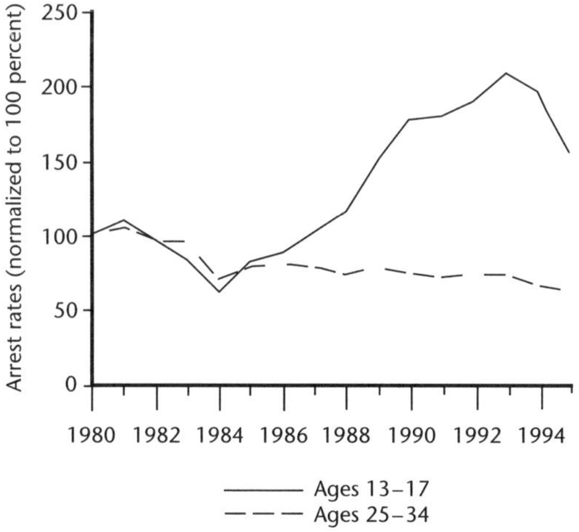

FIGURE 2.5
Trends in Arrest Rates for Murder and Non-negligent Manslaughter, 1980–1995

Source: U.S. Department of Justice, Federal Bureau of Investigation (1980–1993, 1994a, 1995).

spilled over to create more deaths from assault. This suggests that the fluctuations in the older age group could not affect the volume of life-threatening assaults. The similarity of patterns over time of younger and older offenders, then, would suggest that the major reason for movements in the 13-to-17 age group should be the same as for the older group. If so, the major reason for increasing arrest rates in the younger age bracket for assault was not a change in the behaviour of young offenders but a change in the classification of attacks that are close to the line that separates simple from aggravated assaults.

One way to estimate the degree to which police reclassification rather than increasing violent assault drove up aggravated assault rates is to use the trends for the older group as a proxy for reclassification. Since the homicides for this group dropped, we can assume that all of the increases that occurred in both groups were due to reclassification but that increases above and beyond those of the older group were the result of real changes. By this measure, more than 85 percent of the juvenile increase would be presumptive reclassification. (The adult rate increased 67 percent from 1980 to 1995, while the juvenile rate increased 78 percent. The adult increase was 86 percent of the juvenile increase, leaving 14 percent of that increase not accounted for by presumed reclassification.)

Simple Assault

The trends in arrests for simple assault lend strong support to the theory that police standards are shifting toward recording and upgrading assaults. Figure 2.6 shows trends in arrests for the less serious Part II offence of nonaggravated assault for 13- to 17-year-olds and 18- to 34-year-olds. The pattern produced for assaults is similar to that observed for aggravated assaults, only more so. The growth of police recorded assault arrests is larger than for the

FIGURE 2.6
Trends in Arrest Rates for Part II Assaults, 1980–1996

Source: U.S. Department of Justice, Federal Bureau of Investigation (1980–1993, 1994a, 1995–1996).

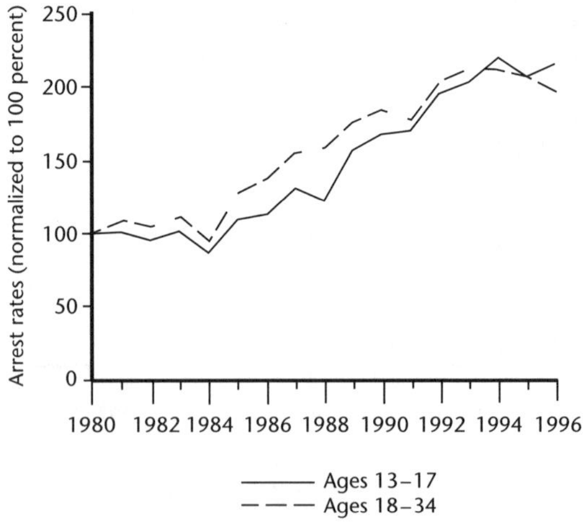

aggravated assault category. The younger and older offenders are almost identical over time, with the two age groups moving in the same direction in thirteen of the sixteen year-to-year comparisons. The data for 1996 are an exception to this pattern, with a 10 percent increase in youth assault arrests and a 5 percent decrease for young adults. The four largest increases for the 13- to 17-year-olds occur in the same years as for the older offenders. It also turns out that three of the four largest year-to-year increases in aggravated assault match the years of the greatest increase in simple assault arrests.

The chances are substantial that a greater police willingness to report and upwardly classify assault crimes and a greater willingness to arrest those who commit assaults are contributing to the increase in arrests for both younger and older offenders. The four largest one-year increases in aggravated assault arrests amount to more than 100 percent of the total increase for aggravated assault (the four one-year jumps were 166.3 per 100 000, whereas the total increase was 160) and 83 percent of the total increase for simple assault up to 1995 (the four one-year increases were 332.4 per 100 000 of a total increase of 399.6). When all or most of the increase is concentrated in a few jumps, the likelihood that reporting thresholds are changing is higher.

Corroboration from Other Sources

A review of available data other than the Uniform Crime Reports on assault reveals three different indications that much of the change in assault statistics stems from changing police standards. The first indication is the divergent trends in assault arrests and the victimization rate reported to the National Crime Survey for assault. Figure 2.7 provides data on trends in assault arrests (combining simple and aggravated assault) and victim-reported assault for 1980–1993.

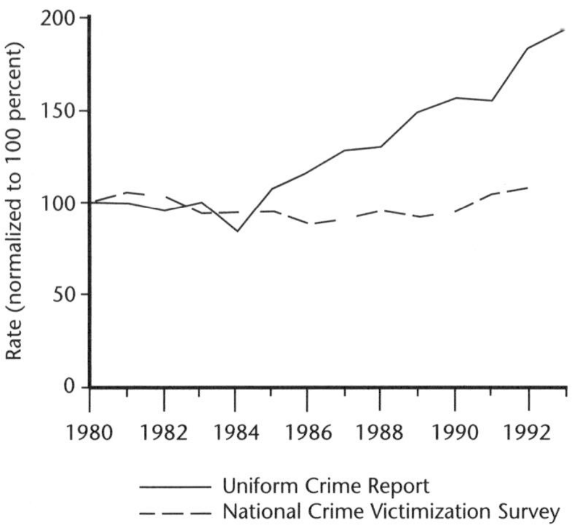

FIGURE 2.7
Trends in Assault, 1980–1993

Source: U.S. Department of Justice, Bureau of Justice Statistics (1980–1992); U.S. Department of Justice, Federal Bureau of Investigation (1980–1993).

The assault arrest rate drops by 14 percent in the early 1980s, then doubles from 1985 through 1993. The reported incidence of assault victimization drops slightly in the early 1980s but then remains steady, never reaching more than 13 percent higher than the 1980 rate. The large climb in assault arrests, therefore, is not reflected in any significant change in assault victimization, a result consistent with a change in standards. Indeed, the reason that national crime survey data after 1992 are not included in Figure 2.7 is also evidence of the power of changing criteria on statistics. In 1993, a new standard was used for the assault category, and the rate immediately jumped more than 80 percent. The reclassification process is not confined to police statistics.

The second piece of evidence that assaults remained more stable than official reports comes from large-scale surveys of high school boys conducted by Lloyd Johnson at the University of Michigan in 1982 and 1992. The first survey occurred at the beginning of the time series reported in Figure 2.4, when aggravated assault arrests were close to the low point in the series. The second survey occurred one year short of the highest rate in the sixteen years, just short of double the official 1982 level. The survey results of involvement in serious assaults are virtually identical for the two periods. Participation in fights with injury held constant at 13 percent in the two surveys, serious fights were 17 percent in 1982 and 18 percent in 1992, and weapon use was 2 percent in 1982 and 3 percent in 1992 (Bachman, Johnston, and O'Malley 1984; 1993).

The third indication of the major role of official reclassification is that the death rate for every type of assault has gone down over time. The gun assault death rate declined from 6.9 percent in 1985 to 5.6 percent in 1994. Using a case-fatality estimate technique created by Philip Cook (1991) and assuming that the additional assaults that are added were the product of reclassification without extra killings, we can see that 19 percent of the gun assaults added between 1985 and 1994 were artifactual. This case-fatality approach also estimates that 40 percent of the increase in knife assaults are probably reclassifications. For the 58 percent of aggravated assaults that involve other weapons and personal force, a declining death rate suggests that 79 percent of the additional assaults are the product of changes in police standards rather than of violent behaviour. Well over half of all the additional assaults in the United States are estimated to be reclassification by this method. Because there is no detailed breakdown of aggravated assaults by age and weapon, a separate estimate only for young offenders cannot be made by using this technique.

PERSPECTIVES ON PREDICTION

Long-range predictions about youth violence are difficult in the best of times because rates of serious offences tend to be cyclical in unpredictable ways. But projections forward from recent trends are also problematic because there are no clear indications for the future of any violent offence to be gleaned from a careful review of current data. There are, however, important lessons about both trends and projections that should inform any discussion of what to expect in the future.

The first important finding from this analysis of recent experience is that there is no unitary trend in the recent history of youth arrests for violent crime. Homicide and assault arrests have increased, but for different reasons. Robbery and rape have fluctuated, without any discernible long-range trend. This lack of pattern has both procedural and substantive implications. The procedural lesson to be learned from the recent past is that patterns of arrest should be carefully examined one at a time rather than aggregated into a single arrest index. The substantive conclusion is that no generalization about the behaviour of the current cohort of youth can be factually supported. The absence of any discernible growth trend in non-firearms homicide, in robbery, and in rape arrest rates just does not fit generalizations about a more violent cohort, about superpredators, and the like.

Furthermore, when the two categories of growing rates are scrutinized, it turns out that youth arrests for homicides and assault have increased for different reasons. A sharp increase in gun homicide cases was the only reason the total homicide rate increased after the mid-1980s. By 1993, the rate of arrests for gun homicides had tripled from its low point, while nongun homicide was flat. Then a sharp downward trend in these arrests eliminated about half of the previous eight years of increases.

What can be applied from current information to homicide predictions is one part cliché and one part question mark. The dynamic force in the coming decade is likely to be trends in gun cases, just as it has been. But the future trend in youth gun homicide is anybody's guess. The most recent decline in gun cases has been steep, but will it be sustained? Although there is suspicion that market changes for drugs in the 1980s produced the initial increase in adolescent gun use (Blumstein 1995), speculations about why gun homicides decreased have not produced a consensus. It is difficult to predict the future course of a trend one cannot explain.

One thing is clear: There will be very little tendency for trends in homicides with guns to reflect big changes in overall rates in assault or aggravated assault. Doubling the total number of aggravated assaults with handguns would produce less than a 20 percent increase in aggravated assaults; cutting gun assaults in half would lead to a 10 percent decrease in aggravated assaults.

The largest statistical mystery of the last decade is the sharp expansion in assault and aggravated assault arrests. The same large increase occurred for the 25-to-34 age group, a group with a decline in homicide. Any reduction in the threshold between simple and aggravated assault and any shift in the minimum standard for recording an offence would have the kind of statistical impact on assault arrests that has occurred since the late 1980s. Although the matter is not beyond doubt, it appears that the willingness of police authorities to give greater priority to assaults has altered the classification of attacks across the board.

Two aspects of this possible reclassification deserve special mention. First, when this sort of reclassification occurs, there is no telling whether the old or the new threshold is the correct one. As I have shown in another work (Zimring 1998, Chapter 2), the verbal description of aggravated assault is not precise, and the large number of attacks near the border between aggravated and simple assaults creates ample opportunity to justify different behavioural standards of what constitutes an aggravated assault. Second, the change in priority that motivates reclassification by the police can be very good news from a policy standpoint. More attention to particular problems often leads to reclassification of cases. Domestic violence incidents are counted as assaults more often when the problem becomes a priority. As police rejection of rape complaints (known as "unfounding") decreases, the number of rape complaints that become officially recorded incidents increases. If similar sentiments have created a higher probability that acts of violence become official statistics about violence, this is good news.

But it is good news that can be badly misinterpreted. A lower threshold for aggravating and reporting assault can produce a totally artificial crime wave in the sense that the statistics increase while the actual behaviour is stable. More than half of the growth in aggravated assault by youth may be a product of this pattern during 1980–1996.

If reclassification is the principal reason for the growth in assault statistics, what further developments can be anticipated in the next decade or so? First, it is not likely that standards for arrests and for considering attacks to be aggravated assaults will revert to previous levels. There is no recurrent, cyclic pattern in crime classification over time to serve as a precedent. The larger social concern with violence that supports the efforts of the police seems to be a long-term development. Thus standards for assault arrest and for aggravated assault arrest will stay at their present levels or perhaps drop further over the coming years.

The result of these developments might well be more arrests of young persons for assault and aggravated assault. The heterogeneity of the offence category will tend to increase, and the overwhelming majority of offences that produce arrests will be at the low end of the seriousness scale. More than ever, it will be necessary to sort out the more serious from the less serious assaults in fashioning sanctions and policy responses.

The statistical portrait of the last sixteen years is not without irony. Between 1980 and 1996, the increasing arrest rate for youth violence was concentrated in the assault category. The aggravated assault arrest rate was 41 percent of the youth violence arrest rate in 1980, yet increases in aggravated assault arrests dominated the growth over time. In 1996, the total rate of juvenile arrests for Index crimes of violence other than aggravated assault was lower than in 1980. With most of those extra aggravated assault arrests clustering at the low end of the seriousness scale, it is very likely that the average Part I arrest for an offender under 18 was for a less serious violent offence in

1996 than in 1980. It is possible that this trend will continue, so that a larger number of violence arrests will be counterbalanced by a smaller proportion at the serious end of the scale. But this kind of expansion at the shallow end of the violent crime pool is far from the growth in crime that is projected in current policy debates.

STUDY QUESTIONS

1. *According to Zimring, why is it misleading to claim that violent youth crime has increased dramatically in the United States in recent years?*
2. *How does Zimring interpret U.S. arrest statistics that show a dramatic increase in arrest rates for assault from the mid-1980s to the mid-1990s?*
3. *Why does Zimring think it is difficult to predict future trends in violent youth crime in the United States?*

REFERENCES

Bachman, Jerald, Lloyd Johnston, and Patrick O'Malley. 1984. *Monitoring the Future.* Ann Arbor, MI: University of Michigan, Institute for Social Research.

———. 1993. *Monitoring the Future.* Ann Arbor, MI: University of Michigan, Institute for Social Research.

Blumstein, Alfred. 1995. "Youth Violence, Guns, and the Illicit Drug Industry." *Journal of Criminal Law and Criminology 86*(1): 10–36.

Cook, Philip J. 1991. "The Technology of Personal Violence." In Michael Tonry, ed., *Crime and Justice: An Annual Review of Research,* 1 – 71. Chicago: University of Chicago Press.

Cook, Philip J., and John Laub. 1998. "The Unprecedented Epidemic in Youth Violence." In Michael Tonry and Mark Moore, eds., *Youth Violence. Crime and Justice: An Annual Review of Research,* 27 – 64. Chicago: University of Chicago Press.

Fox, James A. 1996. *Trends in Juvenile Violence: A Report to the United States Attorney General on Current and Future Rates of Juvenile Offending.* Boston: Northeastern University Press.

Snyder, Howard, and Melissa Sickmund. 1995. *Juvenile Offenders and Victims: A National Report.* Washington, DC: U.S. Government Printing Office.

Zimring, Franklin E. 1968. "Is Gun Control Likely to Reduce Violent Killings?" *University of Chicago Law Review 35*: 721 – 37.

———. 1972. "The Medium Is the Message: Firearms Caliber as a Determinant of the Death Rate from Assault." *Journal of Legal Studies 1*: 97 – 123.

———. 1979. "American Youth Violence: Issues and Trends." In Norval Morris and Michael Tonry, eds., *Crime and Justice: An Annual Review of Research,* 67 – 107. Chicago: University of Chicago Press.

———. 1996. "Kids, Guns, and Homicide: Policy Notes on an Age-Specific Epidemic." *Law and Contemporary Problems 59*(1): 25 – 38.

———. 1998. *American Youth Violence.* New York: Oxford University Press.

CHAPTER THREE

Trends in Youth Crime in Canada, 1977 – 1996

PETER J. CARRINGTON
University of Waterloo, Ontario

In 1991, police-reported youth crime in Canada reached the highest level ever recorded. This peak followed increases in five of the six years since the Young Offenders Act (YOA) came into force in 1985. Not surprisingly, this aroused considerable adverse comment in the media and contributed to public disenchantment with the YOA (Corrado and Markwart 1992: 160 – 63; Bala 1994: 248 – 51; Hylton 1994: 236 – 39; Task Force on Youth Justice 1996: 14 – 19). By 1996, the rate of youth crime had returned to the same level as in 1983, after falling for four of the five years since 1991; this decrease seems to have received less public attention.

Although scholarly commentators did not attribute the rise in youth crime to the YOA, it did occasion debate about the extent to which youth crime was increasing and the extent to which its level exceeded that under the Juvenile Delinquents Act (JDA). Answers to these questions were conditioned by the range of years selected for study by researchers, although most writers cautioned that insufficient time had elapsed since the inception of the YOA to draw definite conclusions about post-YOA trends.

More than a decade has now elapsed since the YOA came into effect. This is therefore an opportune time to review the fluctuations in youth crime over the past twenty years, and to assess the change, if any, in its post-YOA level and the extent to which any change that has occurred is due to the YOA.

Source: Peter J. Carrington, "Trends in Youth Crime in Canada, 1977–1996," excerpt from article of the same title in *Canadian Journal of Criminology* (January 1999): 1 – 32.

PREVIOUS RESEARCH

Has the Level of Youth Crime in Canada Increased Since 1984?

Carrington and Moyer (1994: 8–11) compared quarterly data from the Uniform Crime Reporting (UCR) Survey on rates of young persons apprehended and charged for the periods 1980–84 (under the JDA) and 1985–90 (under the YOA) and concluded that the average per capita rate of police-reported youth crime during 1985–90 was the same as during 1980–84, but that the average rate of young persons charged was 21 percent higher in the post-YOA period. They also noted that there was no upward or downward trend in either rate during 1980–84, but that there appeared to be slight upward trends, which were not statistically significant, in both rates during 1985–90, especially during 1989–90.

Corrado and Markwart (1994: 350–51) concluded from analysis of annual UCR data on young persons charged with Criminal Code offences from 1986 to 1992 that there was a "relatively modest 25 percent increase" over the period. Comparing annual UCR data for 1986–92 with 1980–83, Carrington (1995: 63–64) found a statistically nonsignificant increase of 5 percent in the per capita rate of young persons apprehended, and an increase of 29 percent in the rate of young persons charged. He also reported an apparent upward trend in both rates from 1986 to 1992, which he said required further data for confirmation. Markwart and Corrado (1995: 77–79) compared UCR data on rates of young persons apprehended during 1990–93 and 1980–83, and found a 10 percent increase. They estimated that, after correcting for inflation in the per capita rates for 1980–83, the post-YOA increase was "more likely in the range of 20 percent." Using annual UCR data for 1980 to 1993, Moyer (1996: 16) noted a "steady climb" in rates of young persons apprehended and charged from 1986 to a peak in 1991, followed by declines in 1992 and 1993. Comparing the level in 1993 with the average level in 1980–83, she reported an increase of 5 percent in the rate of young persons apprehended and of 32 percent in the rate of young persons charged.

In summary, there is agreement that the per capita rate of young persons charged has increased significantly since the inception of the YOA, but disagreement as to the size and interpretation of the change, if any, in the per capita rate of young persons apprehended.

What Has Caused the Increase, if Any, in Youth Crime? Is It the YOA?

After comparing the 1985–90 period with 1980–84, Carrington and Moyer (1994) concluded that the observed increase in the per capita rate of young persons charged with offences reflected a change in the police propensity to charge young persons, rather than in the criminal behaviour of young persons, since the average rate of young persons apprehended by police did not change. Furthermore, they speculated that this change in police propensity to charge young persons might be statistical rather than "real" — that is, it might reflect a change in statistical categories rather than in police behaviour. After examining this phenomenon on a province-by-province basis, they suggested that the observed post-YOA increase in police charging could be due to a possibly pre-existing practice of charging 16- and 17-year-old suspects in higher proportions than 12- to 15-year-olds. When these 16- and 17-year-olds were added, in many provinces, to the youth justice system, the average per capita rate of young persons charged would have increased: more "young persons" per capita would be charged (although no more people would actually be charged) due to the legal redefinition of 16- and 17-year-olds as "young persons." Carrington (1998) analyzed age-specific data for Ontario and Saskatchewan and concluded that a substantial part — between one-half and all — of the observed increase in police charging of young offenders in at least those two provinces is not a statistical artifact and reflects a change in actual police behaviour.

None of these writers attributes the observed changes in youth crime since 1985 to the effect of the YOA on the criminal behaviour of young persons. DuWors (1997) and Kong (1997) note that peaks in the early 1990s in overall police-reported crime in Canada are mirrored by similar trends in other countries. As Markwart and Corrado (1995: 84) put it:

> [T]he international evidence seems quite clear that crime control changes in law alone will not have any significant effect on youth crime rates, changes to which, of course, arise as a result of far broader social factors.

THE PRESENT STUDY

The logic of this study is that of the interrupted time-series experiment. It attempts to detect the effects, if any, of the YOA on youth crime by comparing the level and direction of time series of crime data before and after the legislation came into effect. This "natural experiment" has serious weaknesses as a design for establishing cause and effect (Cook and Campbell 1979). In order to attribute any observed changes to the YOA, it is necessary to rule out other possible causes and to establish a plausible conceptual connection with the YOA. This can never be done with certainty. Nevertheless, we believe that a prima facie case for an effect of the YOA can be made on the basis of evidence of sudden changes occurring immediately after 1985 that cannot be attributed to other events. More gradual changes during the period are more likely to be due to the "broader social factors" referred to in the quotation above.

The analyses presented here are based on annual UCR data on young persons apprehended and charged during 1977 to 1996, omitting 1984–85. Differences in average levels under the YOA and the JDA were tested for statistical significance using t-tests in order not to attribute significance to results that could well be due to random year-to-year fluctuations. Trends over time were estimated by regressing the annual rate per 100 000 on the year, separately for the JDA and YOA periods.

Data from the UCR Survey cannot be taken at face value as an indicator of the level of youth crime. The UCR Survey collects its data from police forces and is therefore limited to criminal activity known to police and considered by police to be worth recording. Furthermore, counts of young persons implicated and charged in connection with criminal incidents, which are used in the present study, are necessarily limited to incidents that have been "cleared" — that is, incidents in which the offender(s) have been identified, or "apprehended," by police. Thus, the substantial number of incidents that are known to and recorded by police, but not cleared, are omitted — in 1996, for example, only about 38 percent of incidents known to police in Canada were cleared.

The UCR Survey reports counts of both "young persons charged" and "young persons not charged." Counts of "young persons charged" are probably an accurate indicator of the charging of young persons, since the laying of charges is an official act that must be carefully recorded as the first step in court process. As an indicator of the amount of youth crime, it has the major disadvantage of omitting the substantial number of persons, especially young persons, who are apprehended but not charged — that is, levels of "young persons charged" reflect both criminal activity by young persons (and its detection and recording by police) and the exercise of police discretion to charge or to deal with the apprehended youth by other means. Thus, changes in numbers of young persons charged may confound changes in youth crime with changes in police charging practices. The analyses presented below show that the use of "young persons charged" as an indicator of youth crime (which is a common practice) would lead to seriously erroneous conclusions concerning changes in the level of youth crime after the YOA came into effect. Therefore, in this study, "young persons charged" is interpreted as precisely that: an indicator of the charging of young persons by police.

For an indicator of changes over time in the amount of youth crime, this study uses UCR data on "young persons apprehended" — that is, the sum of police-reported "young persons charged" and "young persons not charged." Numbers of young persons apprehended are a more valid indicator of changes in the level of youth crime than numbers of young persons charged, since they are not filtered by the decision to charge. However, they are less reliable — that is, consistent — because the criteria for classifying a person as "[apprehended but] not charged" are much less precise than for "charged" and vary considerably among police forces reporting to the UCR (Hackler and Paranjape 1983; 1984). Data on young persons apprehended also systematically underestimate the amount of youth crime known to the police, because police tend to underreport minor incidents involving young persons (Doob and Chan 1982).

On the other hand, UCR data are probably reliable enough to be useful for certain purposes. After reviewing research on the production, interpretation, and reliability of police crime statistics, Scanlon (1986: 94–95) concludes:

> Despite these serious limitations, which are associated with the crime *rates* for any given year, official crime *trends* may accurately reflect relative changes in crime over time. Finally, while differences in crime rates between police jurisdictions may be confounded to an unknown extent by differences in levels of police activity and reporting procedures, there is some empirical evidence to suggest that regional comparisons may be valid.

In this study, UCR data are used primarily to trace trends over time and to compare changes over time across regions.*

ANALYSIS AND RESULTS

Young Persons Apprehended by Police

As Figure 3.1 shows, the per capita rate of youth apprehended by police increased rapidly during the late 1970s, which were the last years of a rising trend in officially recorded crime in Canada that had begun in the 1960s (Brantingham 1991: 399). From 1980 to 1988, youth crime remained at about the same level, then it rose to a peak in 1991, and fell back almost to its former level by 1996. During the period of stable rates under the JDA — 1980 to 1983 — the average annual rate of juveniles apprehended was approximately 7891 per 100 000. During 1986–96, the average annual rate of young persons (aged 12 to 17) apprehended was 8413 per 100 000 — a statistically significant increase of 522 per 100 000, or 7 percent, over the annual rate under the JDA.

Thus, the rate of police-reported youth crime was a little higher during the first decade under the YOA than during the last few years under the JDA. Was this increase due to the YOA itself? If the YOA had affected rates of youth crime, we would expect to see one or both of the following phenomena: a jump in level after 1984–85 or a rising trend after 1984–85 that had not existed previously. Changes such as these would indicate that something had affected the rate of youth crime around 1984–85, and if other causes could be ruled out, the changes could be attributed to the YOA.

In fact, there was no jump after 1985, as can be seen from Figure 3.1. There was a slight change in the trend over time. During 1980–83, the trend was an annual increase of 25 per 100 000, but this was not statistically significant — that is, it could represent random fluctuations rather than a "real" trend. During 1986–96, the rising trend increased to 46 per 100 000, but it remained statistically nonsignificant. Thus, we cannot be confident that any real change in trend took place after 1986. The only noteworthy change in

* Peter Carrington's original article contains an additional section in which he addresses the difficulties of using UCR data to estimate rates of youth crime and offers a solution to deal with these difficulties. In the remainder of this chapter, only the results of the author's subsequent data analysis and major findings of the study are described.

FIGURE 3.1

Rates per 100 000 of Juveniles/Young Persons Apprehended and Charged by Police, Canada, 1977–1996

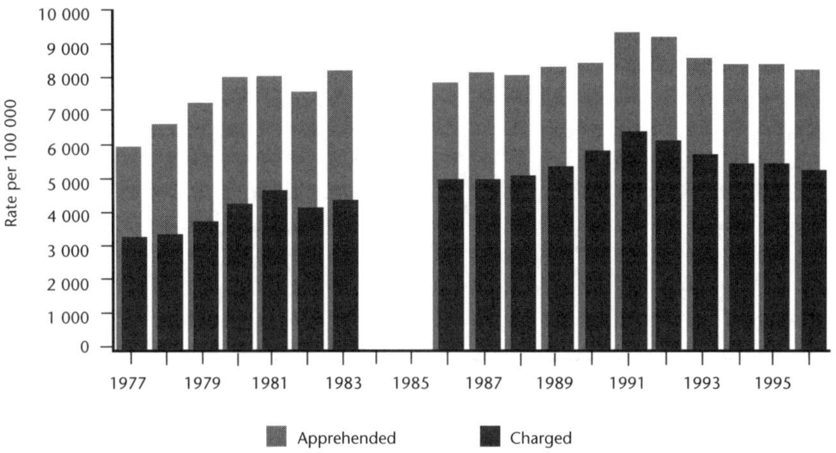

the level of youth crime that took place after 1984–85 was the "hump" in the early 1990s, and this is highly unlikely to have been caused by the YOA since it occurred several years later and was mirrored by similar "humps" in crime in other countries that could not be related to the YOA.

Another way of looking for changes in youth crime due to the YOA is to examine data for individual provinces and territories, since some underwent large changes in age jurisdiction, due to the addition of 16- and 17-year-olds, and others underwent smaller or no changes in age jurisdiction. It is in the provinces and territories that added 16- and 17-year-olds that we would most expect to see changes in the rate of youth crime following 1984–85 (Carrington and Moyer 1994).

The results of this examination are shown in Figure 3.2. In the four Atlantic provinces, there appears to have been a rising trend in youth crime during the entire period 1977–96, with a temporary peak in the early 1990s. New Brunswick is the only province in which there was a (small) jump after 1984–85. Thus, the rate of police-reported youth crime in the Atlantic provinces was much higher during 1986–96 than during 1977–83, but this appears to be due to a pre-existing trend, not to the YOA.

In Quebec, the rate of youth crime was significantly lower during 1986–96 than during 1980–83. This decrease was due to a sudden drop, not to a falling trend: in fact, there was a slight rising trend during both periods. We would speculate that this drop in official youth crime reflects not a sudden change in actual youth crime but rather a change made by the Quebec government in 1984 in the screening procedure for young offenders (LeBlanc

FIGURE 3.2

Rates per 100 000 of Juveniles/Young Persons Apprehended, by Region, 1977–1996

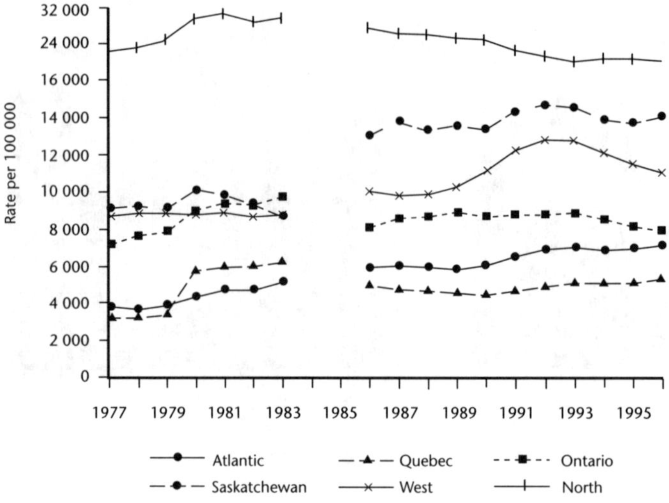

Notes: Rates are modified three-year moving averages. The upper part of the Y-axis is not linear.

and Beaumont 1992) that could have affected the numbers of young persons reported to the UCR as apprehended offenders.

In Ontario, there was also a substantial drop in police-reported youth crime in 1986, and little trend thereafter. As a result, the average rate of youth crime in Ontario was 999 per 100 000 lower during 1986–96 than during 1980–83: a statistically significant decrease of 11 percent. Perhaps some or all of this was due to the YOA, but we are unable to say how.

In Manitoba, Alberta, and British Columbia, rates of police-reported youth crime were fairly stable from 1980 to 1983, then rose steadily from 1988 to peaks in the early 1990s, from which they declined through 1996. In British Columbia, there was a jump in 1986. The large "hump" in youth crime rates during 1986–96 (Figure 3.2), and the post-1985 jump in British Columbia, resulted in average rates for the period that were significantly (16 to 27 percent) higher than during 1980–83. With the possible exception of the jump in 1986 in British Columbia, the timing of these phenomena suggests that they are not related to the YOA.

Saskatchewan is shown separately in Figure 3.2 because of the unique, and spectacular, one-time jump in its rate of official youth crime after 1986, which resulted in an average rate during 1986–96 that was 55 percent higher than during 1980–83, and the highest among the ten provinces. Since this coincided with the introduction of the YOA, it may well have been related to it; however, we are unable to determine from these data the extent to which this sudden increase of more than 50 percent reflects a change in the criminal behaviour of young persons, and whether it reflects a change in police enforcement activity and reporting practices.

Beginning at very high levels, both the Yukon and the Northwest Territories experienced somewhat erratic downward trends in police-reported youth crime from 1980 to 1996, and no jump after 1984–85.

This survey of trends over two decades in police-reported youth crime in the provinces and territories confirms once again the diversity of patterns of criminal behaviour in Canada. With the exception of Quebec, regional youth crime rates rise from east to west and are far higher in the territories. Saskatchewan and British Columbia are the only provinces in which there was a substantial increase in recorded youth crime immediately after the YOA was introduced. Ontario and Quebec experienced drops in police-reported youth crime immediately after 1984–85; this could have been due to changes in the Youth Protection Act (YPA) in Quebec, and may have been related somehow to the introduction of the YOA in Ontario. In the other provinces and territories, there were rising or falling trends, or both, that appear to be unrelated to the YOA.

Young Persons Charged by Police

Figure 3.1 shows that the rate per 100 000 of young persons charged (the "charge rate") tracked the rate of young persons apprehended fairly consistently over the period 1977 to 1996, with one important exception: there was a jump in charging in 1986 that did not occur in apprehensions of young persons. As a result of this jump, the average charge rate during 1986–96 was 27 percent higher than during 1980–83, compared with the 7 percent increase in young persons apprehended. There was practically no rising or falling trend in the charge rate either before or after 1984–85.

Since the rate of young persons apprehended increased by only 7 percent after 1985, most of the 27 percent increase in the charge rate was due to an increase in the proportion of apprehended young persons who were charged (the "charge ratio") and a corresponding reduction in the use by police of informal means — that is, in police discretion (Carrington and Moyer 1994). This is shown in Figure 3.3, in which the proportion of apprehended youth who were charged fluctuated around 55 percent prior to 1984, jumped to about 65 percent in 1986, and fluctuated around that level through 1996. There was practically no trend over time in the charge ratio either before or after 1984–85.

It seems likely that this jump in charging of apprehended youth was due to the YOA, since it occurred immediately after the YOA came into effect, and the charge ratio was stable over the rest of the two decades examined. The following section examines changes in charging of young persons by province, to see if the changes were more pronounced in the eight provinces and territories that experienced the greatest expansion of their youth justice

FIGURE 3.3
Percentage of Apprehended Youth Who Were Charged, Canada, 1977–1996

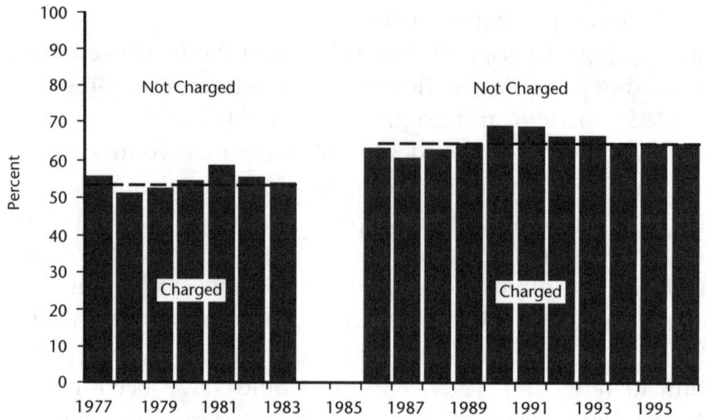

systems due to the addition of 16- and 17-year-olds, as Carrington and Moyer (1994) suggested.

Quebec is the only province in which fewer young persons per capita were charged after 1984–85 than during 1980–83. There was an immediate drop after 1985, similar to the drop in the rate of apprehensions, but then the charge rate declined slowly through 1996; however, the rate of apprehensions rose slightly in Quebec during 1986–96 (Figure 3.2). This divergence in the rates of apprehensions and charging is reflected in a strong downward trend in the charge ratio — the proportion of apprehended youth who were charged — from 80 percent in 1986 to 51 percent in 1996 (Figure 3.4b). While Quebec had the highest proportion of apprehended youth charged during 1980 to 1988, it had the lowest proportion charged, and by far the lowest per capita rate of young persons charged, by 1996. Since these trends are unique to Quebec, it seems likely that they are due to its unique system of diversion for young persons, which was implemented in 1979 by the provincial Youth Protection Act, and whose operation was not greatly changed when the JDA was replaced by the YOA in 1984 (LeBlanc and Beaumont 1988; 1992).

The other provinces and territories all experienced increases after 1985 in rates of young persons charged: in the range of 10 to 30 percent in British Columbia, Newfoundland, Manitoba, the Yukon, and the Northwest Territories, and 70 to 110 percent in the other provinces, except Saskatchewan, in which the rate of young persons charged tripled after 1985. Saskatchewan moved from having the second-lowest rate of youth charged in the country during 1980–83 to having the highest rate, except for the territories, during 1987–96. This spectacular increase was due both to the large increase in the rate of young persons apprehended (Figure 3.2) and to the large increase after

1985 in the proportions of these apprehended youth who were charged: from around 25 percent in 1977–83 to 60 to 70 percent in 1986–96. Both of these increases were mainly in the form of large jumps in 1986, but there were also upward trends after 1986 (Figure 3.4a).

Ontario also experienced a large increase — about 75 percent — after 1985 in the rate of young persons charged, due to a jump from about 3000 per 100 000 in the early 1980s to about 4500 in 1986, rising to 5000–6000 per 100 000 in the early 1990s. This was not due to an increase in apprehensions — which actually declined during the period (Figure 3.2) — but to a jump in the proportion of these apprehended youth who were charged, from about 30 percent in 1983 to about 55 percent in 1986, followed by a steady increase to about 70 percent in the early 1990s (Figure 3.4a).

Indeed, one of the most striking aspects of the transition from the JDA to the YOA in five of the eight provinces and territories that had a maximum age of 15 years under the JDA, and therefore added 16- and 17-year-olds under the Uniform Maximum Age provision of the YOA, is the sudden transition in 1986 from charging relatively low proportions of apprehended youth — that is, high use of police discretion to charging high proportions. This has resulted in greater national homogeneity in police charging practices. This sudden change was particularly pronounced in Saskatchewan and Ontario, but also occurred in Prince Edward Island, Nova Scotia, and the Northwest Territories (Figure 3.4a). The timing suggests the influence of the YOA. Previous research suggests that the increase in proportions charged in Ontario and Saskatchewan applied over the entire YOA age range (12 to 17 years inclusive) and was therefore not simply due to the addition of 16- and 17-year-olds to the jurisdiction of the youth justice system (Carrington 1998).

In Prince Edward Island and Nova Scotia, this increase in charge ratios, combined with the rising trends in both the rate of apprehensions and charge ratios, resulted in rising trends after 1986 in the rates of young persons charged and in average rates of young persons charged that were twice as high as during 1980–83. In the Northwest Territories, the large jump in charge ratio in 1986 (Figure 3.4a) was offset to some extent by a decrease in the rate of apprehensions, resulting in a moderate, statistically nonsignificant, increase in the rate of young persons charged.

On the other hand, the higher average charge ratios for 1986–96 in Alberta and the Yukon are due to rising trends rather than large jumps in 1986, and may be unrelated to the YOA.

In New Brunswick and Manitoba, there were fairly stable, high proportions of apprehended youth charged throughout 1977–96 (Figure 3.4b), so the rate of young persons charged followed the rate of apprehensions.

In Newfoundland, the charge ratio decreased steeply during 1977–83, rose sharply from 1988 to 1993, then fell (Figure 3.4b). Similarly, the rate of young persons charged rose from a rather low level of about 3200 per 100 000 in 1986 to a peak of about 6000 in 1991, then fell to about 5300 in 1996. In

FIGURE 3.4

Percentage of Apprehended Youth Who Were Charged, 1977–1996

(a) Provinces in which the charge ratio jumped in 1986

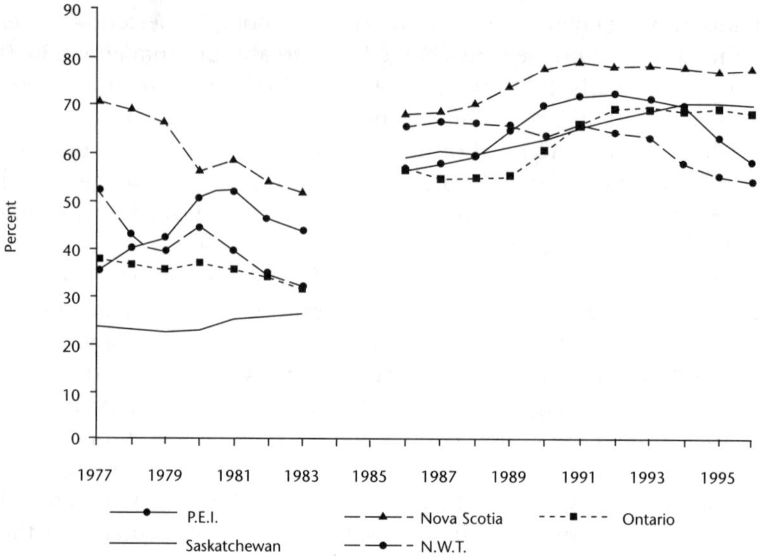

(b) Other provinces

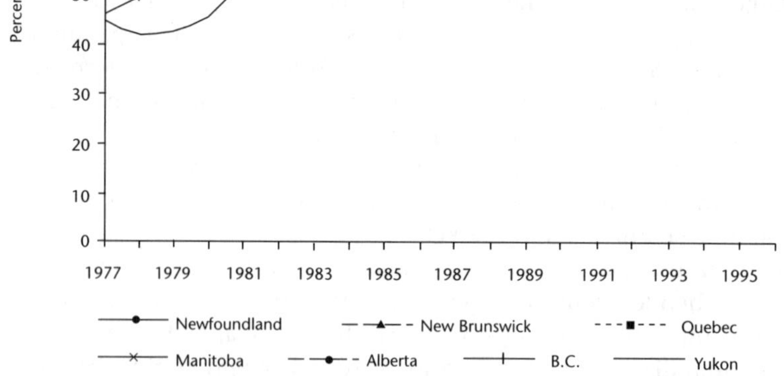

Note: Percentages are modified three-year moving averages.

British Columbia — the other province in which 17-year-olds were added to the youth justice system by the YOA — the charge ratio and the rate of young persons charged increased from 1977 to 1983, then decreased from 1986 to 1996. In neither province was there a significant change in level in 1986, and it is difficult to know to what extent the changes in charging in these provinces might have been affected by the YOA.

CONCLUSION

This chapter has shown that there is no basis in fact for public concern about increased levels of youth crime or the supposed failure of the YOA to control youth crime. Apart from a temporary peak in the early 1990s, the level of police-reported youth crime in Canada has changed very little since 1980. The average per capita rate of police-reported youth crime was 7 percent higher during the first eleven years under the YOA than during the last four years under the JDA. This increase does not appear to be due to the YOA, since it did not occur immediately after 1985, but is largely accounted for by a temporary "hump" in youth crime during the early 1990s, mainly in the Western provinces. There were jumps in police-reported youth crime in Saskatchewan and British Columbia immediately after 1985, which may have been due to the YOA, possibly because of changes in police recording practices rather than the criminal behaviour of young persons. On the other hand, police-reported youth crime was lower under the YOA than during 1980–83 in Quebec and Ontario. Although the drop in Quebec was probably at least partly due to the provincial youth diversion system, which predated the YOA by five years, we cannot account for the drop in 1986 in Ontario.

The average rate of young persons charged by police was 27 percent higher during 1986–96 than 1980–83. Unlike the rate of young persons apprehended, the charge rate jumped immediately after the YOA came into effect. Before and after this, the charge rate followed the rate of apprehensions quite closely.

The jump in young persons charged in 1986 reflects a jump in the proportion of identified young offenders who were charged — that is, to a sudden drop in police diversion of young offenders. This sudden change in the charge ratio, a time series that is otherwise quite stable, suggests the effect of a discrete event: presumably the YOA. The jump in police charging was especially pronounced in Saskatchewan and Ontario but also occurred in Prince Edward Island, Nova Scotia, and the Northwest Territories. All of these jurisdictions were characterized, prior to the YOA, by the charging of relatively low proportions of apprehended youth — that is, by the use of relatively high levels of police discretion. On the other hand, Quebec, which had the highest proportion of apprehended youth charged prior to the YOA, experienced a continuous decline in the charge ratio after 1988. The charging of apprehended youth in the other six jurisdictions appears not to have been affected by the YOA.

During the decade after the YOA came into effect, the rate of police-reported youth crime in Canada increased slightly, but probably not because of the YOA. It decreased in Ontario, Quebec, and the Yukon, and increased elsewhere. The YOA does appear to have caused a substantial increase in the rate of young persons charged in Canada, by causing an increase in the proportion of apprehended youth who are charged — that is, a reduction in the use of police discretion — in some jurisdictions. In other jurisdictions, the rate of young persons charged also increased, but apparently not because of the YOA. Quebec is the only province in which the rate of young persons charged declined after 1985.

In its Declaration of Principle, the YOA recognized the right to the "least possible interference" in the lives of young persons accused of crimes. It encouraged the use of informal processing in preference to formal proceedings against young persons. Quebec is the only province in which formal charging of apprehended young persons decreased under the YOA. It is difficult to see how the increase in the laying of charges against young persons in Ontario, Saskatchewan, Prince Edward Island, Nova Scotia, and the Northwest Territories is consistent with the intent of the YOA. The federal government is now considering changes to the youth justice system to encourage more use of police discretion and other innovative alternatives to formal charging (Department of Justice Canada n.d. [1998]: 19–24). The findings reported in this chapter suggest that such measures are needed.

STUDY QUESTIONS

1. *How does Carrington explain changes in the rate of young persons apprehended and charged by police in Canada from 1977 to 1996?*
2. *According to Carrington, what effect, if any, did the introduction of the Young Offenders Act have on officially recorded youth crime rates in Canada?*
3. *What do Carrington's research findings show about provincial and regional variations in the rates of young persons apprehended and charged in Canada before and after the introduction of the Young Offenders Act?*

REFERENCES

Bala, Nicholas. 1994. "What's Wrong with YOA Bashing? What's Wrong with the YOA? — Recognizing the Limits of the Law." *Canadian Journal of Criminology 36*(3): 247–70.

Brantingham, Paul J. 1991. "Patterns in Canadian Crime." In Margaret A. Jackson and Curt T. Griffiths, eds., *Canadian Criminology*, 371–402. Toronto: Harcourt Brace Jovanovich, Canada.

Carrington, Peter J. 1995. "Has Violent Youth Crime Increased? Comment on Corrado and Markwart." *Canadian Journal of Criminology 37*(1): 61–73.

———. 1998. "Changes in Police Charging of Young Offenders in Ontario and Saskatchewan after 1984." *Canadian Journal of Criminology 40*(2): 153–64.

Carrington, Peter J., and Sharon Moyer. 1994. "Trends in Youth Crime and Police Response, Pre- and Post-YOA." *Canadian Journal of Criminology 36*(1): 1–28.

Cook, Thomas D., and Donald T. Campbell. 1979. *Quasi-Experimentation.* Boston: Houghton Mifflin.

Corrado, Raymond R., and Alan Markwart. 1992. "The Evolution and Implementation of a New Era of Juvenile Justice in Canada." In Raymond R. Corrado, Nicholas Bala, Rick Linden, and Marc LeBlanc, eds., *Juvenile Justice in Canada*, 137–227. Toronto: Butterworths.

———. 1994. "The Need to Reform the YOA in Response to Violent Young Offenders: Confusion, Reality or Myth?" *Canadian Journal of Criminology 36*(3): 343–78.

Department of Justice Canada. n.d. [1998]. *A Strategy for the Renewal of Youth Justice.* Ottawa: Department of Justice Canada.

Doob, Anthony N., and Janet B.L. Chan. 1982. "Factors Affecting Police Decisions to Take Juveniles to Court." *Canadian Journal of Criminology 24*: 25–37.

DuWors, Richard. 1997. "The Justice Data Factfinder." *Juristat 17*(13). Ottawa: Canadian Centre for Justice Statistics, Statistics Canada.

Hackler, Jim, and Wasanti Paranjape. 1983. "Juvenile Justice Statistics: Mythmaking or Measure of System Response." *Canadian Journal of Criminology 25*(1): 209–26.

———. 1984. "Official Reaction to Juvenile Theft: Comparison across Provinces." *Canadian Journal of Criminology 26*(1): 179–98

Hylton, John H. 1994. "Get Tough or Get Smart? Options for Canada's Youth Justice System in the Twenty-First Century." *Canadian Journal of Criminology 36*(3): 229–46.

Kong, Rebecca. 1997. "Canadian Crime Statistics, 1996." *Juristat 17*(8). Ottawa: Canadian Centre for Justice Statistics, Statistics Canada.

Leblanc, Marc, and Hélène Beaumont. 1988. "The Quebec Perspective on the Young Offenders Act: Implementation before Adoption." In Joe Hudson, Joseph P. Hornick, and Barbara A. Burrows, eds., *Justice and the Young Offender in Canada*, 81–92. Toronto: Wall and Thompson.

———. 1992. "The Effectiveness of Juvenile Justice in Quebec: A Natural Experiment in Implementing Formal Diversion and a Justice Model." In R. Corrado, N. Bala, R. Linden, and M. Leblanc, eds., *Juvenile Justice in Canada*, 283–312. Toronto: Butterworths.

Markwart, Alan, and Raymond R. Corrado. 1995. "A Response to Carrington." *Canadian Journal of Criminology 37*(1): 74–87.

Moyer, Sharon. 1996. *A Profile of the Juvenile Justice System in Canada.* Report to the Federal-Provincial-Territorial Task Force on Youth Justice. Ottawa: Department of Justice Canada.

Scanlon, R. Lorcan. 1986. "Canadian Crime Rates: Sources and Trends." In Robert A. Silverman and James J. Teevan, Jr., eds., *Crime in Canadian Society*, 3rd ed., 90–7. Toronto: Butterworths.

Task Force on Youth Justice. 1996. *A Review of the Young Offenders Act and the Youth Justice System in Canada.* Report of the Federal-Provincial-Territorial Task Force on Youth Justice. Ottawa: Department of Justice Canada.

PART TWO
Youth Crime: Theoretical Perspectives

INTRODUCTION

Over the years criminologists have proposed many different theoretical perspectives on youth crime. In fact, while most theories in criminology claim to be general theories of crime, the majority focus mainly on attempting to explain youth crime and delinquency. In addition, as feminist criminologists have noted critically, most of these theories have also focused primarily on male criminality to the exclusion of attempting to account for different levels and patterns of male and female criminality (Comack 1996). The abundance of different theoretical perspectives means, on the one hand, that there is certainly no shortage of theories for students of youth crime to study. On the other hand, this also adds a great deal of complexity to the task of trying to learn about the variety of ways in which criminologists have attempted to explain youth crime and delinquency. Like the theoretical study of crime in general, the theoretical study of youth crime is challenging for most students. Despite this, however, it is also very important. The study of theoretical perspectives on youth crime and delinquency is essential for any person concerned with understanding the causes of youth crime and developing meaningful efforts at youth crime prevention.

As we saw in the David Farrington chapter in Part One, in recent years criminologists have moved increasingly toward developing integrative theories of youth crime that include complementary theoretical propositions from a number of traditionally distinct theories, such as strain theory, control theory, and social learning theory. The following chapters in Part Two highlight other similar integrative and revised theoretical approaches that are now being used by criminologists as a starting point for explaining youth crime.

In Chapter Four, John Laub and Robert Sampson provide a discussion of their important and influential life-course theory of crime and delinquency, which they develop in more detail in their book *Crime in the Making: Pathways and Turning Points through Life* (1993). Sampson and Laub's theory attempts to provide a foundation for explaining variation in criminal behaviour "over the life course," from early childhood to adulthood. The theory focuses in particular on the conditions associated with the onset, maintenance, and desistance of criminal behaviour at various points in a person's life. Sampson and Laub's most important contribution is their identification of the life events that enable young adult offenders to desist from crime. Two of the most important "turning points" they identify are a "cohesive marriage" (or cohabitation) and "attachment to the labour force" (or stable employment). According to Sampson and Laub, life events like this help people build positive relationships with individuals and institutions that lead to a greater stake in conformity, or the development of more "social capital." Sampson and Laub point out that their life-course theory is based on the "central idea of social control theory — that crime and deviance are more likely when an individual's bond to society is weak or broken." In the chapter, they review evidence that supports the basic premises of their theory and pose questions for future research. In recent years, many criminologists, including Sampson and Laub themselves, have undertaken follow-up research to test and extend life-course theory as a way to more adequately explain youth crime (see, for example, Arnold and Kay 1999; Sampson and Laub 1997; Warr 1998). Most importantly, the life-course perspective draws attention to crucial questions about youth crime, including: Why do some troubled youth go on to become adult offenders while others do not? What are the most significant life events associated with the onset, maintenance, and desistance of criminal behaviour? What can be done to turn young offenders away from youth crime? It should also be noted that Sampson and Laub's theory is now one among several theories that are forming the basis of a new perspective in criminology called developmental criminology (Thornberry 1997).

In Chapter Five, Robert Agnew provides a similar overview of his important, recently developed general strain theory of crime and delinquency. Agnew's strain theory has also been called a "social-psychological strain theory" (Brezina 1998: 77) to distinguish it from earlier sociological strain theories popularized in the 1950s by leading U.S. criminologists like Robert K. Merton (see Hackler 1996). Agnew's theory is different from traditional strain theories in that it focuses on the "strain" people feel as a result of their negative treatment from others. Rather than treating strain as something that is generated by social-structural forces (like the gap between culturally prescribed goals and legitimate means of achieving them identified in Merton's theory), Agnew proposes that negative treatment from others (or "strain") tends to generate negative emotions such as anger, frustration, and resentment. In turn, Agnew's theory predicts that individuals may try to alleviate their feelings of anger and resentment toward others by engaging in delinquent or criminal behaviour. This behaviour may take various forms, including theft, vandalism, and aggressive violent acts undertaken for the purpose of revenge. At a more abstract level, in the article chosen here, Agnew attempts to integrate insights derived from developmental theories of crime (like Sampson and Laub's) with his revised strain theory. Agnew argues forcefully that developmental and strain theory concepts are quite consistent with each other and that strain theory has a great deal to offer in helping to further explain adolescent development and crime. In the chapter, Agnew offers a description of adolescent development from a strain theory perspective that complements the work of researchers like Sampson and Laub (Chapter Four; 1993; 1997). In doing so, Agnew's chapter also makes a significant contribution to our understanding of stability and change in offending over the life course.

In Chapter Six, Ross Matsueda and Karen Heimer offer a complementary life-course approach rooted in symbolic interactionism. According to Matsueda and Heimer, integrating ideas from the symbolic interactionist theories developed by sociologists adds another important dimension to the life course perspective. In particular, interactionist theory draws attention to the importance of symbolic meanings attached to the unfolding of role transitions across the life course. In addition, it offers a situational theory of the mechanisms by which life course transitions translate into criminal acts. In the chapter, Matsueda and Heimer summarize Sampson and Laub's (1993) "theory of informal social control" as one example of a developmental theory that focuses on role transitions while ignoring the symbolic meaning that is often attached to them by individuals. Matsueda and Heimer remark that symbolic interactionist theory can augment the life-course perspective in several other ways. This includes, first, drawing attention to the influence of deviant subcultures on the behaviour of individual members. Second, interactionist theory stipulates "how the dynamics of the immediate situation are linked to social roles, meanings, and behaviors, and how individual propensities (personality) are socially reconstituted in interactions." Matsueda and Heimer's approach focuses more on the human agency of individual actors. Specifically, they show how individuals are constantly engaged in a "dialectical relationship" in which "social interaction is conditioned by the life course, which at the same time, is socially constituted in interactions."

The chapters included in Part Two are designed to provide an overview of the most important recent theoretical developments in the study of youth crime and delinquency. Reading these chapters on your own, and discussing them with your colleagues, friends, or instructor, should help you to begin to develop an understanding of some of the most significant causes of youth crime. The readings should also help you to think more critically about youth crime prevention, an important topic we turn to later in the book.

REFERENCES

Arnold, B., and F. Kay. 1999. "Early Transition Stages and Heterogeneity in Criminal Careers among Young Offenders." *Canadian Review of Sociology and Anthropology 36*(2): 157–77.

Brezina, T. 1998. "Adolescent Maltreatment and Delinquency: The Question of Intervening Processes." *Journal of Research in Crime and Delinquency 35*(1): 71–99.

Comack, E. 1996. "Women and Crime." In R. Linden, ed., *Criminology: A Canadian Perspective.* 3rd ed., 139–75. Toronto: Harcourt Brace.

Hackler, J. 1996. "Strain Theories." In R. Linden, ed., *Criminology: A Canadian Perspective.* 3rd ed., 265–91. Toronto: Harcourt Brace.

Sampson, R., and J. Laub. 1993. *Crime in the Making: Pathways and Turning Points through Life,* 133–61. Cambridge: Harvard University Press.

———. 1997. "A Life-Course Theory of Cumulative Disadvantage and the Stability of Delinquency." In T. Thornberry, ed., *Developmental Theories of Crime and Delinquency.* New Brunswick, NJ: Transaction Books.

Thornberry, T., ed. 1997. *Developmental Theories of Crime and Delinquency.* New Brunswick, NJ: Transaction Books.

Warr, M. 1998. "Life-Course Transitions and Desistance from Crime." *Criminology 36*(2): 183–216.

CHAPTER FOUR

Turning Points in the Life Course: Why Change Matters to the Study of Crime

JOHN H. LAUB
Northeastern University, Boston
ROBERT J. SAMPSON
University of Chicago

Several years ago we uncovered 60 cartons of case files in the basement of the Harvard Law School Library. These data constituted the classic longitudinal study of 500 delinquents and 500 nondelinquents initiated by Sheldon and Eleanor Glueck in 1940 (see Glueck and Glueck 1950; 1968). While we were organizing and reconstructing the Gluecks' data, two important books rocked the field of criminology — *Crime and Human Nature* by James Q. Wilson and Richard Herrnstein (1985), and *A General Theory of Crime* by Michael Gottfredson and Travis Hirschi (1990). Although certainly different, the thrust of these books was to redirect criminological attention to the importance of childhood. For example, Gottfredson and Hirschi (1990) argue that effective child rearing in the early formative years of a child's development produces high self-control, which in turn is a stable phenomenon that inhibits crime throughout the life course. The work of Wilson and Herrnstein (1985) pushed the explanation of crime back even earlier in life to constitutional differences (e.g., impulsiveness and temperament) in interaction with familial factors (see also Grasmick et al. 1993; Nagin and Paternoster 1991).

Ironically, then, as we were resurrecting the Gluecks' data, new life was breathed into the primary thesis of the Gluecks — childhood temperament and family socialization matter most, and thus the "past is prologue" (Glueck and Glueck 1968: 167). Although attracted to this renewed emphasis on the importance of children and families to the explanation of delinquency, we were troubled by the profound questions raised by the childhood-stability argument. Are differences in child rearing and temperament all we need to know to understand patterns of adult crime? Are childhood differences in an-

Source: John H. Laub and Robert J. Sampson, "Turning Points in the Life Course: Why Change Matters to the Study of Crime," *Criminology 31*(3) (1993): 301–25. Reprinted by permission of The American Society of Criminology.

tisocial behaviour invariably stable? Why does continuity in deviant behaviour exist? Perhaps most important, what about individual change, salient life events, and turning points in adulthood?

Challenged by these and other questions, we set out to examine crime and deviance in childhood, adolescence, and adulthood in a way that recognized the significance of both continuity and change over the life course. To do so we synthesized and integrated the criminological literature on childhood antisocial behaviour, adolescent delinquency, and adult crime with theory and research on the life course (Sampson and Laub 1992). By also rethinking the findings produced by longitudinal research, we were eventually led to develop an age-graded theory of informal social control to explain crime and deviance over the life span. We then tested this theory on the longitudinal data we reconstructed from the Gluecks' study (Sampson and Laub 1993).

Building on these efforts, we turn to an examination of conceptual issues relating to continuity and change in antisocial behaviour over the life course. With respect to continuity, we highlight the distinction between self-selection and cumulative continuity. We then unite the ideas of state dependence (Nagin and Paternoster 1991) and cumulative continuity (Caspi and Moffitt 1993a; Moffitt 1993) in delineating a developmental, sequential model of crime across the life course. With respect to change, we explicate the relevance of the adult life course and the various meanings of change. Our major thesis is that social capital and turning points are important concepts in understanding processes of change in the adult life course. We illustrate these concepts using qualitative life-history data drawn from the Gluecks' study. Overall, our goal is to advance a framework that challenges theories of crime which "presuppose a developmental determinism in which childhood experiences set the course of later development" (Bandura 1982: 747). To set the stage, we briefly highlight the theoretical framework on change from our recent study (Sampson and Laub 1993).

AN AGE-GRADED THEORY OF INFORMAL SOCIAL CONTROL

The central idea of social control theory — that crime and deviance are more likely when an individual's bond to society is weak or broken — is an organizing principle in our theory of social bonding over the life course.

The life course has been defined as "pathways through the age differentiated life span" (Elder 1985: 17), in particular the "sequence of culturally defined age-graded roles and social transitions that are enacted over time" (Caspi et al. 1990: 15). Two central concepts underlie the analysis of life-course dynamics. A *trajectory* is a pathway or line of development over the life span, such as work life, parenthood, and criminal behaviour. Trajectories refer to long-term patterns of behaviour and are marked by a sequence of transitions. *Transitions* are marked by life events (e.g., first job or first marriage) that are embedded in trajectories and evolve over shorter time spans (Elder 1985: 31–32).

Following Elder (1975; 1985), we differentiate the life course of individuals on the basis of age and argue that the important institutions of both formal and informal social control vary across the life span. However, we emphasize the role of age-graded, informal social control as reflected in the structure of interpersonal bonds linking members of society to one another and to wider social institutions (e.g., work, family, school). Unlike formal sanctions that originate in purposeful efforts to control crime, informal social controls "emerge as by-products of role relationships established for other purposes and are components of role reciprocities" (Kornhauser 1978: 24).

Although rejecting the "ontogenetic" approach dominant in developmental psychology (see Dannefer 1984), our theoretical framework nonetheless follows a developmental strategy (Loeber and LeBlanc 1990; Patterson, DeBaryshe, and Ramsey 1989). The specific developmental approach we take views causality as "best represented by a developmental network of causal factors" in which dependent variables become independent variables over time (Loeber and LeBlanc 1990: 433). Moreover, developmental criminology recognizes both continuity and within-individual changes over time, focusing on "life transitions and developmental covariates . . . which may mediate the developmental course of offending" (Loeber and LeBlanc 1990: 451). This strategy has also been referred to as a "stepping-stone approach" whereby factors are time ordered by age and assessed with respect to outcome variables (see Farrington 1986).

A similar orientation can be found in interactional theory as proposed by Thornberry (1987). Interactional theory embraces a developmental approach and argues convincingly that causal influences are reciprocal over the life course and that delinquency may contribute to the weakening of social bonds over time. Thornberry's perspective is also consistent with a person-centred approach to development as propounded by Magnusson and Bergman (1988; 47). Namely, by focusing explicitly on "persons" rather than "variables" and examining individual life histories over time (see Magnusson and Bergman 1988; 1990), this strategy offers insight into the social processes of intra-individual developmental change in criminal behaviour over the life course.

Although beyond the scope of this analysis, the first building block in our "sociogenic" developmental theory focuses on the mediating role of informal family and school social bonds in explaining childhood and adolescent delinquency (Sampson and Laub 1993; Chapters 4–5). As elaborated on below, the second building block incorporates the subsequent continuity in childhood and adolescent antisocial behaviour that extends throughout adulthood across a variety of life's domains (e.g., crime, alcohol abuse, divorce, unemployment).

Having provided a role for continuity, we nonetheless believe that salient life events and social ties in adulthood can counteract, at least to some extent, the trajectories of early child development. Hence, a third and major thesis of our work is that social bonds in adulthood — especially attachment to the labour force and cohesive marriage (or cohabitation) — explain criminal behaviour regardless of prior differences in criminal propensity. In other words, we contend that pathways to both crime and conformity are modified by key institutions of social control in the transition to adulthood (e.g., employment, military service, and marriage).

In contrast to many life-course models, we emphasize the quality or strength of social ties in these transitions more than the occurrence or timing of discrete life events (cf. Loeber and LeBlanc 1990: 430–32). For example, marriage per se may not increase social control, but close emotional ties and mutual investment increase the social bond between individuals and, all else equal, should lead to a reduction in criminal behaviour (cf. Shover 1985: 94). Employment by itself also does not necessarily increase social control. It is employment coupled with job stability, commitment to work, and mutual ties binding workers and employers that should increase social control and, all else equal, lead to a reduction in criminal behaviour.

In short, our theory attempts to unite continuity and change within the context of a sociological understanding of crime in the life course. A major concept in our framework is the dynamic process whereby the interlocking nature of trajectories and transitions generates turning points, or a change in life course (Elder 1985: 32). Adaptation to life events is crucial because the same event or transition followed by different adaptations can lead to different trajectories (Elder 1985: 35). That is, despite the connection between childhood events and experiences in adulthood, turning points can modify life trajectories — they can "redirect paths." For some individuals, turning points are abrupt — radical "turnarounds" or changes in life history that separate the past from the future (Elder, Gimbel, and Ivie 1991: 215). For most individuals, however, we conceptualize turning points as "part of a process over time and not as a dramatic lasting change that takes place at any one time" (Pickles and Rutter 1991: 134; see also Clausen 1990; McAdam 1989: 745; Rutter 1989a; 1989b). The process-oriented nature of turning points leads us to focus on incremental change embedded in informal social controls.

To evaluate and refine our theory, we analyzed the natural histories of two groups of boys that differed dramatically in childhood antisocial behaviour and delinquency that were followed into adulthood. More specifically, we reconstructed and examined the life histories originally gathered by Glueck and Glueck (1950; 1968) of 500 delinquents and 500 control subjects matched on age, IQ, ethnicity, and neighbourhood deprivation. An exhaustive body of data (e.g., official records, observations, and personal interviews with subjects, parents, spouses, neighbours, and employers) was collected on these individuals in childhood, adolescence, young adulthood, and adulthood. Our analyses involved a multi-method, multi-measurement scheme that used quantitative and qualitative data (for details, see Sampson and Laub 1993).

DISTINGUISHING SELF-SELECTION FROM CUMULATIVE CONTINUITY

Critics will argue that individual differences combine with self-selection to account for patterns of behaviour across the life course. In brief, this counter-argument goes as follows: Individuals with an early propensity to crime (e.g., low self-control) determined mainly by family socialization and individual differences (e.g., impulsiveness) systematically sort themselves throughout adulthood into states consistent with this latent trait. For instance, Gottfredson and Hirschi (1990: 164–67) argue that delinquent and impulsive youth will choose deviant spouses, unstable jobs, and continue their delinquent ways in adulthood. If true, the adult life course is merely a setting within which predetermined lives are played out.

In one sense the self-selection thesis was supported in the Gluecks' study — adolescent delinquents and nondelinquents displayed significant behavioural consistency well into adulthood. Delinquency and other forms of antisocial conduct in childhood were related not only to adult crime, but also to troublesome behaviours across a variety of adult domains (e.g., AWOL in the military, economic dependence, marital discord). This continuity persisted despite the fact that delinquents and controls were originally matched case-by-case on age, intelligence, neighbourhood, and ethnicity.

The hypothesis of self-selection, however, leads to a more fundamental methodological implication — correlations among adult behaviours (e.g., job instability and crime) are completely spurious and should disappear once controls are introduced for prior individual-level differences in criminal propensity or low self-control (see Gottfredson and Hirschi 1990: 154–68). Although rarely examined directly, we believe the data do not support this spuriousness hypothesis. In particular, our quantitative analyses revealed independent effects of marital attachment and job stability on adult crime. These results were consistent for a wide variety of outcome measures, control variables (e.g., childhood and adolescent antisocial behaviour; individual-difference constructs, such as IQ, self-control, mesomorphy, and personality), and analytic techniques — including methods that account for persistent unobserved heterogeneity in criminal propensity (see Nagin and Paternoster 1991). Rutter, Quinton, and Hill (1990) have also shown the independent explanatory power of adult marital cohesion on adult deviance, self-selection notwithstanding.

At the same time, our theory incorporates the causal role of prior delinquency in facilitating adult crime by integrating the concept of state dependence (Nagin and Paternoster 1991) with that of cumulative continuity (Moffitt 1993). Although this role is potentially direct, we emphasize a developmental model wherein delinquent behaviour has a systematic, attenuating effect on the social and institutional bonds linking adults to society (e.g., labour force attachment, marital cohesion). More specifically, the idea of cumulative continuity posits that delinquency incrementally mortgages the future by generating negative consequences for the life chances of stigmatized and institutionalized youth. For example, arrest and incarceration may spark failure in school, unemployment, and weak community bonds, in turn increasing adult crime (Tittle 1988: 80). Serious delinquency in particular leads to the "knifing off" (Caspi and Moffitt 1993a; Moffitt 1993) of future opportunities such that participants have fewer options for a conventional life. The cumulative continuity of disadvantage is thus not only a result of stable individual differences in criminal propensity, but a dynamic process whereby childhood antisocial behaviour and adolescent delinquency foster adult crime through the severance of adult social bonds. In this view, weak social bonding is a mediating and, hence, causal sequential link in a chain of adversity between childhood delinquency and adult criminal behaviour.

The thesis of cumulative continuity was supported in our quantitative analyses. As noted above, job stability and marital attachment in adulthood were significantly related to changes in adult crime — the stronger the adult ties to work and family, the less crime and deviance among delinquents and controls. Moreover, social bonds to employment were directly influenced by state sanctions — incarceration as a juvenile and as a young adult had a negative effect on later job stability, which in turn was negatively related to continued involvement in crime over the life course. Although we found little direct effect of incarceration on subsequent criminality, the indirect "criminogenic" effects through job stability were substantively important. Research by Nagin and Waldfogel (1992) also supports the cumulative continuity thesis in showing a destabilizing effect of convictions on the labour market prospects of a cohort of London boys.

Our synthesis of cumulative continuity and state dependence recasts in a structural and developmental framework the original contentions of labelling theory — that official reactions to primary deviance (e.g., arrest) may create problems of adjustment (e.g., unemployment) that foster additional crime in the form of secondary deviance (Becker 1963; Lemert 1951; Tittle 1988). As Becker (1963: 24–39) has argued, the concept of a deviant career suggests a stable pattern of deviant behaviour, which is sustained by the labelling process. More recently, Hagan and Palloni (1990) suggested that continuity in delinquent behaviour may result from a structural imputation process that begins early in childhood (see also Tittle 1988: 78–81). They show that this process may even extend across generations, thereby explaining the effects of parental conviction on sons' delinquency regardless of family background and propensity to crime.

Cumulative Disadvantage and Structural Background

Hagan's (1991) research further suggests that the deleterious effect of adolescent deviance on adult stratification outcomes is greatest among lower-class boys, especially as mediated by police contacts. Middle-class boys who escaped the negative consequences of official labelling did not suffer impairment in adult occupational outcomes as a result of their adolescent delinquency. In other words, avoiding the snares of arrest and institutionalization provided opportunities for prosocial attachments among middle-class youth to take firm hold in adulthood. Similarly, Jessor, Donovan, and Costa (1991) show that for middle-class youth, delinquency is not a major handicap with respect to adult outcomes. These studies suggest that the concepts of knifing off and cumulative continuity are most salient in explaining the structurally constrained life chances of the disadvantaged urban poor.

In short, there is evidence that cumulative disadvantage, state-dependence, and location in the class structure may interact. Among those in advantaged positions that provide continuity in social resources over time, nondelinquents and delinquents alike are presumably not just more motivated, but better able structurally to establish binding ties to conventional lines of adult activity. If nothing else, incumbency in prosocial middle-class roles provides advantages in maintaining the status quo and counteracting negative life events (e.g., last hired, first fired). Race, class, and crime also pervade the consciousness of American society more generally and employers in particular. Consider the widespread perceptions of blacks as "dangerous" and "criminal" as rationales by employers for discrimination in hiring (Kirschenman and Neckerman 1991). We therefore merge the state-dependence thesis that historical time matters with a concern for structural location. Quite simply, the context of where and how long one has been in prior states is crucial in understanding later adult development.

Self-Selection Reconsidered

Our theoretical conceptualization of cumulative continuity and the causal role of the adult life course does not negate the potential direct or unmediated effect of self-selection through individual differences. In other words, by distinguishing self-selection from cumulative continuity, we incorporate the independent effects of early delinquency (or individual propensity) and the dimensions of adult social bonding on adult crime. This distinction is consistent with recent research on homophily in social choices across the life course. For example, Kandel, Davies, and Baydar (1990) studied mate selection and found considerable homophily — deviant individuals tend to select deviant marriage or cohabitation partners (see also Caspi, Elder, and Herbener (1990). Nevertheless, social causation emerges as a crucial factor even in the face of such social selection. As Kandel, Davies, and Baydar (1990: 221) state, "Although individual choices are made, in part, as a function of the individual's prior attributes, values, and personality characteristics, involvement in the new relationship has further effects and influences on that individual." Similarly, Rutter, Quinton, and Hill (1990) found homophily in the choice of marital partners but also a substantial effect of marital cohesion that held after taking planning of marriage partners into account.

The emergence of significant social causation in tandem with homophily (or self-selection) undermines the theoretical individualism that pervades social scientific thought. We believe that an overemphasis on self-selection stems from a "broadly perpetuated fiction in modern society" (Coleman 1990: 300):

> This fiction is that society consists of a set of independent individuals, each of whom acts to achieve goals that are independently arrived at, and that the functioning of the social system consists of the combinations of the actions of independent individuals.

Consistent with our theory, social interdependence arises from the fact that actors have social investments in events and relationships that are partially under the control of other actors. Hence, the interdependent web of relations characteristic of social collectivities ensures the operation of constraints and opportunities in shaping behaviour notwithstanding individual intentions.

WHY CHANGE STILL MATTERS

Whether generated by self-selection or cumulative continuity, a focus on stability is nonetheless insufficient for understanding crime in the adult life course. First, the stability of antisocial behaviour is far from perfect. As the literature on prediction shows, childhood variables tend to be rather modest prognostic devices. In fact, a large percentage of false positives and false negatives is a common result (see, e.g., Loeber and Stouthamer-Loeber 1987; Farrington and Tarling 1985). The prediction literature thus reinforces the futility of an invariant or deterministic conception of human development (Jessor, Donovan, and Costa 1991; Sampson and Laub 1992).

Second, and equally important, rank-order correlations and other common measures of stability refer to the consistency of between-individual differences over time and consequently rely on an aggregate picture of relative standing. As Huesmann et al. (1984: 1131) note, what remains stable over time is the position of an individual relative to the population. Stability coefficients do not measure the heterogeneity of individual behaviours over time and, hence, do not capture within-individual change.

Life is dynamic; change is clearly possible. Yet the theoretical conceptualization of change has been surprisingly neglected, not just in criminology (see Farrington 1988; Sampson and Laub 1993) but in developmental psychology as well. Indeed, in searching the literature, we found little conceptual work that directly confronts the problem. Moreover, Caspi and Bem (1990: 569) have argued that when the term change does appear, it frequently refers to the mere absence of continuity. We thus consider more explicitly the meaning of change and how it comes about.

Social Capital and Turning Points

Much of the confusion regarding change centres on the various meanings the concept conveys. According to the 1992 edition of *The American Heritage Dictionary of the English Language*, one definition of change is "to cause to be different" — to give a completely different form or appearance, to wholly transform or alter. This definition is most closely related to Caspi and Moffitt's (1993b) notion of "deep" or "real" change (e.g., a high-rate offender who suddenly desists and becomes a productive citizen). But change can also mean a modification, reshaping, or transition from one state, condition, or phase to another. For instance, a high-rate offender who begins to commit fewer crimes than expected based on age and prior criminal propensity changes because his or her trajectory has been modified. A third meaning of change is exchange or replacement with another, usually of the same kind or category. An individual may change from use of beer and wine to use of marijuana and cocaine. Or offenders may change from burglary to robbery.

All of this leads us to think of change along a continuum and to investigate the underlying processes that enable people to change the course of their lives. We believe this may be accomplished by viewing the life course as a probabilistic linkage or chain of events (Rutter, Quinton, and Hill 1990) and by unravelling the mechanisms that operate at key turning points (e.g., when a risk trajectory is recast to a more adaptive path [Rutter 1987: 329]).

In our view, "deep" change and "modified" change are of most interest; both are enhanced when changing roles and environments lead to social investment or social capital (Coleman 1988; 1990; Nagin and Paternoster 1992) in institutional relationships (e.g., family, work, community). As Coleman (1990: 302) argues, the distinguishing feature of social capital lies in the structure of interpersonal relations and institutional linkages. Social capital is created when these relations change in ways that facilitate action. In other words, "social capital is productive, making possible the achievements of certain ends that in its absence would not be possible" (Coleman 1988: 98). By contrast, physical capital is wholly tangible, being embodied in observable material form (1990: 304), and human capital is embodied in the skills and knowledge acquired by an individual. Social capital is even less tangible, for it is embodied in the relations among persons (1990: 304). A core idea, then, is that independent of the forms of physical and human capital available to individuals (e.g., income, occupational skill), social capital is a central factor in facilitating effective ties that bind a person to societal institutions.

Linking Coleman's notion of social capital to social control theory, we have argued that the lack of social capital or investment is one of the primary features of weak social bonds (Sampson and Laub 1993; see also Coleman 1990: 307; Nagin and Paternoster 1992). The theoretical task is to identify the characteristics of social relations that facilitate the social capital available to individuals, families, employers, and other social actors. One of the most important factors is the closure (i.e., "connectedness") of networks among actors in a social system (Coleman 1990: 318–20). In a system involving employers and employees, for example, relations characterized by an extensive set of obligations, expectations, and interdependent social networks are better able to facilitate social control than are jobs characterized by purely utilitarian objectives and nonoverlapping social networks. Similarly, the mere presence of a relationship (e.g., marriage) among adults is not sufficient to produce social capital, and hence, the idea of social capital goes beyond simple structural notions of role change (i.e., married versus not married) to capture the idea of embeddedness.

Our theory thus maintains that adult social ties are important insofar as they create interdependent systems of obligation and restraint that impose significant costs for translating criminal propensities into action. In this scheme, adults will be inhibited from committing crime to the extent that over time they accumulate social capital in their work and family lives, regardless of delinquent background. By contrast, those subject to weak systems of interdependency (see also Braithwaite 1989) and informal social control as an adult (e.g., weak attachment to the labour force or noncohesive marriage) are freer to commit deviance — even if nondelinquent as a youth. This dual premise enables us to explain desistance from crime as well as late onset, and it is consistent with Jessor, Donovan, and Costa's (1991: 160) argument that change is "as much an outcome of the person's embeddedness in a socially organized and structured context of age-related roles, expectations, demands, and opportunities as it is of internal dispositions and intentions."

We also emphasize the reciprocal nature of social capital invested by employers and spouses. For example, employers often take chances in hiring workers, hoping that their investment will pay off. Similarly, a prospective marriage partner may be aware of a potential spouse's deviant background but may nonetheless invest his or her future in that person. This investment by the employer or spouse may in turn trigger a return investment in social capital by the employee or other spouse. The key theoretical point is that social capital and interdependency are reciprocal and embedded in the social ties that exist between individuals and social institutions. This conception may help explain how change in delinquent behaviour is initiated (e.g., an employer's taking a chance on a former delinquent, fostering a return investment in that job, which in turn inhibits the deviant behaviour of the employee).

Sullivan's (1989) research on gangs in New York also provides insight into racial, ethnic, and community differences in the influence of social capital on transitions to work. As they entered young adulthood, the men in the low-income white neighbourhood that Sullivan studied secured better-quality jobs than men in African-American or Hispanic neighbourhoods. Whites were also better able to hold onto these jobs, in part because of their familiarity with the "discipline of the workplace" gained through personal networks and intergenerational ties (1989: 100–5). Networks with the adult community thus differentiated the chances of white youths' escaping environmental adversity from those of their minority counterparts. In a similar vein, Anderson's *Streetwise: Race, Class and Change in an Urban Community* (1990) points to the importance of racial differences in intergenerational ties and the salience of those ties in facilitating employment among young males as they enter adulthood. Anderson (1990) focuses in particular on the sharp decrease over time in African-American "old heads," who socialized boys in the world of work and adulthood more generally. These ethnographies underscore variations by race, ethnicity, and structural context in social capital and its role in promoting successful transitions to young adulthood (see also Short 1990).

Thus, because individual-difference constructs and childhood antisocial behaviour are independent of adult social capital and structural context in fundamental respects, another key aspect of our theory is the partial exogenous nature of the adult life course. This conceptualization opens the door for turning points that can redirect behavioural trajectories in the transition to adulthood. To be sure, we are not implying that individuals in our study became completely different or that they transformed their total personality as a result of social bonding in adulthood. We do not have the data to assess such transformations, nor would we expect that kind of change to occur given what we know about continuities over the life course. But we strongly contend that behavioural changes do occur and that adult life-course patterns are not solely the result of childhood socialization (Bandura 1982).

A PERSON-BASED, LIFE-HISTORY APPROACH TO CHANGE

Our research program has included an intensive qualitative analysis of the life-history records for a subset of men from the Gluecks' study (see Sampson and Laub 1993, Chapter 9). In contrast to the traditional "variables oriented" approach dominant in criminology and the social sciences at large (see especially, Abbott 1992; Katz 1988), we have adopted a "person-oriented" strategy that allows us to explore "patterns or configurations of relevant person characteristics in a developmental perspective" (Magnusson and Bergman 1990: 101). This approach enables one to investigate person–environment interactions, sequences of action, and individual change over time (see Abbott 1992; Cairns 1986; Magnusson and Bergman 1988: 47).

Consistent with our goal of integrating quantitative and qualitative methods, we used quantitative results to identify cases for in-depth qualitative analysis. For example, based on the finding that job stability was an important predictor of desistance from crime, we selected cases that displayed high job stability (e.g., upper 15 percent of the frequency distribution) in combination with no arrest experiences as an adult. Similarly, we selected cases exhibiting low job stability (e.g., bottom quartile of the distribution) and arrest experiences as an adult. When there was a sufficient number of cases in a cell (usually on the diagonal), we randomly selected them for in-depth analysis (e.g., strong job stability and no offending in adulthood). We used a similar selection procedure for marital attachment. In total, we reconstructed and examined 70 life histories from the delinquent sample (for details, see Sampson and Laub 1993).

Integrating divergent sources of life-history data (e.g., narratives, interviews), our qualitative analysis was consistent with the hypothesis that the major turning points in the life course for men that refrained from crime and deviance in adulthood were stable employment and good marriages. As an illustration of our thesis, consider the case history of a subject we call Charlie. Although Charlie had no official arrests during adulthood (ages 17–32), this pattern sharply contrasted with his criminal experiences in childhood and adolescence. As a juvenile, Charlie had ten arrests, primarily for larcenies and burglaries. His first arrest occurred at the age of eight. Moreover, he was incarcerated three times (his first commitment took place when he was 11), and he spent a total of 30 months confined in reform schools.

At the age of 18, Charlie joined the U.S. Maritime Service. He was employed by the same shipping line for two and a half years, working the eastern seaboard from Canada to Cuba. Once every three months, he returned home. Charlie gave virtually all of his earnings to his mother to bank for him. His parole officer speculated that Charlie joined the merchant service to remove himself from detrimental neighbourhood influences that were leading him to delinquency and crime. During this same period (ages 18–20), Charlie began a relationship with a woman who would eventually become his wife. Although classmates together in high school, they began "an active courtship via letters" while Charlie was in the merchant service.

At age 25, Charlie was living with his wife in East Boston. (He was almost 21 at the time of marriage and his wife was 19.) According to interview data, Charlie was devoted to his wife, and the couple appeared especially united in their mutual desire to advance economically. Their goal was to build their own home. Charlie was appreciative of his wife's cooperation and her enduring help and desire to advance economically. When asked for reasons for his reformation, he offered, "I'm married, older, and settled down now."

This portrait of Charlie's life did not change very much at his age-32 interview. He was living with his wife and two children in a suburb close to Boston. Charlie appeared happy and was especially devoted to his two children. In his spare time, he worked on home improvement. Throughout the age 25–32 period, Charlie worked at one job and had recently been promoted to foreman. Previously, he had been a machine operator at the same factory. From interviewer notes, Charlie was described as an industrious worker with no problems on the job whatsoever.

In this chapter, we further advance the life-history, person-based approach to uncovering turning points and processes of change. Specifically, we selected cases for qualitative analyses that demonstrated a change in social bonds (a general measure combining job stability and marital attachment) from age 25 to age 32. Our analysis revealed evidence of both incremental and abrupt change. Incremental change usually occurred over a period of time in the context of an ongoing relationship or institutional affiliation (e.g., marriage); abrupt change was linked to a single event (e.g., entering the military). We also examined the investment processes that are involved as social capital is formed through the development of strong marital ties. Marital investment is a reciprocal process between husbands and wives that, if successful, encourages desistance from crime because of the strength of the social relations that are built up in the family. The life history of the subject we call Tony illustrates these investment processes.

Tony had five arrests during the age 17 – 25 period, including arrests for serious crimes such as armed robbery and burglary. He also served considerable time in penal institutions — 32 months from age 20 to 25. Tony's marital situation at ages 17 – 25 was also rocky. At the time of his marriage, Tony was 22 and his wife was 17. His wife was in high school when she became pregnant, an event that precipitated their marriage. Shortly after the marriage, the couple separated on and off. They continued to experience poor conjugal relations throughout the early period of their marriage.

Despite marital discord and a record of crime as a young adult, Tony had no criminal activity (official or unofficial) during the age 25 – 32 period. What accounted for this change in behaviour? Inspection of his life-history material reveals a distinct change in the marital relationship. At Tony's age-32 interview, his family situation had changed dramatically, to the point that the couple's conjugal relations were cohesive. Tony was described as a rather dependent type who clung to his wife. She was portrayed as a strong, sensible person whose interests were in the home and in her family. The couple had two sons, and overall there was a strong "we feeling" in the household.

According to Tony, his reasons for reformation included: (1) "I have steady work;" (2) "I have family responsibilities now;" and (3) "I have learned my lesson" — he feared returning to prison. According to detailed interviewer notes and additional narratives, the strong influence of Tony's wife was the most important reason for his reform. Indeed, in what appears to be a form of marital social control seen in other cases described below, the interviewer wrote that Tony's wife "gives him good counsel and she sees to it that the subject follows her advice."

Other cases we examined revealed more abrupt change. For instance, one subject, Fred, had no arrests as an adult although he experienced five arrests as a juvenile, mainly for burglaries and larcenies. Fred was incarcerated in reform school for a period of nine months for his crimes. At the age of 16, he left school to go to work in order to support his mother and five siblings. Fred served in the U.S. Maritime Service for about eighteen months at ages 17 – 18. He worked on oil tankers along the East Coast.

Throughout the age 17 – 25 period, Fred remained single. He was living with his mother and siblings in Boston at the age-25 interview. Fred fully supported his mother and two siblings who were still in high school. He worked in several unskilled jobs (e.g., an oil and coal truck helper, an apprentice welder, and a factory worker) over this period. Fred stated that his "home responsibilities forced him to be a stable and regular worker."

A similar pattern is revealed in Frank's life history. Although he had eight arrests during the age 17–25 period, Frank emphasized at age 25 that he intended to marry later that year and was making an earnest effort to reform. He noted how hard it was for him to get a steady job because of his record. At the age-32 interview, Frank had no official or unofficial record of criminal behaviour. He married and was living with his wife and child. He worked in a warehouse and, by all accounts, was a reliable worker (e.g., he had held the same job for the past five years). Frank did admit to some excessive drinking during the period, but he claimed that his drinking had tapered off since his marriage. He stated that his reformation stemmed from a variety of factors: (1) the influence of his wife — according to the interviewer, "she exerts pressure on the subject to conform and holds in check his aggression;" (2) family responsibilities; (3) a long period of probation; (4) fairly steady work since 1957; and (5) fear of being "put away."

For George, a more incremental process of change was evident; it consisted of several circumstances, including leaving the city of Boston, becoming a parent, and finding a steady job. In his interview, George remarked: "Well, for one thing, I got out of Boston — I began to work steadily, and now I have a family — a son whom I always wanted. My father helped me to get back on the road to responsibility and he has lived with us since we moved here. My wife always wanted me to do the right thing and I try to follow her advice. I got away from the old gang and the bookie racket which my uncle runs in the city. In a small town such as this, you have to go straight."

Another set of cases we examined pointed to the military as a "settling influence" or turning point in the life course (see also Elder 1986). Given the available information in the Gluecks' case files, it is hard to uncover exactly what it was about the military experience that facilitated a change in behaviour. Also, our finding of a positive influence is somewhat surprising given our results on the continuity of antisocial behaviour from adolescence into adult domains, including misconduct in the military (see Sampson and Laub 1993, Chapter 6). However, it is not inconsistent that the military can function to turn some men's lives around, even as it disrupts other men's lives (Elder 1986) or provides yet another setting for some men to continue their criminal and deviant behaviour (Gottfredson and Hirschi 1990: 165).

At his age-25 and age-32 interviews, Mickey was living with his wife and children. The subject married when he was almost 22 and his wife was nearly 21. A strong marital attachment between Mickey and his spouse centred around their home and children. Mickey joined the U.S. Navy while on parole from reform school and remained there for thirteen years. According to narrative data, the subject stated that his enlistment in the military changed his outlook on life. "In the navy I was thrown in with guys from all over the country; some of them were well educated and had good backgrounds.

I began to see that my thinking was way out of line and that I was probably wrong. I began to do things their way and things have gone well ever since."

This experience parallels that of another subject who spent a considerable period of time in the navy (seven and a half years) and had strong bonds to his wife and two sons. Similarly, other subjects in the study reported that they "matured in the service" or that the "army taught me a few things." Like Elder (1986), we find that for some men serving in the military can help surmount childhood disadvantage by recasting the past. Bandura (1982: 753) argues that encounters in a closed milieu such as the military "have the greatest potential for branching persons abruptly into new trajectories of life."

We also examined a subset of men who experienced a significant decline in social bonding from ages 25 to 32. In these cases, it was difficult to detect clear turning points, but nevertheless certain patterns did emerge. For some men, a decline in job stability was due to changes in the labour market. Not surprisingly, layoffs, seasonal work, and factory closings all contributed to the weakening of ties to work. For one subject, his troubles in adulthood started when the company he was working for "folded." All employees were let go and his "good job" was simply gone. Macro-level transformations of the economy clearly bear on individual lives.

For several other cases the following scenario emerged. The subject married young, and often the marriage was forced due to pregnancy. Although prior to marriage there was some evidence of excessive drinking by the subject, the subject's wife claimed that the subject had matured into his familial responsibilities, and initially the couple got along well. Work was typically of a seasonal nature (e.g., construction work) and weather dependent. But as the men became older (and while one would normally expect an increasing "conformity" or settling down), ties to marriage and work unravelled. There were separations, followed by reconciliations, followed by further separations. There was often evidence of physical abuse and nonsupport of children. The subject's wife objected to the subject's drinking and was not pleased by the financial uncertainty of seasonal work. The subject resented what he perceived to be "overprotectiveness" on the part of his wife and claimed she "nagged" him. Often the subject's drinking continued to be a problem, exacerbated in part by the fact that in certain jobs drinking seemed to be tolerated or even encouraged so long as one did not drink on the job (Vaillant 1983: 96–97). As a result, crime and deviance became more pronounced over time due to the severing of social ties to work and family.

IMPLICATIONS FOR FUTURE RESEARCH

As Clausen (1990) argues, the idea of turning points is an important concept in the study of lives. Turning points are closely linked to role transitions, and conceptually, they are helpful in understanding change in human behaviour over the life course. We adapted this perspective to explore turning points in the lives of a sample of disadvantaged, persistent adolescent delinquents.

Some positive turning points in the course of their lives were cohesive marriage, meaningful work, and serving in the military. Clear negative turning points were prolonged incarceration, heavy drinking, and subsequent job instability during the transition to young adulthood.

Having established that change does in fact occur, the key research question for the future becomes: Why do some individuals change while others do not? Learning more about turning points — especially in the transition from adolescence to adulthood — is critical for understanding the development of social capital and the facilitation of change in life trajectories. For example, what predicts strong marital attachment in adulthood? How do troubled youth achieve job stability and a strong commitment to work as adults? Is military service an effective vehicle for reshaping the life course of disadvantaged youth? What roles do structural factors and historical context play in determining strong bonds to family and work? More generally, how does one explain differential change among individuals?

Although these questions are complex and form the basis of our current work, we advance some tentative hypotheses. One is simply that there is an element of luck, randomness, or chance operating throughout the course of life. Bandura (1982) argues that chance encounters play a prominent role in shaping life paths. Namely, chance encounters introduce an element of unpredictability in life-course trajectories and thereby opportunities for change to emerge. As Bandura (1982: 749) writes, "Although the separate chains of events in a chance encounter have their own causal determinants, their intersection occurs fortuitously rather than through deliberate plan." A more explicit theorizing of the roles of chance, "adventitious happenings" (Rutter 1989b: 33) or what Short and Strodtbeck (1965) many years ago called "aleatory" elements, may thus help to capture dynamic etiological processes.

The confluence of objective and subjective contingencies is also important in understanding the change process. In all likelihood, transitions involving structural role change, like marriage and employment, do not have the same meaning for everyone (Rutter 1989a: 20). For example, marriage and full-time work provided an opportunity for men in our study to change the direction of their life-course trajectory, but not every man saw it that way (see also Clausen 1990; Elder, Gimbel, and Ivie 1991). In other words, structural role changes only provide the possibility for change to occur — its realization is mediated by individual contingencies. Hence, there is a need to conceptualize and measure objective and subjective elements of turning points.

Although beyond the scope of this analysis, macro opportunity structures for marriage and the labour market also play central roles. As recent research on work and occupations shows, employment outcomes have as much to do with structural features of the labour market (e.g., vacancy chains, segmentation of the labour market, ethnic enclaves) as it does with individual predispositions to work (Rosenbaum 1984; Rosenfeld 1992). Similarly, network and exchange theory emphasize the importance of role multiplexity and interdependence that combine with other structural features of collective life to introduce numerous avenues for positive and negative change (Cook and Whitmeyer 1992). As Dannefer (1987: 216) argues, most research on life-course transitions is too quick to attribute continuity to social-psychological processes of "accentuation" rather than "structured mechanisms of social allocation producing similar differentiating tendencies in successive cohorts." The channelling of prior differences and the tendency toward cumulation of advantage and disadvantage in employment (e.g., increasing inequality over time) are so general that they have been referred to as the "Matthew effect" (see Dannefer 1987: 216). Labour market research thus motivates a deeper appreciation of contextual forces and opportunity structures in the shaping of the life transitions of young adults.

Relatedly, variations in criminal propensity (e.g., low self-control) are incomplete as an explanation of adult crime because the latter's realization is dependent on criminal opportunity (e.g., lack of guardianship or surveillance; suitable targets). Ties to work and family in adulthood restrict many criminal opportunities and thus reduce the probability that criminal propensities will be translated into action. For example, those in stable employment and marital relations are typically subject to more structured routine activities and less free time than those in unstable roles (see the discussion of free time, types of employment, and opportunities that facilitate drinking in Vaillant 1983: 96–97). Some turning points in life may also reflect changes in the availability or profitability of criminal strategies (see Cohen and Machalek 1988).

As noted earlier, cumulative continuity and processes of change are likely to interact with race and structural location (Hagan 1991; Jessor, Donovan, and Costa 1991). In particular, there is increasing evidence that the probability of adolescent risks becoming transmuted into adverse adult circumstances is greatest among those in disadvantaged racial and economic positions. Whether it be environmental traps in the form of unemployment or arrest, research is needed to specify the dependence of trajectories on structural location.

Turning points and developmental change are bounded by historical context as well. The men in the Gluecks' study grew to young adulthood in a period of expanding economic opportunities during the 1950s and 1960s. They were also in a position to take advantage of numerous opportunities offered by the G.I. Bill. Prospects for current cohorts may not be as promising. The industrial base in America has changed dramatically over the past twenty years (Wilson 1987), and there has been an increase in global competition and a decline in expectations for upward social mobility. There is a sense that good jobs are harder to find and keep today than in previous decades. Moreover, the military may not be the vehicle out of poverty in the 1990s as it was during the 1940s and 1950s (Elder 1986). Consistent with the life-course perspective, we thus stress the importance of conceptualizing and measuring secular change at the macrosocial level, especially through explicit cohort comparisons (see Ryder 1965). In this regard we believe a central topic for future research is the interaction of turning points with the varying structural locations and historical contexts within which individuals make the transition to young adulthood.

CONCLUSION

Our dynamic conceptualization of social capital and informal social control at once incorporates stability and change in criminal behaviour. Change is central to our model because we propose that variations in adult crime unexplained by childhood behaviour are directly related to the strength of adult social bonds. Yet, we incorporate the link between childhood and adult outcomes, positing a cumulative, developmental process wherein delinquent behaviour attenuates the social and institutional bonds linking adults to society (e.g., labour force attachment, marital cohesion). As such, we theorize that adult social bonds not only have important effects on adult crime in and of themselves, but help to explain the probabilistic links in the chain connecting early childhood differences and later adult crime.

Perhaps the key idea is ultimately a simple one — the adult life course matters, regardless of how one gets there. We do not deny the reality of self-selection or that persons may sometimes "create" their own environment. But once in place, those environments take on a history of their own in a way that invalidates a pure spuriousness or self-selection argument. Moreover, the self-selection view of the world is, in our opinion, much too deterministic and neglects the role of state sanctions, chance, luck, structural location, historical context, and opportunity structure in shaping the life course.

In sum, by redirecting attention to the significance of both pathways and turning points in the life course, we are optimistic about the possibilities for a new research agenda that has the potential to unify heretofore divergent conceptions of stability and change in human development. For example, Gottfredson and Hirschi (1990: 177–78; Hirschi and Gottfredson 1993) explicitly incorporate the role of opportunity in explaining criminal events. If opportunity matters for criminal events, surely it matters for the establishment of strong employment and marital bonds. More important, at one point Gottfredson and Hirschi (1990: 115) allow for social control in explaining adolescent delinquency. In this sense we see some compatibility between our theory and Gottfredson and Hirschi's theory, especially if one conceptualizes variations in social control as partly influenced by variations in self-control (see also Hirschi 1992; Hirschi and Gottfredson 1993; Nagin and Paternoster 1992). Therefore, while Gottfredson and Hirschi (1990) and Wilson and Herrnstein (1985) start off with a similar premise, they offer quite different possibilities for potential integration with our focus on change and informal social control across the adult life course. Future research is needed to examine these possibilities, especially the relative importance of stability and change throughout lives in varying contexts.

STUDY QUESTIONS

1. *What are the main ideas and themes associated with the life-course perspective on crime?*
2. *How does Sampson and Laub's theory explain why some youth who are involved in crime in their teenage years become law-abiding adults later in life?*
3. *What are the major research questions that Sampson and Laub argue need to be addressed in order to more adequately explain stability and change in criminal behaviour over the life course?*

REFERENCES

Abbott, Andrew. 1992. "From Causes to Events: Notes on Narrative Positivism." *Sociological Methods and Research 20*(4): 428–55.

Anderson, Elijah. 1990. *Streetwise: Race, Class, and Change in an Urban Community.* Chicago: University of Chicago Press.

Bandura, Albert. 1982. "The Psychology of Chance Encounters and Life Paths." *American Psychologist 37*: 747–55.

Becker, Howard. 1963. *The Outsiders.* New York: Free Press.

Braithwaite, John. 1989. *Crime, Shame, and Reintegration.* New York: Cambridge University Press.

Cairns, Robert B. 1986. "Phenomena Lost: Issues in the Study of Development." In Jaan Valsiner, ed., *The Individual Subject and Scientific Psychology,* 97–111. New York: Plenum.

Caspi, Avshalom, and Daryl J. Bem. 1990. "Personality Continuity and Change across the Life Course." In Lawrence Pervin, ed., *Handbook of Personality: Theory and Research,* 549–75. New York: Guilford.

Caspi, Avshalom, Glen H. Elder, Jr., and Ellen S. Herbener. 1990. "Childhood Personality and the Prediction of Life-Course Patterns." In Lee Robins and Michael Rutter, eds., *Straight and Devious Pathways from Childhood to Adulthood,* 13–35. New York: Cambridge University Press.

Caspi, Avshalom, and Terri E. Moffitt. 1993a. "The Continuity of Maladaptive Behavior: From Description to Understanding in the Study of Antisocial Behavior." In Dante Cicchetti and Donald Cohen, eds., *Manual of Developmental Psychopathology,* 472–511. New York: John Wiley & Sons.

———. 1993b. "Continuity amidst Change: A Paradoxical Theory of Personality Coherence." *Psychological Inquiry 4*: 247–71.

Clausen, John. 1990. "Turning Point as a Life Course Concept: Meaning and Measurement." Paper presented at the annual meeting of the American Sociological Association, Washington, DC.

Cohen, Lawrence, and Richard Machalek. 1988. "A General Theory of Expropriative Crime: An Evolutionary Ecological Approach." *American Journal of Sociology 94*: 465–501.

Coleman, James S. 1988. "Social Capital in the Creation of Human Capital." *American Journal of Sociology 94*: 95–120.

———. 1990. *Foundations of Social Theory*. Cambridge, MA: Harvard University Press.

Cook, Karen, and Joseph Whitmeyer. 1992. "Two Approaches to Social Structure: Exchange Theory and Network Analysis." *Annual Review of Sociology 18*: 109–27.

Dannefer, Dale. 1984. "Adult Development and Social Theory: A Paradigmatic Reappraisal." *American Sociological Review 49*: 100–16.

———. 1987. "Aging as Intracohort Differentiation: Accentuation, the Matthew Effect, and the Life Course." *Sociological Forum 2*: 211–36.

Elder, Glen H., Jr. 1975. "Age Differentiation and the Life Course." *Annual Review of Sociology 1*: 165–90.

———. 1985. "Perspectives on the Life Course." In Glen H. Elder, Jr., ed., *Life Course Dynamics*, 23–49. Ithaca, NY: Cornell University Press.

———. 1986. "Military Times and Turning Points in Men's Lives." *Developmental Psychology 22*: 233–45.

Elder, Glen H., Jr., Cynthia Gimbel, and Rachel Ivie. 1991. "Turning Points in Life: The Case of Military Service and War." *Military Psychology 3*: 215–31.

Farrington, David P. 1986. "Stepping Stones to Adult Criminal Careers." In Dan Olweus, Jack Block, and Marian Radke-Yarrow, eds., *Development of Antisocial and Prosocial Behavior*, 359–84. New York: Academic Press.

———. 1988. "Studying Changes within Individuals: The Causes of Offending." In Michael Rutter, ed., *Studies of Psychosocial Risk: The Power of Longitudinal Data*, 158–83. New York: Cambridge University Press.

Farrington, David P., and Roger Tarling. 1985. *Prediction in Criminology*. Albany: State University of New York Press.

Glueck, Sheldon, and Eleanor Glueck. 1950. *Unraveling Juvenile Delinquency*. New York: Commonwealth Fund.

———. 1968. *Delinquents and Nondelinquents in Perspective*. Cambridge, MA: Harvard University Press.

Gottfredson, Michael, and Travis Hirschi. 1990. *A General Theory of Crime*. Stanford, CA: Stanford University Press.

Grasmick, Harold, Charles R. Tittle, Robert J. Bursik, Jr., and Bruce Arneklev. 1993. "Testing the Core Empirical Implications of Gottfredson and Hirschi's General Theory of Crime." *Journal of Research in Crime and Delinquency 30*(1): 5–29.

Hagan, John. 1991. "Destiny and Drift: Subcultural Preferences, Status Attainments, and the Risks and Rewards of Youth." *American Sociological Review 56*(5): 567–82.

Hagan, John, and Alberto Palloni. 1990. "The Social Reproduction of a Criminal Class in Working-Class London, circa 1950–1980." *American Journal of Sociology 96*(2): 265–99.

Hirshci, Travis. 1992. "From Social Control to Self Control." Paper presented at the annual meeting of the American Society of Criminology, New Orleans.

Hirshci, Travis, and Michael Gottfredson. 1993. "Commentary: Testing the General Theory of Crime." *Journal of Research in Crime and Delinquency 30*(1): 47–54.

Huesmann, Rowell, Leonard Eron, Monroe Lefkowitz, and Leopold Walder. 1984. "Stability of Aggression over Time and Generations." *Developmental Psychology 20*: 1120–34.

Jessor, Richard, John E. Donovan, and Frances M. Costa. 1991. *Beyond Adolescence: Problem Behavior and Young Adult Development.* New York: Cambridge University Press.

Kandel, Denise, Mark Davies, and Nazli Baydar. 1990. "The Creation of Interpersonal Contexts: Homophily in Dyadic Relationships in Adolescence and Young Adulthood." In Lee Robins and Michael Rutter, eds., *Straight and Devious Pathways from Childhood to Adulthood,* 221–41. New York: Cambridge University Press.

Katz, Jack. 1988. *Seductions of Crime.* New York: Basic Books.

Kirschenman, Joleen, and Kathryn Neckerman. 1991. "'We'd Love to Hire Them, but . . .' The Meaning of Race for Employers." In Christopher Jencks and Paul Peterson, eds., *The Urban Underclass,* 203–32. Washington, DC: Brookings Institution.

Kornhauser, Ruth. 1978. *Social Sources of Delinquency.* Chicago: University of Chicago Press.

Lemert, Edwin. 1951. *Social Pathology.* New York: McGraw-Hill.

Loeber, Rolf, and Marc LeBlanc. 1990. "Toward a Developmental Criminology." In Michael Tonry and Norval Morris, eds., *Crime and Justice,* vol. 12, 375–473. Chicago: University of Chicago Press.

Loeber, Rolf, and Magda Stouthamer-Loeber. 1987. "Prediction." In Herbert C. Quay, ed., *Handbook of Juvenile Delinquency,* 325–82. New York: John Wiley & Sons.

Magnusson, David, and Lars R. Bergman. 1988. "Individual and Variable-Based Approaches to Longitudinal Research on Early Risk Factors." In Michael Rutter, ed., *Studies of Psychosocial Risk: The Power of Longitudinal Data,* 45–61. New York: Cambridge University Press.

———. 1990. "A Pattern Approach to the Study of Pathways from Childhood to Adulthood." In Lee Robins and Michael Rutter, eds., *Straight and Devious Pathways from Childhood to Adulthood,* 101–15. New York: Cambridge University Press.

McAdam, Doug. 1989. "The Biographical Consequences of Activism." *American Sociological Review 54:* 744–60.

Moffitt, Terrie E. 1993. "Adolescence-Limited and Life-Course-Persistent Antisocial Behavior: A Developmental Taxonomy." *Psychological Review 100*(4): 674–701.

Nagin, Daniel, and Raymond Paternoster. 1991. "On the Relationship of Past and Future Participation in Delinquency." *Criminology 29*: 163–90.

———. 1992. "Social Capital and Social Control: The Deterrence Implications of a Theory of Individual Differences in Criminal Offending." Unpublished manuscript. Carnegie Mellon University, Pittsburgh.

Nagin, Daniel, and Joel Waldfogel. 1992. "The Effects of Criminality and Conviction on the Labour Market Status of Young British Offenders." Unpublished manuscript. Carnegie Mellon University, Pittsburgh.

Patterson, Gerald R., Barbara D. DeBaryshe, and Elizabeth Ramsey. 1989. "A Developmental Perspective on Antisocial Behavior." *American Psychologist 44*: 329–35.

Pickles, Andrew, and Michael Rutter. 1991. "Statistical and Conceptual Models of 'Turning Points' in Developmental Processes." In David Magnusson, Lars Bergman, Georg Rudinger, and Bertil Torestad, eds., *Problems and Methods in Longitudinal Research: Stability and Change*, 133–65. New York: Cambridge University Press.

Rosenbaum, James. 1984. *Career Mobility in a Corporate Hierarchy.* Orlando, FL: Academic Press.

Rosenfeld, Rachel A. 1992. "Job Mobility and Career Processes." *Annual Review of Sociology 18*: 39–61.

Rutter, Michael. 1987. "Psychosocial Resilience and Protective Mechanisms." *American Journal of Orthopsychiatry 57*: 316–33.

———. 1989a. "Age as an Ambiguous Variable in Developmental Research: Some Epidemiological Considerations from Developmental Psychopathology." *International Journal of Behavioral Development 12*: 1–34.

———. 1989b. "Pathways from Childhood to Adult Life." *Journal of Child Psychology and Psychiatry 30*: 23–51.

Rutter, Michael, David Quinton, and Jonathan Hill. 1990. "Adult Outcomes of Institution-Reared Children: Males and Females Compared." In Lee Robins and Michael Rutter, eds., *Straight and Devious Pathways from Childhood to Adulthood*, 135–57. New York: Cambridge University Press.

Ryder, Norman. 1965. "The Cohort as a Concept in the Study of Social Change." *American Sociological Review 30*: 843–61.

Sampson, Robert J., and John H. Laub. 1992. "Crime and Deviance in the Life Course." *Annual Review of Sociology 18*: 63–84.

———. 1993. *Crime in the Making: Pathways and Turning Points through Life.* Cambridge, MA: Harvard University Press.

Short, James F., Jr. 1990. "Gangs, Neighborhoods, and Youth Crime." *Criminal Justice Research Bulletin 5*: 1–11.

Short, James F., Jr., and Fred Strodtbeck. 1965. *Group Process and Gang Delinquency.* Chicago: University of Chicago Press.

Shover, Neal. 1985. *Aging Criminals.* Beverly Hills, CA: Sage.

Sullivan, Mercer. 1989. *"Getting Paid:" Youth Crime and Work in the Inner City.* Ithaca, NY: Cornell University Press.

Thornberry, Terence P. 1987. "Toward an Interactional Theory of Delinquency." *Criminology 25*: 863–91.

Tittle, Charles R. 1988. "Two Empirical Regularities (Maybe) in Search of an Explanation: Commentary on the Age–Crime Debate." *Criminology 26*: 75–86.

Vaillant, George. 1983. *The Natural History of Alcoholism.* Cambridge, MA: Harvard University Press.

Wilson, James Q., and Richard Herrnstein. 1985. *Crime and Human Nature.* New York: Simon & Schuster.

Wilson, William Julius. 1987. *The Truly Disadvantaged: The Inner City, the Underclass, and Public Policy.* Chicago: University of Chicago Press.

CHAPTER FIVE

Stability and Change in Crime over the Life Course: A Strain Theory Explanation

ROBERT AGNEW
Emory University, Atlanta

Strain theory does not play a significant role in recent developmental theories of crime. Such theories are instead dominated by biological and psychological theories and, on the sociological side, by control and social learning theories (e.g., Moffitt 1993; Patterson 1992; Sampson and Laub 1990; 1992; 1993; Thornberry 1987; Tonry, Ohlin, and Farrington 1991; Warr 1993). The neglect of strain theory by developmental theorists is understandable. Strain theory has been heavily criticized in recent years, and one of the leading criticisms contends that the classic strain theories of Merton (1938), Cohen (1955), and Cloward and Ohlin (1960) are unable to explain trends in crime over the life course (Gove 1985; Greenberg 1977; Hirschi 1969; Matza 1964). While such theories may be able to shed light on the increase in crime in early adolescence, they cannot account for the decrease in crime that begins in late adolescence. If anything, these theories would predict an increase in crime during this period since older adolescents should be more aware of their limited prospects for success (Greenberg 1977; also see Simmons and Rosenberg 1971). Paralleling the attack on strain theory by sociologists, psychologists have seriously challenged the "storm and stress" image of adolescence that once dominated the developmental literature (Lerner and Shea 1982; Petersen 1988; Simmons and Blyth 1987: 3–5). This image is very compatible with strain theory, and its demise may also explain the neglect of strain theory by developmental criminologists.

Source: Robert Agnew, "Stability and Change in Crime over the Life Course: A Strain Theory Explanation." In T. Thornberry, ed., *Developmental Theories of Crime and Delinquency*. (New Brunswick, NJ: Transaction Books, 1997): 101–32. Reprinted by permission of Transaction Publishers.

Greenberg (1977) recognized the limitations of classic strain theory, and developed an integrated strain/control theory specifically designed to explain the peak in crime during adolescence. According to Greenberg, adolescents are subject to much strain because (a) they become very concerned with achieving popularity with peers, but often lack the funds necessary to finance their social activities with peers; (b) they develop a strong desire for autonomy, but their autonomy and self-esteem needs are frustrated by the school system; and (c) males are often "prevented from fulfilling male role expectations," particularly by the school system with its expectations of "docility and submission to authority." As a consequence, adolescents often engage in theft, assert their autonomy and masculinity through criminal activity, and vent their hostility against those who frustrate them. As adolescents enter adulthood, however, they become less concerned with popularity with peers, they acquire legitimate sources of funds, and they experience an increase in autonomy — especially as they leave the school system. Greenberg's theory has never received a proper test, although Hirschi and Gottfredson (1983; 1985) argue that certain data cast doubt on it. They point to the fact, for example, that adolescents with legitimate funds are more rather than less likely to steal (see Greenberg 1985). Perhaps as a result, Greenberg's theory has also been neglected by developmental criminologists in recent years.

Strain theory, however, has recently experienced a revival, with new versions of the theory being developed at the social-psychological and macro levels (Alder and Laufer 1995). This chapter argues that certain of the new strain theories have much to say about the relationship between age and crime, and that they should be part of any developmental theory of crime. In particular, these theories point to new sources of stability and change in crime over the life course, and help better organize existing arguments in this area. The focus is on Agnew's (1992) general strain theory (GST). This is the most comprehensive social-psychological strain theory and it has received preliminary empirical support (Agnew and White 1992; Paternoster and Mazerolle 1994). Up to this point, the theory has only been used to explain differences *between* individuals in the level of crime. In this chapter, the theory is used to explain trends in crime *within* individuals over time (see Loeber and LeBlanc 1990; Farrington 1986). The theory, in particular, will be used to explain two fundamental facts about crime that have emerged out of the developmental research.

First, much evidence suggests that there is a small group of offenders who engage in crime and other antisocial behaviour at a high rate over their life course (Farrington 1986; Moffitt 1993; Olweus 1979; Hirschi and Gottfredson 1983; Gottfredson and Hirschi 1990; Sampson and Laub 1992; 1993; Nagin and Land 1993; Wilson and Herrnstein 1985: 240–42; Wolfgang, Figlio, and Sellin 1972; Wolfgang, Thornberry, and Figlio 1987). Moffitt (1993) refers to these individuals as "life-course persistent" offenders. There is some debate over just how stable the behaviour of such individuals is, but most researchers agree that it is reasonably stable and that a central task of any developmental theory is to explain this stability. Several theories have been developed to this end, and in this chapter it will be argued that the GST can form a useful supplement to these theories (Sampson and Laub 1992; 1993; Patterson 1992; Patterson, DeBaryshe, and Ramsey 1989; Gottfredson and Hirschi 1990; Wilson and Herrnstein 1985; Caspi, Bem, and Elder 1989; Moffitt 1993; Farrington 1986; Thornberry 1987).

Second, data also suggest that there is another, larger group of individuals whose criminal behaviour peaks in mid to late adolescence and declines rapidly thereafter (Farrington 1986; Moffitt 1993; Gold and Petronio 1980; Nagin and Land 1993; Sampson and Laub 1992; 1993; Wilson and Herrnstein 1985). Moffitt (1993) refers to these individuals as "adolescent-limited" offenders. Several theories have also been developed to account for their behaviour (Moffitt 1993; Sampson and Laub 1992; 1993; Warr 1993; Greenberg 1977; Thornberry 1987), and the GST will likewise be applied to this issue. There are, of course, additional facts regarding the development of crime that require explanation (see Loeber and LeBlanc 1990; Farrington 1986), but these two are perhaps the most fundamental and well researched.

The chapter begins with an overview of GST, and then applies the theory to the explanation of stability and change in criminal behaviour.

AN OVERVIEW OF GENERAL STRAIN THEORY

GST focuses on negative relationships with others: "relationships in which others are not treating the individual as he or she would like to be treated" (Agnew 1992: 50). Such negative relationships increase the likelihood that individuals will experience negative affect, with anger being an especially important reaction. This negative affect creates pressure for corrective action, and crime is one possible response. Crime may be a method for alleviating strain, seeking revenge, or managing negative affect (through illicit drug use).

There are three major types of negative relations or strain: relations where others (1) prevent or threaten to prevent you from achieving positively valued goals (such as popularity with peers or autonomy from adults); (2) remove or threaten to remove positively valued stimuli that you possess (e.g., the loss of a romantic partner); or (3) present or threaten to present you with negatively valued stimuli (e.g., insult or physically assault you). Strain researchers have only focused on the first type of negative relationship, and here strain has been measured primarily in terms of the disjunction between aspirations and expectations. The GST argues that this type of strain would be better measured in terms of the disjunctions between (a) expectations and actual outcomes and (b) just/fair outcomes and actual outcomes. According to GST, negative relationships are ultimately defined from the perspective of the individual. That is, the individual determines whether a particular relationship is negative or aversive. At the same time, the GST argues that certain types of relationships are likely to be experienced as aversive by most individuals. Given this fact, it is possible to develop a list of "those objective situations that might reasonably be expected to cause adversity" among individuals (Agnew 1992: 62).

While certain events are likely to be experienced as aversive by most individuals, GST recognizes that individuals sometimes differ in their appraisal of a given event. Some individuals may cognitively interpret (or later reinterpret) negative relations in ways that minimize their adversity. This is a central theme in the stress literature, and the cognitive reappraisal of aversive events is recognized as a major method of coping. GST lists several cognitive coping strategies in this area (Agnew 1992: 66–69). Individuals prevented from achieving the goal of monetary success, for example, may cope by lowering the amount of money they desire, claiming that money is unimportant, claiming that other goals are more important than money, exaggerating the amount of money they currently have or expect to have in the future, claiming they are better off than others, focusing on the positive benefits of poverty, or claiming that they are to blame for their poverty. GST contains a discussion of those factors that influence the use of such cognitive coping strategies.

GST also recognizes that there are a variety of ways to cope with events that are interpreted as aversive, and that only some of these coping strategies involve crime. Individuals may engage in several types of behavioural coping, paralleling each of the major types of strain or negative relations. They may seek to achieve positively valued goals, protect or retrieve positively valued stimuli, or terminate or escape from negative stimuli. And their actions in these areas may involve conventional or criminal behaviour. Individuals may also engage in emotional coping, in which they act directly on the negative emotions that result from adversity. Emotional coping may involve criminal behaviour, as in the use of illicit drugs, or conventional behaviour, as in the use of exercise or relaxation techniques. GST also discusses those factors that influence the use of criminal versus noncriminal coping strategies.

GST, then, focuses on three sets of variables: (1) the negative relations experienced by the individual; (2) the individual's appraisal of these negative relations — to what extent are they viewed as aversive (and so contribute to negative affect); and (3) the individual's choice of criminal versus noncriminal coping strategies. These variables are next used to explain stability and change in crime over the life course.

EXPLAINING THE STABILITY OF ANTISOCIAL/CRIMINAL BEHAVIOUR

Control and Social Learning Explanations of Stability

As indicated, much data indicate that a small group of offenders engage in high rates of antisocial/criminal behaviour over the life course. This stability is most often explained in terms of control and learning theories.

Most theorists begin their explanation of stability by pointing to traits that manifest themselves early in the life of the child. Such traits include impulsivity, hyperactivity, attention deficit, low intelligence, insensitivity, difficult temperament, minimal tolerance for frustration, and composite traits that incorporate many of these individual traits, such as low "self-control" (Gottfredson and Hirschi 1990; Wilson and Herrnstein 1985; Moffitt 1993; Sampson and Laub 1992; 1993; Tonry, Ohlin, and Farrington 1991). These traits are usually said to be a function of both biological factors and the child's early socialization in the family, although theorists differ in the relative importance attached to biology and socialization (e.g., Wilson and Herrnstein 1985; Gottfredson and Hirschi 1990; Moffitt 1993).

Such traits may affect crime directly, by increasing the individual's propensity to engage in crime. Gottfredson and Hirschi (1990) explain this propensity in terms of control theory, arguing that people with the above traits are less able to restrain themselves from acting on their impulses or desires. Wilson and Herrnstein (1985) explain this propensity in terms of learning theory, arguing that people with the above traits will be more likely to find crime reinforcing. Both Gottfredson and Hirschi and Wilson and Herrnstein argue that once these traits are formed, later changes in the social environment are unimportant except to the extent that they affect the opportunity to commit crime in particular situations (see Nagin and Farrington 1992 for an examination of "persistent-heterogeneity" and "state-dependent" theories).

Other theorists disagree, and argue that these traits may also affect crime indirectly through their effect on the social environment. These indirect effects have been explained in terms of control and learning theories. Certain theorists argue that these traits promote crime by reducing social control: individuals with these traits are less likely to form close attachments to conventional others — such as parents, teachers, and spouses; learn prosocial beliefs and behaviours; do well in school; and obtain rewarding jobs (Moffitt 1993; Sampson and Laub 1993; Caspi, Bem, and Elder 1989). Theorists have also suggested that these traits promote crime by increasing the likelihood that the individual's deviant behaviour will be reinforced. Individuals with such traits are more likely to associate with deviant peers and, in a manner described by Patterson (1982; 1992), develop interactional patterns with parents that result in the reinforcement of coercive behaviour (Caspi, Bem, and Elder 1989; Sampson and Laub 1993). The impact of such traits has not been explicitly explained in terms of strain theory, although Moffitt (1993), Caspi, Bem, and Elder (1989), and others have advanced explanations compatible with strain theory.

Finally, the stability of crime has been explained in terms of the reciprocal relations between delinquency, social control variables, and social learning variables. Thornberry (1987) is the leading advocate of this position. He argues that these variables are involved in an amplifying loop, such that low social control increases the likelihood of association with delinquent peers and of delinquent behaviour, which in turn lead to a further reduction in social control. For most adolescents, this amplifying loop is interrupted by the transition to adulthood, which involves the development of new commitments to conventional activity, such as commitments to work and family. Thornberry, however, argues that this does not happen in all cases. If initial levels of social control are very weak, the adolescent may not develop adult commitments capable of interrupting the loop (1987: 882). According to Thornberry, this is most likely to happen in the case of lower-class individuals, who start out with lower levels of social control and greater levels of exposure to delinquent values, delinquent peers, and delinquent behaviour. As a result, they are more likely to become involved in delinquency at an early age, setting the amplifying loop described above in motion and leading to extremely high rates of delinquency. Their ties to conventional society may be so weak by late adolescence that they are unable to break out of the loop. Patterson, DeBaryshe, and Ramsey (1989) draw on social learning theory to make a similar argument. Such arguments are not incompatible with the above emphasis on traits conducive to delinquency: these traits may help explain why some individuals get involved in the amplifying loop described by Thornberry and have trouble breaking out of it (see Sampson and Laub 1993; Moffitt 1993; Caspi, Bem, and Elder 1989). Nevertheless, the work of Thornberry and others suggests that some adolescents may develop stable patterns of delinquency even though they do not possess the above-mentioned traits.

The General Strain Theory Explanation of Stability

GST explains the stability of criminal behaviour in ways that parallel the above explanations. Like the above theories, GST argues that the stability of crime is partly due to traits that develop early in the life of the child. While such traits may affect self/social control and the reinforcement of crime, they are also important for reasons that are uniquely related to strain theory. In particular, such traits increase the likelihood that individuals will (a) experience negative relationships; (b) interpret these relationships as aversive; and (c) react to this adversity with criminal behaviour.

THE CONCEPT OF AGGRESSIVENESS

Certain of these traits were mentioned above, such as hyperactivity, attention deficit, impulsivity, insensitivity, minimal tolerance for frustration, and difficult temperament. Minimal tolerance for frustration and difficult temperament are especially relevant to GST. Those with a minimal tolerance for frustration are more likely to experience environmental stimuli as aversive, showing signs of arousal and distress to a wider range of stimuli than others (Garrison and Earls 1987; Bates 1980; Compas 1987b: 394, 399; Van Der Boom 1989). Individuals with difficult temperament have been described as moody, fussy, irritable, argumentative, stubborn, and noncompliant (Bates 1980; Tonry, Ohlin, and Farrington 1991; Landy and Peters 1992; Moffitt 1993). As indicated, these traits emerge very early in the life course, and data suggest that they may be the product of both biological factors and early socialization experiences in the family — especially harsh and inconsistent discipline. Further, many of these traits are positively correlated with one another and so are often found in the same individual (Bates 1980; Garrison and Earls 1987; Landy and Peters 1992; Van Der Boom 1989; Wolfe, Wekerle, and McGee 1992).

Other relevant traits emerge later in childhood, with the individual's problem-solving skills being most relevant to GST. Dodge (1986) lists five steps in effective problem solving: (1) search for cues in the environment; (2) interpret these cues; (3) generate possible responses to the situation; (4) consider the possible consequences of the responses; and (5) enact the chosen response. Individuals differ in their ability to engage in these steps, with data suggesting that delinquents are more deficient in problem-solving skills. Delinquents attend to fewer environmental cues and tend to focus on aggressive cues, more often attribute hostile intentions to the benign or ambiguous acts of others, generate fewer alternative solutions, generate more aggressive responses, fail to recognize the negative consequences of delinquent behaviour, and more often lack the social skills to enact prosocial responses (Dodge and Feldman 1990; Dodge and Newman 1981; Hollin 1991; Kazdin 1987; Morton 1987; Landy and Peters 1992; Nasby, Hayden, and DePaulo 1980; Pepler, King, and Byrd 1991; Slaby and Guerra 1988; Wolfe, Wekerle, and McGee 1992). It is unclear to what extent biological and social factors contribute to problem-solving skills, although the effectiveness of many problem-solving courses suggests that socialization experiences are of major importance (Hollin 1991; Kazdin 1987; Pepler, King, and Byrd 1991). Nevertheless, it is undoubtedly the case that traits like impulsivity and intelligence bear a strong relationship to problem-solving skills. These traits have a large impact on the effectiveness of the socialization process (see Moffitt 1993), and these traits directly underlie many problem-solving skills. Individuals who are low in intelligence and high in impulsiveness, for example, will obviously have more difficulty generating alternative solutions to a problem and evaluating the consequences of these solutions.

In summation, many individuals have one or more of the following traits: irritability, minimal tolerance for frustration, hyperactivity, attention deficit, impulsivity, insensitivity to others, and deficient problem-solving skills. For the purposes of theoretical argument, we can classify individuals who score high on these traits as high in aggressiveness.

THE IMPACT OF AGGRESSIVENESS ON CRIME

GST argues that aggressive individuals are likely to engage in high rates of crime over the life course. Aggressiveness has both direct and indirect effects on crime. Individuals with this trait have a greater propensity to engage in crime, and for that reason they are more likely to respond to a given situation with crime. In particular, their irritability and low tolerance for frustration mean that they are more likely to find a given situation aversive. Their greater tendency to blame adversity on others increases the likelihood that they will react with anger. And this anger, in combination with their limited problem-solving skills, increases the likelihood that they will respond with delinquency. This direct impact of aggressiveness is one reason for the stability of crime.

Aggressiveness also has an indirect effect on crime: individuals with this trait are more likely to be treated negatively by others and the negative affect generated by such treatment increases the likelihood of crime. There are three reasons why aggressive individuals are more likely to be treated negatively. The first reason does not have to do with the causal impact of aggressiveness. As described by Moffitt (1993), many of the traits comprising aggressiveness are partly caused by the aversive behaviour of parents or by factors that are linked to the aversive behaviour of parents. Moffitt, for example, points out that temperamental traits such as activity level and irritability are partly heritable. So children with these traits will tend to have parents who are "impatient and irritable too" (Moffitt 1993). Children with the traits comprising aggressiveness, then, are more likely to be born and raised in aversive family environments — independent of whatever negative reactions their behaviour may elicit. Their behaviour will remain stable, then, to the extent that their aversive environment remains stable.

Second, aggressive individuals are more likely to provoke negative reactions from others in a given situation — leading to interactional continuity over the life course (see Caspi, Bem, and Elder 1989, on interactional continuity; also see Moffitt 1993; Sampson and Laub 1993). These negative reactions often anger the aggressive individual and thereby increase the likelihood of crime. Numerous researchers have argued that many of the traits comprising aggressiveness are likely to elicit negative responses from others (Moffitt 1993; Bates 1980; Garrison and Earls 1987; Caspi, Bem, and Elder 1989; Coie, Dodge, and Kupersmidt 1990). Moffitt argues that children with these sorts of traits are more irritating, less satisfying, and more difficult to discipline. As such, they are likely to be at odds with everyone in their environment. The trait of difficult temperament has been shown to have a negative effect on the quality of mother-infant interaction (Van Der Boom 1989). Children with the above sorts of traits are also more likely to be rejected by peers and to experience problems at school (Coie, Dodge, and Kupersmidt 1990; Vitaro, Gagnon, and Tremblay 1990). And as Caspi, Bem, and Elder (1989) demonstrate, they are more likely to have difficulties with their employers and spouses as well. The stability of criminal behaviour, then, is also partly explained by the fact that aggressive individuals are likely to provoke negative reactions from others over the life course.

Third, aggressive individuals are also more likely to become involved or enmeshed in adversive social environments (see Caspi, Bem, and Elder 1989, on cumulative continuity; also see Moffitt 1993; Sampson and Laub 1993). Such individuals are more likely to be rejected by conventional peers, and so are more likely to enter deviant peer groups that — among other things — are characterized by higher levels of conflict (Cairns et al. 1988; Giordano,

Cernkovich, and Pugh 1986). There is also evidence that such individuals are more likely to obtain less desirable jobs and marry less desirable partners (Caspi, Bem, and Elder 1989). These facts also help explain the stability of criminal behaviour over the life course.

It is important to emphasize that the above processes not only increase the likelihood of criminal behaviour, they also serve to enhance and maintain the trait of aggressiveness (Landy and Peters 1992). The negative reactions of others may lower one's tolerance for adversity by taxing coping resources, may convince the person that their hostile attributions are correct (see Dodge and Newman 1981; Caspi, Bem, and Elder 1989), and may prevent the person from learning prosocial methods of coping with problems (Patterson 1982; 1992; Moffitt 1993). This feedback process, as Moffitt and others emphasize, plays a central role in explaining the stability of antisocial behaviour, for it helps explain the stability of the trait that underlies antisocial behaviour.

To summarize, individuals with the trait of aggressiveness are likely to engage in a high rate of crime over the life course for several reasons. They are more likely to interpret a given situation as aversive and respond to that adversity with antisocial behaviour. They are more likely to be born into aversive family environments and so be the recipients of negative behaviour for at least the first part of their lives, they are more likely to provoke negative responses from others in a given situation, and they are more likely to become exposed to aversive environments. Such individuals, in short, are more likely to be subject to the three types of strain identified in GST. They are more likely to have trouble achieving positively valued goals, like popularity with peers and monetary success; to lose those things they value, like friends and good jobs; and to be presented with negative stimuli, like verbal and physical abuse from parents, teachers, and peers. Further, all of these processes serve to maintain and enhance the trait of aggressiveness.

It should be noted that these processes are not inevitable. While many of the components of aggressiveness appear to emerge early in life and be reasonably stable, they are not perfectly stable. As the work of Rutter (1985) and Sampson and Laub (1993) demonstrate, many individuals are able to break out of the cycle of delinquency. This is often accomplished with the aid of a supportive individual, and often happens during periods of major role transitions — such as the start of adulthood. The focus of the present discussion, however, is on those forces promoting the stability of antisocial/criminal behaviour.

THE URBAN UNDERCLASS AND THE STABILITY OF CRIME

Aggressiveness is seen as the driving force behind the stability of crime in the above discussion: it increases the likelihood of negative treatment by others and of a criminal response to such treatment. Following the lead of Thornberry (1987), however, we may also argue that some individuals may engage in high rates of crime over the life course even though they are not high in aggressiveness. The environment of the urban underclass is conducive to this outcome, since it is not only lower in control and more criminogenic, but more aversive as well. Further, social and cultural forces may increase the sensitivity of the underclass to certain stimuli and increase the likelihood of a criminal response to these stimuli (see Bernard 1990). As a consequence, such individuals may be more likely to turn to delinquency at an early age. This delinquency may then contribute to a further increase in strain. The delinquent acts of the individual, in particular, are likely to anger others and result in negative treatment by such others. Individuals may be negatively treated by the victims of their delinquency, by parents and others responsible for their behaviour, and by others who feel threatened by or upset with their behaviour, such as neighbours and peers. The delinquency of the individual may also reduce the likelihood of escape from the underclass. So, like Thornberry (1987), we can argue that delinquency has consequences which contribute to further delinquency, setting an amplifying loop in motion. This argument goes beyond Thornberry, however, by arguing that delinquency may increase strain as well as reduce control and lead to association with delinquent peers.

EXPLAINING THE CHANGE IN ANTISOCIAL/CRIMINAL BEHAVIOUR

While a small group of individuals engage in high rates of crime over the life course, a much larger group of individuals experience an increase in crime during early to mid-adolescence and a decrease beginning in late adolescence. Numerous explanations have been offered for this fact, although control and social learning explanations once again dominate (Tonry, Ohlin, and Farrington 1991; Sampson and Laub 1990; Farrington 1986; Rowe and Tittle 1977; Warr 1993; Gove 1985; Loeber and LeBlanc 1990; Steffensmeier et al. 1989; Patterson 1992; Thornberry 1987). According to control theory, adolescents are more likely to engage in crime because they are less subject to the familial controls that govern the lives of children but are not yet subject to adult controls. In particular, they are not yet subject to the sanctions of the adult justice system, and have not yet formed close attachments to spouses or strong commitments to work. According to social learning theory, adolescents are more likely to engage in crime because of their increased involvement with delinquent peers. The few empirical studies that have been done in this area tend to confirm that variables like association with delinquent peers, moral beliefs, attachment to family, and commitment to work are able to explain a substantial part of the association between age and crime (Kercher 1987; Rowe and Tittle 1977; Warr 1993; Gold and Petronio 1980; Sampson and Laub 1990; 1993). This section argues that GST can supplement the above explanations, pointing to new variables and shedding additional light on the relationship between age and variables like association with delinquent peers.

According to GST, the peak in crime during adolescence can be explained by changes in (a) the extent of negative relations with others; (b) the tendency to interpret such relations as aversive; and (c) the tendency to cope with adversity through delinquency. For reasons already indicated, aggressive individuals and those in the urban underclass may not experience much change in these variables over the life course. Their individual characteristics and social location lead them to experience negative treatment from others at all ages, and to interpret this negative treatment as aversive and react to it with crime (although adolescence may pose some additional problems). The large majority of adolescents, however, do experience significant changes in these variables.

The Extent of Negative Relations

LOSS OF POSITIVE STIMULI/PRESENTATION OF NEGATIVE STIMULI

The adolescent enters a larger and more demanding social world, and does so with the desire to establish autonomy from adults and popularity with the peers who dominate this world. These facts increase the likelihood that adolescents will be treated negatively by others.

Individuals leave elementary school during early adolescence and enter larger, more impersonal, and more diverse secondary schools (Simmons and Rosenberg 1971; Petersen and Hamburg 1986; Simmons and Blyth 1987). They typically change teachers and classmates several times during the day in such schools, which not only dramatically increases the number of relationships, but means that such relationships are less likely to be governed by established patterns of interaction and less likely to be supervised by teachers. Adolescents, then, must assume more responsibility for managing their own social relationships. The greater diversity of individuals they interact with also challenges their role taking and other social skills. Adolescents also find that such schools are more demanding than elementary school. They are subject to more rules, given more work, and graded in a more difficult manner (Petersen and Hamburg 1986; Simmons and Blyth 1987). Adolescents have greater access to their own transportation, which increases their ability to move through their neighbourhood and city. This further expands the number and diversity of social relationships. Adolescents dramatically increase the extent to which they interact with others away from their parents and other adults. Adolescents, for example, begin to leave the house on their own in the evening and on weekends. Finally, there is an increase in the size of the peer group, contact with the opposite sex, the level of intimacy with same- and opposite-sex peers, and association with delinquent peers (Petersen 1987; Petersen and Hamburg 1986; Lempers and Clark-Lempers 1992; Warr 1993). Interaction with such peers comes to be governed by a more subtle set of social cues. In childhood, for example, peer rejection is a function of highly visible negative behaviours. In adolescence, it is a function of more subtle and differentiated behaviours (Coie, Dodge, and Kupersmidt

1990). Further, status among peers and others becomes increasingly dependent on the adolescent's competence in several spheres — such as athletics and academics (Coie, Dodge, and Kupersmidt 1990).

Adolescents, in short, experience a dramatic increase in the size and complexity of their social world. These changes are likely to be stressful in and of themselves, particularly given the fact that they often occur in tandem with major biological changes (Chumlea 1982). More important for our purposes, however, is that these changes increase the likelihood that adolescents will be treated negatively by others. There are more people to negatively treat the adolescent. These people are freer to treat the adolescent in a negative manner, since they are less likely to be under the supervision of adults and their ties to the adolescent may be less strong. Interaction with these people is more demanding in all the senses described above, so there is a greater likelihood that interactions will break down in ways that result in negative treatment. Adolescents, for example, may have difficulty meeting the academic demands of teachers or the emotional demands of romantic partners, with the result being poor grades or severed relationships. Particularly noteworthy is the increased association with delinquent peers. Delinquent peers may increase the likelihood of delinquency for a number of reasons, one of which is that there tends to be more conflict with such peers (Cairns et al. 1988; Giordano, Cernkovich, and Pugh 1986). Such conflict may anger or provoke the adolescent, thereby leading to crime. Individuals with delinquent peers may also be more likely to be negatively treated by others outside the peer group. Strain theory, then, may explain part of the effect of delinquent peers on crime.

As adolescents become adults, however, their social world begins to narrow again and they have more control over the nature of this world. Their circle of friends becomes smaller, they usually settle with a single romantic partner, and the number of primary and secondary contacts at their job is likely to be smaller than the number at school. They experience less turnover in friends, romantic partners, and co-workers. And they are much less likely to associate with delinquent peers (Warr 1993). Further, adults usually have more choice over their associates than adolescents. Adults, for example, typically have some choice over where they will live and work, and who they will marry. This is likely to reduce the probability of negative treatment by one's associates. GST, then, would argue that the reduction in crime starting in late adolescence is partly due to the narrowing of one's social world and the greater choice over one's associates. There are fewer people to treat the adult in a negative manner, and these people are less likely to engage in negative behaviour.

Certain data support these speculations. Researchers examining adolescent stress have asked adolescents to describe their "personal problems," the "negative events" they have encountered, the situations or events that have "troubled or worried" them, or the "events that irritate, annoy, or upset" them. The answers inevitably focus on interpersonal problems, typically interpersonal problems with parents, siblings, teachers, friends, and romantic partners (Aneshensel and Gore 1991; Brown et al. 1986; Compas 1987a; Compas, Davis, and Forsythe 1985; Kohn and Milrose 1993; Stark et al. 1989; Spirito et al. 1991; Larson and Asmussen 1991). Their responses, in particular, fall into the three categories of strain described in the GST. Most such responses seem to involve the presentation of negative stimuli by others. Respondents report that others have negatively evaluated them, disciplined or sanctioned them, pressured them, overburdened them, fought with or got into conflicts with them, and rejected them. In many cases, teenagers will specifically cite certain of the changes noted above as the source of their problems. In a study by Aneshensel and Gore (1991), for example, almost all teenagers who had recently moved to a new school mentioned this move as problematic, claiming that it was difficult to adapt to the new teachers and that they faced higher expectations and more difficult grading. Adolescents also frequently speak of the loss of positively valued stimuli, such as friends and romantic partners (Aneshensel and Gore 1991). And adolescents often mention the failure or anticipated failure to achieve positively valued goals (more below).

The key question, of course, is whether adolescents are more likely to experience negative relations with others than are children and adults. This is a difficult question to answer at present because of the lack of representative surveys that employ comprehensive measures of negative relations. Also, when we survey individuals we are obtaining data on their *perceptions* of negative relations, rather than data on the actual number of *objective* negative relations they have experienced. As will be discussed, there is reason to believe that adolescents may be more likely to perceive negative relations than children. Certain data, however, suggest negative relations may also be more common among adolescents. Grades become worse during adolescence (Petersen 1987; 1988; Petersen and Hamburg 1986), victimization and association with delinquent peers increase, and certain studies suggest that stressful life events may peak during early and middle adolescence — although these studies typically focus on limited age ranges (Coddington 1972; Larson and Asmussen 1991; Lempers and Clark-Lempers 1992; Newcomb, Huba, and Bentler 1981; Compas, Davis, and Forsythe 1985; Larson and Lampman-Petraitis 1989; Larson and Ham 1993). Further, it should be noted that many of these changes can be tied to the larger, more complex social world of adolescents. Victimization, for example, is more likely in the larger, more diverse schools that adolescents attend (Simmons and Blyth 1987).

The few empirical studies that have tried to account for the relationship between age and crime have not examined variables related to GST, although Gold and Petronio (1980) found that the relationship was partly explained by such variables as poor relationships with parents and negative attitudes toward school. Such variables provide a rough index of negative treatment by others, although they also index level of social control (see Agnew 1995). Further, data from Rutter (1985) and Sampson and Laub (1990; 1993) suggest that crime is most likely to decline among those adolescents who enter satisfying relationships as adults. These data are typically interpreted in terms of social control theory: such relationships increase the costs of crime. They may also index the individual's declining level of strain, however. Finally, as noted above, association with delinquent peers explains a large part of the relationship between age and crime. Such association may contribute to crime, in part, because it is related to an increase in interpersonal conflicts.

GOAL BLOCKAGE IN ADOLESCENCE

Traditional strain theories focus on the inability of adolescents to achieve their goals, and the increase in delinquency during adolescence has been explained in terms of goal blockage. The early strain theories focused on the inability of adolescents to achieve long-range goals like monetary success and middle-class status. The focus on such long-range goals, however, made it difficult for such theories to explain the decline in crime in late adolescence; partly as a result, recent strain theories have focused on more immediate goals. One of the most prominent theories in this area is that of Greenberg (1977), and this section relies heavily on his work.

Researchers in both sociology and psychology have pointed to a large number of adolescent goals or "developmental tasks" (Simmons and Blyth 1987: 13–17; Jackson and Bosma 1990; Olbrich 1990). The GST has not focused on any specific goals. The GST argues that individuals tend to pursue a variety of goals, usually focusing on those they are best able to achieve. Any study of goal-blockage, then, should ideally begin by determining what goals the individual considers important, rather than by assuming in advance that certain goals are considered important. At the same time, it is worth noting that many recent researchers have focused their attention on two adolescent goals: autonomy from adults and popularity with peers. Such goals are at the centre of Greenberg's (1977) strain theory; autonomy is emphasized in Moffitt's (1993) discussion of "adolescent-limited" offenders; and these goals appear in numerous other explanations of delinquency and developmental accounts of adolescence (e.g., Agnew 1984; Compas and Wagner 1991; Smetana et al. 1991). Adolescents are said to focus on such goals for a variety of reasons (Greenberg 1977), and it should be noted that these goals parallel the changing social circumstances of adolescents described above. Adolescents are beginning to leave the restricted world dominated by parents and elementary school teachers, and they are building a new world that centres around peers.

As has often been noted, however, adolescents are systematically denied the autonomy they desire by adults. While adolescents have more freedom than children, their behaviour is still subject to much control — with a broad range of behaviours being prohibited or restricted (see Greenberg 1977; Moffitt 1993; Agnew 1984). The regulations encountered in the school system may be especially difficult to deal with since many of these regulations become more strict during adolescence (see Greenberg 1977). Parents, however, may also continue to restrict the freedom of adolescents. Data support these arguments, suggesting that adolescents often demand greater autonomy from parents and teachers, and that they frequently clash with these individuals over issues involving autonomy (Smetana et al. 1991; Petersen and Hamburg 1986; Gold and Petronio 1980; Petersen 1988; Siegel 1982). It should be noted that these clashes usually do not involve "raucous, open conflict" over major issues. This "storm and stress" view of adolescence has faded. Rather, they usually involve clashes over more mundane issues, like chores, clothing, appearance, schoolwork, the child's activities, interpersonal relations, and rules regarding such things as bedtime and curfew. In short, they involve clashes over the everyday details of life. Such conflicts generate much emotional tension, however, and they are common. Limited data also suggest that they tend to peak in early to mid-adolescence (Smetana et al. 1991). In the only study to examine the relationship between autonomy and delinquency, Agnew (1984) found that adolescents with a strong need for autonomy were higher in delinquency, with part of the effect of autonomy being mediated by a scale measuring anger or frustration. Agnew (1984), Greenberg (1977), Moffitt (1993) and others argue that the denial of autonomy may lead to delinquency for several reasons. Delinquency may be a means of asserting autonomy (e.g., sexual intercourse or disorderly behaviour), achieving autonomy (e.g., stealing money to gain financial independence from parents), or venting frustration against those who deny autonomy.

Data also suggest that adolescents are very concerned about their standing with peers (Newman 1982; Compas and Wagner 1991; Coie, Dodge, and Kupersmidt 1990). The highly competitive nature of adolescent peer groups, however, makes popularity difficult to achieve for many. Standing with peers is dependent on a number of factors, including social skills, appearance, intelligence, athletic ability, and money to buy clothing and finance social activities. Adolescents deficient in these areas may find themselves rejected by others, and they may turn to delinquency for several reasons. They may seek revenge on those who reject them, turn to theft to finance their social activities (see Greenberg 1977; 1985), turn to drug use to alleviate their negative feelings, and turn to delinquent others who are similarly rejected, thereby indirectly increasing their likelihood of delinquency.

When adolescents become adults, they achieve the autonomy that is often denied them as adolescents. Also, popularity with peers becomes less of a concern. Peers are left behind and new sources of self-esteem emerge (Greenberg 1977). The peak in crime during adolescence, then, may be explained in terms of the goals adolescents pursue. This argument, however, assumes that the goals of autonomy and popularity are not replaced by new goals that are just as difficult to achieve. One might argue, for example, that adults shift their focus to the goal of material success and that they often have trouble achieving this goal. Certain theorists have suggested that this does not happen: that adults lower their aspirations and the importance that they attach to goals like material success (see Shover and Thompson 1992;

Tonry, Ohlin, and Farrington 1991: 160). In particular, their increased maturity and experience make them more likely to bring their goals in line with reality. There is limited evidence that aspirations do decline with age (Bachman, O'Malley, and Johnston 1978: 16–18), although more research on the relationship between goal-blockage and age is clearly needed. We currently know little about the absolute and relative importance attached to various goals over the life course, and the extent of goal-blockage experienced.

The Increased Tendency to View the Environment as Adversive

The above discussion focuses on the objective social environment of the adolescent, arguing that there is reason to believe that adolescents are more likely to be treated in a negative manner. There is also reason to believe that adolescents are more likely to define such treatment as aversive. There are several reasons for this, the first of which involve cognitive changes, which make adolescents more aware of their environment. Adolescents, in particular, notice and become upset over things that escape the attention of children. Certain of these cognitive changes are described by Larson and Asmussen (1991: 34–37; see also Rodriguez-Tome and Bariaud 1990):

> With abstract thought teenagers become capable of deeper analysis of social situations; they become sensitive to the thoughts of others, the discrepancy between appearance and reality . . . the more frequent negative experiences among adolescents may not be a result of an objectively harder, harsher world, but of subjective changes that make it *seem* harder. The adolescents as compared to the preadolescents more often explained their negative emotions in terms of a more distal world, including the feelings of others and anticipated future events. This shift resembles a Piagetian shift from a concrete, here-and-now world to a more abstract, hypothetical, and constructed reality . . . The cognitive advances of adolescence lead to the fundamental insight that other people are centers of thinking and feeling. This insight opens the floodgate to sources of anger and anxiety that were not previously perceived. They experience pain through empathic identification with others. They suffer the ups and downs associated with new dimensions of strategic social interactions among peers. Sensitivity to what Suzy told Bob about Jeremy may be beyond the capacity of most fifth graders, yet was a preoccupation of some of our ninth graders.

Other cognitive changes also increase the likelihood that adolescents will experience a given environment as aversive. Larson and Asmussen (1991) argue that the cognitive growth of adolescents leads them to raise "the ante on what they expect from the world . . . to impose a more penetrating set of standards on the events and the people around them" (1991: 24). Elkind (1967: 1029–30) argues that the adolescent passes through an egocentric phase, during which time "he assumes that other people are as obsessed with his behaviour and appearance as he is himself." The adolescent also believes that his or her emotional experiences are unique. This egocentrism is said to diminish at ages 15–16, but it may intensify the adolescent's emotional reactions to the environment while in existence. The problems that befall the adolescent, for example, are magnified by the belief that others are also aware of and deeply concerned with them. Finally, certain researchers have found evidence suggesting that adolescents are more likely to blame others for the problems they experience (Spirito et al. 1991; Larson and Asmussen 1991; Dodge and Feldman 1990). Such blame increases the likelihood that adolescents will react to their negative treatment with anger. These later two cognitive changes are important because not only do they increase in adolescence, they also decrease in adulthood. So even if adolescents occupy the same objective social environment as children and adults, there is reason to believe that adolescents will experience this environment as more aversive.

A potential illustration of this fact was provided in a study of young people's perceptions of the stratification system by Simmons and Rosenberg (1971; see also Seligman, Kamen, and Nolen-Hoeksema 1988). Even though they occupied the same position in the stratification system, teenagers were less likely than children to (a) give favourable ratings to jobs; (b) inflate the prestige level of their father's job and the degree of their parent's success in life; (c) overestimate their own social class; and (d) express optimism about their own personal chances of success. Teenagers were also more likely to perceive economic differences among their peers. Differences in cognitive level are one of the likely explanations for these findings.

Adolescents may also be more likely to experience their environment as aversive because they are more likely to experience several negative events at the same time. Researchers have argued that negative emotional reactions are most likely when individuals experience several negative events at once, and limited data support this proposition (Petersen, Kennedy, and Sullivan 1991; Simmons and Blyth 1987; Larson and Ham 1993). The dramatic changes associated with puberty, while not detrimental in and of themselves, may also increase the sensitivity of adolescents to environmental change (see Simmons and Blyth 1987; Petersen 1987).

Finally, adolescents may have a more difficult time engaging in the cognitive reinterpretation of negative events. Adolescents live in a very public world. Much of the negative treatment they receive occurs before an audience, such as classmates or peers. Other negative treatment, although occurring in private, may be shared with peers and so become part of the public sphere. The public nature of adolescent life makes cognitive reinterpretation more difficult since reinterpretations are more likely to be challenged by others. Adolescent peers, in fact, may not only challenge attempts at cognitive reinterpretation, they may regularly remind the adolescent of the negative treatment he or she has suffered. Children and adults live in more private worlds, and so may have an easier time engaging in cognitive reinterpretation. Children probably have limited skills at this form of coping, but parents may assist them by telling them that the negative events they have experienced are not as bad as they think. Adults have much experience with this coping technique.

These arguments find support in several studies, which suggest that adolescents experience higher levels of emotional distress than children and adults (Siegel 1982; Gove 1985; Larson and Asmussen 1991; Petersen and Hamburg 1986; Siddique and D'Arcy 1984; Larson and Ham 1993; also see Mirowsky and Ross 1989). One of the best of these studies was carried out by Larson and Lampman-Petraitis (1989; also see Larson and Ham 1993). They equipped preadolescents and early adolescents with electronic pagers, which were signalled at random times during the day. Respondents were then asked to record their feelings. The early adolescents reported more occurrences of anger, hurt, and worry than did the preadolescents. This higher instance of negative affect was due to (a) a higher instance of perceived negative events and (b) the fact that these negative events had a much larger effect on the emotional state of young adolescents than preadolescents (see Larson and Ham 1993).

The Increased Tendency to Cope with Adversity through Delinquency

As argued above, adolescents experience a dramatic increase in the size and complexity of their social world and in their tendency to interpret this world as aversive. At the same time, adolescents are poorly equipped to cope with these changes. Data suggest that adolescents are more likely to cope with adversity in "immature" or maladaptive ways, including delinquency (Compas, Malcrane, and Fondacaro 1988; Aneshensel and Gore 1991; Hoffman et al. 1992; Rook, Dooley, and Catalano 1991; Seiffge-Krenke 1990). Certain of these studies, in fact, suggest that their coping efforts exacerbate rather than alleviate their levels of stress. There are several reasons for the greater likelihood of delinquent coping among adolescents.

First, adolescents lack experience at coping. This is not, of course, to claim that children have more experience at coping. Children, however, are under the protection of parents, who cope on their behalf and are a major source of social support. Parents are more likely to be aware of the problems of children, since they supervise children more closely and children are more likely than adolescents to share their problems with parents (Seiffge-Krenke 1990). And parents are more likely to cope for and provide support to children, since they view children as more helpless and fragile than adolescents. As a consequence, adolescents not only confront a much larger and more challenging world, but they must assume much more responsibility for coping with this world. Unfortunately, they have little experience at coping. Many of the coping techniques employed by their parents are unavailable to them, because they lack power or the requisite cognitive skills. Other techniques require practice for effective use. Adolescents, however, typically receive little practice because the changed social circumstances associated with adolescence occur abruptly, often with the transition from elementary to middle or high school. Adolescents may receive increased social support from friends, but as indicated below there is reason to doubt the value of such support. Further, a recent study focusing on adults suggests that social support from friends is less effective than that from family (Jackson 1992). Adolescents, then, often lack the experience and support necessary for effective coping, which increases the likelihood of ineffective coping, including delinquent coping.

Second, coping with strain through nondelinquent means often requires power; power to terminate, alleviate or escape from adversive relations. And as Agnew (1985) argues, one of the distinguishing features of adolescents is that they often lack power and are compelled to remain in relationships they find aversive (see Agnew 1991). Adolescents "are compelled to live with their family in a certain neighbourhood; to go to a certain school; and, within limits, to interact with the same group of peers and neighbours" (Agnew 1985: 156). If any of these contexts is aversive, there is often little that the adolescent can do to legally cope. Except under unusual circumstances, adolescents cannot quit school or change teachers; move to a new neighbourhood; leave their family; or impose restraints on parents, teachers, and others. The result is an increase in negative affect and a greater likelihood of delinquent coping. Adolescents, in particular, often end up coping through one of the few sources of power available to them — physical strength. Adults, however, usually have access to legal means of coping. Adults, for example, can move to a new neighbourhood, quit their job, or get a divorce. Their greater resources also increase their bargaining power when dealing with others who treat them in a negative manner. Children lack power, but parents typically employ their power in behalf of children (see Marwell's 1966 discussion of "power of agency"). Once again, then, we find that adolescents have less access to nondelinquent means of coping.

Third, not only do adolescents lack access to many nondelinquent modes of coping, but they often find themselves in situations that are conducive to delinquent coping. As previously discussed, they are lower in social control — so the costs of delinquent coping are lower. They are much more likely to associate with delinquent peers, who often encourage the use of delinquent coping. Much of their negative treatment occurs before an audience or becomes known to peers, which increases the pressure to engage in a "face-saving" response, which might involve delinquency. And their tendency to blame others for their adversity increases their anger, which makes a delinquent response more likely. In sum, adolescents are both less able and less disposed to cope with their adversity through nondelinquent channels.

The peak in crime during adolescence, then, is due to an increase in negative relations at this time and an increased tendency to interpret such relations as aversive and react with crime. These arguments obviously apply more to some adolescents than to others. Some adolescents, for example, may experience a smaller increase in negative relations because they attend small high schools in homogeneous communities or they possess personality characteristics that limit their interaction with peers. Likewise, some adolescents may be less disposed to respond to negative treatment with crime because they receive much social support from conventional adults or they have less access to delinquent peers (see Moffitt 1993, for a fuller discussion of these and other variables which may limit the delinquency of adolescents).

CONCLUSION

General strain theory, then, has much to say about stability and change in crime over the life course. Stability is partly explained in terms of the trait of aggressiveness, which increases the likelihood that individuals will be treated negatively by others, interpret such treatment as aversive, and react to such adversity with crime. And stability is partly explained by the fact that some individuals are born into highly aversive environments. They respond with delinquency, which elicits negative reactions from others and reduces the likelihood of escape from the adversive environment. So strain and delinquency become involved in an amplifying loop, and escape for many is difficult.

The increase in delinquency during adolescence is explained by arguing that adolescents enter a larger and more demanding social world, which increases the likelihood of negative treatment by others. Further, certain of the cognitive and social changes associated with adolescence increase the likelihood that adolescents will find such treatment aversive and cope with it through delinquency.

These arguments differ from the control and social learning explanations that dominate the literature in two ways. First, GST points to certain variables not explicitly considered by these other theories. While the trait of aggressiveness includes most of the traits previously considered in the literature, it also focuses attention on certain traits that have not been accorded a central role by developmental criminologists — such as problem-solving skills. Also, the GST focuses attention on a much broader range of negative relations than have been considered by control and learning theories. While control and learning theorists often examine negative relations between juveniles, parents, and — to a lesser extent — teachers, they seldom focus on negative relations with others, including peers and neighbours; and they rarely examine the broad range of negative life events and life hassles that are central to GST. Further, GST also considers a range of cognitive and social variables that affect the likelihood that social relations will be interpreted as aversive and that aversive relations will be dealt with through delinquency.

Second, GST differs from these other theories in its specification of intervening processes. There is some overlap between the independent variables considered by GST, control theory, and social learning theory. All three theories, for example, focus on traits like difficult temperament. In particular, there is much overlap between the traits of aggressiveness and low self-control (see

Agnew 1995). Likewise, all three theories focus on negative relations between parents and children, including the harsh and inconsistent discipline by parents. The theories differ dramatically, however, when it comes to explaining why such variables affect crime. For example, control theorists would argue that negative family relations increase delinquency because they reduce attachment to parents, interfere with the internalization of conventional beliefs, and reduce the likelihood that the child will develop a strong attachment to school. Social learning theorists would argue that these negative relations increase delinquency because they expose the child to coercive models, result in the reinforcement of delinquency, implicitly teach the child that coercive behaviour is acceptable in certain circumstances, and increase the likelihood of association with delinquent peers. GST theorists, while acknowledging the validity of these arguments, would also argue that negative relations have another effect. Children subject to harsh and inconsistent discipline are being mistreated on a regular basis. Their punishment is excessive and often undeserved. This fact is likely to anger and frustrate these children, and they may turn to delinquency in an effort to cope. Their delinquency may be a means of escaping from or alleviating their adversity (e.g., running away from home, attacking parents) or managing the negative emotions they are experiencing (e.g., drug use). Agnew (1995) provides a more complete description of the differences between the theories in this area, and describes strategies for testing between the different explanations offered by these theories.

The GST, then, supplements control and social learning theories in explaining the continuity and change in antisocial/criminal behaviour: GST points to certain variables not considered by these theories and offers an additional explanation for the effect of variables that are considered by these theories.

STUDY QUESTIONS

1. *How does Agnew's general strain theory explain the stability of criminal behaviour over time among some individuals?*
2. *How does Agnew's general strain theory explain the impact of aggressiveness on crime?*
3. *How does Agnew's general strain theory explain the peak in crime during adolescence?*

REFERENCES

Agnew, R. 1984. "Autonomy and Delinquency." *Sociological Perspectives 27*: 219–40.

———. 1985. "A Revised Strain Theory of Delinquency." *Social Forces 64*: 151–67.

———. 1991. "Adolescent Resources and Delinquency." *Criminology 28*: 535–66.

———. 1992. "Foundation for a General Strain Theory of Delinquency." *Criminology 30*: 47–87.

———. 1995. "The Contribution of Social-Psychological Strain Theory to the Explanation of Crime and Delinquency." In F. Alder and W. Laufer, eds., *Advances in Criminological Theory, The Legacy of Anomie*, vol. 6, 113–37. New Brunswick, NJ: Transaction.

Agnew, R., and H.R. White. 1992. "An Empirical Test of General Strain Theory." *Criminology 30*(4): 475–99.

Alder, F., and W. Laufer. 1995. *Advances in Criminological Theory, The Legacy of Anomie*, vol. 6. New Brunswick, NJ: Transaction.

Aneshensel, C.S., and S. Gore. 1991. "Development, Stress, and Role Restructuring: Social Transitions of Adolescence." In John Eckenrode, ed., *The Social Context of Coping*, 55–77. New York: Plenum.

Bachman, J.G., P.M. O'Malley, and J. Johnston. 1978. *Youth in Transition: Adolescence to Adulthood — Change and Stability in the Lives of Young Men*, vol. 6. Ann Arbor, MI: Institute for Social Research.

Bates, J.E. 1980. "The Concept of Difficult Temperament." *Merrill-Palmer Quarterly 26*: 299–319.

Bernard, T.J. 1990. "Angry Aggression among the 'Truly Disadvantaged.' " *Criminology 28*: 73–96.

Brown, J.M., J. O'Keefe, S.H. Sanders, and B. Baker. 1986. "Developmental Changes in Children's Cognition to Stressful and Painful Situations." *Journal of Pediatric Psychology 11*: 343–57.

Cairns, R.B., B.D. Cairns, H.J. Neckerman, S.D. Gest, and J.L. Gariepy. 1988. "Social Networks and Aggressive Behavior: Peer Support or Peer Rejection." *Developmental Psychology 24*: 815–23.

Caspi, A., D.J. Bem, and G.H. Elder. 1989. "Continuities and Consequences of Interactional Styles Across the Life Course." *Journal of Personality 57*: 375–406.

Chumlea, W.C. 1982. "Physical Growth in Adolescence." In B.B. Wolman, ed., *Handbook of Developmental Psychology*, 471–85. Englewood Cliffs, NJ: Prentice-Hall.

Cloward, R.A., and L.E. Ohlin. 1960. *Delinquency and Opportunity*. New York: Free Press.

Coddington, R.D. 1972. "The Significance of Etiologic Factors in the Diseases of Children-II. A Study of a Normal Population." *Journal of Psychosomatic Research 16*: 205–13.

Cohen, A. 1955. *Delinquent Boys*. New York: Free Press.

Coie, J.D., K.A. Dodge, and J.B. Kupersmidt. 1990. "Peer Group Behavior and Social Status." In S.R. Asher and J.D. Coie, eds., *Peer Rejection in Childhood*, 17–59. Cambridge: Cambridge University Press.

Compas, B.E. 1987a. "Stress and Life Events During Childhood and Adolescence." *Clinical Psychology Review 7*: 275–302.

———. 1987b. "Coping with Stress During Childhood and Adolescence." *Psychological Bulletin 101*: 393–403.

Compas, B.E., G.E. Davis, and C.J. Forsythe. 1985. "Characteristics of Life Events During Adolescence." *American Journal of Community Psychology 13*: 677–91.

Compas, B.E., V.L. Malcrane, and K.M. Fondacaro. 1988. "Coping with Stressful Events in Older Children and Young Adolescents." *Journal of Consulting and Clinical Psychology 56*: 405–11.

Compas, B.E., and B.M. Wagner. 1991. "Psychosocial Stress during Adolescence: Intrapersonal and Interpersonal Processes." In M.E. Colten and S. Gore, eds., *Adolescent Stress: Causes and Consequences*, 67–85. New York: Aldine De Gruyter.

Dodge, K.A. 1986. *Social Competence in Children*. Chicago: University of Chicago Press.

Dodge, K.A., and E. Feldman. 1990. "Issues in Social Cognition and Sociometric Status." In S.R. Asher and J.D. Coie, eds., *Peer Rejection in Childhood*, 119–55. Cambridge: Cambridge University Press.

Dodge, K.A., and J.P. Newman. 1981. "Biased Decision-Making Processes in Aggressive Boys." *Journal of Abnormal Psychology 90*: 375–79.

Elkind, D. 1967. "Egocentrism in Adolescence." *Child Development 38*: 1025–34.

Farrington, D.P. 1986. "Age and Crime." In M. Tonry and N. Morris, eds., *Crime and Justice*, vol. 7, 189–250. Chicago: University of Chicago Press.

Garrison, W.T., and F.J. Earls. 1987. *Temperament and Child Psychopathology.* Newbury Park, CA: Sage.

Giordano, P.G., S.A. Cernkovich, and M.D. Pugh. 1986. "Friendships and Delinquency." *American Journal of Sociology 91*: 1170–1202.

Gold., M., and R.J. Petronio. 1980. "Delinquent Behavior in Adolescence." In J. Adelson, ed., *Handbook of Adolescent Psychology*, 495–535. New York: John Wiley and Sons.

Gottfredson, M.R., and T. Hirschi. 1990. *A General Theory of Crime*. Stanford, CA: Stanford University Press.

Gove, W.R. 1985. "The Effect of Age and Gender on Deviant Behaviour: A Biopsychological Perspective." In A.S. Rossie, ed., *Gender and the Life Course*, 115–44. New York: Aldine.

Greenberg, D.F. 1977. "Delinquency and the Age Structure of Society." *Contemporary Crises 1*: 189–223.

———. 1985. "Age, Crime, and Social Explanation." *American Journal of Sociology 91*: 1–27.

Hirschi, T. 1969. *Causes of Delinquency*. Berkeley, CA: University of California Press.

Hirschi, T., and M. Gottfredson. 1983. "Age and the Explanation of Crime." *American Journal of Sociology 89*: 552–84.

———. 1985. "Age and Crime, Logic and Scholarship: Comment on Greenberg." *American Journal of Sociology 91*: 22–27.

Hoffman, M.A., R. Levy-Shiff, S.C. Sohlberg, and J. Zarizki. 1992. "The Impact of Stress and Coping: Developmental Changes in the Transition to Adolescence." *Journal of Youth and Adolescence 21*(4): 451–69.

Hollin, C.R. 1991. "Cognitive Behavioural Modification with Delinquents." In M. Herbert, ed., *Clinical Child Psychology*, 293–308. Chichester: John Wiley.

Jackson, P.B. 1992. "Specifying the Buffering Hypothesis: Support, Strain, and Depression." *Social Psychology Quarterly* 55(4): 363–78.

Jackson, S., and H. Bosma. 1990. "Coping and Self in Adolescence." In H. Bosma and S. Jackson, eds., *Coping and Self-Concept in Adolescence*, 1–11. Berlin: Springer-Verlag.

Kazdin, A.E. 1987. *Conduct Disorders in Childhood and Adolescence*. Newbury Park, CA: Sage.

Kercher, K. 1987. "Explaining the Relationship Between Age and Crime: The Biological vs. Sociological Model." Presented at the annual meeting of the American Society of Criminology, Montreal.

Kohn, P.M., and J.A. Milrose. 1993. "The Inventory of High-School Students' Recent Life Experiences: A Decontaminated Measure of Adolescents' Hassles." *Journal of Youth and Adolescence 22*(1): 43–55.

Landy, S., and R.D. Peters. 1992. "Toward an Understanding of a Developmental Paradigm for Aggressive Conduct Problems During the Preschool Years." In R. Peters, R.J. McMahon, and V.L. Quinsey, eds., *Aggression and Violence Throughout the Life Span*, 1–30. Newbury Park, CA: Sage.

Larson, R., and L. Asmussen. 1991. "Anger, Worry, and Hurt in Early Adolescence: An Enlarging World of Negative Emotions." In M.E. Colten and S. Gore, eds., *Adolescent Stress: Causes and Consequences*, 21–41. New York: Aldine De Gruyter.

Larson, R., and M. Ham. 1993. "Stress and 'Storm and Stress' in Early Adolescence: The Relationship of Negative Events with Dysphoric Affect." *Developmental Psychology 29*(1): 130–40.

Larson, R., and C. Lampman-Petraitis. 1989. "Daily Emotional States as Reported by Children and Adolescents." *Child Development 60*: 1250–60.

Lempers, J.D., and D.S. Clark-Lempers. 1992. "Young, Middle, and Late Adolescents' Comparisons of the Functional Importance of Five Significant Relationships." *Journal of Youth and Adolescence 21*(1): 53–96.

Lerner, R.M., and J.A. Shea. 1982. "Social Behavior in Adolescence." In B.B. Wolman, ed., *Handbook of Developmental Psychology*, 503–25. Englewood Cliffs, NJ: Prentice-Hall.

Loeber, R., and M. LeBlanc. 1990. "Toward a Developmental Criminology." In M. Tonry and N. Morris, eds., *Crime and Justice: A Review of Research*, vol. 12, 375–473. Chicago: University of Chicago Press.

Marwell, G. 1966. "Adolescent Powerlessness and Delinquent Behavior." *Social Problems 14*: 35–47.

Matza, D. 1964. *Delinquency and Drift*. New York: John Wiley.

Merton, R. 1938. "Social Structure and Anomie." *American Sociological Review 3*: 672–82.

Mirowsky, J., and C.E. Ross. 1989. *Social Causes of Psychological Distress*. New York: Aldine de Gruyter.

Moffitt, T.E. 1993. "Adolescence-Limited and Life-Course-Persistent Antisocial Behavior: A Developmental Taxonomy." *Psychological Review 100*(4): 674–701.

Morton, T. 1987. "Childhood Aggression in the Context of Family Interaction." In D.H. Crowell, I.M. Evans, and C.R. O'Donnell, eds., *Childhood Aggression and Violence*, 117–58. New York: Plenum.

Nagin, D.S., and D.P. Farrington. 1992. "The Onset and Persistence of Offending." *Criminology 30*(4): 501–23.

Nagin, D.S., and K.C. Land. 1993. "Age, Criminal Careers, and Population Heterogeneity: Specification and Estimation of a Nonparametric, Mixed Poisson Model." *Criminology 31*(3): 327–62.

Nasby, W., B. Hayden, and B.M. DePaulo. 1980. "Attributional Bias Among Aggressive Boys to Interpret Unambiguous Social Stimuli as Displays of Hostility." *Journal of Abnormal Psychology 89*: 459–68.

Newcomb, M.D., G.J. Huba, and P.M. Bentler. 1981. "A Multidimensional Assessment of Stressful Life Events Among Adolescents: Derivation and Correlates." *Journal of Health and Social Behaviour 22*: 400–15.

Newman, P.R. 1982. "The Peer Group." In B.B. Wolman, ed., *Handbook of Developmental Psychology*, 526–36. Englewood Cliffs, NJ: Prentice-Hall.

Olbrich, E. 1990. "Coping and Development." In H. Bosma and S. Jackson, eds., *Coping and Self-Concept in Adolescence*, 35–47. Berlin: Springer-Verlag.

Olweus, D. 1979. "Stability of Aggressive Reaction Patterns in Males: A Review." *Psychological Bulletin 86*: 852–57.

Paternoster, R., and P. Mazerolle. 1994. "General Strain Theory and Delinquency." *Journal of Research in Crime and Delinquency 31*(3): 235–63.

Patterson, G.R. 1982. *Coercive Family Process*. Eugene, OR: Castalia.

———. 1992. "Developmental Changes in Antisocial Behavior." In R.D. Peters, R.J. McMahon, and V.L. Quinsey, eds., *Aggression and Violence Throughout the Life Span*, 52–82. Newbury Park, CA: Sage.

Patterson, G.R., B.D. DeBaryshe, and E. Ramsey. 1989. "A Developmental Perspective on Antisocial Behavior." *American Psychologist 44*: 329–35.

Pepler, D.J., G. King, and W. Byrd. 1991. "A Social Cognitively Based Social Skills Training Program for Aggressive Children." In D.J. Pepler and K.H. Rubin, eds., *The Development and Treatment of Childhood Aggression*, 361–79. Hillsdale, NJ: Lawrence Erlbaum.

Petersen, A.C. 1987. "The Nature of Biological-Psychosocial Interactions: The Sample Case of Early Adolescence." In R.M. Lerber and T.T. Foch, eds., *Biological-Psychosocial Interactions in Early Adolescence*, 35–61. Hillsdale, NJ: Lawrence Erlbaum.

———. 1988. "Adolescent Development." *Annual Review of Psychology 39*: 583–607.

Petersen, A.C., and B.A. Hamburg. 1986. "Adolescence: A Developmental Approach to Problems and Psychopathology." *Behavior Therapy 17*: 480–99.

Petersen, A.C., R.E. Kennedy, and P. Sullivan. 1991. "Coping with Adolescence." In M.E. Colten and S. Gore, *Adolescent Stress: Causes and Consequences*, 93–110. New York: Aldine De Gruyter.

Rodriquez-Tome, H., and F. Bariaud. 1990. "Anxiety in Adolescence: Sources and Reactions." In H. Bosma and S. Jackson, eds., *Coping and Self-Concept in Adolescence*, 167–86. Berlin: Springer-Verlag.

Rook, K., D. Dooley, and R. Catalano. 1991. "Age Differences in Workers' Efforts to Cope with Economic Distress." In J. Eckenrode, ed., *The Social Context of Coping*, 79–105. New York: Plenum.

Rowe, A.R., and C.R. Tittle. 1977. "Life Cycle Changes and Criminal Propensity." *Sociological Quarterly 18*: 223–36.

Rutter, M. 1985. "Resilience in the Face of Adversity." *British Journal of Psychiatry 147*: 598–611.

Sampson, R.J., and J.H. Laub. 1990. "Crime and Deviance Over the Life Course: The Salience of Social Bonds." *American Sociological Review 55*(5): 609–27.

———. 1992. "Crime and the Life Course." *Annual Review of Sociology 18*: 63–84.

———. 1993. *Crime in the Making*. Cambridge, MA: Harvard University Press.

Seiffge-Krenke, I. 1990. "Developmental Processes in Self-Concept and Coping Behavior." In H. Bosma and S. Jackson, eds., *Coping and Self-Concept in Adolescence*, 49–68. Berlin: Springer-Verlag.

Seligman, M.E.P., L.P. Kamen, and S. Nolen-Hoeksema. 1988. "Explanatory Style Across the Life Span: Achievement and Health." In E.M. Hetherington, R.M. Lerner, and M. Perlmutter, eds., *Child Development in Life-Span Perspective*, 91–114. Hillsdale, NJ: Lawrence Erlbaum Associates.

Shover, N., and C.Y. Thompson. 1992. "Age, Differential Expectations, and Crime Desistance." *Criminology 30*: 89–104.

Siddique, C.M., and C. D'Arcy. 1984. "Adolescence, Stress, and Psychological Well-Being." *Journal of Youth and Adolescence 13*: 459–73.

Siegel, O. 1982. "Personality Development in Adolescence." In B.B. Wolman, ed., *Handbook of Development Psychology*, 537–48. Englewood Cliffs, NJ: Prentice Hall.

Simmons, R.G., and D.A. Blyth. 1987. *Moving into Adolescence*. New York: Aldine De Gruyter.

Simmons, R.G., and M. Rosenberg., 1971. "Functions of Children's Perceptions of the Stratification System." *American Sociological Review 36*: 235–49.

Slaby, R.G., and N.G. Guerra. 1988. "Cognitive Mediators of Aggression in Adolescent Offenders: 1. Assessment." *Developmental Psychology 24*: 580–88.

Smetana, J.G., J. Yau, A. Restrepo, and J.L. Braeges. 1991. "Conflict and Adaptation in Adolescence: Adolescent-Parent Conflict." In M.E. Colten and S. Gore, eds., *Adolescent Stress: Causes and Consequences*, 43–65. New York: Aldine De Gruyter.

Spirito, A., L.J. Stark, N. Grace, and D. Stamoulis. 1991. "Common Problems and Coping Strategies Reported in Childhood and Early Adolescence." *Journal of Youth and Adolescence 20*(5): 531–44.

Stark, L.J., A. Spirito, C.A. Williams, and D.C. Guevremont. 1989. "Common Problems and Coping Strategies I: Findings with Normal Adolescents." *Journal of Abnormal Child Psychology 17*: 203–21.

Steffensmeier, D.J., E.A. Allan, M.D. Harer, and C. Streifel. 1989. "Age and the Distribution of Crime." *American Journal of Sociology 94*: 803–31.

Thornberry, T.P. 1987. "Toward an Interactional Theory of Delinquency." *Criminology 25*: 863–91.

Tonry, M., L.E. Ohlin, and D.P. Farrington. 1991. *Human Development and Criminal Behavior*. New York: Springer-Verlag.

Van Der Boom, D.C. 1989. "Neonatal Irritability and the Development of Attachment." In G.A. Kohnstamm and J.E. Bates, eds., *Temperament in Childhood*, 299–318. Chichester, England: John Wiley.

Vitaro, F., C. Gagnon, and R.E. Tremblay. 1990. "Predicting Stable Peer Rejection from Kindergarten to Grade One." *Journal of Clinical Child Psychology 19*(3): 257–64.

Warr, M. 1993. "Age, Peers, and Delinquency." *Criminology 31(1)*: 17–40.

Wilson, J.Q., and R.J. Herrnstein. 1985. *Crime and Human Nature*. New York: Touchstone.

Wolfe, D.A., C. Wekerle, and R. McGee. 1992. "Developmental Disparities of Abused Children: Directions for Prevention." In R.D. Peters, R.J. McMahon, and V.L. Quinsey, eds., *Aggression and Violence throughout the Life Span*, 31–51. Newbury Park, CA: Sage.

Wolfgang, M., R. Figlio, and T. Sellin. 1972. *Delinquency in a Birth Cohort*. Chicago: University of Chicago Press.

Wolfgang, M., T.P. Thornberry, and R. Figlio. 1987. *From Boy to Man, From Delinquency to Crime*. Chicago: University of Chicago Press.

CHAPTER SIX

A Symbolic Interactionist Theory of Role-Transitions, Role-Commitments, and Delinquency

ROSS L. MATSUEDA
KAREN HEIMER
University of Iowa

Recent criminological research has emphasized the importance of viewing crime and delinquency within the framework of the life-course or life-span development (Hagan and Palloni 1988; Elliott, Huizinga, and Menard 1989; Loeber and LeBlanc 1990; Sampson and Laub 1992; 1993; Farrington 1992). A life-course perspective opens new puzzles and questions for the study of deviance, such as the role of pathways, trajectories, and life-course transitions in deviance, hypotheses about duration-dependent processes, questions about ontogenetic versus sociogenic causal mechanisms, and issues in modelling longitudinal data. The empirical research on these topics suggests that trajectories, pathways, and transitions are important, and that a general theory of crime should incorporate a life-course view (Sampson and Laub 1992; 1993; Farrington 1992; Hagan and Wheaton 1993). This chapter explores the potential contribution of symbolic interactionism to a life-course theory of crime. We argue that such a view provides a theory of the meaning of life-course transitions and a situational theory of the mechanisms by which such transitions translate into criminal acts. It also provides a slant on the ontogenetic-sociogenic debate, and can help specify duration-dependent hypotheses about crime. The remainder of this chapter is divided into three parts: First, we briefly review the importance of a life-course perspective in crime and delinquency, highlighting important issues, theoretical questions, and tentative empirical findings. Next, we sketch a symbolic interactionist approach to crime in the life course. Third,

Source: Ross L. Matsueda and Karen Heimer, "A Symbolic Interactionist Theory of Role-Transitions, Role-Commitments, and Delinquency." In T. Thornberry, ed., *Developmental Theories of Crime and Delinquency* (New Brunswick, NJ: Transaction Books, 1997): 163–213. Reprinted by permission of Transaction Publishers.

we apply the theory to three stages of the life course: early child development, adolescence, and adulthood.

LIFE COURSE, DEVELOPMENT, AND CRIME

Life-course perspectives generally view life events in the context of life stages, transitions, turning points, and pathways, which are embedded in social institutions (Elder 1985). According to Elder (1985), pathways or trajectories refer to long-term trends or patterns of events, such as occupational careers or family trajectories. In contrast, transitions refer to short-term changes that can redirect a trajectory, such as getting married, becoming divorced, or entering the labour force. For example, Sampson and Laub (1993) argue that it is not life transitions per se that affect criminality, but rather the extent of informal social control associated with such transitions that lead to changes in crime. That is, life events effect change in crime by influencing the strength of social ties, which reflect investments in institutional relationships or social capital (Laub and Sampson 1993).

Sampson and Laub's Theory of Informal Social Control

Applied to crime and delinquency, the life-course approach has fallen centre stage amidst controversy in criminology (Hagan and Palloni 1988). In perhaps the most promising program of research on deviance within the life course, Sampson and Laub (1990; 1992; 1993; Laub and Sampson 1993) specify a theory of informal social control. Their theoretical view combines low self-control theory and social control theory: criminal behaviour is due in large part to a stable trait of childhood antisocial propensity, which causes adult deviance and adult problems with conventional institutions like education, family, military, and employment. But net of antisocial propensity, they argue that adult ties to conventional institutions and individuals reduce adult criminality. For Sampson and Laub, it is not education, marriage, or employment per se that is important, but rather the level of commitment and attachment to those conventional roles. Here they draw parallels between adult social bonds and Coleman's (1990) concept of social capital. Their empirical results find that early childhood antisocial behaviour is linked to adult deviant behaviour as well as adult social bonding — marital attachment, job stability, and occupational commitment. Moreover, net of child and antisocial behaviour, marital attachment and job stability (but not occupational commitment) affect adult crime and the time to desistance from crime (Sampson and Laub 1993).

Sampson and Laub's work has set an important theoretical and research agenda for examination of crime in the life course. Nevertheless, we believe that a symbolic interactionist perspective can augment their theoretical argument in two important ways. First, by relaxing the assumptions made by control theories that the motivation for crime is constant across persons, that subcultures are impotent, and that only conventional culture matters, a symbolic interactionist theory can provide a more complete and nuanced theory of the content of culture — one that specifies a theory of the meaning of social roles, and links the life course to criminal and deviant subcultures. Second, by providing a situational theory of action, interactionism can stipulate how the dynamics of the immediate situation are linked to social roles, meanings, and behaviours, and how individual propensities (personality) are socially reconstituted in interactions. Third, the theory of meaning within interactions specifies a dialectical relationship between the life course and interaction: social interaction is conditioned by the life course, which at the same time, is socially constituted in interactions.

A SYMBOLIC INTERACTIONIST FRAMEWORK

Symbolic interactionism is a useful framework for developing a life-course theory of crime for several reasons. First, unlike structural functionalism, which underlies anomie and social control theories of crime, symbolic interactionism does not take a static view of society, social organization, and social order. Instead, interactionism builds on the philosophical position of American Pragmatism, beginning with a process model of society: society consists of an ongoing process of interactions, which fit together and constitute social organization and social order. Such a model is compatible with a life-course perspective that begins with a dynamic view of individual, group, and societal biographies. Second, symbolic interactionism takes a clear and consistent position on the ontogenetic-sociogenic debate. We follow George Herbert Mead's (1934) view of "biosocial man," in which the impulses, instincts, and genotypes of human biological organisms are translated into behaviour through a social process consisting of interaction with others. Third, life-course perspectives emphasize the importance not only of role-transitions, but also of the meanings of such transitions to individuals (Elder 1985). Symbolic interactionism provides an explicit theory of meaning and a way of linking roles to meanings, identities, and subcultures (Stryker 1980). Finally, symbolic interactionism can stipulate specific mechanisms of population heterogeneity and state dependence within a unified framework. Thus, we can apply these mechanisms to crime without having to resort to ad hoc mixing of contradictory theories, like social control and labelling. To specify the mechanisms explicitly requires a brief review of a symbolic interactionist view of crime. We build upon statements made by Matsueda (1992) and Heimer and Matsueda (1994) in applying the principles to life-course issues.

Culture and Subcultures

Symbolic interactionism rejects the assumptions of sociology's structural functionalists, and criminology's social control theorists, that society consists of a single moral order and that subcultures are irrelevant to the motivation of crime and delinquency (Kornhauser 1978; Hirschi 1969). Instead, interactionists assume that pluralist societies consist of a diversity of perspectives organized along lines of communication. These perspectives at times crystallize into distinct social worlds, in which groups organize around a common set of concerns and viewpoints. These subcultures can give rise to new ways of solving problems or adapting to the environment. At the same time, they can give rise to a parochialism that generates deviant behaviour from the standpoint of other groups.

A dominant culture in pluralist societies consists of the intersection of various perspectives, and is socially constituted in interaction. In general, a dominant culture consists of norms, beliefs, and behaviour patterns that facilitate success in conventional realms and proscribe deviant and criminal behaviour. In a market economy, various forms of capital investment increase the likelihood of individual market success, including investments in human capital, such as schooling and job training (Becker 1964), social capital, which inheres in social relations such as obligations and expectations, information channels, and norms (Coleman 1990), and cultural capital, defined as competence in elite status cultures, including elite attitudes, behaviours, and habits (Bourdieu 1977). These forms of capital are resources that can be translated into material rewards through conventional institutions. Moreover, capital investments should reduce the likelihood of criminality by increasing conventional role commitments, identities, and reference groups, and by reducing incentives for crime.

Furthermore, within criminal subcultures, one can speak of rudimentary criminal counterparts to conventional culture. That is, success in a criminal subculture may be increased by investing in criminal counterparts to human, social, and cultural capital. Thus, members of these subcultures might gain greater monetary returns, prestige, and status through investing in criminal skills, training, obligations, information channels, norms, attitudes, and habits. Because such structures and norms foster behaviour proscribed by the larger social system — which mobilizes resources to combat the behaviour — they will remain comparatively rudimentary, weak, and ineffectual relative to conventional structures. Nevertheless, in contrast to disorganization and control theorists, we do not view these structures and cultures as entirely impotent (Matsueda 1988). For individuals unable to attain success in conventional ways, criminal structures may be important determinants of crime (e.g., Cloward and Ohlin 1960). We use the term "criminal capital" to refer to forms of human, social, and cultural capital that foster returns to criminal behaviour. Both conventional and criminal capital investments vary across the life course and are critical variables in explaining the timing and sequence of behaviours and roles. We argue that investments in various forms of capital and the resulting decisions based on those investments are in part conditioned by taking the role of significant others in problematic situations.

Social Process and Transactions: Role-Taking

Symbolic interactionism assumes that society is an ongoing process of social transactions, consisting of interactions between two or more individuals. Transactions are built up by participants' adjustments to each other and their situations. When adjustments are smooth and routine, they occur without self-consciousness. When they are temporarily blocked, the situation becomes problematic and the individuals engage in role-taking, solving the problematic situation by taking the role of others, viewing themselves as objects from the standpoint of others, and considering alternative lines of action from the standpoint of others (Mead 1934). When an act or impulse is blocked by a physical or social barrier, an emotion is released, and the impulse is transformed into an image, including a plan of action and the anticipated reactions of others to the action. This image is then reacted to by another impulse, which either follows the plan into overt behaviour, combines the plan with another, or blocks the plan, causing the situation to remain problematic. Mead (1934) referred to the image as the "me," the reacting impulse as the "I," so that cognition is an internal dialogue or conversation between two phases of the self, the "I," and the "me." This process continues until the problem is solved or the transaction ends. Once the problem is solved, the "me" is incorporated into the self in memory, and can be called up in future problematic situations. When problematic situations are solved repeatedly in similar ways, they become less problematic, and behaviour becomes more habitual, nonreflective, and scripted (Matsueda 1992; Heimer and Matsueda 1994). Specifically, consistent with some psychological research, situations that are encountered repeatedly become routine and do not trigger deep cognitive processing; behaviour, therefore, appears relatively "mindless" and unfolds in a scripted fashion (Shiffrin and Schneider 1977; Langer 1989). Thus, successive solutions to problematic situations — solutions that are rewarded (to use the terms of social learning theories), — lead to continuity in behaviour, whether legal or illegal, across similar situations. For example, within turf gangs, violence may be automatic and nonreflective, whereas within a church choir, violence would rarely result and only after considerable reflection.

The self, then, is the critical locus of social control, and consists of a dialectical relationship between the "I" and the "me." The "me" consists of the portion of the self rooted in one's organized groups; the "I" consists of impulses, some of which are socially conditioned. Moreover, the "I" contains a variable element of novelty or emergence, so that the response of the "I" can never be predicted perfectly by the "me."

From this standpoint, criminal acts refer to specific directions of ongoing behaviours. The probability of such behaviours occurring is a function of the situation into which interactants self-select, and the contributions of each interactant to the direction of that behaviour. Those contributions in turn are a function of the individual biographical histories of each interactant relevant to criminality. This includes stable views of the self (as a criminal or conformist) from the standpoint of others, attitudes and motives about crime, and anticipated reactions of others toward crime (Heimer and Matsueda 1994).

Role-Commitment and Differential Social Control

Because the self consists of a dialectic between the "I" and the "me," behaviour is patterned, but not completely determined. Stability in the self results from stability in the organization of attitudes in the "me," or the generalized other, which leads to continuity in behaviour within individuals. This organization of the self results from participation in organized groups, which implies that those individuals who participate in similar organized groups will display similarities in behaviour relevant to the particular group. For example, youth who participate in delinquent peer groups are likely to take the role of delinquents when considering whether to engage in delinquent behaviour. If role-taking involving this generalized other repeatedly solves problematic situations, the delinquent group is likely to constitute an important element of a youth's "me" and the youth is likely to become increasingly committed to the group, which becomes an important generalized other. Thus, self-control is social control because social organization enters behaviour through the process of taking the role of the other (Matsueda 1992).

With respect to unlawful behaviour it is important to emphasize that social control varies in strength and meaning. In a pluralistic society, members participate in multiple groups, which vary not only in the degree to which they control the behaviour of a given member, but also in the meaning or content of control — either encouraging or dissuading criminal behaviour through the process of role-taking. Therefore, social control of criminal versus conventional behaviour is a process of differential social control — either toward conventional or criminal habits and solutions to problematic situations (Matsueda 1992; see also Elliott, Huizinga, and Menard 1989). Differential social control includes stable views of the self (as a criminal or conformist) from the standpoint of others, attitudes and motives about crime, and anticipated reactions of others to crime (Heimer and Matsueda 1994).

A Biosocial View of Human Behaviour

Most symbolic interactionists, following Blumer (1969) and others, have ignored the role that genetic, biological, and constitutional factors play in behaviour, and instead have assumed that social processes are sufficient to account for behaviour. We take a different view, beginning with Mead's view of humans as biosocial organisms (see also Shibutani 1961). In this view, genetics alone do not determine criminality (i.e., there is no crime gene), but inheritance does play an important role in the process leading to crime, operating indirectly through social interaction. This view is generally consistent with twin and adoption studies of crime. Twin studies show that correlations between delinquency of identical twins (e.g., .70) are consistently higher than those of fraternal twins (e.g., .50), suggesting that both genetics and shared environments play an important role in accounting for behaviour (e.g., Rowe 1983). Adoption studies show that criminality of adoptees resembles the criminality of biological parents slightly more than that of adoptive parents (e.g., Mednick, Gabrielli, and Hutchings 1984). Although these studies have been criticized on methodological grounds (e.g., Walters and White 1989; Gottfredson and Hirschi 1990), it is hard to deny that inheritance plays some role (Walters and White 1989; Plomin 1986).

But what are the specific mechanisms by which genes influence criminal behaviour? Scarr and McCartney (1983) argue that the way in which genetic traits influence behavioural outcomes is by affecting the environment. They identify three mechanisms by which genotypes select environments: (1) passively, in which parents select environments of their children (because parents' genotypes are correlated with children's genotypes, the result is a correlation between child's genotypes and environment); (2) evocatively, in which the physical and social environment responds to a child's genotypes; and (3) actively, in which a child's genotype directly selects the environment. Moreover, these are age-dependent effects: passive selection is emphasized in infancy, when parents determine a child's environment; and active selection is increasingly emphasized in adolescence and adulthood.

This conception of the interplay between genetics and environments can be consistent with an interactionist framework. From an interactionist standpoint, human beings are biosocial organisms that adjust to changing environments; the ability to engage in self-reflective behaviour, in which the attitudes of organized groups enter behaviour, is the highest evolutionary form of adjustment because it gives humans the capacity to change the environment to which they must adjust. Thus, human beings are born with genotypes, constitutions, and temperaments, but these do not directly determine behaviour. Instead, they restrict the range of behaviours possible, and affect the likelihood that certain environments are selected. The most important element of the environment is role-taking, in which adjustments to the environment are self-conscious. In the case of infants and young children, parents help determine environments in part unintentionally, due to their structural limitations (e.g., resources), and in part intentionally, as they exercise their discrimination, tastes, and values. The physical and social environment selected will affect a child's behaviour by circumscribing the child's social transactions. But the environment's response to the child's constitution and evolving social self is more critical. Here the self emerges through reciprocal role-taking in social transactions. From an interactionist standpoint, the evocative and active mechanisms of selecting environments are not discrete. Rather, they emerge jointly out of interaction: the self is built up from appraisals of oneself by others, and the self in turn actively selects future lines of action to adapt to present problematic situations.

An example of how a genetic characteristic affects criminality is given in Caspi, Elder, and Bem's (1987) work on child temper tantrums. This work shows how early child temper tantrums can lead to later problems in life (e.g., downward occupational mobility, erratic work lives, and divorce) through one of two mechanisms: cumulative continuity, in which the maladaptive behaviour selects individuals into negative environments (e.g., dropping out of school) that perpetuate the maladaption; and interactional continuity, in which reciprocal interaction with the environment leads to sustained maladaptive behaviours. From an interactionist standpoint, these two mechanisms derive from a continuous social process, in which reciprocal role-taking produces a self that selects future environments. Thus, early child tantrums can lead to criminality through a labelling process: temperamental outbursts lead to problems in conventional settings, like preschool and kindergarten, causing adults to discipline and label the child as a troublemaker or problem-child, which alters the child's views of self, increasing the likelihood of sustained troublesome behaviour. This, in turn, can increasingly channel a child into situations conducive to deviance, foreclose conventional opportunities, and leave the child with a deviant identity.

SYMBOLIC INTERACTION, LIFE COURSE, AND DELINQUENCY

Symbolic Interaction and the Life Course

We can use a symbolic interactionist framework to examine delinquency within the life course. The most important phases of the life course include infancy, childhood, adolescence, and adulthood. Within these phases are age-graded or development-graded social roles including the roles of dependent child, student, adolescent peer, employee, criminal, spouse, parent, military employee, etc. When viewed within a person and across time, these roles trace out life-course trajectories for individuals.

From an interactionist standpoint, there exists a dialectical relationship between the life course, consisting of age-graded and developmentally graded organized social roles, and social interactions (Wells and Stryker 1986). On the one hand, the life course, like other aspects of social organization, is constituted in social interaction; on the other hand, social interactions are in part conditioned by the life course. But how exactly is behaviour conditioned by the life course, and how exactly is the life course constituted in interaction? We can posit two mechanisms: (1) an endogenous process in which actors consider aspects of the life course in carrying out meaningful, self-conscious behaviour; and (2) an exogenous social structuring that may or may not condition the consciousness of actors.

Drawing on our earlier discussion of role-taking within problematic situations and Mead's theory of temporality, we can specify an endogenous process by which the life course is constituted. One can think of features of the life course as abstract objects whose meaning is constituted in social interactions. Although we can speak of a life course as an objective phenomenon existing independent of consciousness, it is an indefinite object; what is important in behaviour is the specific meaning of features of the life course as constituted in interactions. Thus, an individual's biographical history — including the content of identities, definitions of situations, and role-expectations — is limited by his or her specific life-course roles, transitions, and trajectories. In the process of engaging in meaningful action, individuals take the role of the other, call up elements from the past to solve problematic situations in the present in light of future consequences. When individuals consider aspects of their biographical past or consider the future consequences of action that have implications for future role-transitions and trajectories, they are taking into self-conscious consideration features of the life course. For example, a high school dropout may consider whether he wants to pursue drug dealing as a major source of income, or instead delay gratification, take a low-paying conventional job, and attend an evening trade school. The decision may involve considering the attitudes of peers toward drug dealing, the risks and future potential involved, as well as imagining the probability of garnering a high-paying job after completing trade school, and the meaning of such a job. The life course as a whole consists in part of the aggregation of interactions such as these that involve self-conscious attention to some of its constituent features.

But the life course also is constituted partly exogenously in interactions, without self-consciousness. When the features of a nonproblematic situation (including role relationships of interactants, the objective opportunities to engage in behaviour, such as crime, and the resources available to interactants) are age-graded or developmental, they directly constitute the life course in social interaction. Finally, the life course also constrains social interaction, and thus behaviour. Here age-graded or development-graded roles affect behaviour by delimiting opportunities, and affecting the generalized other and identities by affecting communication networks, peer associations, and subcultural affiliation.

Role Transitions and Crime

The life course can be viewed as a series of transitions, representing choice points, or branches in a time-ordered tree diagram. Each choice made at one point opens up opportunities and choices at a future time point, as well as closing off other opportunities (Atchley 1975; Wells and Stryker 1986). For example, dropping out of high school reduces the likelihood of obtaining a job that requires a college degree, while increasing the likelihood of pursuing criminal careers, such as dealing drugs. For our purposes, an important distinction is between conventional and criminal roles. Conventional roles entail predominantly law-abiding behaviour; when crime is called for, it is exceptional and transient. Criminal roles entail predominantly law-abiding behaviour as well; but it also includes criminal behaviour as a major defining feature. For example, most of the day-to-day behaviour of persons occupying the roles of pimp or drug dealer is law-abiding behaviour, but nevertheless the roles are defined by sustained criminal role expectations of organizing prostitution and selling drugs, respectively. Most acts of crime are probably transient rather than role behaviour.

A symbolic interactionist perspective can help explain why some individuals undergo life-course transitions at particular times, while others do not, and how such transitions may affect the probability of illegal behaviour. According to interactionism, role transitions and continuity are each an outcome of social interaction. That is, within social transactions, individuals self-select into social roles — including age-graded roles — and are selected by social groups into social roles. Most importantly, self-selection and other selection into roles occurs simultaneously in social interaction.

At an abstract level of explanation, we can specify the major determinants of role-continuity versus role-transition, given a decision point between two or more age-graded social roles. This entails factors that push one out of a social role and factors that pull one into another role. These determinants include the context of the decision, particularly its location in social structure, and the facts that affect the direction of role-taking, including impulses, habits, commitments, reference groups, attitudes, and anticipated reactions. The immediate context of the decision conditions the outcome by framing possible objective alternatives. Here, structural position, defined by access to resources and power in society, becomes important. The greater the resources and power, the greater the range of alternative roles, and the greater the likelihood of selecting a role that maximizes tangible rewards and minimizes aversive outcomes. An individual located in an advantaged social class with greater human capital (education, experience, and skills) and social capital (network connections, obligations and authority, norms and sanctions, and information) will have access to a wider range of social roles, such as high-paying desirable jobs, than a lower-class person lacking capital. By determining the objective possibilities, social structure will exert a direct effect on the likelihood of individual role-transitions. This holds for criminal as well as conventional roles. For criminal roles, criminal capital (network connections, information, and obligations associated with criminal subcultures) are particularly important (Letkemann 1973; Steffensmeier 1986).

In addition to these direct effects, structural location may affect role-transitions indirectly. Here symbolic interactionism can help specify selection mechanisms. From an interactionist standpoint, social structure conditions alternatives, but selection into a role is dependent on perceptions of alternatives and their meanings, which are formed through role-taking in interactions. People are likely to remain in roles if they do not perceive the opportunity to change, even if opportunity exists objectively. Here the situation does not become problematic, and people will continue engaging in habitual behaviour associated with existing roles. However, once alternative roles are under consideration, the situation becomes problematic and persons engage in role-taking. The outcome of this role-taking process will be affected by the relative meanings of the present and prospective roles. These meanings, in turn, are determined by perceived appraisals of others, salience of the role-identities, and strength of habits and attitudes corresponding to the roles. It follows that role-continuity is more likely for individuals who have experienced a restricted range of roles, a restricted set of generalized others, and a restricted range of information about new roles.

Selection into roles is often a joint transaction carried out between two or more individuals. For example, employment is typically a joint decision between employer and employee (Sørensen and Kalleberg 1981), college entrance is a joint decision between student applicants and college admission committees, and entrance into professional crime rings is often a joint process of inquiry and recruitment (Sutherland 1937; Letkemann 1973). Similarly, selection out of roles can also be a joint decision: for example, the decision to divorce or separate at a particular time is often determined jointly by spouses, or the decision to leave a criminal organization may be a joint decision among members. In each case, the transaction entails role-taking, as interactants take the role of the other in a process of developing a joint definition of the situation, and work toward a given outcome. The outcome will be governed by the emergent dynamics of the interaction, in which interactants consider the perspectives of the other in light of the immediate circumstances, drawing upon past experiences to fit behaviour together and attain a future objective.

Individuals lacking qualities or skills that social roles require will be unlikely to be selected into such roles. Through the interactional process of being denied entrance into various roles, the individual is likely to adjust by externalizing failure, devaluing the role, or internalizing failure, and blaming himself. They may have no alternatives to less desirable positions, and may also develop a preference for such positions. The clearest example of this is given by Gottfredson and Hirschi (1990), who argue that persons who are impulsive, unskilled, unable to plan or delay gratification, and preoccupied with risk-taking are unlikely to succeed at conventional activities, such as school, jobs, and family life, and at the same time unable to control their criminality. But for Gottfredson and Hirschi (1990), the effects of life-course transitions are spuriously related to criminal behaviour: each is entirely determined by a stable individual personality trait they term "low self-control." We argue that selection into life-course events such as high school dropout, unemployment, and divorce may result from an interactional process that reflects in part prior individual characteristics (including mutable elements of the self), but that those events and their attendant roles directly effect criminality by changing opportunities, resources, reference groups, and therefore, elements of the self that in part selected the events in the first place (Thornberry 1987). Thus, there may be a long-term tendency toward cumulative continuity, in which individual characteristics select for roles and events which reinforce those characteristics (Caspi, Elder, and Bem 1987).

Role Trajectories and Duration-Dependent Mechanisms

For a theory of crime to take a developmental or life-course approach, it must specify not only the effects of roles and transitions on crime, but also specify duration-dependent casual mechanisms (Featherman and Lerner 1985). One way of framing this discussion is to follow Daniel Nagin's (Nagin and Paternoster 1991; Nagin and Farrington 1992) lead and apply Heckman's (1981) distinction between state dependence versus population heterogeneity to crime (see also Sampson and Laub 1993). Heckman (1981) argued that continuity in events, like spells of unemployment or poverty, can be explained by individual differences that remain stable over time (population heterogeneity) or by changes directly brought about by the earlier event, like changes in preferences, constraints, or prices (state dependence). Nagin and his colleagues apply this to crime, noting that persistent criminality can be due to individual characteristics that select for crime (heterogeneity), like low self-control, biological characteristics, or relatively stable structure characteristics like social class, as well as mechanisms that result from the *event* of committing a crime, such as secondary deviance, specific deterrence, and social learning. They find support for state dependence and rule out inertia or mere habit (Nagin and Paternoster 1991), but elsewhere find more support for heterogeneity over state dependence (Nagin and Paternoster 1991).

State dependence can be further decomposed into two components identified by Caspi, Elder, and Bem (1987): cumulative continuity, in which maladaptive behaviour increasingly channels an individual into environments that sustain the behaviour; and interactional continuity, in which maladaptive behaviour is responded to by others (in reciprocal social interaction) in ways that maintain the behaviour (see also Sampson and Laub 1993). The former refers to a sorting process into structural positions, while the latter refers to sorting into interactional sequences. We argued above that a symbolic interactionist perspective implies that both selection into social roles (due to individual heterogeneity) and the social role itself (state dependence) should affect subsequent role transitions and behavioural outcomes, like crime and deviance. Moreover, the mechanism by which individuals select into roles and positions is the self, which itself is in part socially constituted in interactions. This is consistent with Moffitt's (1993) view that life-course persistent delinquents may begin with neuropsychological deficits and temperament problems, which selects them into structural positions conducive to labelling and antisocial behaviour, and results in interactions in which they fail to learn prosocial alternatives. She suggests that adolescence-limited delinquents tend to imitate the delinquent acts of life-course persistent peers in an effort to establish autonomy and maturity. Our view is also consistent with Sampson and Laub's (1993) findings that adult social roles affect adult criminality net of childhood delinquency, temperament, and low self-control, and contrasts with the position of Gottfredson and Hirschi (1990), who argue that stability in crime should be the result of heterogeneity in the form of the trait of low self-control.

CHILD DEVELOPMENT AND ANTISOCIAL BEHAVIOUR

Interaction, Identity Formation, and Deviant Behaviour in Early Childhood

Social control rests on the ability to take the role of the other, which requires the acquisition of language, or significant symbols that call out the functionally identical response in self and others (Miller 1973). After young children have developed language skills, an important development with respect to antisocial behaviour is the learning of the significant symbol, the directive, "No," which distinguishes appropriate and inappropriate behaviour from the standpoint of others. In addition, the social self begins to emerge through rudimentary role-taking, in which children begin to label and differentiate themselves from others (Hewitt 1989). As children experience a wider range of situations, particularly those outside the family setting (e.g., preschool or play with other children), their ability to take the perspectives of others improves (Denzin 1972). Role-taking now takes the form of play-acting, in which children perform discrete roles serially, such as playing mother, doctor, nurse (Mead 1934). At this stage, the child is not cognizant of the larger social group in which the role is embedded and takes the role of the other without considering relationships to larger social groups, such as the family or hospital staff. Social control, then, at the age of 3 or 4, consists of a serial process of considering the reactions of concrete significant others, like mother, father, best friend, teacher, and so on. The identities that emerge at this stage are restricted largely to gender identity, body image, and personal characteristics (Keller, Ford, and Meacham 1978). Such embryonic identities are unstable, changing easily with situational context. Nevertheless, they can set up patterns of self-reflection that extend throughout the life course (Demo 1992). Indeed, the identities that begin to form during the preschool years can be consequential for future roles and identities. It follows that young children who become accustomed to seeing themselves as "bad kids" or "troublemakers" through the eyes of others are likely to perceive negative appraisals from others as they age, which can increase the chances for forming a delinquent identity in later years.

By the time children are 5 or 6 years old, their cognitive capabilities have matured to the point where they can view situations from the perspectives of a variety of others, including teachers, peers, and parents, and anticipate the reactions of others to certain lines of action (Entwistle et al. 1987). Their developing cognitive capabilities also allow for the emergence of a stable set of attitudes toward the self by this time, which we can think of as the "core" self-concept (Demo 1992). Research shows that children who have developed a core self-image as a "bad kid" through taking the roles of their parents, teachers, and peers are more likely than children who view themselves as "good kids" to intentionally break rules at home and school because misbehaviour is consistent with their identities (Matsueda 1992). Misbehaviour, of course, perpetuates others' appraisals and reflected appraisals as a "bad kid," increasing the chances of future deviance (Matsueda 1992). Conversely, children who have come to see themselves as "good kids" through the eyes of others will be relatively unlikely to violate rules and norms, prompting further appraisals by others and reflected appraisals as a good kid and making future rule violation less likely. This labelling process occurring early in life can lead to self-fulfilling prophecies.

From our perspective, labelling of children does not occur in a vacuum but reflects objective characteristics of children, like abilities, temperaments, and constitutions. For example, intelligent, sociable preschoolers tend to have more positive interactions with caretakers than other children, which can produce positive labels and self-images (MacKinnon and King 1988). The relationship between objective characteristics and interactional environments reflects a three-pronged selection process (e.g., Scarr and McCartney 1983). First, when children are very young, parents likely play a large role in creating the association between characteristics and interactional environments. Parents presumably share with their children genotypes related to intelligence and sociability and therefore select environments for their children that to some extent are "matched" to such characteristics. Second, intelligent, sociable children may themselves evoke positive responses from others because of the value given to these characteristics in our culture. By contrast, less intelligent, reticent children may evoke fewer positive responses and more negative responses. Third, bright, sociable children may themselves seek out positive interactions with others. The outcome is that intelligent and sociable children are more likely to find themselves in social environments that reward these attributes and accordingly begin to develop corresponding identities. By contrast, less intelligent, less socially skilled, and temperamental children may receive negative sanctions rather than rewards for these attributes, and thus, develop negative identities.

We can imagine that parents will channel temperamental children into interactions that reinforce such tendencies, and that temperamental children will evoke negative responses from others and will themselves initiate or select into interactions in which others perceive them to be "difficult children" or "troublemakers." Indeed, research finds that temperamental, aggressive children who are not socially responsive tend to evoke coercive and erratic responses from parents, which increases antisocial behaviour (Keller and Bell 1979; Patterson 1982; Lytton 1990; Patterson, Reid, and Dishion 1992). We argue that such responses to children increase negative labelling, which can set in motion a self-fulfilling prophecy leading to behavioural trajectories that "move against the world," including later delinquency (see Caspi, Elder, and Bem 1987; Moffitt 1993). A similar process may account for the greater likelihood of future delinquency among children with attention deficit disorders (Moffitt 1990; White et al. 1990). In short, characteristics that lead to selection into particular environments during early childhood can have implications for labelling and reflected appraisals. When reflected appraisals from a variety of sources converge on a common self-image, they become a core part of self and thus have significant consequences for future trajectories of deviance versus conformity.

Another clear example of the selection process is the influence of sex on interactional environments. Parents view and treat infants differently on the basis of sex from the time they are born, thereby creating different social environments for males and females and initiating the formation of gender identity (see Cahill 1980). After gender identity emerges, children become active agents in gender role construction by seeking out situations in which they test and learn to express gender identity. Also, the biological fact of being male or female evokes quite different reactions and expectations from the others with whom children interact, such as families, teachers, and peers (see Goffman 1977; Cahill 1980). As in the case of ability and temperament, this three-pronged selection process leads to the formation of gender identity. Because our culture defines female antisocial behaviour more negatively than male antisocial behaviour, strong gender identity should reduce the chances of future delinquency among females but not males (Schur 1983; Heimer 1996).

Such selection processes are conditioned by social structure. Parents with greater access to financial resources can mitigate the negative consequences for their temperamental children. And, differences in parenting styles across social class are likely consequential when parents select environments for their children based on children's attributes, like intelligence, sociability, or attention deficit disorders.

Consequently, abilities, temperaments, constitutions, and social structure influence selection into interactional environments, which influence children's reflected appraisals, definitions of deviance, and anticipated reactions for deviance. For example, selection into an environment in which parental supervision is lax can attenuate the learning of moral principles from parents and increase the learning of antisocial motives from peers. Research provides partial support for this argument: (1) Difficult children, with histories of temper tantrums, are supervised less closely than other children and are more likely to break rules and laws (Sampson and Laub 1993: 91); and (2) selection processes result in less supervision for boys than girls and, hence, higher rates of male than female delinquency (Jensen and Eve 1976; Hagan, Simpson, and Gillis 1987). The weaker supervision of boys and temperamental children increases delinquency by reducing the learning of conventional morals and enhancing the learning of delinquent definitions from peers. Also, the stronger the emotional connection between parent and child, the more likely the child is to consider the parent's reactions to delinquency — which presumably would be negative, averaged across persons — when they negotiate definitions of situations through role-taking (Heimer and Matsueda 1994; see also Hewitt 1989: 118).

Overall, we can specify a developmental hypothesis based on the discussion in this section. In early childhood, the negotiation of antisocial definitions of situations are influenced largely by impulses of the "I" and concrete others who are present in the immediate situation, but not abstract others who are not present. So, in a group of peers playing aggressively, children will be apt to behave similarly regardless of potential reactions by parents. By middle childhood (ages of 9 to 11), children's cognitive capabilities have developed sufficiently to allow them to grasp the notion of multiple explanations for behaviour (Demo 1992). Here the child can recognize multiple and perhaps competing definitions of rule and norm-violating behaviours. Thus, children negotiate definitions of situations by simultaneously considering the perspectives of a variety of others, such as parents, teachers, and peers, who may be physically absent.

Generalized Others, Social Networks, Peer Groups, and Delinquency

By middle childhood, then, youth are capable of taking the perspective of generalized others or reference groups. During the game stage of the development of self, a child is able to take the role of an abstract organized group, locate him or herself within the group, and consider the attitudes, rules, and expectations relating the child to other group roles. Mead's (1934) favourite example of the game is a baseball game, in which a pitcher must hold the attitudes of all incumbents of positions, including the batter, the catcher, the managers, and the other fielders. He is able to take the role of the abstract group, including the rules, norms, and expectations to organize the various roles. Involvement in antisocial peer groups has parallel consequences. Thus, the member of an antisocial peer group will be more likely to engage in group delinquency because the generalized other is organized around deviant behaviour. As the child participates in increasingly diverse and broad groups, its generalized other broadens and diversifies. Continuity in generalized others (the "me") results in stability in self. But, the self also changes over time with changes in group participation and novel solutions (the "I") to problematic situations.

Children's generalized others likely reflect the perspectives of both families and peers, which at times conflict (Hewitt 1989: 118; Heimer and Matsueda 1994). By middle childhood, however, the influence of peer groups is intensified and the influence of parents wanes (Thornberry et al. 1991; Demo 1992). Peer interactions become crucial contexts for children's interpretations of their worlds, resulting in peer cultures that are essential for the development of the knowledge and skills necessary to participate in the adult world. In short, peers become at least as important as adults in the socialization process (Corsaro 1992: 162).

From a symbolic interactionist perspective, peer groups are essential to antisocial behaviour during childhood and adolescence because they shape identities and communicate cultural definitions of deviance. Once again, selection is important. Although parents influence selection into peer groups through supervision (Matsueda and Heimer 1987), selection by the peer groups and self-selection become more important by middle and late childhood. Thus, highly aggressive boys are rejected by conventional peer groups (Dishion 1990) and are likely to associate with other antisocial children (Dishion et al. 1991; Vuchinich, Bank, and Patterson 1992). They are less likely to consider the perspectives of conventional peer groups and are more likely to take the role of the antisocial peer group in problematic situations. Consequently, these youth will continue to react to difficult situations aggressively and their antisocial and aggressive behaviour will appear stable over time. When selection into deviant peer groups is systematic rather than random, stability in antisocial behaviour may be due in large part to pre-existing individual differences, or heterogeneity.

At other times, selection can be stochastic. For example, youth may be "falsely accused" of being troublemakers in school or fortuitously sorted into an antisocial peer group. If such stochastic processes lead youth to enact deviant or antisocial roles, the mere fact of role-occupancy itself can create stability in antisocial behaviour through processes producing state dependence. By virtue of their group status, these youth may be further labelled as troublemakers, come to identify with the delinquent group, and learn delinquent attitudes and values.

Similarly, when youth select into peer groups that are organized against law violation, taking the role of these groups produces attitudes and identities that conflict with antisocial behaviour. Again, such selection may be based on strong matching between the characteristics of youth and conventional groups and at other times may be approximately random. Strong selection into these groups would occur when youth have learned to conform to the expectations of authority figures, when youth's scholastic performance is encouraged and they develop commitments to academics, or when other characteristics of youth are strongly compatible with those of peer groups organized against delinquency. Interestingly, gender plays a strong role here. Boys' peer groups are integrated by the excitement derived from rule-violation, while girls' groups are integrated by sharing intimacies and secrets with each other (Thorne and Luria 1986). Boys gain status in their peer groups through the display of "toughness" and "coolness," while girls gain status through their physical appearances, social skills, and academic success (Adler, Kless, and Adler 1992). Consequently, girls are more likely than boys to select into groups that are organized against antisocial behaviour.

Finally, the more systematic the role selection, the greater the match between the individual and the group, and therefore, the greater the future role-commitments and role-continuity. And, the longer the duration in a role, the greater the future continuity — until a major triggering event occurs. This is because the identities formed in interaction with groups become stable over time, persons are motivated to maintain stable self-images, and consequently, seek further interaction with these groups. It is also because other reference groups, such as parents and teachers, label youth, reducing the chances of transitions out of peer group roles. And, role transitions also become more difficult the longer one enacts a role because behaviour becomes scripted, automatic, and nonreflective (Heimer and Matsueda 1994). This suggests that youth who have developed strong conventional or deviant role-identities will be likely to continue such trajectories during adolescence unless some major events occur to alter such trajectories. Other youth may be more susceptible to transitions across deviant and conventional groups.

ADOLESCENCE, DELINQUENCY, AND YOUTH CRIME

Pubertal change is often viewed as an important trigger in the transition from childhood to adolescence. Indeed, adolescence is commonly seen as a period in which biological changes dramatically outpace social development, thus requiring great social adjustment. In addition, the transition from childhood to adolescence also involves a transition from elementary school to middle school and high school environments. These major biological and social changes create stress and contribute to the "difficulties" of adolescence (Simmons and Blyth 1987). One of the major adjustments that occurs during this period is the development of a stable identity (Erikson 1968) that allows the youth to align previous conceptions of self with current social, physical, and physiological changes. This requirement causes adolescents to be unusually egocentric and preoccupied with the evaluations and thoughts of their significant others and reference groups (Elkind 1967).

Understanding adolescence, then, requires a perspective that acknowledges the importance of biological as well as social development. A symbolic interactionist perspective can recognize both. From this viewpoint, biological tendencies, such as those accompanying puberty, set the context in which social interactions unfold. Indeed, physical and hormonal changes can create impulses, needs, or desires, which trigger role-taking; yet, the potency of such impulses is determined by the meaning that they are given when youth take themselves as objects from the perspectives of others (see Simmons and Blyth 1987). Thus, biological factors shape behaviour principally through reflective thought, in which they are defined and examined by the individual.

This means that the dramatic physical and physiological changes that occur during this period create impulses or needs that are symbolized in identity crises, preoccupation with appraisals by others, and psychological stress, which in turn prompt delinquency when role-taking suggests that impulses and needs may be satisfied by delinquency. Physiological changes will have the largest impact on identity crises, reflected appraisals of self, and stress when they are "off-time." For instance, children who mature earlier or later than their peers must negotiate identities in light of off-time hormonal changes, growth spurts, voice changes, and the development of acne. Given that most youth emancipate from parents during this time (Montemayor

1983), the peer group becomes an especially important generalized other for giving meaning to physical changes (or lack of change). In some cases, the meaning given to maturational processes increases the chances of delinquency. Youth who experience early growth spurts may feel more comfortable interacting with older peers, who are of similar physical size, and may be more willing to engage in delinquency (if this translates into acceptance by the group). For example, Caspi et al. (1993) find that early onset of pubertal changes (menarche) increases adolescent female delinquency in coed schools but not all-girl schools. They hypothesize that girls experiencing early menarche in coed schools associate with older delinquent boys, who influence them into delinquency. This mechanism does not occur in all-girl schools, since girls lack opportunities to associate with older boys. We would argue that the association and learning process entails role-taking with a reference group of older boys. In general, the important arenas for role-taking during adolescence are the school and peer group (e.g., Demo 1992).

Student Roles and the Social Organization of the School

Since the advent of mandatory education and child labour laws, the role of student and the social institution of the school have become central to the lives of adolescents, and thus constitute a primary arena in which identities are formed (Coleman 1961; Greenberg 1977; Platt 1977). The social organization of the school, as a haven of development and learning, has a positive impact on the identities of most youth. For instance, the school provides youth with opportunities to develop academic skills within the classroom and social skills within extracurricular activities, such as organized sports, band, special interest, and leadership groups. When youth have experienced repeated successes in these arenas earlier in childhood, they will have developed identities premised on commitments to student roles, which they seek to maintain during adolescence. Consequently, the trajectories of conventional students, initiated in previous years, can continue into adolescence when youth continue to work for good grades and become further involved in extracurricular activities (Schafer and Polk 1967; Wiatrowski et al. 1982). These youth are relatively unlikely to adopt delinquent lines of action when they consider the perspectives of their teachers, other committed students, and the school (Heimer and Matsueda 1994).

By contrast, when youth have failed in the classroom or in extracurricular activities, they are less likely to view themselves positively from the perspectives of teachers and schools. Indeed, poor performance in the classroom and the absence of positive experiences with extracurricular activities can have devastating consequences for self-esteem, given the importance of the school and student roles during adolescence. This can be exacerbated when poor performance leads to failure to be promoted to the next grade and the youth is off-time in terms of age-graded transitions in comparison to peers. Under these circumstances, we can expect weak commitment to student roles, lack of motivation to perform well academically, and generally, alienation from school. Teachers are likely to view these youth in a negative light, which youth perceive through role-taking. This, in turn, heightens alienation and increases the chances of selection into groups of other alienated students (Menard and Morse 1984) in an attempt to repair a damaged identity (Kaplan 1980). In groups of similarly alienated peers, then, youth encourage one another to "reject the rejecters" (Sykes and Matza 1957), and innovate attitudes and behaviours that are counter to those supported by the school. When confronted with problematic situations, these youth are more likely than committed students to jointly negotiate delinquent lines of action.

The outcome of this labelling process can be seen in studies of academic tracking in schools. Students assigned to college tracks perform better and have a greater chance of high school graduation, even when factors that account for initial selection into track (e.g., ability) are controlled (Gamoran and Mare 1989). Net of social class and ability, students assigned to low- and average-ability tracks are viewed more negatively by teachers and classmates, have lower aspirations, have more negative self-images, are more alienated, and are more likely to drop out than their high-track counterparts (e.g., Oakes 1985; Schafer and Olexa 1971). From an interactionist perspective, students in lower tracks are more likely than those in higher tracks to form reflected appraisals as poor students, which can be expected to hinder the development of strong commitments to academic roles and schooling. These youth, then, are more likely to drop out of school and more likely to select into peer groups that encourage law violation. The general practice of ranking students may cause identity problems for students ranked on the bottom. In some ways, schools, like total institutions, seek to break down the identities youth bring to school, and reconstitute them in ways consistent with the ideology of achievement and the social control requirements of the school (Goffman 1961). Ironically, the degradation ceremonies in schools often exacerbate the problems of control, causing threats to identity and encouraging rebellion to restore self-images (Greenberg 1977).

Other aspects of the social organization of schooling contribute to alienation from conventional school roles. The first of these stems from our cultural definitions of adolescence, which emphasize conflicting values like moral maturity versus social irresponsibility, social concern versus egocentrism, and laudable ideals versus childish misbehaviour (Kett 1977). While we expect children to be obedient, we expect adolescents to begin exercising their own judgment at times, but not yet at others. Such contradictions are embodied in the social organization of the school. For example, through policies such as hall passes, bathroom monitoring, and dress codes, the school strips youth of autonomy and denies them the opportunity to demonstrate moral and social responsibility (Greenberg 1977). This presents a dilemma for youth when they take the perspective of the school in general, and specific teachers in particular: they are aware that the school simultaneously expects maturity and immaturity from them. Concretely, this means that when youth encounter novel situations, the likely social consequences for any given line of action will be unclear — sometimes responsibility and independence may be rewarded, and at other times, it may be negatively sanctioned. When the consequences for behaviour are unclear, the likelihood of deviant behaviour increases.

Social class can condition the interactionist process linking the school, role-taking, and delinquency. For instance, based on his study of working class British students, Willis (1977) argues that working-class cultural capital (norms, values, skills, speech patterns, demeanour, and practices) is devalued in schools, which instead reward and value middle-class cultural capital. Indeed, some argue that the typical language patterns used in schools are compatible with middle-class but not working-class socialization, thereby communicating to youth a devaluing of working-class cultural capital from the outset (Mehan 1992). Through taking the role of teachers and the school itself, working-class youngsters become aware that their cultural capital is not valued highly and that success in the school setting would be difficult. Youth then act upon this knowledge by selecting into oppositional peer groups, which reproduce and revel in working-class culture and reject the academic achievement orientation of the school (Cohen 1955; Willis 1977). Eventually, the peer group becomes a much more important generalized other than teachers and schools, and these youth engage in activities that produce skills associated with working-class rather than middle-class jobs. Finally, the emergent normative codes of oppositional peer groups may promote rejection of other middle-class values, such as the value given to private property, which increases the chances of delinquency among working-class youth (Cohen 1955).

Peer Roles and the Social Organization of Peer Groups

Within adolescent peer groups, attention is largely focused on acceptance, status, and group solidarity (Corsaro and Eder 1990). Gossip and evaluation of group members becomes a primary activity, reinforcing membership and definitions of appropriate behaviour from the perspective of the group (Eder and Enke 1991). Indeed, daily interactions with peer groups allow youth to constitute norms about appearance, friendship, sexuality, and achievement, which youth subsequently consider through role-taking when they negotiate identities and lines of action. In this way, peer groups are an important source of social control during adolescence.

In addition to reinforcing group solidarity and controlling members' behaviours, a common theme in adolescent peer groups is resistance and rebellion against adult rules (Wulff 1988). Reactance against adult authority may be due to the inherent contradictions in adolescence, such as pressures to conform and exert independence. Because it affords youth with autonomy and personal control, such reactance may be a "universal feature of peer culture" during adolescence (Corsaro and Eder 1990). Thus, when youth consider the perspectives of peer groups, they are quite likely to rebel against rules. And, because delinquency represents an extreme form of resistance to authority, peer group processes may explain part of the peak in crime during adolescence (Warr 1993). These arguments are consistent with the empirical finding that association with delinquent peers is a robust and powerful predictor of law violation during adolescence (e.g., Warr and Stafford 1991; Matsueda and Heimer 1987). Moreover, delinquent peers can increase the likelihood of delinquency via role-taking by fostering identities as troublemakers and transmitting definitions favourable to delinquency (Heimer and Matsueda 1994).

But what determines selection into delinquent peer groups? A critical factor is prior behaviour. Indeed, deviant youth actively seek out similar peers (Billy and Udry 1985) and, therefore, actively shape their own future role-taking and delinquent behaviour (Heimer and Matsueda 1994). Other social psychological factors contribute to the selection of peer groups: youth who are strongly committed to student roles, whose families disapprove of law violation, and whose parents offer warm and supportive emotional environments will be less likely to select into delinquent groups (Elliott, Huizinga, and Ageton 1985; Elliot, Huizinga, and Menard 1989; Thornberry et al. 1991).

Structural features of community organization also affect selection into delinquent peer groups. For instance, the opportunity structures of communities, such as the opportunities for getting a good education and landing a job that pays well, are consequential for the emergence of delinquent groups and gangs (Vigil 1985; Hagedorn 1985; Sullivan 1989; Hagan 1991). Specifically, when opportunities for economic success through legitimate avenues are not available, youth may adapt by forming deviant subcultures (Cohen 1955; Cloward and Ohlin 1960). Youth who live in communities where legitimate opportunities are blocked and delinquent gangs are common are more likely to interact with and take the perspectives of persons who favour law violation as a way to satisfy needs. Thus, a structural feature of communities (the availability of educational and occupational opportunities) is consequential for the formation of delinquent groups, which in turn, influence role-taking and delinquency.

Cultural features of communities also may be consequential for delinquent group formation and role-taking. In structurally disadvantaged communities where adults do not sanction delinquency, crime can come to be defined as an acceptable mechanism for generating income or acceptable "work" (Sullivan 1989). In some structurally disadvantaged communities, characteristics such as toughness, smartness, and machismo become valued cultural capital, which can be translated into status in subcultures and lead to delinquency (see Miller 1958; Vigil 1985). Entrance into gangs can then involve a matching process, focused on norms of toughness, risk-taking, courage, honour, and negative attitudes toward law enforcement (Horowitz

1983). Once a tradition of delinquent groups is established in a community, the likelihood that other youth will come into contact with such groups, and consider their perspective through role-taking, is increased. And, there may be significant pressures to affiliate with gangs in communities where long-standing traditions exist. For example, many youth are recruited into gangs by older siblings or other relatives and move through the gang in a series of age-graded cliques. Indeed, gang membership often is viewed as indicating commitment to the larger community, neighbourhood, and even ethnic group (Vigil 1985).

ADULTHOOD, ADULT ROLES, AND CRIME

Adulthood marks a series of significant changes for individuals, as they take on more responsibility, develop commitments to adult social roles, and accommodate to the effects of physiological aging. At the same time, however, the transition to adulthood is marked by continuity with adolescence. Patterns of behaviour in adolescence trace a trajectory that influences the transition to adulthood by affecting access to resources, selection into adult roles, and consequently the likelihood of adult crime. The most important adult roles, family and work, are important for criminality in two ways: as causal forces that affect criminal behaviour net of individual characteristics, and as noncausal states that are spuriously correlated with criminality due to causal characteristics of individuals selecting both crime and adult roles.

Family Roles: Marriage and Parenthood

Conventional wisdom suggests that getting married and becoming a parent will have a negative effect on criminality. Some research supports this proposition that marriage reduces crime and antisocial behaviour (Gibbens 1984; Rand 1987), although the effect may be age-graded, applying more to delayed than early marriages (West 1982; Farrington 1986). Sampson and Laub (1993) argue that the key to adult criminality is the degree of bonding to conventional institutions, which operate to control individual behaviour. They find that criminality is affected not by marriage per se, but instead by attachment to spouse, measured by attitudes toward marital responsibility, attitudes about the conjugal relationship, and the absence of divorce, separation, and desertion. Similarly, Quinton et al. (1993) find that having a supportive spouse reduces adult criminality for both males and females (see also Pickles and Rutter 1991).

From our perspective, the important dimension of adult family roles is the meaning of the role to spouses, particularly as it is relevant to criminality. For most individuals, the greater the commitment to spousal and parental roles — including a greater respect for the institution of marriage, a greater affection for and attachment to family members, and a stronger investment in familial activities — the lower the likelihood of criminality, since crime entails the risk of jeopardizing the functioning of the family. When confronted with opportunities for crime, the family is likely to enter role-taking as a generalized other. Committed family members are likely to take the role not only of family members, but the role of the family as a conventional institution intertwined with other institutions, and are thereby unlikely to jeopardize the family through crime. In contrast, individuals who lack commitments to family roles are less likely to share the family as a generalized other, and thus less likely to be controlled by the family. For example, some members of the urban underclass have little belief in the sanctity of the family and little commitment to the roles of parent and spouse, and thus are vulnerable to criminalistic influences. Commitment to parenthood is perhaps the most important family influence on crime. Because crime is so counternormative and carries serious sanctions, nearly all committed parents desire that their children refrain from most crimes, particularly serious crimes. Such desires will affect their attitudes and behaviours, as they seek to be positive influences and role models, which in turn will reduce the likelihood of their own criminality.

Although commitment to family roles — a conventional set of roles — will on average reduce the likelihood of criminality, there are instances in which commitment to family roles increases the likelihood of crime. For example, in the relatively uncommon case in which spouses together commit crimes such as robbery, greater commitment to the spousal unit may increase the likelihood of a commitment to crime. Indeed, it is conceivable that a spouse who holds criminalistic attitudes may influence a straight spousal partner into crime. We hypothesize that such an effect, if it exists, would operate through role-taking: the straight partner would learn criminal attitudes from their spouse by taking the role of the other and considering him or herself from their standpoint. Thus, husbands holding criminalistic attitudes may influence the criminality of their wives. Sampson and Laub (1993), however, found that the opposite does not occur: deviant wives do not significantly affect the deviance of their husbands, when marital attachment is controlled. Given the gender differences in power and types of deviance, this finding is perhaps not surprising.

The timing of transitions into or out of family roles may also be critical to one's life chances and criminality. For example, teenage pregnancy can result in material needs that are beyond reach, or curtail one's educational attainment. The difficulty of such off-time transitions varies dramatically by context. When accompanied by substantial investments in social capital, such as a supportive spouse, a supportive kinship network, an adequate income, and advanced education and career opportunities, teenage pregnancy may pose few additional problems, and thus may be unrelated to criminality. In contrast, in the absence of social capital — no spouse or kinship, few marketable skills, and an inadequate income — and in the presence of other risk factors, such as a delinquent history, explosive temper, or history of drug use, teenage pregnancy can lead to continuous problematic situations. Such problems may increase the likelihood of crime.

From an interactionist perspective, the stigma of these off-time, early transitions to parenthood can solidify deviant or marginalized identities developed during earlier life stages and thus increase alienation from other conventional roles, such as legitimate work roles, and encourage entry into less legitimate roles, such as welfare and even criminal roles. This implies that the high rates of school dropout, teenage pregnancy, unemployment, welfare dependency, and crime among the urban underclass (Wilson 1987) may involve trajectories of commitments to deviant identities and roles that begin early in the life course, continue through adulthood, and are ultimately rooted in structural conditions.

CONCLUSION

This chapter has argued that symbolic interactionism can provide a fruitful way of examining crime and delinquency throughout the life course. The interactionist perspective developed here has several important features. First, it assumes a biosocial view of human behaviour such that behaviour occurs at the intersection between biological and environmental processes. Second, it specifies specific ways in which ontogenetic mechanisms are constituted in interactions with others. Third, it emphasizes the importance of criminal and deviant counterparts to conventional culture and organization, including criminal capital. Fourth, it implies several duration-dependent mechanisms linking social roles and criminal behaviour through the major life-course transitions from childhood to adolescence and finally, to adulthood.

STUDY QUESTIONS

1. *What are the main ideas and themes associated with the symbolic interactionist perspective on crime and delinquency?*
2. *According to Matsueda and Heimer, how does membership in a delinquent subculture reinforce delinquent behaviour?*
3. *According to Matsueda and Heimer, how does the symbolic interactionist perspective help explain how life-course transitions may affect the probability of delinquent and later criminal behaviour?*

REFERENCES

Adler, Patricia A., Steven J. Kless, and Peter Adler. 1992. "Socialization in Gender Roles: Popularity among Elementary School Boys and Girls." *Sociology of Education* 65(3): 169–87.

Atchley, R. 1975. "The Life Course, Age Grading, and Age Linked Demands for Decision Making." In N. Datan and L. Ginsberg, eds., *Life-Span Developmental Psychology: Normative Life Crises*, 261–78. New York: Academic Press.

Becker, Gary S. 1964. *Human Capital.* New York, National Bureau of Economic Research: Columbia University Press.

Billy, John O.G., and J. Richard Udry. 1985. "Patterns of Adolescent Friendships and Effects on Sexual Behavior." *Social Psychology Quarterly 48*: 27–41.

Blumer, Herbert. 1969. *Symbolic Interactionism: Perspective and Method.* Englewood Cliffs, NJ: Prentice-Hall.

Bourdieu, Pierre. 1977. "Cultural Reproduction and Social Reproduction." In J. Karabel and A.H. Halsey, eds., *Power and Ideology in Education*, 487–511. New York: Oxford University Press.

Cahill, Spencer E. 1980. "Directions for an Interactionist Study of Gender Development." *Symbolic Interaction 3*: 123–38.

Caspi, Avshalom, Glen H. Elder, Jr., and Daryl J. Bem. 1987. "Moving against the World: Life-Course Patterns of Explosive Children." *Developmental Psychology 23*: 308–13.

Caspi, Avshalom, Donald Lynam, Terrie E. Moffitt, and Phil A. Silva. 1993. "Unraveling Girls' Delinquency: Biological, Dispositional, and Contextual Contributions to Adolescent Misbehavior." *Developmental Psychology 29*(1): 19–30.

Cloward, Richard. A., and Lloyd. E. Ohlin. 1960. *Delinquency and Opportunity.* New York: Free Press.

Cohen, Albert K. 1955. *Delinquent Boys.* Glencoe, IL: Free Press.

Coleman, James S. 1961. *The Adolescent Society.* Glencoe, IL: Free Press.

———. 1990. *Foundations of Social Theory.* Cambridge, MA: Harvard University Press.

Corsaro, William A. 1992. "Interpretive Reproduction in Children's Peer Cultures." *Social Psychology Quarterly 55*(2): 160–77.

Corsaro, William A., and Donna Eder. 1990. "Children's Peer Cultures." *Annual Review of Sociology 16*: 197–220.

Demo, David H. 1992. "The Self-Concept over Time: Research Issues and Directions." *Annual Review of Sociology 18*: 303–26.

Denzin, Norman K. 1972. "The Genesis of Self in Early Childhood." *Sociological Quarterly 13*: 291–314.

Dishion, Thomas J. 1990. "The Family Ecology of Boys' Peer Relations in Middle Childhood." *Child Development 61*: 874–92.

Dishion, Thomas J., Gerald R. Patterson, M. Stoolmiller, and M.L. Skinner. 1991. "Family, School, and Behavioral Antecedents to Early Adolescent Involvement with Antisocial Peers." *Developmental Psychology 27*(1): 172–80.

Eder, Donna, and Janet Lynn Enke. 1991. "The Structure of Gossip: Opportunities and Constraints on Collective Expression among Adolescents." *American Sociological Review 56*(4): 494–508.

Elder, Glen H., Jr. 1985. "Perspectives on the Life Course." In Glen H. Elder, Jr., ed., *Life Course Dynamics*, 23–49. Ithaca: Cornell University Press.

Elkind, D. 1967. "Egocentrism in Adolescence." *Child Development 38*: 1025–34.

Elliott, Delbert S., David Huizinga, and Suzanne Ageton. 1985. *Delinquency and Drug Use*. Beverly Hills: Sage.

Elliott, Delbert S., David Huizinga, and Scott Menard. 1989. *Multiple Problem Youth: Delinquency, Substance Use, and Mental Health*. New York: Springer-Verlag.

Entwistle, D.W., K.L. Alexander, A.M. Pallas, and D. Cadigan. 1987. "The Emergent Academic Self-Image of First Graders: Its Response to Social Structures." *Child Development 58*: 1190–1206.

Erikson, Erik H. 1968. *Identity: Youth and Crisis*. New York: Norton.

Farrington, David P. 1986 "Unemployment, School Leaving, and Crime." *British Journal of Criminology 26*: 335–56.

———. 1992. "Explaining the Beginning, Progress, and Ending of Antisocial Behavior from Birth to Adulthood." In J. McCord, ed., *Facts, Frameworks, and Forecasts: Advances in Criminological Theory*, vol. 3, 253–86. New Brunswick, NJ: Transaction.

Featherman, David, and Richard Lerner. 1985. "Ontogenesis and Sociogenesis: Problematics for Theory and Research about Development and Socialization across the Lifespan." *American Sociological Review 50*: 659–76.

Gamoran, Adam, and Robert D. Mare. 1989. "Secondary School Tracking and Educational Inequality: Compensation, Reinforcement, or Neutrality?" *American Journal of Sociology 94*: 1146–83.

Gibbens, T.C.N. 1984. "Borstal Boys after 25 Years." *British Journal of Criminology 24*: 49–62.

Goffman, Erving. 1961. *Asylums*. Garden City, New York: Anchor.

———. 1977. "The Arrangement between the Sexes." *Theory and Society 4*: 301–31.

Gottfredson, Michael, and Travis Hirschi. 1990. *A General Theory of Crime*. Palo Alto: Stanford University.

Greenberg, David F. 1977. "Delinquency and the Age Structure of Society." *Contemporary Crises: Crime, Law, and Social Policy 1*: 189–223.

Hagan, John. 1991. "Destiny and Drift: The Risks and Rewards of Youth." *American Sociological Review 56*: 567–82.

Hagan, John, and Alberto Palloni. 1988. "Crimes as Social Events in the Life-course: Reconceiving a Criminological Controversy." *Criminology 26*: 87–100.

Hagan, John, John Simpson, and A.R. Gillis. 1987. "Class in the Household: A Power-Control Theory of Gender and Delinquency." *American Journal of Sociology 92*: 788–816.

Hagan, John, and Blair Wheaton. 1993. "The Search for Adolescent Role Exits and the Transition to Adulthood." *Social Forces 71*(4): 955–80.

Hagedorn, John M. 1985. *People and Folks: Gangs, Crime and the Underclass in a Rustbelt City*. Chicago: Lakeview Press.

Heckman, James. 1981. "Statistical Models for Discrete Panel Data." In Charles F. Manski and David McFadden, eds., *Structural Analysis of Discrete Panel Data with Econometric Applications*, 114–78. Cambridge, MA: MIT Press.

Heimer, Karen. 1996. "Gender, Interaction, and Delinquency: Testing a Theory of Differential Social Control." *Social Psychology Quarterly 59*(1): 39–61.

Heimer, Karen, and Ross L. Matsueda. 1994. "Role-Taking, Role Commitment, and Delinquency: A Theory of Differential Social Control." *American Sociological Review 59*(3): 365–90.

Hewitt, John P. 1989. *Self and Society: A Symbolic Interactionist Social Psychology.* Boston: Allyn and Bacon.

Hirschi, Travis. 1969. *Causes of Delinquency.* Berkeley: Free Press.

Horowitz, Ruth. 1983. *Honor and the American Dream: Culture and Identity in a Chicano Community.* New Brunswick, NJ: Rutgers University Press.

Jensen, Gary F., and Raymond Eve. 1976. "Sex Differences in Delinquency: An Examination of Popular Sociological Explanations." *Criminology 13*: 427–48.

Kaplan, Howard B. 1980. *Deviant Behavior in Defense of Self.* New York: Academic.

Keller, A., L.H. Ford, and J.A. Meacham. 1978. "Dimensions of Self-Concept in Pre-School Children." *Developmental Psychology 14*: 483–99.

Keller, B., and R.Q. Bell. 1979. "Child Effects on Adults' Method of Eliciting Altruistic Behavior." *Child Development 50*: 1004–10.

Kett, Joseph F. 1977. *Rites of Passage: Adolescence in America, 1977 to the Present.* New York: Basic.

Kornhauser, Ruth R. 1978. *Social Sources of Delinquency.* Chicago: University of Chicago Press.

Langer, Ellen J. 1989. "Minding Matters: The Consequences of Mindless-Mindfulness." In L. Berkowitz, ed., *Advances in Experimental Social Psychology,* vol. 22, 137–73. San Diego, CA: Academic.

Laub, John H., and Robert J. Sampson. 1993. "Turning Points in the Life Course: Why Change Matters to the Study of Crime." *Criminology 31*(3): 301–25.

Letkemann, Peter. 1973. *Crime as Work.* Englewood Cliffs, NJ: Prentice-Hall.

Loeber, Rolf, and Marc LeBlanc. 1990. "Toward a Developmental Criminology." In Michael Tonry and Norval Morris, eds., *Crime and Justice,* vol. 22, 375–437. Chicago: University of Chicago Press.

Lytton, Hugh. 1990. "Child and Parent Effects in Boys' Conduct Disorder: A Reinterpretation." *Developmental Psychology 26*(5): 683–97.

MacKinnon, C.E., and D. King. 1988. "Day Care: A Review of Literature, Implications for Policy, and Critique of Resources." *Family Relations 37*: 229–36.

Matsueda, Ross L. 1988. "The Current State of Differential Association Theory." *Crime and Delinquency 34*: 277–306.

———. 1992. "Reflected Appraisals, Parental Labelling, and Delinquency: Specifying a Symbolic Interactionist Theory." *American Journal of Sociology 97*(6): 1577–1611.

Matsueda, Ross L., and Karen Heimer. 1987. "Race, Family Structure and Delinquency: A Test of Differential Association and Social Control Theories." *American Sociological Review 52*: 826–40.

Mead, George H. 1934. *Mind, Self and Society*. Chicago: University of Chicago.
Mednick, S.A. W.F. Gabrielli, and B. Hutchings. 1984. "Genetic Influences in Criminal Convictions: Evidence from an Adoption Cohort." *Science 224*: 891–94.
Mehan, Hugh. 1992. "Understanding Inequality in Schools: The Contribution of Interpretive Studies." *Sociology of Education 65*(1): 1–20.
Menard, Scott, and Barbara J. Morse. 1984. "A Structuralist Critique of the IQ–Delinquency Hypothesis: Theory and Evidence." *American Journal of Sociology 89*: 1347–78.
Miller, David L. 1973. *George Herbert Mead: Self, Language and the World.* Chicago: University of Chicago Press.
Miller, Walter. 1958. "Lower Class Culture as a Generating Milieu of Gang Delinquency." *Journal of Social Issues 14*: 5–19.
Moffitt, Terrie E. 1990. "Juvenile Delinquency and Attention Deficit Disorder: Developmental Trajectories from Age 3 to 15." *Child Development 61*: 893–910.
———. 1993. "Adolescent-Limited and Life-Course-Persistent Antisocial Behavior: A Developmental Taxonomy." *Psychological Review 100*(4): 674–701.
Montemayor, R. 1983. "Parents and Adolescents in Conflict: All Families Some of the Time and Some Families Most of the Time." *Journal of Early Adolescence 3*: 83–103.
Nagin, Daniel S., and David P. Farrington. 1992. "The Stability of Criminal Potential from Childhood to Adulthood." *Criminology 30*: 235–60.
Nagin, Daniel S., and Raymond Paternoster. 1991. "On the Relationship of Past and Future Delinquency." *Criminology 29*: 163–90.
Oakes, Jeannie. 1985. *Keeping Track: How Schools Structure Inequality*. New Haven: Yale University Press.
Patterson, Gerald R. 1982. *Coercive Family Process*. Eugene, OR: Castalia.
Patterson, Gerald R., John B. Reid, and Thomas J. Dishion. 1992. *Antisocial Boys: A Social Interactional Process*. Eugene, OR: Castalia Publishing Co.
Pickles, Andrew, and Michael Rutter. 1991. "Statistical and Conceptual Models of 'Turning Points' in Developmental Processes." In David Magnusson, Lars Bergman, Georg Rudinger, and Bertil Torestad, eds., *Problems and Methods in Longitudinal Research: Stability and Change*, 133–65. New York: Cambridge University Press.
Platt, Anthony M. 1977. *The Child Savers: The Invention of Delinquency*. Chicago: University of Chicago Press.
Plomin, Robert. 1986. *Development, Genetics, and Psychology*. Hillsdale, NJ: Lawrence Erlbaum.
Quinton, David, Andrew Pickles, Barbara Maughan, and Michael Rutter. 1993. "Partners, Peers, and Pathways: Assortative Pairing and Continuities in Conduct Disorder." *Developmental Psychopathology 5*: 763–83.
Rand, Alicia. 1987. "Transitional Life Events and Desistance from Delinquency and Crime." In Marvin Wolfgang, Terence P. Thornberry, and Robert M. Figlio, eds., *From Boy to Man, From Delinquency to Crime*, 134–62. Chicago: University of Chicago Press.

Rowe, David. 1983. "Biometrical Genetic Models of Self-Reported Delinquent Behavior: A Twin Study." *Behavior Genetics 13*: 473–89.

Sampson, Robert J., and John H. Laub. 1990. "Crime and Deviance over the Life Course: The Salience of Adult Social Bonds." *American Sociological Review 55*(5): 609–27.

———. 1992. "Crime and Deviance in the Life Course." *Annual Review of Sociology 18*: 63–84.

———. 1993. *Crime in the Making: Pathways and Turning Points through Life.* Cambridge: Harvard University Press.

Scarr, Sandra, and Kathleen McCartney. 1983. "How People Make Their Own Environments: A Theory of Genotype — Environment Effects." *Child Development 54*: 424–35.

Schafer, Walter E., and Carol Olexa. 1971. *Tracking and Opportunity: The Looking Out Process and Beyond.* Scranton: Chandler Publishing Co.

Schafer, Walter E., and Kenneth E. Polk. 1967. "Delinquency and the Schools." In *Task Force Report: Juvenile Delinquency and Youth Crime*, 222–27. Washington, DC: Government Printing Office.

Schur, Edwin M. 1983. *Labeling Women Deviant.* New York: McGraw-Hill.

Shibutani, Tamotsu. 1961. *Society and Personality.* Englewood Cliffs, NJ: Prentice-Hall.

Shiffrin, Richard M., and Walter Schneider. 1977. "Controlled and Automatic Human Information Processing: II. Perceptual Learning, Automatic Attending, and a General Theory." *Psychology Review 84*: 127–90.

Simmons, Roberta G., and Dale A. Blyth. 1987. *Moving Into Adolescence: The Impact of Pubertal Change and School Context.* New York: Aldine de Gruyter.

Sørensen, Aage B., and Arne L. Kalleberg. 1981. "An Outline of a Theory of the Matching of Persons to Jobs." In I. Berg, ed., *Sociological Perspectives on Labor Markets*, 49–74. New York: Academic Press.

Steffensmeier, Darrell J. 1986. *The Fence: In the Shadow of Two Worlds.* Totowa, NJ: Rowman and Littlefield.

Stryker, Sheldon. 1980. *Symbolic Interactionism: A Social Structural Version.* Menlo Park, CA: Benjamin/Cummings.

Sullivan, Mercer L. 1989. *"Getting Paid": Youth Crime and Work in the Inner City.* Ithaca: Cornell University Press.

Sutherland, Edwin H. 1937. *The Professional Thief.* Chicago: University of Chicago Press.

Sykes, Gresham M., and David Matza. 1957. "Techniques of Neutralization: A Theory of Delinquency." *American Sociological Review 22*: 664–70.

Thornberry, Terence P. 1987. "Toward an Interactional Theory of Delinquency." *Criminology 25*: 863–91.

Thornberry, Terence P., Alan J. Lizotte, Marvin D. Krohn, Margaret Farnworth, and Sung Joon Jang. 1991. "Testing Interactional Theory: An Examination of Reciprocal Causal Relationships among Family, School and Delinquency." *Journal of Criminal Law and Criminology 82*: 3–35.

Thorne, Barrie, and Zella Luria. 1986. "Sexuality and Gender in Children's Daily Worlds." *Social Problems 33*: 176–90.

Vigil, James Diego. 1985. *Barrio Gangs*. Austin, TX: University of Texas Press.

Vuchinich, Samuel, Lew Bank, and Gerald R. Patterson. 1992. "Parenting, Peers, and the Stability of Antisocial Behavior in Preadolescent Boys." *Developmental Psychology 28*(3): 510–21.

Walters, Glenn D., and Thomas W. White. 1989. "Heredity and Crime: Bad Genes or Bad Research? (Review of the Literature)." *Criminology 27*: 455–85.

Warr, Mark. 1993. "Age, Peers, and Delinquency." *Criminology 31*(1): 17–40.

Warr, Mark, and Mark Stafford. 1991. "The Influence of Delinquent Peers: What They Think or What They Do?" *Criminology 29*: 851–66.

Wells, L. Edward, and Sheldon Stryker. 1986. "Stability and Change in Self over the Life Course." In P.B. Baltes, D.L. Featherman, and R.M. Lerner, eds., *Life Span Development and Behavior*, vol. 7, 191–229. Hillsdale, NJ: Lawrence Erlbaum.

West, Donald J. 1982. *Delinquency: Its Roots, Careers, and Prospects*. London: Heinemann.

White, Jennifer L., Terrie E. Moffitt, Felton Earls, Lee N. Robbins, and Phil A. Silva. 1990. "How Early Can We Tell? Predictors of Childhood Conduct Disorder and Adolescent Delinquency." *Criminology 28*: 507–33.

Wiatrowski, Michael D., Stephen Hansell, Charles R. Massey, and David L. Wilson. 1982. "Curriculum Tracking and Delinquency." *American Sociological Review 47*: 151–60.

Willis, Paul E. 1977. *Learning to Labor*. London: Routledge and Kegan Paul.

Wilson, William J. 1987. *The Truly Disadvantaged: The Inner City, the Underclass, and Public Policy*. Chicago: University of Chicago Press.

Wulff, Helena. 1988. *Twenty Girls: Growing Up, Ethnicity, and Excitement in a South London Microculture*. Stockholm: University of Stockholm Press.

PART THREE
Street Kids and Crime: Causes, Consequences, and Intervention

INTRODUCTION

The next two parts of the book cover the topics of street kids and crime and youth gangs. Although these topics are closely related — most obviously, because many homeless and abandoned youth who end up on the street also become members of youth gangs — it is important to look separately and in some detail at the research that has been done on each topic. This will help in understanding the different causes and consequences of street life and gang involvement. In Part Three, you are given the opportunity to read some of the most important recent research on the topic of street kids and crime. Each of the chapters in Part Three is written by a Canadian criminologist and presents the findings of research carried out on street kids and crime in different central Ontario and Western Canadian cities.

Chapter Seven, by Bill McCarthy and John Hagan, outlines the situational theory they have developed to explain the relationship between youth homelessness and street crime. McCarthy and Hagan argue that most contemporary sociological theories of delinquency fail to give adequate attention to the situational factors that lead homeless youth to engage in different kinds of criminal behaviour. To overcome this weakness, McCarthy and Hagan develop an integrative theory that combines elements of social-psychological strain theory (Agnew 1985) and control theory (Hirschi 1969), while also theorizing the possible role that adverse situational factors experienced by youth on the street play in delinquent behaviour. McCarthy and Hagan undertake a preliminary empirical test of this theory using data they obtained from their survey of street youth and other school-aged youth in Toronto in the late 1980s. In essence the authors argue that, after background and street exposure variables are controlled for, and after comparing the types of delinquency self-reported by street youth and other school-aged youth, there is consistent evidence that the adverse situational conditions youth experience on the street are linked to specific types of delinquent behaviour. Specifically, their evidence suggests that, implicated as situational factors, hunger causes theft of food, problems of hunger and shelter lead to serious theft, and problems of unemployment and shelter produce prostitution. Importantly, while traditional sociological theories have often focused on background factors like poverty and lack of education as causes of delinquent behaviour, McCarthy and Hagan show that the everyday "situational pressures" experienced by street youth may be more immediate important causes of youth street crime. More recently, this situational theory of youth street crime has been used by Hagan and McCarthy as part of the theoretical foundation to their widely acclaimed book *Mean Streets: Youth Crime and Homelessness* (Hagan and McCarthy 1997). There they add further evidence to support their view that street youth often become involved in crime as a means of surviving on the street. In addition, the authors report the findings of several follow-up studies they undertook with homeless and runaway youth in Toronto and Vancouver in the early 1990s. These studies provide a rich source of related qualitative and quantitative data on the reasons youth give for leaving home, as well as their accounts of what it is like to try to survive on the street. Hagan and McCarthy (1997) find a pattern in the reasons given by youth for leaving home. A large percentage of youth came from disrupted (divorced or single-parent) family backgrounds, and most had parents or guardians who used physical discipline in the home. Consistent with other research on the topic (cf. MacLaurin 1996), Hagan and McCarthy (1997) also point out that there are many other unfortunate risks associated with street life for youth who either decide to run away or are abandoned by their families. These include crime victimization, drug and alcohol abuse, illnesses tied to lack of adequate diet and hygiene, depression and other mental health problems, along with frequent involvement in criminal behaviour.

Chapter Eight, by Stephen Baron and Timothy Hartnagel, presents the findings of their research on criminal violence among homeless male street youth in Edmonton. Drawing on data collected from qualitative interviews with 200 homeless male street youth, Baron and Hartnagel examine the factors that lead street youth to commit violent criminal acts. The findings presented in the chapter reveal that factors associated with the street subculture, including long-term homelessness and criminal peers, increase the likelihood of violent criminal acts being committed by individual respondents. In addition, Baron and Hartnagel found that victimization on the street and a history of physical abuse in the home are related to the violent behaviour of respondents. In the chapter, the authors attempt to explain their findings by developing a theoretical perspective that combines subcultural and routine activities theories.

In Chapter Nine, Bernard Schissel and Kari Fedec examine factors that have led street kids in Saskatoon and Regina to become juvenile street prostitutes. In addition, Schissel and Fedec's research documents the effect that involvement in street prostitution has on the lives of street youth in Saskatoon and Regina, many of whom are Aboriginal. Using Social Services data on 400 young offenders from the two Saskatchewan cities, the authors examine the connections between abusive childhoods, personal and educational success, and involvement in the youth sex trade. In line with the findings of comparable studies carried out in other jurisdictions, the authors report that there is a strong and consistent relationship between particular types of child abuse and neglect at home and involvement in prostitution. Concerning the effect of this involvement, Schissel and Fedec argue that a culture of violence encompasses the lives and well-being of many young prostitutes. In addition to being routinely exposed to external threats of violence, many young prostitutes are also the victims of self-inflicted violence, often through self-abusive slashing and suicide attempts. Schissel and Fedec also discuss the policy implications that emanate from their research findings, including the need for more well-thought-out intervention strategies and cooperation involving schools, child-welfare agencies, police, and First Nations communities.

Although all of the chapters in Part Three are Canadian studies, this is more coincidental than intended. In the search for representative studies to include in Part Three, a wide range of Canadian and non-Canadian literature was consulted. In the end, the chapters included here were chosen because they are arguably among the best North American studies to date that have examined the serious and widespread problem of street kids and crime.

REFERENCES

Agnew, R. 1985. "A Revised Strain Theory of Delinquency." *Social Forces* *64*(1): 151–67.

Hagan, J., and B. McCarthy. 1997. *Mean Streets: Youth Crime and Homelessness*. Cambridge: Cambridge University Press.

Hirschi, T. 1969. *Causes of Delinquency*. Berkeley: University of California Press.

MacLaurin, B. 1996. "Runaway and Homeless Youth in Canada." In J. Winterdyck, ed., *Issues and Perspectives on Young Offenders in Canada*, 175–93. Toronto: Harcourt Brace Jovanovich.

CHAPTER SEVEN

Mean Streets: Situational Delinquency among Homeless Youths

BILL MCCARTHY
University of California, Davis
JOHN HAGAN
University of Toronto

The idea that adverse situations cause crime and delinquency was once a fundamental theoretical principle of sociological criminology. Early European criminologists including Russell (1847), Fletcher (1849), and Bonger (1916) recognized the significance of adverse situations and attributed crime and delinquency to sudden fluctuations in food prices and the availability of jobs. During the Great Depression in the United States, Sellin (1937) similarly adopted a situational perspective to explain changes in crime rates. He emphasized the sudden onset of unemployment and discounted the longer-term influence of chronic poverty. However, this situational emphasis did not endure or prosper in sociological criminology; instead, theoretical attention to immediate problems of day-to-day survival diminished, as if the relative prosperity of post-Depression society eliminated adverse situations as causes of crime and delinquency. Gradually, sociological theories of criminogenesis moved from the foreground to the background of the criminal experience.

FROM PAST TO PRESENT IN THE CAUSATION OF CRIME

Three contemporary tendencies reflect an underestimation of situational adversity as a cause of crime; two of these are theoretical, the other methodological. The first tendency is to discount situational effects and focus instead on background and development. The second incorporates situational effects but emphasizes the inducements, opportunities, or attractions of crime, to

Source: Bill McCarthy and John Hagan, "Mean Streets: The Theoretical Significance of Situational Delinquency among Homeless Youths," *American Journal of Sociology 98*(3) (1992): 597–627.

the neglect of more pressing circumstances. The third involves studying self-reports of delinquency by adolescents living at home and attending school; that is, adolescents who live in institutionally protected situations.

The first inclination of modern sociological theories of crime is to focus on background and developmental factors while disregarding situational circumstances: strain theory locates the motivation for crime in cumulative frustrations arising from structural inequality; control theory focuses on the failure of family and school experiences to establish social bonds; differential association theory emphasizes prior exposure to deviant beliefs; and labelling theory concentrates on successive stages of stigmatization. These theories assume that crime and delinquency are predetermined by background experiences and developments that cumulate over time. This is one reason that their focus is on the formative years of adolescence.

In a variation on this first tendency, some theorists give limited attention to situational variables. The vocabulary varies, but consideration is sometimes given to pressures, inducements, or motivations for crime, variously described as situational, mechanistic, dynamic, endogenous, or contemporaneous. However, these factors are not given extensive consideration and most usually are dismissed. For example, in an early and influential statement, Sutherland and Cressey (1978) acknowledge and then minimize the significance of situational effects by asserting that although situations may contribute to crime, the primary definitions of these situations are determined through differential exposure to competing norms. Thus, they argue that "while a person could define a situation in such a manner that criminal behavior would be the inevitable result, past experiences would, for the most part, determine the way in which he or she defined the situation" (Sutherland and Cressy 1978: 80).

Briar and Piliavin (1965), and more recently Gottfredson and Hirschi (1990), arrive at a similar conclusion, although these authors argue it is the lack of commitment to conformity or self-control that determines whether situational factors will lead to crime. So a predominant view, even among those who acknowledge the presence of situational factors, is to assign them a secondary role in the causation of crime and delinquency.

Alternatively, a few writers argue for the importance of situational effects. Although these writers give greater attention to situational variables, their work dwells on opportunities or attractions to crime. For example, Gibbons (1971) argues that there are external motivations for crimes that result from opportunities that accompany "criminogenic conditions." According to Gibbons (1971: 271), "in many cases, criminality may be a response to nothing more temporal than provocations and attractions bound up in the immediate circumstances."

Katz (1988) echoes this view in an evocative articulation of the situational approach. According to Katz, traditional theories neglect the "seductions of crime" that result from attempts to maximize pleasure (e.g., thrills) or satisfaction (e.g., from overcoming challenges to one's authority or moral position) in intensely felt situations. Katz (1988: 4) focuses on situational events that immediately precede crimes and propel offenders, since "something causally essential happens in the very moment in which crime is committed." Like Gibbons's, Katz's emphasis is restricted to particular situational factors: the opportunities or the sensual attractiveness of situations that seduce people to offend. This argument is more persuasive in situations that present opportunities or temptations for crime than in situations that pose problems of day-to-day survival; focusing on the former instead of the latter obscures much of the force of the situational argument.

The neglect of more pressing circumstances is institutionalized by the third tendency noted above: a shift to self-report surveys of school students for tests of crime and delinquency theories. Data collection through home and school-based self-report surveys (from Nye and Short 1957, through Hindelang, Hirschi, and Weis 1981, to Nagin and Paternoster 1991) was an important innovation because it freed researchers from reliance on official records and allowed the systematic and extensive measurement of background and developmental variables. However, as Sullivan (1989: 6) notes, "there is doubt about the extent to which such surveys ever reached the population of serious delinquents." Moreover, exclusive reliance on school and home samples has diverted attention from less protected settings, like the street, that once formed an important focal point for delinquency research (from Thrasher 1927 to Short and Strodtbeck 1965).

It is perhaps not surprising, given the tendencies we have outlined, that circumstances that pose problems of survival and well-being have come to occupy a secondary position, at best, in sociological theory and research on crime.

BACK TO THE STREETS

Our purpose is to re-examine the role of adverse situations in crime causation. We accept the place of background and developmental variables in our re-examination and are guided by an integration of background and developmental variables from strain and control theories. However, we also extend these theories by incorporating situational variables that derive from our attention to the conditions of homeless youth on the streets. Our premise is that reconceptualizing strain and control to include the adverse circumstances of homeless street youth draws more attention to the role of these situational factors than is currently acknowledged in theories of delinquency causation.

Our integration links Agnew's (1985) strain theory with Hirschi's control theory (see Hirschi 1969). Classical Mertonian strain theory asserts that delinquency is a response to encounters with structural impediments to the attainment of socially determined success goals. Agnew (1985) recasts this conceptualization by suggesting that delinquency may also be a response to living in painful or punishing environments. This perspective is particularly relevant in the present context because homeless youth may have fled from one set of adverse situations (i.e., abuse in the home and conflict at school) only to find themselves in another (i.e., the difficult circumstances of life on the street).

Meanwhile, youth who encounter strain in the home and on the street may also experience little social control in these settings. In more conventional terms, they may experience neglect at home and have few attachments or involvements in conventional activities on the street; thus, they may have weak social bonds. Our integration of strain and control theory reflects our assumption that both the presence of strain and the absence of control can push youth to delinquency as well as free them from it. However, to the extent that either or both theoretical sources of this integration operate, it is important to establish the relative contribution of each and that the influence of one set of factors is not a spurious product of the other.

ADVERSE SITUATIONS

Many homeless adults live in conditions of great difficulty (see Rossi 1989; Momeni 1989). Many adolescents who leave and stay away from home encounter conditions similar to adults, including unemployment, poverty, hunger, and lack of shelter (Kufeldt and Nimmo 1987; McCarthy 1990; Stephenson 1989). So the conditions confronted by youth on the streets can clearly be adverse in the theoretical sense that Agnew suggests.

Although the great majority of studies on the homeless and on runaways have not collected data on crime (for reviews, see Brennan, Huizinga, and Elliott 1978; Rossi 1989), there is also some evidence that homelessness is conducive to crime. For example, police arrest records from Austin, Texas, were used in a study by Snow, Baker, and Anderson (1989), who found that the arrest rate for homeless males (aged 18–68) was significantly greater than for males who were not homeless. They reported an arrest rate for property offences of 179 per 100 000 for homeless males, compared with 130 per 100 000 for men who have homes (also see Fischer 1988; Gelberg, Linn, and Leake 1988).

Several studies on runaways also point to criminogenic aspects of street life. In a study using data on youth from Colorado and from a national sample of adolescents, Brennan, Huizinga, and Elliott (1978) found that 33 percent of runaways admitted to stealing after leaving home (15 percent indicated that they stole objects worth $50 or more) and 20 percent reported selling drugs. Brennan, Huizinga, and Elliott (1978) also note that these activities were positively associated with the length of time away from home and with the number of previous departures. In a more recent investigation of 489 runaway youth in Edmonton, Alberta, Kufeldt and Nimmo (1987) indicate that 71 percent of runaways reported being encouraged by others to participate in crime while on the street; moreover, 49 percent admitted to using unspecified illegal means to satisfy their needs. Several other studies also suggest that crime is common among runaways, particularly those with extensive street careers; unfortunately, these studies provide insufficient data to document this possibility fully (see Janus et al. 1987; Palenski 1984; Shellow et al. 1967). In the sample of homeless youth analyzed below, we find that 46 percent made drug sales, 49 percent stole goods valued up to $50, and 27 percent broke into homes or businesses. The respective figures reported by Hindelang, Hirschi, and Weis (1981), which is stratified to overrepresent adolescents with police contacts, are 32 percent, 13 percent, and 13 percent. Larger differences characterize more representative studies based on school or home samples (e.g., see Hirschi 1969; Elliott and Ageton 1980; Paternoster and Triplett 1988).

Although less commonly reported, comparisons of the frequency of offending also suggest that homeless youth are disproportionately involved in crime. For example, in a study of 1544 eleventh-grade students, Paternoster and Triplett (1988) report that, among those committing at least one offence, the median frequency of petty theft is 3 and for smoking marijuana it is 10. In our sample of homeless youth, the median frequency of more serious theft (over $50) while on the street, is 8, and for selling hard drugs, it is 10. So, even though homeless youth constitute a relatively small proportion of all adolescents, they are involved in a substantial and disproportionate share of crime (see also Hagan and McCarthy 1992). However, the causal relationship between crime and homelessness has not been adequately specified. The importance of understanding the relationship between street life and crime is heightened by the growing numbers of youth who are leaving and staying away from home. According to recent estimates, there are 750 000 to 1 500 000 homeless youth in the United States (Shane 1989).

DATA, VARIABLES, AND METHODS

We propose that adverse circumstances in themselves can compel people to commit crimes. However, a meaningful test of this proposition requires a sample of individuals exposed to such circumstances, indicators of these difficulties, and measures of other variables that may account for a possibly spurious association between indicators of adversity and delinquency among street youth.

Data

In the main part of our analysis, we study Canadian youth surveyed in the city of Toronto during 1987 and 1988. These adolescents were not living with their families (nor were they from homeless families), nor did they have a permanent or fixed address; in other words, they were "living on the street" or "homeless."

Note that we do not refer to these street youth as "runaways." This term is of questionable applicability here. It implies that leaving home is inappropriate and that a return is both possible and desirable. Yet previous research reveals that many youth who leave home are forced out by parents (i.e., they are "throwaways") or are escaping from abusive environments; not surprisingly, many are unwilling to return home (Adams, Gullotta, and Clancy 1985; Janus et al. 1987; Stephenson 1989). Furthermore, the term runaway is commonly used as a legal classification. As noted by Sellin, Sutherland, and others, it is often misleading to use a legal classification for sociological research, especially when the classification has no legal application. In Great Britain (see Liddiard and Hutson 1991) and the province of Ontario, adolescents can legally leave home at age 16; thus, being a runaway is not a criminal or delinquent offence for these youth.

We used a two-pronged procedure to collect anonymous self-report data from adolescents at social service agencies and in nonagency settings. Toronto offers a unique opportunity for studying "street" or homeless youth because it has a number of social service agencies that provide free services for homeless people; moreover, many of these services are reserved explicitly for adolescents. Although these agencies provide necessities of life (e.g., shelter, food, clothing, and companionship), some youth do not use them (i.e., agency use is voluntary, like their adult counterparts) (Rossi 1989), some youth avoid social service agencies because they find agencies have too many rules and limit their freedom of movement and activity.

To include a wide cross-section of clients, we surveyed youth in nine social agencies: a short-term hostel (maximum stay, five days) restricted to adolescents under the age of 21; a "drop-in" agency that provided a place for homeless youth to socialize; a long-term shelter (maximum stay, three months) for people under 21; a drop-in agency for adolescent prostitutes; three gender-specific shelters; one hostel for youth 16 and under; and one shelter without client restrictions.

The nonagency locations included inner-city parks, street corners, and places for sleeping. In these places, we distinguished homeless youth through observation and conversation. We approached only adolescents who were panhandling or preparing to sleep in a public place. We subsequently screened these youth on their knowledge of general "street topics" (e.g., could they recommend a place to sleep or panhandle) and to determine their ages (the study was limited to those aged 19 and under).

We used a weekly schedule to survey youth in both settings. However, every visit did not provide respondents. Instead, a considerable amount of time was spent "hanging out" in agencies, parks, and on street corners talking with workers and street youth. Interested adolescents completed a consent form and an anonymous 30-minute survey, for which they received $10 in restaurant coupons. The instrument required about a Grade 7 reading level (Laubach and Koschnick 1977; Lorge 1959) and 32 respondents needed reading assistance. Over a one-year period, we approached 475 adolescents; of these, 390 completed usable surveys (an 82 percent response rate).

Demographic data reveal that 67 percent of our respondents were male and 33 percent female; at the time of the survey, 12 percent were under 16 years old (the youngest was 13), 35 percent were 19, and the remaining 63 percent were almost evenly distributed across ages 16, 17, and 18. Of our respondents, 62 percent were staying in a hostel, 23 percent were living on the street, 12 percent were temporarily residing with friends or relatives, and 3 percent were living elsewhere (e.g., in a hotel). While we cannot be certain that our sample of street youth is representative, comparisons with accounts of other Canadian street youth (Janus et al. 1987; Kufeldt and Nimmo 1987; Stephenson 1989) and demographic data from social service agencies indicate that our sample does not differ significantly from the population of homeless youth (see McCarthy 1990).

In a second part of our analysis we introduce data from a supplementary sample of adolescents living at home and attending school. We randomly selected one school from each of three areas in Toronto and distributed survey invitations and parental permission forms to all students in randomly chosen ninth- through twelfth-grade classes. A 30-minute instrument designed to parallel that used with the street youth was administered in classrooms and cafeterias, with a maximum of 40 students at a sitting. We offered popular music tapes as inducements and obtained 562 usable questionnaires with a response rate of 68 percent. This level of response falls within the range of 60–75 percent commonly reported for comparable school-based surveys (e.g., Hindelang, Hirschi, and Weis 1981; Elliott and Ageton 1980).

Dependent Variables

Our primary interest is in explaining street youth involvement in several kinds of delinquency. Our first dependent variable is a measure that asks about stealing food since leaving home. Our second measure, serious theft, includes responses to seven items asking how often the respondent did the following since leaving home: (1) took things worth over $50; (2) took things from a car (tape deck, etc.); (3) took things from a store worth less than $50; (4) used a bank card or credit card without the owner's permission; (5) took things from a store worth more than $50; (6) took a stranger's automobile; and (7) broke into and took things from a house or building. Our final dependent variables, prostitution, is based on the question, "How often have you had sex for money since leaving home?"

We use these particular measures of street crime for two reasons. First, previous research on homeless adults (Rossi 1989; Snow, Baker, and Anderson 1989) and youth (Janus et al. 1987; Kufeldt and Nimmo 1987) points to the disproportionate level of more serious crime on the street; although theft of food might still be considered a minor form of delinquency, prostitution and serious theft are not. The potential economic returns combined with the costs of detection clearly separate serious theft and prostitution from theft of food and other status offences or crimes of mischief commonly used to measure delinquencies among high school youth. These distinctions are made clear in the public rankings of these activities in crime-seriousness scales (see, for example, Rossi et al. 1974) and in conversations with street and school youth. Second, we include the theft and prostitution measures because they are likely to reveal gender-specific patterns, with situational concerns and difficulties more likely to cause male involvement in theft and female participation in prostitution. That is, strains of the street are most likely to exert their effects along previously observed lines of gender specialization in crime (see, for example, Steffensmeier 1980; Harris 1977).

Independent Variables

We use three kinds of items to tap situational difficulties on the street. The first item inquires about present and past unemployment since leaving home. We use this information to categorize respondents as continuously employed since leaving home, employed since leaving home but presently unemployed, or unemployed since leaving home. Our second measure is of hunger and asks how frequently the respondent has spent entire days without food since leaving home. Our final indicator of situational problems, shelter, uses information on the living conditions the respondent has experienced since leaving home. Our coding of shelter uses four categories that are ordered in increasing levels of risk and decreasing levels of security: living exclusively with friends or relatives (coded "1"); staying in public hostels and shelters (coded "2"); living on the street as well as in hostels (coded "3"); and staying on the street, in hostels and hotels (coded "4"). The kinds of private hotels street youth use may be especially hazardous in exposing them to sites of ongoing criminal activity (e.g., drugs and prostitution).

In addition to measures of adversity, we also include information on strain and control at home. Our first set of background variables measure family class position and are indicators of structurally induced strain transmitted through the family. This conceptualization uses information on parental employment, supervisory responsibilities, and ownership to divide families into the following classes: unemployed surplus population, workers, supervisors, the petty bourgeoisie, and employers. Our measures of family class position use information on both parents (if present) to determine the parent with the greater class power (we use the remaining parent in single-parent families). We assume that families with the least class power (i.e., surplus population families) experience the most strain.

We include two additional indicators of familial strain: a scale measuring coercive control and a single item tapping sexual abuse. The former is based on questions that ask, "Did your parents or guardians ever use physical forms of discipline?" and "Have you ever been intentionally struck so hard by a parent or guardian that it caused a bruise or bleeding?" Street workers argued the inappropriateness of inquiring directly about sexual abuse (especially without follow-up counselling); instead we asked respondents to describe problems they experienced at home and coded responses reflecting sexual abuse as a dummy variable. Consequently, this measure may underestimate sexual abuse.

Our measures of familial control include indicators of family structure and parental control. We measure family structure with an indicator of intactness; that is, the presence of two biological parents in the respondent's family. Parental control is conceptualized along two dimensions: relational control and instrumental control (Hagan, Gillis, and Simpson 1988). The former involves attachment and identification within the family, whereas the latter concerns supervision and surveillance. Four separate maternal and paternal relational control measures ask, "Did you talk with your mother/father about your thoughts and feelings?" and "Would you like to be the kind of person your mother/father is?" The four maternal and paternal instrumental control measures ask, "Did your mother/father know your whereabouts/who you were with when you were away from home?"

Our indicators of school experiences include measures of school control and school-induced strain. We measure two elements of the former, involvement and commitment, with items that inquire about time devoted to homework while in school and educational aspirations (see Hirschi 1969; Wiatrowski, Griswold, and Roberts 1981). We measure school-induced strain by asking about the frequency of problems with teachers.

Although we have measured a wide range of concepts, we may still have misspecified the causation of crime in some way; this could result in spuriously attributing causal significance to situational variables. To guard further against this, we include several omnibus controls: length of time on the street (the length of time at risk), number of times the respondent left home (previous street experiences), criminal support at home (the number of home friends arrested) and on the street (the number of street friends arrested), and respondent's participation in crime and delinquency while at home.

Our indicators of delinquency at home are comparable to our measures of street delinquency introduced above. For example, we measure serious theft and prostitution at home with items parallel to those used for the street. However, since we do not have an indicator of theft of food at home, we use a two-item scale measuring minor theft. This scale utilizes items that ask how often the respondents took things valued at less than $5, and between $5 and $10.

Controls for crime at home are important because compared with non-runaways, runaways may have more extensive criminal backgrounds before leaving home (see Brennan, Huizinga, and Elliott 1978). Compared with at-home samples used in other research, our homeless youth have higher prevalence rates of crime while living at home (see Hindelang, Hirschi, and Weis 1981; Hirschi 1969; Paternoster and Triplett 1988). Nonetheless, the prevalence of crime on the street is significantly higher than crime at home (McCarthy and Hagan 1991).

Descriptive Statistics

The descriptive statistics inform us about youth at home and on the street. Our sample of homeless youth is, on average, older, with a greater proportion of males. The class backgrounds of these two groups are similar, but there is a larger representation of surplus worker parents among the homeless. More prominent contrasts occur for measures of family control and strain. Compared with youth at home, homeless youth are more likely to have lived in a family lacking one or both biological parents, and they have experienced lower amounts of parental relational and instrumental control and greater amounts of coercive control and sexual abuse.

The mean measures of school experience reveal that homeless adolescents did significantly less homework, had lower academic aspirations than their at-home counterparts, and had more problems with teachers. These youth also had greater exposure to crime while living at home. Compared with those at home, youth on the street had more extensive networks of arrested peers and reported more minor and serious theft (neither group reported much home prostitution).

On average, homeless youth had left home on a number of occasions and had not lived at home for a period of six months or more. During this period, the average street adolescent worked but was unemployed at the time of the study and had spent an entire day without food at least once or twice. These youth were also more likely to have used the street and public hostels for shelter, rather than have relied on friends and relatives.

Since taking to the street, the majority of homeless youth had replaced their delinquent friends from home with a comparable group on the street. Street youth also report extensive participation in criminal activities: 45 percent reported stealing food, 75 percent indicated they had committed a serious theft, and 30 percent reported working in prostitution since leaving home.

In sum, our data indicate that, compared with adolescents still as home, street youth are disproportionately drawn from families characterized by aversive strain and an absence of control. That is, the latter have a substantially greater likelihood of being the victims of physical and sexual abuse and parental neglect. Not surprisingly, they are also more likely to have experienced problems at school, have delinquent friends, and to have violated the law. These factors are important in understanding the etiology of leaving home (see Brennan, Huizinga, and Elliott 1978; Janus et al. 1987; Kufeldt and Nimmo 1987; Hagan and McCarthy 1992). Although it is not central here, we will discuss this process later when we examine the results from a probit analysis of leaving home.

Unfortunately, our cross-sectional data do not allow us to temporally order the relationships between background variables; thus, in our analysis we enter these variables simultaneously. However, we do feel comfortable in assuming that familial abuse and neglect precede delinquency. Although parents may neglect their adolescent children or use physical force as a response to their childrens' delinquencies or contacts with delinquent friends, we know of no literature that demonstrates that previously nonviolent parents begin to use force when their children reach adolescence and misbehave in the ways just described. Rather, the research literature suggests the primacy of abuse that we also assume (Wauchope and Straus 1990; Wilson and Daly 1987; Wilson, Daly, and Weghorst 1980).

RESULTS

Adversity and Crime

The bivariate correlations reported in Table 7.1 between independent variables and the dependent measures of theft of food, serious theft, and prostitution reveal that the strongest and most consistent relationships involve two measures of situational problems and two street control variables: hunger and shelter, and length of time on the street and arrests of street friends. In contrast, our third situational measure, unemployment, is significantly associated with only one indicator of street crime — prostitution. There is also evidence of gender specialization in street crime; gender is positively related to theft of food and serious theft but negatively associated with prostitution. This indicates that, as expected, males are more likely to steal while females are more likely to work in the sex trade.

The bivariate effects also reveal several significant correlations between strain and control variables and street crime, but the pattern of relationships is less clear. Perhaps all we can say to this point is that situational variables are at least as (if not more) prominently associated with street crime as background and developmental variables are, even though situational variables are rarely measured in crime or delinquency research; furthermore, gender appears to channel involvement in street crime.

In our more detailed research (McCarthy and Hagan 1992), we undertake a multivariate analysis, testing models of the relationship between homelessness and the theft of food. In doing so, we introduce three measures of situational problems (unemployment, hunger, and shelter) together with three measures of street control variables (length of time on the street, number of previous street experiences, and street friends arrested). Although all these measures, except unemployment, are significantly related to theft of food at the bivariate level, hunger alone has a substantial and statistically significant effect on theft of food when they are introduced together.

A Further Test

Our results suggest that adverse situations are prominent in the causation of street crime. However, thus far we have considered only youth who are on the street, and we have had no means of taking into account the process of how they got there. The final part of our analysis brings that process into the picture by incorporating data from a sample of Toronto school youth. This involves using a response-based sampling strategy (see Xie and Manski 1989) that brings a relatively rare outcome-defined population (i.e., street youth)

TABLE 7.1 *Bivariate Coefficients for Street Crime (Theft of Food, Serious Theft, and Prostitution) for Homeless Sample*

	Dependent Variables		
Independent Variables	*Theft of Food*	*Serious Theft*	*Prostitution*
Age	-0.048	0.026	-0.008
Gender	0.160***	0.180***	-0.096**
Surplus workers	-0.001	0.017	0.048
Workers	-0.039	-0.018	-0.123***
Petite bourgeoisie	-0.034	-0.082*	-0.062
Employers	0.075	-0.022	0.031
Intact family	-0.003	0.010	0.034
Maternal instrumental control	-0.135***	-0.162***	-0.042
Paternal instrumental control	-0.026	-0.040	-0.075*
Maternal relational control	-0.011	-0.092**	-0.004
Paternal relational control	-0.029	-0.046	-0.064
Coercive control	-0.019	-0.021	0.105**
Sexual abuse	-0.003	-0.038	0.129***
Homework	-0.276***	-0.236***	0.101**
School goals	0.027	0.035	-0.030
Conflict with teachers	0.171***	0.251***	0.018
Home friends arrested	0.212***	0.252***	-0.039
Minor theft scale (at home)	0.308***	0.319***	0.011
Serious theft scale (at home)	0.303***	0.461***	0.011
Prostitution (at home)	-0.008	0.036	0.184***
Unemployed	-0.034	-0.045	0.103**
Hunger	0.369***	0.262***	0.194***
Shelter	0.169***	0.164***	0.230***
Number of times left home	0.086**	0.036	0.203***
Length of time on street	0.128***	0.251***	0.227***
Street friends arrested	0.197***	0.394***	0.168***

Note: N = 390. All significant tests are two-tailed.
* $P \leq 0.10$, ** $P \leq 0.05$, *** $P \leq 0.01$

together with the remaining larger population (i.e., youth not on the street). Based on this sampling strategy, our conservative estimate is that over the approximate year of the study, for every twenty youth in school in Toronto, there was one on the street. Consistent with previous research, the findings included in our more detailed study (McCarthy and Hagan 1992) show that the likelihood of leaving home increases with age, coercive control, sexual abuse, conflict with teachers, and having delinquent friends; conversely, it decreases with being in an intact family and having high academic aspirations (see Brennan, Huizinga, and Elliott 1978; Shellow et al. 1967). The stability of the effect of delinquent friends suggests that they are not the prior cause of other problems (e.g., with parents) that mediate their effect on leaving home; rather, the presence of delinquent friends is either a closely adjacent intervening cause or a direct cause of leaving home.

CONCLUSION

Contemporary sociological criminology is characterized by its focus on background and developmental factors that are assumed to generate delinquent and criminal behaviour (see Matza 1964; Gottfredson and Hirschi 1990). The result is an array of theoretical orientations that highlight preadolescent and adolescent life experiences that take place in the family, at school, and among peers, that lead to delinquency. In the background of this orientation is an unanswered question of just how far back such causes might be traced (see, for example, White et al. 1990). This question animates a renewed interest among criminologists in the role of sociobiological predispositions and propensities in the causation of crime.

Our purpose here is to push sociological criminology in precisely the opposite direction: toward foreground causes of delinquency and crime, through the study of criminogenic situations. Such situations were once central in the study of crime, as exemplified in Sellin's (1937) study of crime during the Great Depression. The Chicago tradition of field research provided a means of incorporating street situations into the study of delinquency that lasted from Thrasher's (1927) investigation of *The Gang* through to Short and Strodtbeck's (1965) work *Group Process and Gang Delinquency*. This important tradition made street settings central to the collection of data and the organization of delinquency research. However, the emergence of the contemporary self-report paradigm had the unintended consequences of moving crime and delinquency research away from the street and into the schools, and of shifting attention away from the criminogenic nature of situations in which youth on the street often find themselves. The timing of this shift (in the late 1950s and early 1960s) may be significant because this was a period of relative prosperity in America, when it was perhaps possible to believe that conditions of the city were more malleable and the prospects of the urban underclass more benign. Yet, the 1980s and 1990s have made many citizens more sensitive to the harsh conditions that often characterize inner-city life and the potentially criminogenic conditions of contemporary street life. It is time to return our research to these street settings.

Our return to the street builds on what we have learned about background and developmental factors as causes of leaving home for the street, and of crime and delinquency. We propose that an integration of strain and control theories can span background, developmental, and foreground factors. A key to this integration is a focus on adverse conditions at home and in school because taking to the street and subsequent criminal activity are often responses to successive and causally linked adverse conditions, as, for example, when parental abuse and neglect at home lead to youth taking to the street. Our integration also acknowledges that absence of family and school ties can lead to the adoption of street life, so that the presence of strain and absence of control can lead to street crime indirectly as well as directly. We see no contradiction in the integration of these theoretical orientations. Indeed, our perspective on strain is in some ways reminiscent of the focus on conditions of overcontrol and undercontrol found in early versions of control theory (see, for example, Durkheim [1897] 1951; Nye 1958). For example, coercive parental control of children can be conceived as either a source of strain or as overcontrol.

Our findings provide empirical support for our integration of strain and control theory. This support is most apparent in the final stage of our combined analysis of separately sampled school youth and street youth. This analysis supports the premise that background and developmental variables — especially, but not exclusively, including coercive parental control, sexual abuse, and delinquency at home — directly influence taking to the street and indirectly influence theft and prostitution. In effect, this indicates that the youth who are most likely to become homeless are also the most likely to engage in theft and prostitution while on the street.

Meanwhile, variables measuring adverse situations exercise strong direct effects on street crime, apart from the mediating role they can also play. These effects vary somewhat by type of crime and gender, but overall, situational variables play a prominent role in the causation of street crime. This is true even when street variables are pitted against each other with a wide range of background/developmental and control variables and when sample-selection effects are taken into account. Consistently, hunger causes theft of food, problems of hunger and shelter lead to serious theft, and problems of shelter and unemployment produce prostitution. These situational effects gain plausibility from the comprehensive range of control measures we have imposed.

The finding that variables measuring situational adversity are salient in the causation of street delinquency is important not only because it redirects and broadens our theoretical perspective on crime and delinquency, but also because it extends our understanding of street life more generally. That is, this study confirms that many of the most serious problems of the street derive from the conditions of street life itself, including the problems of sustenance and security that street life produces. There is, of course, policy relevance in the fact that street situations can be changed.

STUDY QUESTIONS

1. *What are the key distinguishing features of McCarthy and Hagan's situational perspective on homelessness and youth crime, and why do they argue that it is important to adopt this type of perspective?*
2. *According to McCarthy and Hagan's research findings, how is homelessness linked to different types of delinquent behaviour?*
3. *Assuming that McCarthy and Hagan are correct in arguing that adverse situational factors are a significant cause of delinquent behaviour by street youth, what are some specific types of youth-oriented social welfare programs that could be introduced to try to reduce youth street crime? Should youth street crime prevention efforts directed at addressing situational factors also take into account background and developmental factors that have been traditionally linked to delinquent behaviour? Why or why not?*

REFERENCES

Adams, Gerald, Thomas Gullotta, and Mary Clancy. 1985. "Homeless Adolescents: A Descriptive Study of Similarities and Differences between Runaways and Throwaways." *Adolescence 20*: 715–24.

Agnew, Robert. 1985. "A Revised Strain Theory of Delinquency." *Social Forces 64*: 151–67.

Bonger, Willem. 1916. *Criminality and Economic Conditions*. Boston: Little, Brown.

Brennan, Tim, David Huizinga, and Delbert Elliott. 1978. *The Social Psychology of Runaways*. Lexington, MA: Heath.

Briar, Scott, and Irving Piliavin. 1965. "Delinquency, Situational Inducements, and Commitment to Conformity." *Social Problems 13*: 35–45.

Durkheim, Émile. (1897) 1951. *Suicide*, translated by John A. Spaulding and George Simpson. Glencoe, IL: Free Press.

Elliott, Delbert, and Susan Ageton. 1980. "Reconciling Race and Class Differences in Self-Reported and Official Estimates of Delinquency." *American Sociological Review 45*: 95–119.

Fischer, Pamela. 1988. "Criminal Activity among the Homeless: A Study of Arrests in Baltimore." *Hospital and Community Psychiatry 39*: 46–51.

Fletcher, Joseph. 1849. "Moral and Educational Statistics of England and Wales." *Journal of the Statistical Society of London 12*: 151–76; 189–335.

Gelberg, Lillian, Lawrence Linn, and Barbara Leake. 1988. "Mental Health, Alcohol and Drug Use, and Criminal History among Homeless Adults." *American Journal of Psychiatry 145*: 191–96.

Gibbons, Donald. 1971. "Observations on the Study of Crime Causation." *American Journal of Sociology 77*: 262–78.

Gottfredson, Michael, and Travis Hirschi. 1990. *A General Theory of Crime*. Stanford, CA: Stanford University Press.

Hagan, John, A.R. Gillis, and John Simpson. 1988. "Feminist Scholarship, Relational and Instrumental Control, and a Power-Control Theory of Gender and Delinquency." *British Journal of Sociology 39*: 301–36.

Hagan, John, and Bill McCarthy. 1992. "Street-Life and Delinquency." *British Journal of Sociology 43*(4): 533–61.

Harris, Anthony. 1977. "Sex and Theories of Deviance: Toward a Functional Theory of Deviant Type-Scripts." *American Sociological Review 42*: 3–16.

Hindelang, Michael, Travis Hirschi, and Joseph Weis. 1981. *Measuring Delinquency.* Beverly Hills, CA: Sage.

Hirschi, Travis. 1969. *Causes of Delinquency.* Berkeley: University of California Press.

Janus, Mark-David, Arlene McCormack, Ann Wolbert Burgess, and Carol Hartman. 1987. *Adolescent Runaways.* Toronto: Heath.

Katz, Jack. 1988. *Seductions of Crime: Moral and Sensual Attractions in Doing Evil.* New York: Basic.

Kufeldt, Kathleen, and Margaret Nimmo. 1987. "Youth on the Street: Abuse and Neglect in the Eighties." *Child Abuse and Neglect 11*: 531–43.

Laubach, Robert, and K. Koschnick. 1977. *Using Readability Formulas for Easy Adult Materials.* Syracuse, NY: New Readers.

Liddiard, Mark, and Susan Hutson. 1991. "Homeless Young People and Runaways: Agency Definitions and Processes." *Journal of Social Policy 20*: 365–88.

Lorge, I. 1959. *The Lorge Formula for Estimating Difficulty of Reading Materials.* New York: Columbia University Press.

Matza, David. 1964. *Delinquency and Drift.* New York: Wiley.

McCarthy, Bill. 1990. "Life on the Street: Serious Theft, Drug-Selling, and Prostitution among Homeless Youth." Ph.D. dissertation. University of Toronto, Department of Sociology.

McCarthy, Bill, and John Hagan. 1991. "Homelessness: A Criminogenic Situation?" *British Journal of Sociology 31*(4): 393–410.

———. 1992. "Mean Streets: The Theoretical Significance of Situational Delinquency among Homeless Youths." *American Journal of Sociology 98*(3): 597–627.

Momeni, Jamshid, ed. 1989. *Homelessness in the United States.* New York: Greenwood.

Nagin, Daniel, and Raymond Paternoster. 1991. "On the Relationship of Past to Future Participation in Delinquency." *Criminology 29*: 163–89.

Nye, F. Ivan. 1958. *Family Relationships and Delinquent Behavior.* New York: Wiley.

Nye, F. Ivan, and James Short. 1957. "Scaling Delinquent Behavior." *American Sociological Review 22*: 326–31.

Palenski, Joseph. 1984. *Kids Who Run Away.* Saratoga, CA: R.E. Publishers.

Paternoster, Raymond, and Ruth Triplett. 1988. "Disaggregating Self-Reported Delinquency and Its Implications for Theory." *Criminology 26*: 591–625.

Rossi, Peter. 1989. *Down and Out in America: The Origins of Homelessness.* Chicago: University of Chicago Press.

Rossi, Peter, Emily Waite, Christine Bose, and Richard Berk. 1974. "The Seriousness of Crimes: Normative Structure and Individual Differences." *American Sociological Review 39*: 224–37.

Russell, Whitworth. 1847. "Abstract of the 'Statistics of Crime in England and Wales from 1839 to 1843.'" *Journal of the Statistical Society of London 10*: 38–61.

Sellin, Thorsten. 1937. *Research Memorandum on Crime in the Depression.* New York: Social Science Research Council.

Shane, Paul. 1989. "Changing Patterns among Homeless and Runaway Youth." *American Journal of Orthopsychiatry 59*(2): 208–14.

Shellow, Robert, Juliana Schamp, Elliott Liebow, and Elizabeth Unger. 1967. *Suburban Runaways of the 1960s,* vol. 32, no. 3, Monographs of the Society for Research in Child Development. Chicago: University of Chicago Press.

Short, James, and Fred Strodtbeck. 1965. *Group Process and Gang Delinquency.* Chicago: University of Chicago Press.

Snow, David, Susan Baker, and Leon Anderson. 1989. "Criminality and Homeless Men: An Empirical Assessment." *Social Problems 36*: 532–49.

Steffensmeier, Darrell. 1980. "Sex Differences in Patterns of Adult Crimes, 1965–77: A Review and Assessment." *Social Forces 58*: 1080–1108.

Stephenson, Marylee. 1989. "A Study of the Vancouver Reconnect Program and Vancouver Street Youth." *Research Report.* Vancouver, CS Resors.

Sullivan, Mercer. 1989. *"Getting Paid": Youth Crime and Work in the Inner City.* Ithaca, NY: Cornell University Press.

Sutherland, Edwin, and Donald Cressey. 1978. *Principles of Criminology,* 10th ed. Philadelphia: Lippincott.

Thrasher, Frederick. 1927. *The Gang.* Chicago: University of Chicago Press.

Wauchope, Barbara, and Murray Straus. 1990. "Physical Punishment and Physical Abuse of American Children: Incidence Rates by Age, Gender, and Occupational Class." In Murray Straus and Richard Gelles, eds., *Physical Violence in American Families,* 133–48. New Brunswick, NJ: Transaction.

White, Jennifer, Terrie Moffitt, Felton Earls, Lee Robins, and Phil Silva. 1990. "How Early Can We Tell? Predictors of Childhood Conduct Disorder and Adolescent Delinquency." *Criminology 28*: 507–28.

Wiatrowski, Michael, David Griswold, and Mary Roberts. 1981. "Social Control and Delinquency." *American Sociological Review 46*: 525–41.

Wilson, Margo, and Martin Daly. 1987. "Risk of Maltreatment of Children Living with Step Parents." In R. Gelles and J. Lancaster, eds., *Child Abuse and Neglect: Biosocial Dimensions,* 215–32. New York: Aldine de Gruyter.

Wilson, M., M. Daly, and S. Weghorst. 1980. "Household Composition and the Risk of Child Abuse and Neglect." *Journal of Biosocial Science 12*: 333–40.

Xie, Yu, and Charles Manski. 1989. "The Logit Model and Response-Based Samples." *Sociological Methods and Research 17*: 283–302.

CHAPTER EIGHT

Street Youth and Criminal Violence

STEPHEN W. BARON
University of Windsor, Ontario
TIMOTHY F. HARTNAGEL
University of Alberta

The term street youth usually refers to youth who have run away or been expelled from their homes and/or who spend some or all of their time in various public locations (Kufeldt and Nimmo 1987a; 1987b; McCullagh and Greco 1990; Smart et al. 1990). Most of these street youth are underemployed/unemployed, often lack a permanent residence, and spend significant amounts of time without shelter (Hagan and McCarthy 1992; Kufeldt and Nimmo 1987a; 1987b; McCarthy and Hagan 1991; 1992a; 1992b; Palenski 1984; Webber 1991). Their lives are characterized by poverty, hunger, and other conditions of extreme deprivation (Hagan and McCarthy 1992; Kufeldt and Nimmo 1987a; 1987b; McCarthy and Hagan 1991; 1992a; 1992b; Palenski 1984; Webber 1991).

Past research suggests this population is heavily involved in criminal activity (Brennan, Huizinga, and Elliott 1978; Janus et al. 1987; Kufeldt and Nimmo 1987a; 1987b; McCarthy and Hagan 1991; 1995; Palenski 1984; Radford, King, and Warren 1989; Rothman 1991; Smart et al. 1990) and indicates that these activities are influenced by various family, school, and street factors (Brennan, Huizinga, and Elliott 1978; Gullotta 1979; Hagan and McCarthy 1992; Kufeldt and Nimmo 1987a; 1987b; McCarthy and Hagan 1992a; Palenski 1984; Rothman 1991). However, McCarthy and Hagan (1991; 1992a; 1995; see also Palenski 1984) argue that street youth participation in crime is most likely the result of the homeless experience itself, and not the direct effect of predisposing background variables.

Source: Stephen W. Baron and Timothy F. Hartnagel, "Street Youth and Criminal Violence," *Journal of Research on Crime and Delinquency* 35 (May 1998): 166–92. Reprinted by permission of Sage Publications, Inc.

Yet, little research has explored just what aspects of street life lead to criminal behaviour. Hagan and McCarthy (1992) suggest that at a minimum, the relationship between homelessness and crime and delinquency is poorly specified, arguing that street life is something of a "black box," and they call for researchers to demonstrate the specific conditions, experiences, and aspects of life on the street that cause delinquency.

Limited research suggests that street youth are active participants in group fights, robbery, and other serious assaults (Baron 1989a; 1989b; 1995; Kennedy and Baron 1993; McCarthy and Hagan 1991). But the specific conditions and experiences of the street leading to street youth violence are poorly understood in that most research on this population tends to focus on understanding the background factors that led these youth to the street and documenting their utilitarian behaviours (theft and prostitution) once there (Brennan, Huizinga, and Elliott 1978; Gullotta 1979; Hagan and McCarthy 1992; Kudfeldt and Nimmo 1987a; 1987b; McCarthy and Hagan 1991; 1992a; 1992b; 1995; Palenski 1984; Radford, King, and Warren 1989; Rothman 1991).

The literature does, however, point to a number of intersections between the characteristics of street youth and the conditions others argue are conducive to violent crime, including poverty, unemployment, substance abuse, and victimization (Fagan and Jones 1984; Fagan, Piper, and Moore 1986; Hartstone and Hansen 1984). However, a review of the other available literature reveals a historical inclination to adopt "unicausal" explanations (Fagan and Jones 1984) of violence. The tendency has been for researchers to focus on only one of the many possible causal paths (i.e., family violence, poverty, subcultural support) while ignoring the influence of other probable factors (Fagan and Jones 1984). As a result, the field has been left with a number of competing accounts of limited explanatory power. Further, this work has failed to explore how these frameworks work to explain different forms of violence, focusing instead on more general explanations. Finally, the applicability of findings from other populations to homeless street youth is an open issue because the street population has been all but neglected in other individual-level research (Hagan and McCarthy 1992; Inciardi, Horowitz, and Pottieger 1993).

The current research draws from several criminological perspectives in an effort to identify the specific aspects of street life that lead to several varieties of criminal violence. Specifically, subcultural, economic deprivation, and routine activities theories will be used to develop hypotheses regarding these causal processes. Furthermore, given the evidence of the effect of family abuse on later violence (Elliott 1994; Hartstone and Hansen 1984; Hotaling, Straus, and Lincoln 1989; McCord 1979; Sedgely and Lund 1979; Smith and Thornberry 1995; Straus 1985; Widom 1989), we distinguish further between prior family and recent street experiences of violent victimization as possible causal variables in youth street violence. We will also explore whether four different forms of violence in this population have different antecedents.

THEORETICAL PERSPECTIVES

Street Subculture and Lifestyle

A popular explanation for the violent behaviour of youth has drawn from a subculture of violence perspective. Fagan and Jones (1984) note that the highest rates of aggressive behaviour are located in environments where aggressive role models are abundant and where aggressiveness is a positive attribute. The peer group offers a climate where violent behaviours are modelled, practised, and reinforced. Some have suggested that the violent crime in these groups is a product of conformity to a distinctive culture. Those who are in intimate contact with groups organized in favour of violent criminal activities become exposed to definitions favourable to this unlawful behaviour, and, given their extensive associations with such definitions, such individuals are likely to act in terms of them, committing violent crimes (Curtis 1975; Gastil 1971; Wolfgang and Ferracuti 1967).

In this tradition, Horowitz (1983) suggests that violence revolves around insult and honour. Horowitz argues that honour is a normative code that "stresses the inviolability of one's manhood and defines breaches of etiquette, in an adversarial idiom." Honour sensitizes members of the subculture to violations that are interpreted as "derogations of the self" and must be responded to with physical violence.

At a broader level, Inciardi, Horowitz, and Pottieger (1993) argue that criminal behaviour is a "definitional characteristic" of a street lifestyle and subculture for those who spend considerable amounts of time on the street. Over time, contacts become increasingly limited to other street people, values become altered to fit behaviours, and crime becomes an accepted part of life.

Part and parcel of this street lifestyle is the use of drugs and alcohol (Inciardi, Horowitz, and Pottieger 1993), substances that tend to be associated with aggressive behaviour (Elliott, Huizinga, and Ageton 1985; Fagan 1990; Fagan, Piper, and Moore 1986; Hartstone and Hansen 1984; Tinklenberg et al. 1981; White, Pandina, and LaGrange 1987). Inciardi, Horowitz, and Pottieger (1993) note that substance use is a major requirement for successfully participating in the street lifestyle and reaping its benefits and satisfactions. They argue that being under the influence while committing a crime is something to be expected for those heavily involved in a street lifestyle. In fact, they suggest that the critical factor in the move from trivial to serious crime on the street is drug and alcohol use. Drugs and alcohol can directly affect crime by making risky or otherwise difficult offences easier (Inciardi and Russe 1977). These substances can create feelings of omnipotence, which, in tandem with the sheer youth of many street participants, can distort perceptions of risk. This suggests that the street lifestyle and the substance abuse linked to the street subculture might serve to increase violent criminal activity.

Economic Deprivation

Research assessing the capacity of these subcultural explanations to account for violent behaviour has generated inconsistent results (Ball-Rokeach 1973; Bankston and Allen 1980; Blau and Blau 1982; Curtis 1975; Danziger and Wheeler 1975; Doerner 1979; Gastil 1971; Hackney 1969; Huff-Corzine, Corzine, and Moore 1986; Loftin and Hill 1974; Messner 1983; Rosenfeld 1986; Sampson 1985; Williams 1984), leading to a focus on structural explanations of violent behaviour. A number of researchers have argued that violent behaviour stems from inequality, the uneven distribution of resources, and the deprivation of some relative to others. Perceptions of inequality and relative deprivation are thought to generate feelings of resentment and hostility, which in turn stimulate impulses that are ultimately expressed as violent crime (Blau and Blau 1982; Braithwaite 1979; Danziger and Wheeler 1975; Hawkins 1983; Messner and Tardiff 1986). Furthermore, the likelihood of aggression is increased by the chronic stress of poverty and lower-class life, which further reduces the ability to cope with arousal, which in turn can generate more violence and angry aggression (Bernard 1990).

The conditions outlined by the structural perspective can lead to the creation of an aggressive environment, particularly if the poor are socially isolated (Bernard 1990). An atmosphere is created where there is the constant threat of physical injury or death. These realities produce additional arousal that is probably chronic, leaving a socially isolated group extremely at risk to exhibit angry aggression.

Poverty may also lead to more utilitarian types of violence. Desroches (1997) argues that robbery may be viewed as an offence that is primarily motivated by the desire or need for money. He suggests that limited access to legitimate monetary and material sources may lead to violent offences that meet offenders' immediate requirements (Desroches 1995).

A number of researchers have called for greater attention to be paid to the variables linking poverty, particularly unemployment, to crime (Baron and Hartnagel 1997; Box 1987; Box and Hale 1985; Horwitz 1984; Wright 1981). These scholars have pointed out that people's interpretation of their labour and life situations play a large role in shaping their responses to unemployment and poverty. These interpretations may be contingent on what people believe causes their poverty and unemployment and the actual duration of these conditions (Baron and Hartnagel 1997; Box and Hale 1985; Horwitz 1984; MacLeod 1987; Pearlin et al. 1981).

This may be most important for understanding a more utilitarian type of offence like robbery. Cloward and Ohlin (1961) argue that the failure to achieve socially approved goals can lead to alienation and a "withdrawal of attributions of legitimacy" for dominant norms. The most significant step in the development of this alienation is "the attribution of the cause of failure to the social order rather than to oneself" (Cloward and Ohlin 1961: 112). In short, the link between occupational deprivation and utilitarian criminal activity may be contingent upon the degree of acceptance of the meritocratic ideology. Robbery may be more likely when persons experiencing economic deprivation and employment difficulties believe the system is at fault (Box 1987; Hartnagel 1990; Merton 1957; Stack 1984).

Routine Activities

Sampson and Lauritsen (1990; Lauritsen, Sampson, and Laub 1991) suggest that mere opportunity can lead to an increase in crime independent of the structural or cultural conditions that might motivate individuals to engage in crime. From this perspective, violent street crime is a product of opportunity that arises in the ongoing activities that occur on the street. The probability of crime increases with the convergence in space and time of motivated offenders, suitable targets, and absent guardianship (Cohen and Felson 1979; Felson and Cohen 1980; Lauritsen, Sampson, and Laub 1991; Sampson and Lauritsen 1990; Sampson and Wooldredge 1987). It is argued that the lifestyles that lead one to go to bars and to being on the street lead to situations in which these factors coincide to present offenders with opportunities to commit crime (Jensen and Brownfield 1986; Kennedy and Forde 1990a; 1990b).

Routine activities theorists suggest further that the chances of violence may increase through the "principle of homogamy" (Sampson and Lauritsen 1990). Individuals increase their likelihood of violence the more frequently they come into contact with, or associate with, members of demographic groups that contain a disproportionate share of violent offenders. For example, young males leading "risky lifestyles" out on the street are more likely to become involved in violent altercations because they are more likely to come in contact, and associate, with other young males who are themselves involved in offending (Kennedy and Forde 1990b; Lauritsen, Sampson, and Laub 1991; Sampson and Lauritsen 1990).

There is evidence to suggest that the social hazards of leading these risky lifestyles are reflected in greater risks of experiencing violent victimization. Victimization within this environment in turn leads to greater violent offending behaviour (Fagan, Piper, and Cheng 1987; Fagan, Piper, and Moore 1986; Singer 1981; 1986). People are expected to legitimate more readily the use of violence because of their victimization experience (Singer 1986), and there may also be subcultural expectations that condone retaliation (Lauritsen, Sampson, and Laub 1991; Sampson and Lauritsen 1990).

Another form of violent victimization takes place in the family. A consistent theme in the criminological and family violence literature is the relationship between experiencing violence in the home and later antisocial behaviour (Elliott 1994; Hartstone and Hansen 1984; Hotaling, Straus, and Lincoln 1989; McCord 1979; Sedgely and Lund 1979; Smith and Thornberry 1995; Straus 1985; Widom 1989). It is argued that children in these circumstances come to model the behaviour of their parents (Fagan and Jones 1984;

Fagan and Wexler 1987; Farrington 1978; Sorrels 1977) and adopt violence as an interpersonal strategy and/or tactic. The violent experience encourages the youth to use aggression as a means of problem solving and/or of gaining compliance from others (Fagan and Wexler 1987; Siegal and Senna 1994).

Abusive histories are also said to diminish people's ability to cope with stress or develop empathy for others, resulting in a greater tendency to victimize others and strike out in anger during times of stress (Siegal and Senna 1994; Wooden 1995). Regoli and Hewitt (1991) argue that these violent experiences also influence youth to seek out and create violent situations including joining peers who approve of, require, and encourage violence while providing a sense of belonging. Evidence also suggests that these violent experiences leave abused youth vulnerable to the aggression and violence in the larger culture (Siegel and Senna 1994). They are more likely to be swayed by expectations for, or tolerations of, violence. This may result from the microinfluence of peers or from placement in structural locations where violence is expected.

HYPOTHESES

Drawing from these theoretical perspectives and the supporting research, we can specify several hypotheses regarding the influences of subcultural, economic, routine activities, and family abuse predictors on the violent behaviour of street youth:

1. Beginning with the role of subculture, we expect that street youth who spend more time with criminal peers will engage in more violent behaviour.
2. Further, the street youth literature suggests that the condition of homelessness itself is criminogenic. Therefore, we expect that youth who have lived on the street for a longer time period should report more violent crime net of their other experiences.
3. As part of this street lifestyle, we also anticipate that youth who are more often under the influence of drugs and/or alcohol will be more at risk for violent behaviour.
4. We also expect that long-term unemployment, living with few financial resources, the anger associated with unemployment, and perceptions of an unfair social structure will lead to more violent behaviour.
5. Further, we expect that youth who have suffered violent victimization on the street will be at an increased risk for violent offending.
6. Finally, we believe that the physical abuse that characterizes the home experiences of many street youth will increase their tendency towards violent behaviour.

We will test these predictions with four specific types of violence — robbery, aggravated assaults, group fights, and simple assaults — as well as an index of general violence to assess the various processes that underlie these behaviours. We expect to discover that some predictors have stronger effects on certain offences in that the four types of violence vary among themselves. Robbery is a utilitarian offence mainly committed for monetary gain. Group fights have a collective character that may reflect certain aspects of the street subculture including peers and conflict over status. Assaults may also involve such conflict and peer influence, though in other instances assaults may arise more in the context of alcohol and other drug use and/or the experience of violent victimization.

METHODS

A problem that plagues researchers studying street youth is the difficulty in setting an appropriate definition or criteria for selection into a study. Past research suggests that the street population is made up of a heterogeneous group of youth from preteens to mid-20s. The street is populated by students and dropouts, employed and unemployed youth, regulars who "hang out" on the street on a permanent basis, and those whose presence is sporadic (Kufeldt and Nimmo 1987a; 1987b; McCullagh and Greco 1990; Smart et al. 1990).

Recognizing the heterogeneity of this population, 200 male respondents were identified based on four sampling criteria:

1. Participants must be male.
2. They must be aged 24 and under.
3. They must have left or finished school.
4. They must spend at least three hours a day, three days a week "hanging around" on the street or in a mall.

The rationales for these criteria were (a) to avoid the potential ethical and methodological problems of a male researcher inquiring about intimate areas of female respondents' lives (sexual abuse, sexual assault, and prostitution); (b) to cover the age range of those described as street youth (Caputo and Ryan 1991: 8–10); (c) to eliminate those not eligible for full-time employment; and (d) to obtain a sample of "serious," "at-risk" youth and avoid the "weekend warriors." Although criterion four left the door open for the inclusion of less at-risk youth, the data showed the average respondent to be a full-time street youth who had been homeless for about four months in the prior year.

Data Collection

The data were collected over a six-month period from January through June of 1993, in Edmonton, Alberta, a large western Canadian city with a population of 800 000. The violent crime rate for the area, in 1993, was 1151 per

100 000, a number somewhat higher than the national average of 1079 per 100 000 for that year (Statistics Canada 1994). Further, the labour market at the time of data collection was extremely difficult for those younger than 24, with the youth unemployment rate reaching 20.2 percent in 1993.

The study took place in and around the downtown business core of the city, which is bordered by the local skid row and the "inner city." Thus, the area contained a mix of commercial and financial establishments surrounded by bars, pawnshops, hotels, shelters, detox centres, rooming houses, rundown residential units, and abandoned buildings.

Unlike other research where appropriate samples reflecting target population parameters are drawn from exhaustive population lists, the fluid and mobile nature of the street population makes estimations of composition and size a difficult if not impossible task. Therefore, the study used a snowball sampling technique. This strategy is often employed in field research of little-known or hard to reach subjects (Hagan 1993; Inciardi et al. 1991; Johnson et al. 1985; Maxfield and Babbie 1995). This process begins with the identification of a single or small group of respondents who are then asked to identify, or recruit, other suitable candidates who might be willing to participate in the study. Larger sample sizes can capture the variability of the researched population and reduce some of the sampling error inherent in this method (McCarthy 1990).

Sample selection began with one of the researchers situating himself in this geographical area. The researcher approached potential respondents, informed them of the project, and screened them for study eligibility. Those youth meeting the selection criteria were then provided additional information on the study and invited to participate. Subsequent to granting consent, the respondents were taken to be interviewed in the more comfortable and sheltered conditions of one of the many malls in the downtown core. The interview contained a combination of forced-choice and open-ended questions pertaining to the issues under study. The youth were interviewed for an average of an hour and ten minutes and were rewarded for their participation with $10 in food coupons to a popular fast-food restaurant.

Additional contacts were initiated by youth who were made aware of the researcher's presence and solicited interviews or through introductions from previously interviewed subjects. Following these advances, informed consent was obtained from each new respondent, who was then interviewed and rewarded.

The researcher began and ended each day by returning to the locations where he had come into contact with previous respondents. This allowed him to follow up on the youths' situations and observe and gather more information on their behaviours, which was recorded in field notes at the end of each day. This process also filled periods of down time when there were no new people to be approached or found.

These procedures provided us with a sample of 200 youth of an average age of almost 19. All but fifteen of these youth had spent some time during the year living away from their parents, and a full three-quarters of the sample had been with no fixed address during the last year ($N = 153$). Those who had been homeless had spent on average almost five months in total living on the street in the previous year.

MEASURING CRIME

Information on a number of measures of criminal behaviour including robbery, aggravated assault, group fights, and common assault was obtained via self-report. After each self-report item, youth who admitted to an offence were then asked in an open-ended question to explain circumstances that led to the most recent offence in each category.

The totals generated by the responses to each of the closed-ended questions revealed a large number of violent offences. An inspection of the raw frequency distributions for these various measures suggested a high degree of skewness. This condition stemmed from most respondents reporting a small number of offences, with a few reporting large numbers of offences. Data on the four offence types were aggregated to create a violent crime index.

Independent Variables

Information was obtained in the interviews on a range of subcultural, economic, and victimization variables hypothesized to be important in explaining the violent behaviour of street youth. To explore the effects of the street subculture, respondents were asked about the length of their homelessness, their criminal peers, and peer pressure, as well as their use of alcohol and drugs. To examine the effects of economic deprivation and reactions to structural conditions, respondents were queried about the length of their unemployment, their financial status, their anger over their unemployment, and whether they felt the social structure was fair. To explore the role of victimization on subjects' violent behaviour, they were asked to self-report how many times in the past year they had been the victims of a robbery, aggravated assault, and a common assault. Because we are examining different types of violent crime, it was decided to explore the effect of the various types of victimization on the various categories of violent behaviour. Finally, the youth's history of physical abuse within the family was determined. The youth were also asked in an open-ended question to describe any problems they encountered in their family.

FINDINGS

Street Subculture

Beginning with an examination of the effects of the street subculture and lifestyle variables, we find that peer influence has an unanticipated effect on a variety of violent behaviours. Those youth who reported that friends never or rarely pressured them to engage in criminal activities reported greater participation in robbery, aggravated assaults, and total violent crime net of the other predictors. However, the results also reveal that those youth who reported having more criminal peers also indicated greater participation in simple assaults and total violent crime. These findings suggest that there is a self-selection or mutual attraction of like-minded youth to form friendships. Reiss and Farrington (1991) note that there is a strong tendency for like-minded youth to have friends whose attitudes and behaviours are congruent with their own. If this is the case, there is little need to socially coerce others into criminal behaviour. Further, it is likely that on the street these youth are able to choose from a number of potential criminal peers. As Tremblay (1993) notes, a concentration of offenders increases the likelihood that a given offender will find other like offenders. Thus, violent offenders on the street should select one another as friends because of their similar conflict styles and their greater opportunities for contact and communication.

Reiss and Farrington (1991) also note that high-rate offenders tend to be criminal recruiters who take on the role of social instigator. Low-rate offenders are more likely to require pressure than are willing chronic offenders. Thus, they may recruit others for robberies and act as third parties in other situations that evolve into violence.

Although the quantitative data indicated little pressure to engage in violence, the qualitative data did suggest the presence of group norms regarding protection and guardianship. Many of the group fights described by respondents began as altercations between two disputants that escalated when youth from one group came to the aid of their friend, necessitating the inclusion of people from the other group. Similarly, there were situations where a number of youth attacked a single victim, which rallied respondents to enter the battles as guardians.

> Too many of the others so I joined in to even it up.
> Couple of buddies got into a fight. Some other people jumped in on the other side.
> I was ambushed, and my friends came to help.
> Jocks came up and jumped me, so my friends helped me out.

Responses also revealed that group altercations provided these youth with avenues for retribution to avenge the victimization of friends. Group members who had been robbed or who had been physically assaulted, often by more than one person, enlisted the support of their peers, and together they sought out the offenders and their groups in an attempt to even up the score.

> Somebody rolled one of my friends, so we beat the shit out of them.
> My friend got rolled.

> Some people jumped a friend of mine.
> Somebody beat up one of our friends.

Finally, in their responses, the members indicated that group rivalries, including territorial and turf disputes, provided the impetus for recent group altercations. The idea that these youth would bind together and do battle for each other again suggests certain normative expectations concerning violence for group members.

> Long hairs against the skins.
> Against some bangers before NIA.
> Downtown versus Bonnie Doon.
> Turf, Northside.

These findings suggest that although the youth under study may not acknowledge peer pressure to engage in violent activities, they do enter into peer alliances and appear to give normative assent to requirements for violent participation in defence of their peers. As Thrasher (1927) and Suttles (1968) note, delinquent street groups are often formed to defend against conflict (see also Kornhauser 1978).

Moving to other aspects of the street lifestyle, we find that the experience of homelessness is significantly related to respondents' violent behaviours. The longer these youth had been without a fixed address, the greater their involvement in robbery and total violent crime in general. Spending time on the street may isolate these youth from conventional society as they become immersed in a street lifestyle. This immersion appears to provide them with access to criminal peers perhaps while breaking down standards of behaviour and restrictions on the use of violence.

Furthermore, there may be cultural expectations of violence on the street. Although our quantitative analysis does not do justice to this idea, the qualitative data indicate that a great deal of street youth violence appears to be guided by rules of honour and retributive justice, characteristics often noted by researchers who argue for the existence of a subculture of violence (Horowitz 1983; Wolfgang and Ferracuti 1967).

If a respondent was wronged in terms of business dealings or derogations of self, he was expected to avenge this with violence. For example, when asked to explain the circumstances leading up to their most recent robbery, many youth indicated that unpaid debts led to robbery episodes. On the street, youth who were owed money, particularly for fronted drugs, forced victims to settle accounts by robbing them.

> Screwed me over for a large amount of money.
> I got ripped off. Justice must be served.
> Ripped me off. Let him know you don't fuck me around.
> Ripped me off. Show him you can't have that.

This theme of being owed money or being "ripped off" also figured prominently in explanations of the circumstances surrounding the recent aggravated assaults. Failed business transactions appeared to lead respondents to exact retribution for their losses through physical injury. Retribution for other transgressions, including informing on respondents, also figured prominently as explanations for extreme violent behaviour.

Another popular explanation provided by respondents for seriously injuring others (aggravated assault) revolved around violations of honour and name calling. People who verbally offended respondents with derogatory or offensive names were attacked so severely that respondents believed their victims required medical attention.

> Some guy called me a goof, so he deserved it.
> 'Cause a guy called me a fucking Indian.
> Name calling. Called me a goof.
> Called me a homeless bastard.

In terms of explanations for recent simple assaults, the violation of honour again appears to be an important impetus for violent reactions. In this case, respondents added "the look" and people "kicking attitude" and not showing the proper respect to the list of stimuli that drew out violent reactions. Thus, whereas verbal assaults led to severe attacks resulting in victims needing medical attention, visual assaults provoke less severe attacks.

> The guy had been kicking attitude, so I solved his problem.
> I just didn't like him. His attitude. "I'm big shit."
> The guy looked at me, so I decided to punch him in the mouth.
> Just looked at me funny. I snapped and jumped on him.

Together this suggests that on the street, there may exist a subculture of violence where certain verbal and visual stimuli are viewed as provocative and reacted to with violence. We would expect that those who have spent the most time on the street would be the most vulnerable for adopting these cultural expectations existing on the street (Regoli and Hewitt 1991).

It is also true that spending a great deal of time on the street presents the respondents abundant opportunities to witness different styles of conflict management. They may learn from being on the street that violence is the method most often used to settle conflict. Furthermore, the experience of living on the street provides these youth with ample opportunities to attack attractive targets. Being on the street exposes street youth to more potential victims from which they can pick and choose according to risk and desired items.

As full participants in the street lifestyle (Inciardi, Horowitz, and Pottieger 1993), street youth are heavy users of alcohol and/or drugs. However, alcohol emerges as a significant predictor of only simple assaults, and drug use is not a significant predictor of street youth violence. The failure of drug and alcohol use to reach significance might be explained by the minimal variation in these variables due to this population's heavy substance use. This makes the significance of alcohol use in the assault model more impressive. Although the literature remains unclear about the physiological effects of these substances on violent behaviour, we might speculate that these youth exhibit violent responses while using alcohol in certain settings (Zinberg 1984) and under certain conditions. For example, the simple assault question asks, "How many times have you got into a fight for the hell of it?" This suggests that alcohol use may be linked to less serious forms of recreational violence.

The qualitative data support this speculation. When asked about their involvement in common assaults, respondents often simply indicated that they got into a fight because they were "drunk." This type of response did not regularly emerge in their explanations of other types of violence.

> I was drunk, I wanted to fight.
> I was drunk, so the first person I see.
> Just drunk and stupid in a bar.
> When I get pissed.

Economic Deprivation

Moving from our exploration of the street subcultural lifestyle to the role of economic deprivation in the generation of street youth violence, we discover that poverty is consistently an important predictor. Respondents lacking financial resources were more likely to have high robbery, aggravated assault, common assault, group fight, and overall violence totals. If the others who inhabit the area of the city where the study took place suffer from similar economic situations and react in the same fashion to these situations, it is likely that our respondents are living in a milieu of angry aggression (Bernard 1990). Therefore, conditions regarding a street subculture of violence should be tempered somewhat by the acknowledgment that a number of the described violent behaviours are the result of living under negative economic conditions. In fact, length of time on the street probably reflects to some extent the economic deprivation experienced by these youth.

In the qualitative data, many respondents indicated that they participated in fights to help relieve stress and frustration that is possibly related to their poverty. Some of the respondents indicated that getting into a fight was also "something to do." Thus, for those without disposable income for leisure, violence provided a recreational avenue.

> Stress relief.
> For fun. Let some frustration off.
> Just for something to do.
> Something to do.

The qualitative data also indicate that a lack of financial resources provides an important impetus for more utilitarian violence as well. Respondents indicated that the bulk of their robberies were to obtain money and other material articles.

> Just for fucking things, just for fucking money.
>
> Needed money really really bad to get a hotel room to sleep.
>
> I was in need.
>
> Get clothes and money.

In addition to a lack of income, attitudes toward economic deprivation also proved to be a significant predictor of some violent behaviour. Those youth who perceived the social structure to be blocked were more likely to rob people. From a traditional strain perspective, youth who thought they could not get a fair shake in the legitimate labour market used violent, illegitimate means to secure monetary resources. Thus, the lack of resources and perceptions of inequality appear to stimulate impulses expressed as utilitarian violence.

We do not find the length of the respondents' unemployment to be a significant predictor of violence net of income. This likely stems from the fact that the average respondent had been without legitimate employment for eight out of the previous twelve months. Therefore, there is little variation in most respondents' employment circumstances.

Victimization

In our hypotheses, it was also recognized that risky lifestyles expose actors to victimization, and this experience might increase offending behaviour. It appears that being the victim of an aggravated assault in particular, or to a lesser degree a simple assault, helps to explain a number of violent behaviours. Those youth who had been victims of aggravated assaults were more likely to have participated in aggravated assaults and group fights and to have accumulated a greater number of overall violent behaviours, whereas the victims of common assaults tended to have higher robbery and aggravated assault totals. This suggests that victimization on the street is related to serious violent behaviour. Victimizations can lead to retaliation in both the group and individual setting. Further, respondents may be learning from their victimization experiences on the street that extreme violence is an effective method of dispute settlement and conflict management. Finally, the environment of angry aggression may have left these youth seeking out their victimizers to settle the score regardless of learning experiences and subcultural expectations.

We must also acknowledge that heavy involvement by youth in violent activity may have led to others retaliating against, and injuring, them. Similarly, assaultive behaviours require more than one person, so that the risk of injury in a dispute despite being the initial offender (striking the first blow) is at a maximum (Lauritsen, Sampson, and Laub 1991; Sampson and Lauritsen 1990). Thus, these offenders may have seriously injured someone in the past and then been grievously damaged in return, or they may have received their injuries in the course of battle in various individual and gang fights. Alternatively, they may have been seriously injured and sought out, either alone or with peers, to injure others. In sum, the street provides the social experiences that guide respondents' behaviour as well as the locales, environments, and situations where violence is more likely.

Finally, the experience of familial physical abuse is related to a range of offences including robbery, aggravated assault, and the total violent crime index. Youth who have experienced violent victimization in the home may be more likely to model this type of behaviour and use violence as a method of gaining compliance and seriously injuring others. An indication of the impact these experiences had on the respondents is revealed in the graphic depictions of their violent home life. These episodes were not the accidental result of a parent who "inadvertently" uses too much force in physically disciplining the child. The events were serial and extremely intense and displayed a savageness that could only serve to physically damage the child. This appears to have led to long-term harm.

> Pretty much my dad beating me up and that. Basically treating me like shit.
> Yes there was problems. If we got along it was a shot in the mouth and a good boot fuck.
> Just my dad was a problem. Physical abuse. Bounced me off the walls.
> The only serious problem was my stepdad . . . My stepdad used to beat the shit out of me all the time. I couldn't beat him so . . .

Thus, a history of violent victimization seems to be a fertile breeding ground for the creation of violent offenders. This abusive experience appears to provide these youth with models of behaviour that they then replicate on the street.

CONCLUSION

Our results reveal that aspects of the street subcultural lifestyle, economic deprivation, and victimization work together to explain street youth violence. For the index of total violence, being the victim of family abuse or serious assault, having few financial resources, spending more time on the street, and associating with criminal friends results in more violence.

However, the results also show that different combinations of the street subculture, economic deprivation, and victimization help to explain the different types of violent behaviour. Robbery is best predicted by spending more time on the street, having few financial resources, perceiving a lack of legitimate opportunities, and experiencing victimization in the home as well as on the street. Because robbery is usually a utilitarian or instrumental offence committed to obtain money, it is not surprising that several of these predictors reflect economic factors. Lack of income can be at least temporarily solved by robbing others. Youth who believe the social system is stacked against them can respond with violent means to obtain financial rewards denied them by the legitimate or conventional opportunity structure. Lengthy homelessness can increase the extent of material deprivation experienced by these street youth for whom robbery is a means of survival. These youth also learn from their abusive home experiences that using force is a practical and effective method of gaining compliance, increasing the odds that they will use coercion to gain financial or material rewards.

Low income is also the only consistent significant predictor across the four types of violent crime. This finding lends support to the view that extreme or absolute deprivation can lead to a variety of serious violent behaviours. The average available legal income reported by respondents was $328, and the level of state support for a single employable was $470. This suggests that even minimal amounts of legal financial resources might be able to negate the influences of deprivation on violence. However, the qualitative data suggest that such motives as retribution also play a role even in robbery and that the stresses of a life in poverty are also important in explaining nonutilitarian violence.

Predictive accuracy was weakest for group fights. In addition to low income, the only other significant predictor was serious street victimization. However, qualitative data indicate that youth with similar conflict management strategies enter into peer networks that stress norms of protection and guardianship. These norms required street youth to engage in battle over turf and group identity and to retaliate for the victimization of group members, while at the same time providing for guardianship that minimizes their own victimization. Group conflicts, then, can be distinguished from the other types of violence by the centrality of concerns over territoriality, protection, and group identity.

Aggravated assault is heavily influenced by the experience of serious street victimization and abusive family relationships. The experience of victimization in the home and on the street, along with the stresses of poverty, appear to be vital to an understanding of these serious violent behaviours. Highly injurious violence appears to be linked to retaliation and retribution in response to violence or status threats and perceived violations of honour. The experience of violence can lead to an escalation in violence, and participation in violence can in turn lead to victimization. It is likely that youth learn from these experiences that violence is a method of conflict resolution and that seriously injuring harm doers is an acceptable mode of resolving disputes.

In contrast, simple assaults do not appear to involve the experience of victimization. Rather, involvement in simple assault is best explained by alcohol use, association with criminal peers, and the stresses of poverty. It appears that street youth often become involved in these more minor incidents of violence for recreational purposes when using alcohol, or to "blow off some steam." Drinking and fighting in the company of like-minded peers appears to characterize those street youth reporting more involvement in simple assaults.

We have attempted to go beyond previous research on youth violence by focusing on a population "missing" (Hagan and McCarthy 1992) from traditional data sources and exploring the conditions, experiences, and aspects of life on the street that can lead to violent crime. Although the street subculture, economic deprivation, and violent victimization are elements in the explanation of street violence, our research has shown that no single explanation will suffice for several different types of violence. As expected, economic factors are predominant in the case of robbery, whereas elements of a culture of violence acquired from experience with violence in the home and on the street are more applicable to group fights and serious assaults. Minor violence, on the other hand, appears to be somewhat more spontaneous and linked to excessive drinking with similarly situated peers. Because violence itself is not uniform, neither are its explanations. Future research should explore further the distinctive causes of different types of violent crime, using both at-risk and conventional samples of youth.

STUDY QUESTIONS

1. *To what extent were the male street youth interviewed by Baron and Hartnagel involved in committing particular kinds of violent crime?*
2. *How do Baron and Hartnagel explain the frequent involvement of street youth as both perpetrators and victims of violent crime?*
3. *How does Baron and Hartnagel's research move beyond the findings of earlier research on street youth and criminal violence?*

REFERENCES

Ball-Rokeach, Sandra J. 1973. "Values and Violence: A Test of the Subculture of Violence Thesis." *American Sociological Review 31*: 736–49.

Bankston, William B., and H. David Allen. 1980. "Rural Social Areas and Patterns of Homicide: An Analysis of Lethal Violence in Louisiana." *Rural Sociology 45*: 223–37.

Baron, Stephen W. 1989a. "The Canadian West Coast Punk Subculture: A Field Study." *Canadian Journal of Sociology 14*(3): 289–316.

———. 1989b. "Resistance and Its Consequences: The Street Culture of Punks." *Youth and Society 21*: 207–37.

———. 1995. "Serious Offenders." In James Creechan and Robert A. Silverman, eds., *Canadian Delinquency*, 135–47. Toronto: Prentice-Hall.

Baron, Stephen W., and Timothy F. Hartnagel. 1997. "Attributions, Affect, and Crime: Street Youths' Reactions to Unemployment." *Criminology 35*(3): 409–34.

Bernard, Thomas J. 1990. "Angry Aggression among the 'Truly Disadvantaged.' " *Criminology 28*: 73–95.

Blau, Judith R., and Peter M. Blau. 1982. "The Costs of Inequality: Metropolitan Structure and Violent Crime." *American Sociological Review 47*: 114–29.

Box, Steven. 1987. *Recession, Crime and Punishment*. Basingstoke, UK: Macmillan.

Box, Steven, and Chris Hale. 1985. "Unemployment, Imprisonment and Prison Overcrowding." *Contemporary Crises 9*: 209–28.

Braithwaite, John. 1979. *Inequality, Crime and Public Policy*. London: Routledge & Kegan Paul.

Brennan, Tim, David Huizinga, and Delbert S. Elliott. 1978. *The Social Psychology of Runaways*. Toronto: Lexington.

Caputo, Tullio, and Collen Ryan. 1991. *The Police Response to Youth at Risk*. Ottawa: Solicitor General.

Cloward, Richard A., and Lloyd E. Ohlin. 1961. *Delinquency and Opportunity*. New York: Free Press.

Cohen, Lawrence E., and Marcus Felson. 1979. "Social Change and Crime Rate Trends." *American Sociological Review 44*: 588–607.

Curtis, Lynn A. 1975. *Violence, Race, and Culture*. Lexington, MA: D.C. Heath.

Danziger, Sheldon, and David Wheeler. 1975. "The Economics of Crime: Punishment or Income Redistribution." *Review of Social Economy 33*: 113–31.

Desroches, Fredrick J. 1995. *Force and Fear: Robbery in Canada*. Toronto: Nelson.

———. 1997. *Behind the Bars: Experiences in Crime*. Toronto: Canadian Scholars Press.

Doerner, William G. 1979. "The Violent World of Johnny Reb: An Attitudinal Analysis of the Regional 'Culture of Violence' Thesis." *Sociological Forum 2*: 61–71.

Elliott, Delbert S. 1994. "Serious Violent Offenders: Onset, Developmental Course, and Termination." *Criminology 32*(1): 1–22.

Elliott, Delbert S., David Huizinga, and Suzanne Ageton. 1985. *Explaining Delinquency and Drug Use*. Beverly Hills, CA: Sage.

Fagan, Jeffrey A. 1990. "Intoxication and Aggression." In Michael Tonry and James Q. Wilson, eds., *Drugs and Crime, Crime and Justice: A Review of Research*, 241–320. Chicago: University of Chicago Press.

Fagan, Jeffrey A., and Sally Jo Jones. 1984. "Toward a Theoretical Model for Intervention with Violent Juvenile Offenders." In Robert Mathias, Paul DeMuro, and Richard S. Allinson, eds., *Violent Juvenile Offenders: An Anthology*, 53–70. San Francisco: National Council on Crime and Delinquency.

Fagan, Jeffrey A., Elizabeth S. Piper, and Yu-Teh Cheng. 1987. "Contributions of Victimization to Delinquency in Inner Cities." *Journal of Criminal Law and Criminology 78*: 586–609.

Fagan, Jeffrey A., Elizabeth S. Piper, and Melinda Moore. 1986. "Violent Delinquents and Urban Youths." *Criminology 24*: 439–71.

Fagan, Jeffrey A., and Sandra Wexler. 1987. "Family Origins of Violent Delinquents." *Criminology 25*: 643–69.

Farrington, David P. 1978. "Family Backgrounds and Aggressive Youths." In Lionel A. Hersov, M. Berger, and David Shaffer, eds., *Aggression and Anti-Social Behaviour in Childhood and Adolescence*, 73–93. Oxford: Pergamon.

Felson, Marcus, and Lawrence E. Cohen. 1980. "Human Ecology and Crime: A Routine Activities Approach." *Human Ecology 4*: 389–406.

Gastil, R.D. 1971. "Homicide and a Regional Culture of Violence." *American Sociological Review 36*: 412–37.

Gullotta, Thomas P. 1979. "Leaving Home: Family Relationships of the Runaway Child." *Social Casework 60*: 111–14.

Hackney, Sheldon. 1969. "Southern Violence." *American Historical Review 39*: 906–25.

Hagan, Frank E. 1993. *Research Methods in Criminal Justice and Criminology*, 3rd ed. Toronto: Maxwell Macmillan Canada.

Hagan, John, and Bill McCarthy. 1992. "Streetlife and Delinquency." *British Journal of Sociology 43*(4): 533–61.

Hartnagel, Timothy F. 1990. "Under/Unemployment and Crime among Youth: A Longitudinal Study of Recent High School Graduates." Discussion Paper 23, University of Alberta, Centre for Criminological Research.

Hartstone, Eliot, and Karen V. Hansen. 1984. "The Violent Juvenile Offender: An Empirical Portrait." In Robert Mathias, Paul DeMuro, and Richard S. Allinson, eds., *Violent Juvenile Offenders: An Anthology*, 83–112. San Francisco: National Council on Crime and Delinquency.

Hawkins, Darnell F. 1983. "Black and White Homicide Differentials: Alternatives to an Inadequate Theory." *Criminal Justice and Behaviour 10*: 407–40.

Horowitz, Ruth. 1983. *Honor and the American Dream*. New Brunswick, NJ: Rutgers University Press.

Horwitz, Allan V. 1984. "The Economy and Social Pathology." *Annual Review of Sociology 12*: 109–58.

Hotaling, Gerald T., Murray A. Straus, and Alan J. Lincoln. 1989. "Intrafamily Violence, and Crime and Violence Outside the Family." In Michael Tonry, ed., *Crime and Justice: A Review of Research*, vol. 11, 315–75. Chicago: University of Chicago Press.

Huff-Corzine, Lin, Jay Corzine, and David C. Moore. 1986. "Southern Exposure: Deciphering the South's Influence on Homicide Rates." *Social Forces 64*: 906–24.

Inciardi, James A., Ruth Horowitz, and Anne E. Pottieger. 1993. *Street Kids, Street Drugs, Street Crime*. Belmont, CA: Wadsworth.

Inciardi, James A., Anne E. Pottieger, Mary A. Forney, Dale D. Chitwood, and Duanne C. McBride. 1991. "Prostitution, IV Drug Use, and Sex-for-Crack among Serious Delinquents: Risks for HIV Infection." *Criminology 29*(2): 221–35.

Inciardi, James A., and Brian R. Russe. 1977. "Professional Thieves and Drugs." *International Journal of Addictions 12*: 1087–95.

Janus, Mark-David, Arlene McCromick, Ann W. Burgess, and Carol Hartman. 1987. *Adolescent Runaways*. Toronto: Lexington.

Jensen, Gary F., and David Brownfield. 1986. "Gender, Lifestyles, and Victimization: Beyond Routine Activity." *Violence and Victims 1*: 85–99.

Johnson, Bruce D., Paul J. Goldstein, Edward Preble, James Schmeiler, Douglas S. Lipton, Barry Spunt, and Thomas Miller. 1985. *Taking Care of Business: The Economics of Crime by Heroin Abusers*. Lexington, MA: Lexington.

Kennedy, Leslie W., and Stephen W. Baron. 1993 "Routine Activities and a Subculture of Violence: A Study of Violence on the Street." *Journal of Research in Crime and Delinquency 30*(1): 88–113.

Kennedy, Leslie W., and David R. Forde. 1990a. "Routine Activities and Crime: An Analysis of Victimization in Canada." *Criminology 28*: 137–52.

———. 1990b. "Risky Lifestyles and Dangerous Results: Routine Activities and Exposure to Crime." *Sociology and Social Research 74*(4): 208–11.

Kornhauser, Ruth R. 1978. *Social Sources of Delinquency*. Chicago: University of Chicago Press.

Kufeldt, Kathleen, and Margaret Nimmo. 1987a. "Kids on the Street They Have Something to Say: Survey of Runaway and Homeless Youth." *Journal of Child Care 3*: 53–61.

———. 1987b. "Youth on the Street: Abuse and Neglect in the Eighties." *Child Abuse and Neglect 11*: 531–43.

Lauritsen, Janet L., Robert J. Sampson, and John Laub. 1991. "The Link between Offending and Victimization among Adolescents." *Criminology 29*: 265–91.

Loftin, Colin, and R. Hill. 1974. "Regional Subculture and Homicide." *American Sociological Review 39*: 714–24.

MacLeod, Jay. 1987. *Ain't No Makin' It*. Boulder, CO: Westview.

Maxfield, Michael G., and Earl Babbie. 1995. *Research Methods for Criminal Justice and Criminology*. Toronto: Wadsworth.

McCarthy, Bill. 1990. "Life on the Streets: Serious Theft, Drug Selling, and Prostitution among Homeless Youth." Ph.D. dissertation, University of Toronto, Department of Sociology.

McCarthy, Bill, and John Hagan. 1991. "Homelessness: A Criminogenic Situation?" *British Journal of Criminology 31*(4): 393–410.

———. 1992a. "Mean Streets: The Theoretical Significance of Situational Delinquency among Homeless Youths." *American Sociological Review 98*(3): 597–627.

———. 1992b. "Surviving on the Street: The Experience of Homeless Youth." *Journal of Adolescent Research 7*(4): 412–30.

———. 1995. "Getting into Street Crime: The Structure and Process of Criminal Embeddedness." *Social Science Research 24*(1): 63–95.

McCord, Joan. 1979. "Some Child-Rearing Antecedents of Criminal Behaviour in Adult Men." *Journal of Personality and Social Psychology 37*: 1477–86.

McCullagh, John, and Mary Greco. 1990. *Servicing Street Youth: A Feasibility Study*. Toronto: Children's Aid Society.

Merton, Robert K. 1957. *Social Theory and Social Structure*. Glencoe, IL: Free Press.

Messner, Steven F. 1983. "Regional and Racial Effects on the Urban Homicide Rate: The Subculture of Violence Revisited." *American Journal of Sociology 88*: 997–1007.

Messner, Steven F., and Kenneth Tardiff. 1986. "Economic Inequality and Levels of Homicide: An Analysis of Urban Neighbourhoods." *Criminology 24*: 297–317.

Palenski, Joseph E. 1984. *Kids Who Run Away*. Saratoga, CA: R & E.

Pearlin, Leonard I., Morton A. Lieberman, Elizabeth G. Menaghan, and Joseph T. Mullan. 1981. "The Stress Process." *Journal of Health and Social Behaviour 22*: 337–56.

Radford, Joyce L., Alan J.C. King, and Wendy K. Warren. 1989. *Street Youth and AIDS*. Ottawa: Health and Welfare Canada.

Regoli, Robert M., and John D. Hewitt. 1991. *Delinquency in Society*. New York: McGraw-Hill.

Reiss, Albert J., and David P. Farrington. 1991. "Advancing Knowledge about Co-Offending: Results from a Prospective Longitudinal Survey of London Males." *Journal of Criminal Law and Criminology 82*: 360–95.

Rosenfeld, Richard. 1986. "Urban Crime Rates: Effects of Inequality, Welfare Dependency, Region, and Race." In J. Byrne and Robert Sampson, eds., *The Social Ecology of Crime*, 116–30. New York: Springer-Verlag.

Rothman, Jack. 1991. *Runaway and Homeless Youth*. New York: Longman.

Sampson, Robert J. 1985. "Structural Sources of Variation in Race-Age-Specific Rates of Offending across Major U.S. Cities." *Criminology 23*: 647–73.

Sampson, Robert J., and Janet L. Lauritsen. 1990. "Deviant Lifestyles, Proximity to Crime, and the Offender–Victim Link in Personal Violence." *Journal of Research in Crime and Delinquency 27*: 110–39.

Sampson, Robert J., and John Wooldredge. 1987. "Linking the Micro- and Macro-Level Dimensions of Lifestyles Routine Activity and Opportunity Models of Predatory Victimization." *Journal of Quantitative Criminology 3*: 371–93.

Sedgely, Jeanie, and Dale Lund. 1979. "Self-Reported Beatings and Subsequent Tolerance for Violence." *Review of Public Data Use 7*: 30–38.

Siegal, Larry J., and Joseph J. Senna. 1994. *Juvenile Delinquency: Theory Practice and Law,* 5th ed. New York: West.

Singer, Simon. 1981. "Homogeneous Victim–Offender Populations: A Review of Some Research Implications." *Journal of Criminal Law and Criminology 72*: 779–88.

———. 1986. "Victims of Serious Violence and Their Criminal Behaviour: Subcultural Theory and Beyond." *Violence and Victims 1*: 61–69.

Smart, Reginald G., Edward M. Adlaf, Karen M. Porterfield, and Margaret D. Canale. 1990. *Drugs, Youth and the Street*. Toronto: Addiction Research Foundation.

Smith, Carolyn, and Terrence P. Thornberry. 1995. "The Relationship between Childhood Maltreatment and Adolescent Involvement in Delinquency." *Criminology 33*(4): 451–82.

Sorrells, James M. 1977. "Kids Who Kill." *Crime & Delinquency 23*: 312–20.

Stack, Steven. 1984. "Income Inequality and Property Crime: A Cross National Analysis of Relative Deprivation Theory." *Criminology 22*: 222–57.

Statistics Canada. 1994. *Canadian Crime Statistics 1993*. Ottawa: Canadian Centre for Justice Statistics.

Straus, Murray A. 1985. "Family Training in Crime and Violence." In Alan J. Lincoln and Murray A. Straus, eds., *Crime and the Family*, 164–85. Springfield, IL: Charles C. Thomas.

Suttles, Gerald. 1968. *Social Order of the Slum*. Chicago: University of Chicago Press.

Thrasher, Frederick M. 1927. *The Gang*. Chicago: University of Chicago Press.

Tinklenberg, J.R., P. Murphy, P.L. Murphy, and A. Pfefferbaum. 1981. "Drugs and Criminal Assaults by Adolescents: A Replication Study." *Journal of Psychoactive Drugs 13*: 277–87.

Tremblay, Pierre. 1993. "Searching for Suitable Co-Offenders." In Ronald V. Clarke and Marcus Felson, eds., *Routine Activity and Rational Choice*, vol. 5, *Advances in Criminological Theory*, 17–36. New Brunswick, NJ: Transaction.

Webber, Marlene. 1991. *Street Kids: The Tragedy of Canada's Runaways*. Toronto: University of Toronto Press.

White, Helen Raskin, Robert J. Pandina, and Randy L. LaGrange. 1987. "Longitudinal Predictors of Serious Substance Abuse and Delinquency." *Criminology 25*: 715–40.

Widom, Cathy S. 1989. "Child Abuse, Neglect, and Violent Criminal Behaviour." *Criminology 27*: 251–71.

Williams, Kirk. 1984. "Economic Sources of Homicide. Re-estimating the Effects of Poverty and Inequality." *American Sociological Review 49*: 283–89.

Wolfgang, Marvin E., and Franco Ferracuti. 1967. *The Subculture of Violence*. London: Tavistock.

Wooden, Wayne S. 1995. *Renegade Kids, Suburban Outlaws*. Toronto: Wadsworth.

Wright, Kevin N. 1981. *Crime and Criminal Justice in a Declining Economy*. Cambridge, MA: Oelgeschlager, Gunn & Hain.

Zinberg, Norman E. 1984. *Drug, Set, and Setting: The Social Bases of Controlled Use*. New Haven, CT: Yale University Press.

CHAPTER NINE

The Selling of Innocence: The Gestalt of Danger in the Lives of Youth Prostitutes

BERNARD SCHISSEL
KARI FEDEC
University of Saskatchewan

Cruelty inflicted upon children, especially in the form of sexual exploitation, has the power to generate passionate public disapproval. Despite public indignation, the sex business continues to flourish. Sex has become a multibillion-dollar industry, and today, children are bought, sold, and traded like any other mass-produced article (Sachs 1994). Various inquiries and studies have been commissioned at both the federal and local levels (Badgley 1984; Fraser 1985; Brannigan, Knafla, and Levy 1989; Brannigan and Caputo 1993; Mayor's Task Force 1996; McCarthy 1996), as social policy proponents continue to focus their attentions on the centuries-old problem of child prostitution. But the dilemma they face in addressing the exploitation of children from a causal paradigm is that the majority of research has focused on the factors that force youth to become and stay in the sex trade. What is missing, in a sensitive and complex understanding of the youth sex trade, is a focus on the detrimental effects that young people's participation in such a trade has on their overall well-being, not only on their prospects for escaping a life on the streets but also on their prospects for actual physical survival.

Previous research has addressed the general state of danger in which street prostitutes live (Badgley 1984; Canadian Panel on Violence Against Women 1993; Lowman and Fraser 1995; Boritch 1997; McNairn 1997); much of the focus for youth has been on violence by pimps and, for adults, on violence on the streets. Further, recent research on adult prostitution suggests that, in some cases, prostitution is a profession of choice and that street prostitute cultures develop occupational practices that minimize the dangers of

Source: Bernard Schissel and Kari Fedec, "The Selling of Innocence: The Gestalt of Danger in the Lives of Youth Prostitutes," *Canadian Journal of Criminology* (January 1999): 33–56.

the sex trade (Shaver 1996; Fraser 1985). While these foci are important, they tend to circumvent the direct danger to well-being that the sex trade poses to children and youth. In cities like Saskatoon and Regina, where youth prostitution is not routine and there is not a well-developed youth sex trade culture, the conventions of protection are generally absent. The dangers for such children and youth go well beyond those described in contemporary research.

We focus, therefore, on two dimensions of youth prostitution: first, on previously identified factors that directly influence youth involvement in prostitution as an empirical test of the causation literature, and second, on the effects that being involved in the sex trade has on multiple dimensions of well-being. It is our intention to document and test an oft-forgotten reality of research on youth prostitution: that involvement in the sex trade has dire consequences for an individual's physical, emotional, and social well-being.

HYPOTHETICAL ISSUES RELATING TO YOUTH PROSTITUTION

Family Trauma

The majority of recent literature concerning the topic of youth involvement in prostitution revolves around two issues: runaway behaviour and child sexual abuse as the most significant precursors to involvement in the sex trade (Badgley 1984; Lowman 1987; Seng 1989; Chesney-Lind and Shelden 1992; Van Brunschot 1995; Brannigan 1996). Although child sexual abuse is regarded by some as a direct link to youth engagement in prostitution (Brannigan, Knafla, and Levy 1989; Van Brunschot 1995; McCarthy 1996; Boritch 1997), runaway behaviour is believed by some theorists to be an intervening or mediating variable (Seng 1989). In an attempt to escape a home where parents do not seem to care or where long-term conflict occurs, some children may view the streets as their only option for survival as they seek to obtain food, shelter, and financial capital. Furthermore, a large proportion of youth who run away do so to escape sexual abuse at home (Chesney-Lind and Shelden 1992; Webber 1991). Once on the street, their only means of survival is routine engagement in criminal activities such as prostitution. According to Webber, "ironically, they run to save themselves, yet typically end up in as much, if not more, trouble than they were in at home. While most kids come to the street as victims, many can survive only by becoming perpetrators of crime" (Webber 1991: 31). The grim reality is that "their lives on the streets are almost always even more abusive in nature because they often become trapped in the sordid trafficking of children for sexual gratification" (Chesney-Lind and Shelden 1992: 37). We hypothesize that runaway behaviour does directly influence prostitution involvement; runaway kids end up in conditions that are conducive to engagement in the sex trade.

The direct causal link between childhood physical and sexual abuse and the decision to enter the sex trade has been well documented (McMullen 1987;

Seng 1989; Simons and Whitbeck 1991; Chesney-Lind and Shelden 1992; Van Brunschot 1995; Boritch 1997). The basic thesis is that childhood victimization, especially in terms of sexual abuse, leads to the future sexual exploitation of youth who have been made vulnerable to sexual advances. According to McMullen (1987), there is a psychological connection between child sexual abuse and prostitution: when youth have been abused in the past by family members, they are more likely to believe that strangers can use and abuse them also. The reasoning is that abusive families normalize abusive treatment in the minds of victimized youth. Furthermore, as a result of their sexual abuse, they may perceive themselves to be debased sexual objects. They often hold a "distorted image of their own bodies," which may "lead them to expect that their worth will only be acknowledged when they permit sexual access" (Boyer and James 1982, quoted in Chesney-Lind and Shelden 1992: 38). In effect, they may see themselves as commodities that can be bought and sold at the whim of those who have the financial capital (Simons and Whitbeck 1991; Boyer and James 1982). In addition, as they are used as sexual objects by men, they learn that they have the ability to manipulate men through sexual contact (McGinnes 1994). Because of socio-cultural factors, the level of abuse and its damaging effects may not be experienced equally by all prostitutes. For example, Lowman states that First Nations girls face many of the same problems that other teen prostitutes experience, but they encounter them in accentuated form. Not only do they enter into the sex trade at younger ages, they are also "more likely to be the victims of both family violence and trick or pimp violence" (Lowman 1986: 36). We argue, as a result, that childhood physical and sexual abuse are strong precursors to involvement in prostitution (McCarthy 1996; Chesney-Lind and Shelden 1992), and the effects of abuse on involvement in prostitution differ across racial categories.

Personal and Education Success

Since many of the youth who are involved in the sex trade have less than adequate educational backgrounds, their access to the job market is restricted, often positioning prostitution as the only logical way by which runaways have the ability to secure an income (Badgley 1984; Gibson-Ainyette, Templer, and Brown 1988; Seng 1989; Boritch 1997). We argue that poor educational achievement is due primarily to the fact that these youth have dropped out of school at an early age and that lack of educational achievement is coincident with negative attitudes toward education (Badgley 1984; Sullivan 1987). Because the majority of these young people have negative attitudes toward school, their escape from the street is jeopardized, for they have no means to obtain the marketable skills that will secure employment. We test to see if indifference to education and low educational achievement foster engagement in prostitution-related activities.

As related issues, personal capabilities may influence decisions about career choices and life chances. The developmental psychology literature in criminology is inundated with research that links abilities like self-esteem and social skills to conventional success (Hill et al. 1996; Campagna and Poffenberger 1988; Boyer and James 1982). Personal competencies and adequate self-concepts affect life outcomes either directly (as matters of personal empowerment) or indirectly through occupational and educational success. The reasoning is that such personal characteristics ultimately affect choices about engaging in conventional avenues of support or in unconventional activities like the sex trade.

High-Risk Behaviour, Victimization, and Self-Injury

The incidence of drug use and addiction (including alcohol as well as other illegal drugs) is inordinately high among street prostitutes (Shaver 1993; Boritch 1997). One explanation for this is that substance abuse causes prostitution when youth turn to alcohol and drugs as a way of dealing with stressful life problems such as coping with prior physical and sexual abuse. In order to support a drug habit that helps them cope with life, they turn to prostitution as a means of financial support (Brannigan, Knafla, and Levy 1989; Gibson-Ainyette, Templer, and Brown 1988; Inciardi et al. 1991). In contradistinction, it is also plausible that some prostitutes use drugs and alcohol as an escape, to help them endure the humiliation and negative consequences of their work (Fraser 1985; Lowman 1987; Lau 1989; Inciardi et al. 1991; Heinrich 1995). We analyze substance abuse and prostitution as coterminous and hypothesize that substance abuse is associated with youth involvement in the sex trade.

We are also concerned in this research with exploring the psychologically and physically damaging effects of the sexual exploitation of youth. We argue that self-injurious dispositions like suicidal thoughts are associated with involvement in prostitution (Seng 1989; McMullen 1987; Griffin and Sheehan 1994). The reasoning is that children and youth are deeply traumatized by their experiences on the streets, and perhaps due to despair or humiliation, are prone to suicide. We hypothesize that involvement in prostitution increases the chance of suicidal thoughts and actual suicide attempts.

We extend this analysis by investigating whether the trauma of life in the sex trade leads to other forms of high-risk and self-injurious behaviour, specifically slashing and teen pregnancy. Slashing has been studied primarily in the context of women in prison. The conventional wisdom is that the psychic damage of prison isolation, especially isolation from family, compels some women inmates to self-injure in an attempt to mask their emotional pain (Boritch 1997; Schissel 1995; Faith 1993). Using the same reasoning, we test whether youth prostitutes engage in the same emotion-masking behaviour.

We also analyze the sexual risks that youth in the sex trade take by testing the effects of prostitution on pregnancy. Unprotected sex is a valuable commodity in the sex trade and the highest profits are obtained from the prostitution of young girls who are willing to engage in unprotected sex (Chesney-Lind and Shelden 1992; Sachs 1994; Nyland 1995). We measure the exposure to the dangers of unprotected sex by analyzing whether female youth prostitutes have a higher incidence of pregnancy than other youth in the survey. We do not have measures of incidence of sexually transmitted diseases, and, therefore, are restricted to utilizing pregnancy as the sole indicator of high-risk sexual activity.

The last two issues relate to direct external victimization of youth in the sex trade. We analyze youth prostitute victimization by assessing the degree to which they have been both physically and sexually assaulted. A wealth of research addresses issues of risky lifestyles and victimization (Cohen and Felson 1979; Kennedy and Forde 1990; Lowman and Fraser 1995) and we test the degree to which a lifestyle of prostitution places youth at risk from violent assailants.

Race

Especially in the cities of Saskatoon, Winnipeg, and Regina, the majority of youth prostitutes are believed to be of First Nations background (Fraser 1985; Lowman 1987; Brannigan, Knafla, and Levy 1989; Webber 1991; Shaver 1993; Goulding 1994; Mayor's Task Force 1996; Boritch 1997). Based on the widespread acknowledgement of this fact, we analyze the causal origins of youth prostitution in the context of culture, indicated by youth of Aboriginal versus non-Aboriginal ancestry.

METHODOLOGY

Data Description

The data were gathered from youth probation files on young offenders compiled by the Department of Social Services in both Regina and Saskatoon. Although the files are only from these two cities, youth from throughout the province come under the jurisdiction of both urban social services bureaus and are therefore represented in the final results. The files cover the years from 1980 to 1996 and were randomly selected from all files on youth who had at least some contact with the young offender system. Involvement in the legal system included any act for which the individual was required to report to a probation officer. The offences ranged from break and entry and driving while impaired to armed robbery. Several files contained offences related to soliciting for the purposes of prostitution. Additional files on individuals who had been involved in prostitution-related activities but had been charged with other offences were supplied by probation officers upon request.

The official court documents were relied upon as much as possible as they indicated not only the offence but also other information such as the type of facility (open, closed, or group home custody), the type of sentence, and background information documented in the predisposition reports (family biographies and previous involvement in the justice system). Unofficial reports that were documented in the written reports of the probation officers were accessed for additional biographical and legal information including school performance, details about family life, pregnancy, personal feelings, and employment activity.

As a result, the data set covers a wide array of social, legal, and psychological variables and we use only those that directly relate to this project. Because the data set contains mostly nominal level data, the analysis is based primarily on multivariate contingency tables.

The sample consists of 401 youth, 52 of whom have been involved in the sex trade. Of the 52 youth involved in prostitution, 7 are male and 45 female. Of these same youth, 38 are Aboriginal and 14 are non-Aboriginal. The age range of onset of prostitution for the 52 is from 9 to 18. Lastly, of the 52 youths involved in prostitution, 16 were at one time or another connected with a pimp/boyfriend.

Variables in the Analysis

DEPENDENT VARIABLES

Involvement in prostitution is the first dependent variable in this chapter (Tables 9.1 and 9.2) and is defined as engagement at any time in the sex trade, even if the youth has not been charged. The variables that we examine as associated with involvement in the sex trade (Table 9.3) include:

a. substance abuse (which groups all types of illegal and nonprescription chemicals into the category of drugs while also including alcohol in a separate category);
b. severity of alcohol use as an assessment of the degree to which the young offender is dependent on alcohol;
c. suicidal thoughts defined as the degree to which the youth thinks of committing a suicidal act;
d. suicide attempts defined as whether or not the young offender has attempted suicide and been hospitalized as a result;
e. self-abuse defined as whether the subject has slashed or injured him/herself to the point of requiring medical intervention;
f. physical health based on the social worker's rating of the actual physical health of the youth;
g. teen pregnancy, whether or not the youth has been pregnant (including full-term pregnancy, abortion, and miscarriage);
h. physical assault based on whether or not the youth has been physically assaulted outside the home; and,
i. sexual assault as a recorded incident of sexual assault outside the home.

All of these variables are presented as direct correlations with involvement in the sex trade.

INDEPENDENT VARIABLES

A number of independent variables are used in Tables 9.1 and 9.2 and are presented as direct causal influences on involvement in the sex trade. Their inclusion in the analyses is based on the relevant literature (which has been discussed in the previous section), obvious relevant issues con-

TABLE 9.1 *Percentages of Youth Involved in Prostitution by Childhood Trauma*

	Involvement in Prostitution			
	Non-Aboriginal		*Aboriginal*	
Predetermined Variables	*Yes (N = 14)*	*No (N = 240)*	*Yes (N = 38)*	*No (N = 100)*
Childhood physical abuse				
None	1.6	98.4	19.8	80.2
Some	3.8	96.2	36.8	63.2
Severe	6.5	93.5	41.9	58.1
Chi-square	2.78		6.6*	
Childhood psychological abuse				
None	2.4	97.6	24.2	75.8
Some		100.0	66.7	33.3
Severe	8.3	91.7	28.6	71.4
Chi-square	2.13		7.64*	
Childhood sexual abuse				
None	1.0	99.0	18.5	81.5
Some		100.0	47.1	52.9
Severe	16.0	84.0	44.4	55.6
Chi-square	21.15*		10.97*	
Childhood neglect				
None	2.0	98.0	15.3	84.7
Some	5.3	94.7	41.3	58.7
Chi-square	1.40		11.41*	
Runaway from home				
None		100.0	13.2	86.8
Some	6.5	93.5	24.3	75.7
Often	14.8	85.2	51.4	48.6
Chi-square	23.188*		16.15*	

Note: *Chi-square significant at the 0.05 level.

cerning youth prostitution, and availability of data from the social services data set. The independent variables utilized in this analysis are based on ratings by social service youth workers and the categories of assessment are indicated in Tables 9.1 and 9.2. The variables for the analysis in Table 9.1 include:

a. child physical abuse (which may have been inflicted by a parent, stranger, or other family member);
b. childhood psychological abuse (psychological ratings by youth workers and doctors regarding family experiences);

TABLE 9.2 *Percentages of Youth Involved in Prostitution by Educational and Personal Attributes*

	Involvement in Prostitution			
	Non-Aboriginal		*Aboriginal*	
Predetermined Variables	*Yes (N = 14)*	*No (N = 240)*	*Yes (N = 38)*	*No (N = 100)*
Attitudes to education				
Negative		100.0	30.8	69.2
Neutral	3.1	96.9	28.6	71.4
Positive	3.4	96.6	20.0	80.0
Chi-square	1.26		1.52	
Educational achievement				
Expelled	6.7	93.3	25.0	75.0
Dropped out	6.8	93.2	42.5	57.5
Failing		100.0	26.3	73.7
Doing well	1.4	98.6	14.3	85.7
Doing very well	3.2	96.8	33.3	66.7
Returned to school	4.2	95.8	6.7	93.3
Chi-square	4.58		10.60*	
Social skills				
Loner		100.0	20.0	80.0
Poor		100.0	9.1	90.9
Moderate	1.7	98.3	26.8	73.2
Very good	4.7	95.3	35.1	64.9
Chi-square	3.03		3.12	
Self-esteem				
Low	3.2	96.8	33.0	66.1
Medium	2.0	97.1	22.2	77.8
High		100.0		100.0
Chi-square	1.46		4.84*	

Note: *Chi-square significant at the 0.05 level.

TABLE 9.3 *The Effects of Prostitution on High-Risk Behaviour, Self-Destructive Behaviour, and Violent Victimization*

	Involvement in Prostitution			
	Non-Aboriginal		*Aboriginal*	
Outcome Variables	*Yes (N = 14)*	*No (N = 240)*	*Yes (N = 38)*	*No (N = 100)*
Substance abuse				
None	12.5	48.1	7.9	28.3
Alcohol	25.0	75.0		8.1
Alcohol/drugs	62.5	34.3	92.1	63.6
Chi-square	4.08		11.23	
Severity of alcohol abuse				
Not severe		50.6	13.5	33.7
Somewhat severe	41.9	35.1	40.5	30.6
Severe	57.1	14.2	45.9	35.7
Chi-square	11.77*		5.40*	
Suicidal tendencies				
None	78.2	50.0	52.6	75.8
Some	15.1	50.0	13.1	11.1
Severe	6.7		24.2	13.1
Chi-square	5.49*		8.65*	
Suicide attempts				
No	30.8	90.8	57.9	81.0
Yes	69.2	9.2	42.1	19.0
Chi-square	41.40*		7.77*	
Self abuse/slashing				
No	38.5	93.3	68.4	92.0
Yes	61.5	6.7	31.6	8.0
Chi-square	43.24*		12.35*	
Physical health				
Poor	33.3	5.0	17.1	4.1
Moderate	16.7	24.3	42.9	42.9
Very good	50.0	70.7	40.0	53.0
Chi-square	8.71*		6.53*	
Teen pregnancy				
No	37.5	71.4	55.9	64.3
Yes	62.5	28.6	44.1	35.7
Chi-square	3.10*		0.288	
Physical assault (outside of home)				
No	83.3	90.6	58.3	78.4
Yes	16.7	9.4	41.7	21.6
Chi-square	0.362		5.33*	
Sexual assault (outside of home)				
No	50.0	89.4	62.9	87.4
Yes	50.0	10.6	37.1	12.6
Chi-square	8.83*		9.89*	

Note: *Chi-square significant at the 0.05 level.

c. child sexual abuse (also inflicted by a parent, family member, or non-family member);
d. childhood neglect by families or guardians; and,
e. the prevalence of running away from home.

The variables for Table 9.2 include:

a. educational attitudes (based on youth worker assessments of how the youth defines her/his feelings toward schooling);
b. educational achievement (based on information from the social service files, which tracks the behaviour of youth only while involved in the system, not once they are released); and,
c. social skills and self-esteem assessments based on social services rating scales for young offenders.

Finally, the factor of race has been included in all of the analyses as a control variable, based on prior findings from a number of cross-Canada studies (Badgley 1984; Fraser 1985; Lowman 1987; Brannigan, Knafla, and Levy 1989; Shaver 1993; McCarthy 1996; Mayor's Task Force 1996; Boritch 1997). Race has been divided into two categories, including First Nations (which includes individuals who are either Status Indian or of Métis ancestry), and non-Aboriginal (which includes individuals who are Caucasian, or are from other ethnic minorities — the vast majority in this category self-define as Caucasian, i.e., 95.7 percent).

RESULTS

Childhood Trauma

Table 9.1 presents the results for the childhood trauma variables including indicators of abuse and neglect. The causal variables are listed on the left side of the table. The table is presented in the contexts of Aboriginal and non-Aboriginal ancestry.

Most noticeable, in general, in this table are the strong, consistent effects of forms of abuse on involvement in prostitution. For example, for both Aboriginal and non-Aboriginal youth, greater levels of childhood physical abuse are associated with greater involvement in prostitution. Although the relationship for non-Aboriginal youth is not significant, the percentage differences illustrate the nature of the association which is significant for Aboriginal youth; simply put, childhood physical abuse increases the likelihood of involvement in prostitution. Similar results occur for childhood sexual abuse. Important here, however, are the similar effects on prostitution for the categories of some and severe sexual abuse for Aboriginal youth. These findings suggest quite clearly that it is the act of sexual violation that predisposes children to prostitution, rather than the severity or the amount, especially for Aboriginal youth. For non-Aboriginal youth, it is primarily severe sexual abuse that leads to involvement in prostitution. Despite these racial differences, it is manifest that childhood sexual abuse has a large influence on future involvement in prostitution.

The results for psychological abuse are much less convincing than are those for the two previous physical forms of abuse. For example, for Aboriginal youth, 66.7 percent of those who suffer some degree of psychological abuse are involved in prostitution, compared with 28.6 percent who suffer severe abuse. In contradistinction, non-Aboriginal youth who suffer severe abuse have the greatest degree of involvement in prostitution (8.3 percent), as would be expected. These ambiguous results may, in part, be a function of the inability of youth workers to identify and categorize psychological abuse, which is certainly a problem in social research on family violence (Storrie and Poon 1996; Dekeseredy and Hinch 1991). The categorizations of abuse are based on how the youth characterizes abusive situations when providing information to probation officers. While these categorizations may be somewhat subjective, they are corroborated by psychiatric assessments based on information supplied to the doctor by the young offender.

The last two variables present a most convincing argument for influence of childhood trauma on prostitution. For Aboriginal youth especially, the effect of childhood neglect on involvement in prostitution is strong, and, as expected, indicates that high levels of neglect result in high involvement in prostitution (41.3 percent of Aboriginal youth involved in the sex trade experience some neglect, compared with 5.3 percent of non-Aboriginal youth). One of the behavioural manifestations of neglect, running away, also influences prostitution; 13.2 percent of the Aboriginal youth who never run away become involved in prostitution, compared with 44.4 percent of those who do run away. Similarly for non-Aboriginal youth, those who run away the most often have the highest levels of involvement in the sex trade. As Seng (1989) has hypothesized, however, runaway behaviour may in fact have an indirect effect on prostitution-related activities, with actual engagement resulting from other factors such as abuse.

Overall these findings regarding abuse and home context are not unexpected. They do, however, paint a convincing picture that youth and child prostitutes generally suffer family-based childhood trauma; their victimization on the streets is preceded by victimization in the home. The connections between home life and street life are complex, but certainly must involve the reality that abused children may internalize their abuse as normal. If so, they are much more psychologically disposed to accept further abuse than those who have not suffered similar childhood trauma.

Personal Development

Table 9.2 presents the influences that psychological and educational deficits have on engagement in prostitution. We argue that personal and psychological success will dispose children and youth to resist prostitution as a debasing although somewhat lucrative activity in the face of economic despair.

It is unclear from the two education variables whether success in school does prevent, to some extent, involvement in prostitution. For example, the effect of attitudes to education on prostitution for both racial categories is not significant and not terribly strong. On turning to educational achievement, however, we see that for Aboriginal youth, being expelled from, dropping out of, or failing school does increase the chances of being involved in prostitution. So does doing very well in school. Both of these variables present inconclusive results regarding the connection between school and prostitution. The one exception to this is the expected finding that returning to school results in low involvement in prostitution for both non-Aboriginal and Aboriginal youth (95.8 percent and 93.3 percent noninvolvement respectively).

The psychological measures of self-esteem and social skills reveal some interesting and somewhat perplexing findings. The youth in this study with the best social skills were those most involved in prostitution, and this is the case for both racial categories of youth. Although the findings are not statistically significant, the percentage differences reveal trends that indicate that low social skills prevent or discourage youths from the sex trade. The results for the self-esteem variable, on the other hand, reveal associations that are more consistent with the literature on psychic well-being and vulnerability. For both Aboriginal and non-Aboriginal youth, high levels of self-esteem tend to prevent involvement in prostitution; in fact, no youth in this study who was assessed with high self-esteem was involved in prostitution at any time, as compared with 33 percent of Aboriginal youth with low self-esteem who were involved in the sex trade.

EFFECTS OF INVOLVEMENT IN PROSTITUTION

Table 9.3 illustrates the behavioural manifestations of the psychic trauma produced by involvement in the youth sex trade. Essentially, we analyze the effects of engagement in prostitution on victimization, both self-imposed and perpetrated by predators.

As we maintain in this chapter, youth prostitutes use drugs and alcohol, in part to help them bear the humiliation and potential danger of their work (Fraser 1985; Lowman 1987; Lau 1989; Inciardi et al. 1991; Heinrich 1995). The two substance abuse variables show quite consistently that alcohol and drug abuse are high for those youth engaged in prostitution. Alcohol alone, however, does not seem to be the crutch that youths use. For example, almost all Aboriginal youth (92.1 percent) involved in prostitution use a combination of drugs and alcohol, as do a majority of non-Aboriginal youth (62.5 percent). These figures are appreciably higher than those for the youth not involved in prostitution. As for alcohol use alone, the most severe use of alcohol occurs for youth involved in prostitution, and this is found in both racial categories. These results indicate quite clearly that prostitution is associated with indirect self-imposed harm as measured by exposure to high-risk substance abuse.

On turning to the variables that measure the degree to which youth are exposed to direct self-imposed harm, we observe that, first of all, involvement in prostitution is related to greater suicidal tendencies and to more suicide attempts. Most strikingly, 69.2 percent of non-Aboriginal youth involved in prostitution have attempted suicide, compared with 9.2 percent who are not involved. Although not as dramatic a contrast, similar results appear for Aboriginal youth (42.1 percent and 19.0 percent respectively). These findings suggest that involvement in prostitution is correlated with suicidal tendencies and is also strongly correlated with suicide attempts for all youth, but especially so for non-Aboriginal youth.

We also use slashing or self-abusive behaviour as another indicator of direct self-imposed harm and obviously as a proxy measure of emotional well-being. Much like the findings for suicide, the results here suggest a severe effect of prostitution on well-being. For non-Aboriginal youth, slashing seems to be a reality primarily for youth involved in prostitution (61.5 percent compared with 6.7 percent not involved in prostitution). The results for Aboriginal youth are similar although the relationship is less strong (31.6 percent compared with 8.0 percent). The stronger effect of prostitution on well-being for non-Aboriginal youth is consistent with the findings for suicide.

The physical health variable endorses the findings from the previous discussions on well-being. For both racial categories of youth, poorer health is characteristic of most youth involved in prostitution. For example, for non-Aboriginal youth involved in prostitution, 33.3 percent are assessed with poor physical health, compared with 5 percent of those not involved. The results are similar for Aboriginal youth (17.1 percent and 4.1 percent respectively) but less pronounced.

While the outcome variables in this table to this point have shown the indirect effects of prostitution on well-being, the last two variables measure direct victimization. As mentioned previously, one of the dire realities of prostitution is that johns will pay more for sex without the use of protective measures. The teen pregnancy variable illustrates quite clearly that non-Aboriginal youth involved in prostitution are being coerced or encouraged to engage in unsafe sex, or, possibly, they are unaware or indifferent to the consequences of unsafe sexual practices. Such youth involved in prostitution are much more likely to have been pregnant than their counterparts not involved in the sex trade (62.5 percent compared with 28.6 percent). Interestingly, the relationship between prostitution and pregnancy is not significant for Aboriginal youth, essentially showing little effect.

The physical and sexual assault variables illustrate directly the physical vulnerability of youth involved in the sex trade. For physical assault, unlike several of the previous variables, the dangerous effect of prostitution on well-being occurs primarily for Aboriginal youth. Here, 41.7 percent of youth involved in prostitution have been physically assaulted compared with 21.6 percent not involved. For non-Aboriginal youth, the relationship is not significant and the percentage differences indicate little or no effect. For sexual assault, on the other hand, the vulnerability of youth is apparent for both racial groups. The youth involved in prostitution are more prone to sexual assault than their counterparts who are not involved in the sex trade. This finding, we contend, is indicative not only of the dangerousness of the sex trade but also of the inherent danger of the street life that attends involvement in prostitution.

CONCLUSION

In this research, we have sought, first, to understand some of the experiential and psychic circumstances of youth involved in the sex trade. Second, we have analyzed how prostitution may endanger the well-being of youth both directly through victimization and indirectly through creating the opportunities and pre-conditions for self-destructive behaviour. In summary, this research is an attempt to understand the gestalt of danger that encompasses the lives of youth involved in prostitution as it examines the context of non-Aboriginal and Aboriginal young offenders.

The results show clearly that, in the first instance, youth are involved in prostitution partly because their early lives were characterized by neglect and abuse. The question remains whether such early damage traumatizes children, who are then unable to cope in a conventional world, or whether such damage normalizes abuse and sexual exploitation in the minds of these young victims. A partial answer to this question can be found in the results on psychological skills and education. Our evidence suggests that a child's self-concept and affective abilities, likely associated with early sexual and/or physical abuse, determine involvement in the sex trade. Part of our reasoning is that, with some ambiguity, prostitution is the result of lack of conventional psychic tools that lead to conventional avenues of success, such as success in the education system. Furthermore, childhood abuse damages self-perception that allows children and youth to resist exploitation (Finkelhor 1987; Finkelhor and Browne 1988) and it patterns behaviour that exposes individuals to dangerous individuals and events (Simons and Whitbeck 1991).

Most importantly, for this chapter, however, are the results surrounding the dangers inherent in the sex trade. Quite clearly, teenage prostitution is enhanced by acute sexual and physical victimization, and the sex trade is related to predispositions to self-destructive behaviour. Prostitution creates a context in which those youth who are involved will run a high risk of being damaged by a predator or by themselves—either directly through assault and self-injury or indirectly through high-risk behaviour. These findings are offered in a street context, in which subcultural norms for protection are absent and in which children and youth are coerced and trapped in the sex trade and are not there by choice (Chesney-Lind and Shelden 1992; Campagna and Poffenberger 1988).

It is important to stress that the correlations between prostitution and social, physical, and psychological well-being are somewhat different depending on whether the youth are Aboriginal or non-Aboriginal. In this regard, there is some evidence to suggest that although prostitution predisposes all youth to self-injury, it does so especially for the non-Aboriginal youth in this sample. On the other hand, while all youth involved in the sex trade are especially vulnerable to direct victimization, young Aboriginal prostitutes are more vulnerable to stranger violence than are young non-Aboriginal prostitutes. These conclusions are offered in a context in which First Nations and Métis youth are more vulnerable to sexual exploitation on the streets than their non-Aboriginal counterparts (Badgley 1984, Lowman 1987, McCarthy 1996; Mayor's Task Force 1996).

The social policy implications that emanate from research such as this are clear. Young prostitutes develop and live in contexts of constant danger. Without caring intervention, the risk that these youth run, probably unparalleled anywhere else in society, will shorten their lives. Given that their supposed criminality is not one of choice but of coercion and victimization, an immediate, nonlegalistic, noncondemnatory intervention strategy is crucial, not only for the welfare of the youth involved but also for the integrity of a society that so far has failed to stop adult predators of children and youth.

The specific types of caring intervention need to include not only safe houses where street youth can find sanctuary but also attendant counselling programs that deal with issues of health and safety, personal trauma, family problems, and financial and educational opportunity. Obviously, what we are advocating here is not just token shelters but ongoing, well-financed programs of one-to-one support as well as educational and employment programs that obviate the need to prostitute. Government policy needs to make it easier for destitute and disaffiliated youth to access financial and physical resources. Schools need to provide flexible education models that account for the remedial needs of street youth, physical spaces in which marginalized youth feel safe and secure, and a nonpunitive, nonauthoritarian model of learning and development in which the wishes and opinions of street youth are considered in school policy development. They also need to address issues of sexual exploitation of children, the social problem of destitute children and youth, and the reality of street life.

A most important step is intervention within the school setting, especially in inner-city neighbourhoods. Schools with at-risk children and youth may, for example, address the issues directly by bringing in former prostitutes who are able to tell young people the reality and dangers of street life, and not a glamorized portrait of riches and money. As for outreach and intervention, programs and services must be culturally significant especially in cities where the majority of children and youth in the sex trade are of Aboriginal ancestry. As stated in the 1996 Royal Commission on Aboriginal Peoples, Aboriginal street youth look for Aboriginal faces in helping agencies (Canada 1996). In light of our research and the Royal Commission (Canada 1996), more trusting and effective helping relationships occur when services and programs are culturally relevant.

Lastly, and probably most importantly, the police need to assume the mandate of frontline social workers as well as peace and crime control officers. Street youth need to trust police officers as guardians and protectors, and it is obvious from our research that they need the protection that should be afforded to all citizens. At present, the "policing of child prostitution" role is anathema to the needs of vulnerable youth. Inner-city police officers understand street life and the inherent dangers and they are on the front lines. It is certainly within the realm of possibility for officers to be advocates for children and youth involved in the sex trade. This, however, would involve changing the mandate and training of the police, allowing them to create and work in an atmosphere of trust of and by street children and youth.

STUDY QUESTIONS

1. *According to the research findings reviewed by Schissel and Fedec, how exactly is childhood physical and sexual abuse related to involvement in prostitution?*
2. *According to Schissel and Fedec's findings, what were the effects of involvement in prostitution on young non-Aboriginal and Aboriginal prostitutes in Saskatoon and Regina?*
3. *What do Schissel and Fedec suggest needs to be done in order to more adequately address the problem of child and youth prostitution?*

REFERENCES

Badgley, R. (Chair). 1984. *Committee on Sexual Offences Against Children and Youth.* Ottawa: Supply and Services Canada.

Boritch, H. 1997. *Fallen Women: Female Crime and Criminal Justice in Canada.* Toronto: ITP Nelson.

Boyer, D., and J. James. 1982. "Easy Money: Adolescent Involvement in Prostitution." In S. Davidson, ed., *Justice for Young Women,* 73–98. Seattle: New Directions for Young Women.

Brannigan, A. 1996. "The Adolescent Prostitute: Policing Delinquency or Treating Pathology?" In J.A. Winterdyck, ed., *Issues and Perspectives on Young Offenders in Canada,* 195–217. Toronto: Harcourt Brace Jovanovich.

Brannigan, A., and T. Caputo. 1993. *Studying Runaways and Street Youth in Canada: Conceptual and Research Design Issues.* Ottawa: Supply and Services Canada.

Brannigan, A., L. Knafla, and C. Levy. 1989. *Street Prostitution: Assessing the Impact of the Law, Calgary, Regina, Winnipeg.* Ottawa: Supply and Services Canada.

Campagna, D.S., and D.L. Poffenberger. 1988. *The Sexual Trafficking in Children.* Dover, MA: Auburn House.

Canada. 1996. *Report of the Royal Commission on Aboriginal Peoples: Gathering Strength.* Ottawa: Minister of Supply and Services Canada.

Canadian Panel on Violence Against Women. 1993. *Changing the Landscape: Ending Violence and Achieving Equality.* Ottawa: Minister of Supply and Services.

Chesney-Lind, Meda, and Randall Shelden. 1992. *Girls, Delinquency and Juvenile Justice.* Pacific Grove, CA: Brooks/Cole Publishing.

Cohen, Lawrence E., and Marcus Felson. 1979. "Social Change and Crime Rate Trends: A Routine Activity Approach." *American Sociological Review 44*: 588–608.

Dekeseredy, Walter, and Ron Hinch. 1991. *Woman Abuse: Sociological Perspectives.* New York: Thompson Educational Publishing, Inc.

Faith, Karlene. 1993. *Unruly Women: The Politics of Confinement and Resistance.* Vancouver: Press Gang Publishers.

Finkelhor, David. 1987. "New Myth about Child Sexual Abuse." Address presented at the symposium on child sexual abuse. Ottawa, RIFAS.

Finkelhor, David, and Angela Browne. 1988. *Impact of Child Sexual Abuse: A Review of the Research.* Ottawa: Supply and Services.

Fraser, P. (Chair). 1985. Special Committee on Pornography and Prostitution. *Pornography and Prostitution in Canada.* Ottawa: Supply and Services Canada.

Gibson-Ainyette, I., D.I. Templer, and R. Brown. 1988. "Adolescent Female Prostitutes." *Archives of Sexual Behaviour 17*(5): 431–38.

Goulding, W. 1994. "Younger Hookers Oblivious to Danger." *StarPhoenix.* 26 October: A1.

Griffin, K., and A. Sheehan. 1994. "Children in the Sex Trade." *Vancouver Sun.* 15 November: A8.

Heinrich, K. 1995. "Law Fails to Protect Child Prostitutes, Expert Charges." *Calgary Herald.* 30 August: B2.

Hill, Hope, Fernando Soriano, S. Andrew Chen, and Teresa LaFramboise. 1996. "Sociocultural Factors in the Etiology and Prevention of Violence among Ethnic Minority Youth." In L. Eron, J. Gentry, and P. Schlegel, eds., *Reason to Hope: A Psychosocial Perspective on Violence and Youth,* 59–97. Washington, DC: American Psychological Association.

Inciardi, J., A.E. Pottieger, M.A. Forwey, D.D. Chitwood, and D.C. McBride. 1991. "Prostitution, IV Drug Use, and Sex-for-Crack Exchanges among Serious Delinquents: Risks for HIV Infection." *Criminology 29*(2): 221–35.

Kennedy, Leslie, and David Forde. 1990. "Risky Lifestyles and Dangerous Results: Routine Activities and Exposure to Crime." *Sociology and Social Research 74*(4): 208–11.

Lau, Evelyn. 1989. *Runaway: Diary of a Street Kid.* Toronto: Harper & Collins.

Lowman, J. 1986. "Prostitution in Canada." *Resources for Feminist Research 14*(4): 35–37.

———. 1987. "Taking Young Prostitutes Seriously." *Canadian Review of Sociology and Anthropology 24*(1): 99–115.

Lowman, J., and L. Fraser. 1995. *Violence Against Persons Who Prostitute: The Experience in British Columbia*. Vancouver: Department of Justice and Solicitor General Canada.

Mayor's Task Force on Child Prostitution. 1996. *Action Plan for the Elimination of Child Prostitution in the City of Saskatoon*. Saskatoon.

McCarthy, B. 1996. *On the Streets: Youth in Vancouver*. Victoria: Queen's Printer.

McGinnes, R. 1994. *High Heels and Teddy Bears*. Calgary: Street Teams.

McMullen, R.J. 1987. "Youth Prostitution: A Balance of Power." *Journal of Adolescence 10*(1): 35 – 43.

McNairn, K. 1997. "Child Prostitutes Need Support, Say Ex-Hookers." *StarPhoenix*. 6 October: A1.

Nyland, B. 1995. "Child Prostitution, and the New Australian Legislation on Paedophiles in Asia." *Journal of Contemporary Asia 25*(4): 546 – 60.

Sachs, A. 1994. "The Last Commodity: Child Prostitution in the Developing World." *World Watch* (July/August): 24 – 30.

Schissel, Bernard. 1995. "Degradation, Social Deprivation and Violence: Health Risks for Women Prisoners." In B. Singh Bolaria and Rosemary Bolaria, eds., *Women, Minorities and Health*, 287 – 300. Halifax: Fernwood Books.

Seng, M.J. 1989. "Child Sexual Abuse and Adolescent Prostitution: A Comparative Analysis." *Adolescence 24*(95): 664 – 75.

Shaver, F.M. 1993. "Prostitution: A Female Crime?" In E. Adelberg and C. Currie, eds., *In Conflict With the Law: Women and the Canadian Justice System*, 153 – 73. Vancouver: Press Gang.

———. 1996. "The Regulation of Prostitution: Setting the Morality Trap." In B. Schissel and L. Mahood, eds., *Social Control in Canada: Issues in the Social Construction of Deviance*, 203 – 26. Don Mills, ON: Oxford University Press.

Simons, R.L., and L.B. Whitbeck. 1991. "Sexual Abuse as a Precursor to Prostitution and Victimization among Adolescent and Adult Homeless Women." *Journal of Family Issues 12*(3): 361 – 79.

Storrie, Kathy, and Nancy Poon. 1996. "Deconstructing Spousal Violence: A Socialist Feminist Perspective." In Bernard Schissel and Linda Mahood, eds., *Social Control in Canada: Issues in the Social Construction of Deviance*, 241 – 60. Don Mills, ON: Oxford University Press.

Sullivan, T. 1987. "Juvenile Prostitution: A Critical Perspective." *Marriage and Family Review 12*(1 & 2): 113 – 34.

Van Brunschot, E.G. 1995. "Youth Involvement in Prostitution. Canadian Delinquency. In R.A. Silverman and J.H. Creechan, eds., *Canadian Delinquency*, 298 – 310. Scarborough: Prentice Hall.

Webber, Marlene. 1991. *Street Kids: The Tragedy of Canada's Runaways*. Toronto: University of Toronto Press.

PART FOUR
Youth Gangs: Varieties, Causes, and Intervention

INTRODUCTION

It seems that every generation of adults has chosen to label "youth gangs" as the source of many of society's problems. In his famous study of "mods" and "rockers" in England in the mid-1960s, Stanley Cohen (1972) looked at claims reported in the media that youth gangs were threatening the moral fabric of English society. Cohen argued that, in reality, these claims were evidence of a growing "moral panic" in which adults treated nonconforming youth as "folk devils," or scapegoats whom they could blame for the perceived ills of modern society. In a similar study, Geoffery Pearson (1983) looked at England, covering the period from the 1850s to the 1950s, and found periodically recycled claims by adults and the media about the problem of "hooligans" and other crime-committing youth gangs. A number of more recent historical studies of youth gangs in Canada, the United States, and Britain add support to the argument that youth gangs have routinely been perceived by adults to be a problem, and also, that these perceptions tend to give rise to periodic cycles of heightened concern about youth gang–related crime (cf. Adamson 1998; Davis 1998a; 1998b; Young 1993).

In the same way that general adult concern about youth gangs appears to be cyclical (Klein 1995b), it seems that the amount of attention criminology researchers have given to youth gangs has also been cyclical. Various textbook discussions suggest that research on youth gangs flourished in the 1950s and 1960s, declined in the 1970s and 1980s, and began to expand again in the 1990s (Branch 1999; Covey, Menard, and Franzese 1997; Howell 1998; Siegel and Senna 1997; Shelden, Tracy, and Brown 1997). This putative re-emergence of interest in youth gangs in the 1990s is reflected in the publication of several new studies on a wide range of related topics, including causes of gang formation (Decker and Van-Winkle 1996; Klein 1995a); precursors and consequences of gang membership (Dukes, Martinez, and Stein 1997; Huff 1998); the connection between gang membership and delinquency (Battin et al. 1998; Matsueda and Anderson 1998); gang violence (Hagedorn 1998); female gang involvement (Esbensen and Deschenes 1998; Miller 1998); youth gangs and hate crimes (Douglas 1992; Hamm 1993; Kube 1994); comparative cross-national gang research (Hazlehurst and Hazlehurst 1998); and evaluations of gang-prevention and -suppression strategies (Fritsch, Caeti, and Taylor 1999). Although comparatively little research has been done on youth gangs in Canada, a number of significant studies have been completed in recent years (cf. Baron 1989; 1997; O'Bireck 1996; Young 1993).

The recent profusion of research on youth gangs has made the selection of chapters for Part Four a challenging task. From this wealth of literature, the three chapters chosen for this text are fairly representative of the current state of research on youth gangs in the United States and Canada.

In Chapter Ten, Daniel Flannery, Ronald Huff, and Michael Manos provide a comprehensive overview of youth gang research in the United States. As with any non-Canadian research, caution must be taken in generalizing the findings of American studies to Canada. This is especially so with the authors' data on the incidence of gun-related crimes committed by gang members. Since access to guns is much more restricted in Canada, the data provided on the use of firearms are most useful for purposes of contrast. Flannery, Huff, and Manos review the state of research on a number of issues, including: What is a youth gang? What are the risk factors linked to youth involvement with gangs? How widespread are youth gangs? What is the racial and ethnic composition of gangs? Is female gang involvement increasing? Is it possible to prevent youth from becoming involved in gangs?

In addressing these questions, Flannery, Huff, and Manos offer a developmental perspective on youth gangs that draws attention to the importance of individual, family, and macrosocial risk factors that either increase or deter the likelihood of youth involvement in gangs. According to the authors, the most crucial thing from a developmental perspective "is understanding that early childhood behaviour is the marker for who is at risk for early adolescent gang involvement and for participation in the aggressive, criminal, and violent behaviour characteristic of many gang-involved youth." Acceptance of this perspective leads the authors to endorse a primary prevention approach whose goal is to reduce child aggressive and antisocial behaviour before it leads to gang involvement.

Flannery, Huff, and Manos's discussion of research on prevention and intervention also raises questions about the success of efforts aimed at getting youth to leave gangs after they have joined. In particular, they look at the problems associated with "peer-focused interventions," such as group therapy for antisocial youth, as part of youth gang awareness and gang-resistance strategies. This discussion also provides a good introduction to more general research on youth crime prevention and intervention, which will be the focus of the last part of this book.

In Chapter Eleven, David Curry reviews recent research literature on female gang involvement. Curry argues that a review of the literature on female gang involvement raises three key research questions: Is a feminist perspective required for understanding female gang involvement? Is female gang involvement increasing? Is female gang involvement "liberating" for young females? Curry draws on work that has addressed these questions to develop an agenda for future research that emphasizes the need for a "gender-conscious perspective" as a prelude to developing more useful theories of both male and female gang involvement.

In Chapter Twelve, Robert Gordon outlines Canadian research on youth gangs to the mid-1990s. Although Gordon does not discuss more recent Canadian research on youth gangs (cf. Baron 1997; O'Bireck 1996), he succeeds in addressing essential research issues. Gordon points to the relative lack of research addressing the topic of gangs from a Canadian perspective, and raises the issue of how little attention Canadian researchers have given to distinguishing between youth-related "street gangs" and "criminal business organizations." Drawing on his own research, Gordon provides examples of both types of gangs and stresses the cyclical nature of gang activity in Vancouver, where he carried out most of his research. He argues that while street gang activity appeared to peak in Vancouver in the late 1980s and early 1990s, instability and transience were the hallmarks of most Vancouver street gangs and "wannabe" groups during this period: "gangs and groups appeared and disappeared with breathtaking speed, some disbanding almost as quickly as they were formed." Gordon also offers data, consistent with research findings from other countries (cf. Decker and Van-Winkle 1996; Klein 1995a), about the reasons young people give for joining crime-oriented street gangs and about the high degree of ethnic diversity reflected in the membership of Vancouver-based street gangs.

Although they incorporate only a sample of work that has been done on youth gangs in recent years, the chapters included in Part Four cover many of the important research topics and issues that are now being addressed by criminologists concerned with the study of youth gangs. The next, and final, part of the book will turn to an examination of the more general, but related, topic of youth crime prevention, intervention, and evaluation.

REFERENCES

Adamson, C. 1998. "Tribute, Turf, Honor and the American Street Gang: Patterns of Continuity and Change since 1820." *Theoretical Criminology* *2*(1): 57–84.

Baron, S. 1989. "The Canadian West Coast Punk Subculture: A Field Study." *Canadian Journal of Sociology 14*(3): 289–316.

———. 1997. "Canadian Male Street Skinheads: Street Gang or Street Terrorists?" *Canadian Review of Sociology and Anthropology 34*(2): 125–54.

Battin, S., K. Hill, R. Abbott, R. Catalano, and D. Hawkins. 1998. "The Contribution of Gang Membership to Delinquency beyond Delinquent Friends." *Criminology 36*(1): 93–116.

Branch, C., ed. 1999. *Adolescent Gangs: Old Issues, New Approaches*. Philadelphia: Brunner/Mazel.

Cohen, S. 1972. *Folk Devils and Moral Panics*. London: MacGibbons and Kee.

Covey, H., S. Menard, and R. Franzese. 1997. *Juvenile Gangs*, 2nd ed. Springfield, Ill.: Charles Thomas.

Davis, A. 1998a. "Youth Gangs, Masculinity and Violence in Late Victorian Manchester and Salford." *Journal of Social History 32*(2): 349–70.

———. 1998b. "Street Gangs, Crime and Policing in Glasgow during the 1930s." *Social History 23*(3): 251–68.

Decker, S., and B. Van Winkle. 1996. *Life in the Gang: Family, Friends, and Violence*. Cambridge: Cambridge University Press.

Douglas, M. 1992. "Auslander Raus! Nazi Raus! An Observation of German Skins and Jugendang." *International Journal of Comparative and Applied Criminal Justice 16*: 129–34.

Dukes, R., R. Martinez, and J. Stein. 1997. "Precursors and Consequences of Membership in Youth Gangs." *Youth and Society 29*(2): 139–65.

Esbensen F., and E. Deschenes. 1998. "A Multisite Examination of Youth Gang Membership: Does Gender Matter?" *Criminology 36*(4): 799–827.

Fritsch, E., T. Caeti, and R. Taylor. 1999. "Gang Suppression through Saturation Patrol, Aggressive Curfew, and Truancy Enforcement: A Quasi-Experimental Test of the Dallas Anti-Gang Initiative." *Crime and Delinquency 45*(1): 122–39.

Hagedorn, J. 1998. "Gang Violence in the Postindustrial Era." In M. Tonry and M. Moore, eds., *Youth Violence. Crime and Justice: A Review of Research*, vol. 24. Chicago: University of Chicago Press.

Hamm, M. 1993. *American Skinheads: The Criminology and Control of Hate Crime*. Westport, CT: Praeger.

Hazlehurst, K., and C. Hazlehurst, eds. 1998. *Gangs and Youth Subcultures: International Explorations*. New Brunswick, NJ: Transaction Books.

Howell, J. 1998. "Recent Gang Research. Program and Policy Implications." In P. Sharp and B. Hancock, eds., *Juvenile Delinquency: Historical, Theoretical and Societal Reactions to Youth*. 2nd ed. Upper Saddle River, NJ: Prentice Hall.

Huff, R. 1998. "Comparing the Criminal Behavior of Youth Gangs and At-Risk Youths." *National Institute of Justice. Research in Brief.* Washington, DC: U.S. Department of Justice, Office of Justice Programs.

Klein, M. 1995a. *The American Street Gang: Its Nature, Prevalence, and Control*. New York: Oxford University Press.

———. 1995b. "Street Gang Cycles." In J.Q. Wilson and J. Petersilia, eds., *Crime*. San Francisco: ISC Press, Institute for Contemporary Studies.

Kube, E. 1994. "Collective Violence among Young People: A Serious Challenge to Government and Society." *Eurocriminology* 7: 39–51.

Matsueda, R., and K. Anderson. 1998. "The Dynamics of Delinquent Peers and Delinquent Behavior." *Criminology 36*(2): 269–308.

Miller, J. 1998. "Gender and Victimization Risk among Young Women in Gangs." *Journal of Research in Crime and Delinquency 35*(4): 429–53.

O'Bireck, G. 1996. " 'Ya Gotta Walk That Walk and Talk That Talk': Youth Subcultures and Gang Violence." In G. O'Bireck, ed., *Not a Kid Anymore: Canadian Youth, Crime, and Subcultures*. Toronto: ITP Nelson.

Pearson, G. 1983. *Hooligan: A History of Respectable Fears*. London: MacMillan Press.

Shelden, R., S. Tracy, and W. Brown. 1997. *Youth Gangs in American Society*. Belmont, CA: Wadsworth.

Siegel, L., and J. Senna. 1997. *Juvenile Delinquency: Theory, Practice and Law*, 6th ed. St. Paul, MN: West Publishing Co.

Young, M. 1993. "The History of Vancouver Youth Gangs, 1900–1985." Unpublished M.A. thesis. School of Criminology, Simon Fraser University.

CHAPTER TEN

Youth Gangs: A Developmental Perspective

DANIEL J. FLANNERY Kent State University, Ohio
C. RONALD HUFF Ohio State University
MICHAEL MANOS Case Western Reserve University, Ohio

Adolescence as a developmental period is characterized by significant changes and transformations in family and peer relationships (Montemayor and Flannery 1990; Paikoff and Brooks-Gunn 1991; Steinberg 1989). Peers often gain influence during adolescence, usually at the expense of parents. Youth seek out more time with their peers and report a high degree of satisfaction from their peer relations (Larson and Richards 1989). For some youth, spending time with peers has a positive influence on socialization, providing opportunities to become more involved in community organizations and activities like Boy Scouts, school band, athletics, or church activities. For others, spending time with peers becomes a mechanism for opportunity to engage in deviant behaviour such as truancy, substance use, theft, or assault (Gottfredson and Hirschi 1990).

For better or worse, peers are an important influence in adolescence, affecting development in multiple domains. The purpose of this chapter is to provide an overview of one specific form of peer group relationship, the youth gang, and to provide a developmental framework for understanding what gangs are, why adolescents in particular may become gang members, and how developmental issues can inform prevention and intervention efforts. We begin by providing a general definition of gangs. This is followed by a discussion of different kinds of gang activity, including recent data on the role of drugs in gangs. We then examine gangs from a developmental perspective, focusing on reasons why some kids may join gangs (including risk

Source: Daniel J. Flannery, C. Ronald Huff, and Michael Manos, "Youth Gangs: A Developmental Perspective." In T. Gullotta, G.R. Adams, and R. Montemayor, eds., *Delinquent Violent Youth* (Beverly Hills: Sage, 1998): 175–204. Reprinted by permission of Sage Publications, Inc.

factors), the developmental needs that gangs may meet for some youth, and the role of parents and families in gang activity. Where pertinent, we discuss the role of gender and ethnicity in gangs and gang-member activity. We also provide a brief overview, within a developmental framework, of factors associated with successful prevention and intervention programs, and we discuss programs that have shown treatment effects. Finally, we review some of the macrosocial or individual factors that appear to preclude youth involvement in prosocial settings or prohibit attachment to school and other institutions, and why socially appropriate groups have lost their appeal to many youth.

DEFINING GANGS

As Howell (1994) and Klein (1995) state, no accepted standard definition of a gang currently exists. State and local jurisdictions tend to develop their own definition and form policies based on those local criteria. However, several common criteria are typically used to define gangs: (a) There exists a formal organizational structure; (b) the group has an identified leader or leadership hierarchy; (c) the group is usually, but not always, identified with a specific territory or turf; (d) there exists recurrent interaction among the members of the group; and (e) the members of the group engage in delinquent or criminal behaviour. The last criterion, participating in delinquent or criminal behaviour, is the characteristic that distinguishes gangs from other, more prosocially focused adolescent groups.

Who belongs to a gang? Gang members typically range in age from 14 to 24, with the peak age of gang membership around age 17, although in some cities the gang members are somewhat older. Evidence exists that children as young as 8 are gang involved or gang "wannabes" (Embry et al. 1996; Huff 1996). To some degree, gang membership depends on where one lives. In established gang cities such as Los Angeles or Chicago, the majority of gang members tend to be adults, whereas in cities reporting recent or emerging gang problems, up to 90 percent of gang members are estimated to be juveniles. Certainly not every youth is involved in gang activity. Most reports estimate that between 5 percent and 8 percent of youth are at high risk for engaging in violent, gang-related activities (Tolan and Guerra 1994). Although no reliable national data exist, a recent Denver study estimated that 7 percent of inner-city, high-risk juveniles were gang involved (Esbensen and Huizinga 1993).

Based on research in Colorado, Florida, and Ohio, Huff (1996) identified a developmental progression from "hanging out" with the gang (being a gang "wannabe") to joining the gang and getting arrested. Gang members responded that they first began associating with the gang at about age 13 and joined, on average, about six months later. They were then arrested for the first time at about age 14, one year after beginning to associate with a gang and about six months after joining. Arrests for property crimes peaked one to two years before arrests for either drug offences or violent offences. Rather than gang membership providing protection, Huff found that a high percentage of gang leaders' declining arrest rates were due to incarceration and homicide. The gang lifestyle places individuals at much higher risk than would normally be expected.

Gangs are also appearing in more and more cities, particularly smaller communities (Maxson and Klein 1996). Curry, Ball, and Fox (1994) reported that more than 90 percent of the nation's largest cities report youth gang problems, up from about 50 percent in 1983. This increase is mostly due to family migration and local gang genesis rather than to relocation, suggesting that gang formation is not due solely to the recruitment of youth to "other city" gangs. Even very young children report exposure to gang activity at school (Embry et al. 1996). In Tucson, 42 percent of youth in Grades K through 5 reported seeing gang activity at school in a given week (Embry et al. 1996). This trend among young people is of concern because the Tucson data were collected from self-contained elementary schools, limiting the possibility that youth were reporting gang activity of older peers, or, conversely, suggesting that older peers were coming to elementary schools to recruit younger members.

The racial and ethnic composition of gangs is rapidly changing. Until the mid-1900s, the majority of gangs in the United States were white and composed of various European backgrounds. By the 1970s, an estimated 80 percent of gang members were either African American or Hispanic, and in the past few years, Asian groups have been emerging rapidly. The ethnic composition and social class position of gang members have remained fairly constant, with gangs comprised of recently migrated youth and those of lower socioeconomic status (Howell 1994; Miller 1982; Spergel 1991).

Female gang membership is also increasing (Chesney-Lind, Shelden, and Joe 1996), although girls still account for a relatively small percentage of gang-involved youth (3.5 percent to 6 percent; Curry, Ball, and Fox 1994). In 1992, 40 cities reported female gangs with an estimated 7205 members (Curry et al. 1992). Historically, the stereotype of girls in gangs and delinquent girls in general was that these girls were either tomboys or sex objects (Campbell 1990) or a form of male property (Jankowski 1991). Girls' delinquency was viewed as interpersonal and sexual, whereas boys' offending was viewed as aggressive and more criminal in nature (Chesney-Lind and Shelden 1992). Recent data on girls' participation in gangs, their activities, and their motivations for joining are discussed below.

ACTIVITY: WHAT DO GANGS AND GANG MEMBERS DO?

In this section, we provide an overview of gang member activity, including the social role of the gang and the role of firearms and drugs in gangs. Huff (1996) recently completed several studies of current and former gang-involved youth compared to at-risk youth in Cleveland, metropolitan Denver, and south Florida. He used detailed, semistructured, individual interviews conducted by graduate students and youth workers. For the Cleveland sample, Huff found that gang-involved youth were, on average, younger when first arrested (age 14 for gang members vs. never arrested for most nongang members) and had been arrested more often than their at-risk peers (median of three arrests for gang members vs. zero for nongang youth). Gang-involved youth were significantly more likely to have guns or knives in school, carry a concealed weapon, use or sell drugs, and engage in theft and property crimes. These trends also held for comparisons of the collective criminal behaviour of gangs and nongang peer groups (Huff 1996). These results reflect the criminogenic nature of gangs and the powerful socializing influence of the peer group in a gang member's life.

The Social Role of Gangs

Joe and Chesney-Lind's (1995) interviews with gang members in Hawaii show the social role of the gang for young people. They identified two primary mechanisms for group solidarity through gangs, particularly in disorganized and chaotic neighbourhoods. First, boredom with lack of resources and high visibility of crime in neglected communities create the conditions for turning to others who are similarly situated, that is, peer groups that offer a social outlet. Second, the stress on families from living in marginalized areas combined with financial struggles create tension and, in many cases, violence at home. Patterson and his colleagues have demonstrated the role of economic stress and violence on disrupted family management practices that lead to school failure and delinquency (Patterson, DeBaryshe, and Ramsey 1989). In these families, high levels of physical and sexual abuse and assault, particularly among siblings (Finkelhor and Dziuba-Leatherman 1994), exist. The group or gang, then, is perceived by both girls and boys as providing safe refuge and a surrogate family.

With respect to "normative" adolescent activities, Huff's recent data shed some light on what gang members and nongang members have in common and how they differ. The only activity that is more common for nongang members is involvement in sporting activities. Although varying proportions of nongang youth engage in these activities, gang members are significantly more likely to "party"; attend musical concerts; "hang out"; "cruise" for the opposite sex; engage in fighting, drinking, drug use, and drug sales; and put up and cross out graffiti. These data illustrate how the activities of youth gang members are in some respect very similar to activities of nongang-member youth.

Activities of Boys Versus Girls

Recent analyses of arrest patterns have shown consistently that for boys suspected of gang activity, the most common arrest was "other assaults," mostly fighting with other males (Federal Bureau of Investigation 1994). Boys also report engaging in frequent drinking, cruising, and looking for trouble (Huff

1996). Female suspected gang members tend to be chronic, but not serious, offenders who are arrested most commonly for larceny theft, followed by status offences such as running away. Serious violent offences (murder, sexual assault, robbery, and aggravated assault) accounted for 23 percent of the most serious offences of boys suspected of gang membership, but none of the girls' most serious offences. Girls are three times more likely than boys to be involved in "property offences," an important consideration given Huff's (1996) recent findings that property offences are often a major precursor of more serious gang activity. In jurisdictions that track female gang activity, girls accounted for 13.6 percent of gang-related property offences, 12.7 percent of the drug crimes, but only 3.3 percent of the crimes of violence (Curry, Ball, and Fox 1994). Joe and Chesney-Lind (1995) report that, if anything, the presence of girls in a gang tends to depress the occurrence of violence. They quote one 14-year-old Filipino boy: "If we not with the girls, we fighting. If we not fighting, we with the girls" (Joe and Chesney-Lind 1995: 424).

In 1994, girls accounted for about 25 percent of all arrests of youth in the United States (Federal Bureau of Investigation 1995). As with boys, arrests of girls for violent crimes have increased steadily and significantly in the past decade. From 1985 to 1994, arrests of girls for murder were up 64 percent, robbery arrests were up 114 percent, and aggravated assault arrests were up 136 percent. Similar to males, however, serious crimes of violence represent a small proportion of all girls' delinquency: 2.3 percent in 1984 and 3.4 percent in 1993. Girls are more likely to fight with a parent or sibling, for example, whereas boys are more likely to fight with friends or strangers.

For girls, fighting and violence are part of their life in the gang but not necessarily something they seek out. In qualitative interviews, girls consistently mention protection from neighbourhood and family violence as major reasons why they join gangs (Chesney-Lind et al. 1996). Chesney-Lind and her colleagues assert that, in general, female gang activity is not an expression of "liberation," nor are female gang members the hyperviolent, amoral individuals portrayed in popular media accounts. Rather, gang membership reflects the attempts of young women to cope with a bleak and harsh present as well as a dismal future. This sense of hopelessness about the future and need to cope with the here and now permeate both male and female gang activity and youth's motivations for membership.

Use of Firearms

Gangs and gang members are engaging in more violent offences, experiencing more serious injuries, and using more lethal weapons in the commission of delinquent and criminal acts. Sheley and Wright (1993) recently surveyed male incarcerated offenders and males in ten inner-city high schools about their use of and access to firearms. Although their findings cannot be generalized to other populations, they were somewhat sobering. Approximately 83 percent of inmates (average age 17) and 22 percent of students said that they possessed guns, and more than half of the inmates said that they had carried guns all or most of the time in the year or two before being incarcerated. This compared to 12 percent of high school students who reported regularly carrying guns to school; nearly one in four reported that they did so "now and then." Perhaps even more disconcerting was the ease with which both incarcerated and high school males reported they could acquire a gun. Only 13 percent of inmates and 35 percent of high school males said they would have a lot of trouble getting a gun; nearly half of all respondents indicated that they would "borrow" one from family or friends, more than those who said they would get one "off the street" (54 percent of inmates and 37 percent of students). The most frequently endorsed reason for owning or carrying a gun was self-protection. These inner-city youth were convinced they were not safe in their neighbourhoods and their schools.

Although not a primary focus of their study, Sheley and Wright (1993) identified members of the incarcerated and student cohorts who reported being in quasi-gangs, unstructured gangs, and structured gangs. Especially for the inmates but to some extent for students, moving from nongang member to gang member was associated with increased frequency of possessing and carrying guns. For members of both structured and unstructured gangs, the most commonly owned weapon was a revolver. Ownership of military-style weapons among gang-affiliated inmates was high, averaging 53 percent across gang types. In the street environment inhabited by these juvenile offenders, owning and carrying guns were virtually universal behaviours (Sheley and Wright 1993). Furthermore, the inmate respondents reported that they regularly experienced both threats of violence and violence itself. A total of 84 percent reported that they had been threatened with a gun or shot at during their lives; 45 percent of the student sample reported being threatened or shot at on the way to or from school. The researchers also found that firearms were a common element in the drug business; 89 percent of inmates and 75 percent of students who dealt drugs carried guns regularly.

Drug Use and Gang Activity

Recent research has demonstrated that although some gang members are involved in the distribution and sale of drugs, and although some gangs have evolved specifically for the purpose of drug distribution, drug trafficking is not a primary gang activity (Klein, Maxson, and Cunningham 1991; Huff 1996). Furthermore, most of the homicides involving gang members are over turf battles, not drug violence. In a study conducted in two smaller cities outside Los Angeles, Klein, Maxson, and Cunningham (1991) found that gang members were involved in about 17 percent of arrests for cocaine sales and about 12 percent of arrests connected to other drug sales. Firearms were involved in only about 10 percent of the cases, and violence was present in only about 5 percent of the incidents. Block and Block's (1994) Chicago study of the city's four largest and most criminally active street gangs found only

8 out of 285 gang-motivated homicides between 1987 and 1990 to be related to drugs. Approximately 90 percent of violent crimes, including homicides, involving youth gangs in the Boston area between 1984 and 1994 were unrelated to drug dealing or drug use.

Drugs and Firearms

The combination of drugs and firearms appears to contribute a great deal to both the contextual and situational determinants of violence and gang activity. Youth involved in gangs who carry weapons for self-protection and status seeking and who also may be involved with drugs are at high risk for violence. These youth are often impulsive and frequently lack the cognitive problem-solving skills to settle disputes calmly. Fistfights turn into more lethal confrontations because guns are present. This "sequence" can be exacerbated by the socialization problems (e.g., poor parental monitoring) associated with extreme poverty, the high proportion of single-parent households, educational failures, and the pervasive sense of hopelessness about one's life and economic situation (Blumstein, 1995). The number of murders by adolescents, gun-related homicides by 10- to 17-year-old offenders, the homicide arrest rates for 14- to 17-year-old males, and the number of drug arrests have all increased significantly in the past decade.

Huff (1995; 1996) found a significant disparity in profit from drug selling between gang and nongang youth. The typical gang member was much more likely than his at-risk peers to be selling drugs, usually on a daily basis. At-risk youth who sold drugs also did so on a daily basis. However, gang members reported, on average, nearly 50 percent more in earnings per week ($1000 vs. $675) with far fewer customers (30 vs. 80 per week). Thus, the average earnings per transaction for gang members was $33.33 compared to $8.44 for nongang/at-risk youth. Gang membership has high potential for profit making and presents an additional motivation for remaining in a gang.

Wilkinson and Fagan (1996; Fagan, 1996), using detailed individual interviews with incarcerated and at-risk youth, have found alcohol to be present in nearly 40 percent of violent incidents, with subjects reporting that the use of alcohol prior to conflict increased the chances of the conflict being handled violently. Respondents also characterized violent events as "shocking" life experiences, where alcohol "juiced up" a seemingly harmless situation into a physical assault. Furthermore, problematic alcohol use predicted involvement in violent behaviours for both males and females, regardless of gang involvement (Fagan 1990).

In addition to alcohol use, other situational factors significantly affect the onset, escalation, desistance, and injury outcomes of assaults (Sampson and Lauritsen 1993). Third parties, for example, are important to how a situation is handled. In Fagan's (1996) recent work, individuals explained how disputes that could have been "squashed" or "deaded" were continued by third parties who would provoke combatants with comments like "don't let him play you like that," appealing to courage, respect, and power as reasons to fight back. Even if events were squashed one day, disputes were often continued at school or in the neighbourhood at a later time.

DEVELOPMENTAL PERSPECTIVE

A developmental perspective of youth gangs needs to ground itself in understanding what is normal for children and adolescents as a framework for understanding how normal development may have gone "awry." Recent advances in research on adolescent violence show promise in this regard. Specifically, the study of individual risk factors has focused recently on understanding the cognitive underpinnings of antisocial behaviour (e.g., attitudes, beliefs, and information-processing skills; Kendall and Hollon 1979) and has moved from a dependence on static, simplistic definitions of outcome to an articulation of the sequence of behaviours that mark increasing risk for chronic and serious antisocial behaviour (Loeber and Hay 1994). An emphasis on how developmental sequences are altered rather than a focus on changing static behavioural outcomes has helped advance our thinking about prevention and intervention (Kellam and Rebok 1992). Furthermore, there has been a growing recognition of the impact of context on individual risk (Tolan and Loeber 1993), particularly with emphases on family factors in the etiology of antisocial behaviour and how family factors interact with and unfold in specific cultural and community contexts (Henggeler and Borduin 1990).

There are many developmental tasks and transformations for adolescents that may influence whether a young person joins a gang. For most youth, delinquent and violent behaviour does not suddenly emerge in adolescence. Although risk for gang membership is multifactored, multifaceted, and complex in its etiology, there are several factors that exert a great deal of influence on determining who is at highest risk for gang involvement. We briefly review some of the risk factors at the individual, family, and neighbourhood levels. Individual risk includes exposure to and victimization from violence. Under family risk, we include a discussion of peer group influence. Macrosocial risk factors are also examined. Gang membership and gang-related violence are strongly associated with local economic, school, and peer group factors that need to be taken into account (Klein 1995; Spergel 1991; 1995). Several excellent reviews of risk for youth violence and delinquency are available (Earls 1994; Fraser 1996; Reiss and Roth 1993; Yoshikawa 1994).

Individual-Level Risk Factors

At the individual level, those youth who exhibit an antisocial personality at an early age are most at risk for becoming delinquent adolescents and antisocial adults (Elliott 1994; Farrington et al. 1993). Aggressive behavoiur in kindergarten and first grade is an important predictor of delinquency in adolescence (Huesmann et al. 1984; Tremblay et al. 1992), and, in one longitudinal study, this relationship persisted until the age of 30 (Eron and Huesmann 1990). A child's early aggressive behaviour interacts with family factors to place young children at high risk for delinquency and gang membership. Children who have histories of coercive, intimidating social relations from a very early age experience limited social opportunities with other children and adults (Kupersmidt and Coie 1990). Of course, not all aggressive children end up becoming delinquent or gang-involved adolescents (Tolan, Guerra, and Kendall 1995).

Young children who suffer from a combination of a mood disorder (e.g., major depression, bipolar disorder), conduct disorder, and associated attention deficit hyperactivity disorder are at particularly high risk for criminal offending, school failure, and incarceration as adolescents and young adults (Farrington 1991; Loeber 1982). In the longitudinal studies that have followed young children through adolescence and into adulthood, low verbal intelligence has been shown to be the best predictor of aggressive behaviour at age 8 (as rated by both teachers and parents), delinquent behaviour in adolescence, and violent criminal offending in late adolescence (Huesmann et al. 1984). The effects of IQ on later delinquency remain even after controlling for the effects of socioeconomic status on delinquent behaviour. There is also growing evidence of prenatal factors being associated with adolescent delinquency. Low birth weight, being small for gestational age, and anoxia at birth have all been associated with adolescent delinquency and violence (Kandel and Mednick 1991).

One cannot discuss gangs from an individual developmental perspective without mentioning the significant link between exposure to violence, victimization from violence, and risk for violence perpetration (Martinez and Richters 1993; Richters and Martinez 1993), particularly among African American youth (DuRant et al. 1994; Fitzpatrick and Boldizar 1993). The developmental impact of chronic exposure to violence and victimization by violence can be significant for children and adolescents (Flannery et al. 1996). In general, males are more likely than females to be victims of assault and violence and to witness violent acts. Furthermore, symptoms of post-traumatic stress are commonly reported among children and adolescents exposed to violence (Bell and Jenkins 1991; Garbarino et al. 1992; Singer et al. 1995).

Family conflict and assault also have been linked to increases in interpersonal assaultive behaviour among youth. Sibling assault is one of the most commonly reported forms of youth victimization (Finkelhor and Dziuba-Leatherman 1994). Coupled with high family conflict and poor parental management, violence between siblings creates a home environment with high potential for child victimization and exposure to violence, and for learning interaction styles that lead to further violent behaviour (Cicchetti and Lynch 1993). Other family factors related to victimization and violent youth behaviour include poor parental monitoring (Patterson, DeBaryshe, and Ramsey 1989; Steinberg 1987) and accessibility of firearms in the home (Ropp et al. 1992).

Family-Level and Peer-Related Risk

Patterson and his colleagues have a model of early versus late starters in delinquent activity that incorporates child antisocial behaviour as a precursor to early childhood behaviour problems and poor parent management. These lead to school failure and rejection by peers, precursors of adolescent delinquency and violence. According to Patterson and Yoerger (1993), there exist two primary routes to delinquency, each with a different set of determinants and long-term outcomes. The critical determinant is age at first arrest. If a child is arrested prior to age 14, he or she is considered an early starter. If arrested after the age of 14, the child is considered to be a late starter. The primary assumptions of both models is that disrupted parenting practices directly determine a child's antisocial behaviour, and that these, in turn, place a child at risk for early arrest (Patterson, DeBaryshe, and Ramsey 1989). Second, it is assumed that the majority of adult criminal offenders are early starters. This latter assumption is consistent with the evidence for the chronicity and stability of aggressive, violent behaviour shown across longitudinal studies (Eron and Huesmann 1990; Farrington 1991; Patterson, Reid, and Dishion 1992).

Several other findings and assumptions that underlie their coercion model are important to mention. First is the assumption that, as the frequency of antisocial behaviour increases, the severity shifts from the trivial to more severe acts (Patterson and Bank 1989). Second, Patterson and colleagues have found that parents of antisocial children are noncontingent in many of their interactions with their children. They are essentially ineffective disciplinarians who punish frequently, inconsistently, and ineffectively, and they tend to ignore or fail to reinforce prosocial behaviours. Patterson, Reid, and Dishion's model focuses on five parenting constructs shown to be important predictors of antisocial and delinquent child behaviour; discipline, monitoring, family problem solving, involvement, and positive reinforcement (Patterson, Reid, and Dishion 1992).

Their program of research has demonstrated how child antisocial behaviours directly determine school failure, rejection by peers, and involvement with deviant peers and indirectly determine depressed mood and substance use. All of these factors place youth at greater risk for gang involvement. In the coercion model, child antisocial behaviour is viewed as merely the first step in a long-term dynamic process resulting in adolescent delinquency and adult antisocial behaviour. What is crucial, from a developmental perspective, is understanding that early childhood behaviour is the marker for who is at risk for early adolescent gang involvement and for participation in the aggressive, criminal, and violent behaviour characteristic of many gang-involved youth.

The influence of peers on gang involvement and activity is significant. Goldstein (1991) asserts that establishing a stable sense of identity and striving for peer acceptance are two central features of adolescent development fostered by gang involvement. Contacts with deviant peers are readily available to most adolescents. Cairns and Cairns (1991) showed that most adolescents develop support networks of some kind. For most adolescents, the peer group provides at least one of those social networks. For some adolescents, the gang becomes the primary support network, made up mostly of other deviant peers and rejected youth who are not attached to school or home, and who live in families where parents are not interested in or are unable to monitor effectively who they are with and what they are doing. In their struggle to establish an identity, the gang can provide a context for establishing a system of values, beliefs, and goals.

Physical, emotional, cognitive, and social developmental tasks merge during early and middle adolescence, forcing young people to cope with many issues, expectations, and responsibilities that they may not yet be capable of handling on their own. For gang-involved youth, it is the peer group that provides both girls and boys with a safe refuge and a surrogate family. Patterson and others have shown that the most antisocial youth are those most committed to a deviant peer group. Being relatively free from adult supervision and free from any attachment to school, religion, or family, hanging out with other rejected youth provides a great deal of opportunity to engage in delinquent activity (Gottfredson and Hirschi 1990; O'Donnell, Hawkins, and Abbott 1995). The sooner the antisocial child is out on the streets, the more exposed he or she is to higher levels of antisocial behaviour and violence and the more opportunities he or she has to perpetrate criminal acts.

Macrosocial/Community-Level Risk

Several macrosocial or community-level factors contribute to gang membership, gang activity, crime rates, and violence. Examples of macrolevel risk factors include neighbourhood resident mobility, levels of disorganization, population density, heterogeneity, unemployment, and income inequality (e.g., the spatial proximity of middle class and poor). Each of these has been related to higher levels of gang activity, crime, and violence (Coulton, Korbin, and Su 1996; Sampson and Lauritsen 1993). A major dimension of social disorganization relevant to violence is the ability of a community to supervise and control teenage peer groups, particularly gangs (Sampson and Groves 1989). There is much evidence that adolescent delinquency is most often a group activity, and thus the capacity of the community to control group-level dynamics is a key theoretical mechanism linking community characteristics with crime and gang activity (Sampson and Lauritsen 1993).

Skogan (1986) reviews some of the "feedback" processes that may further increase levels of crime and gang activity in a community. These include (a) physical and psychological withdrawal from community life; (b) weakening of the informal social control processes that inhibit crime; (c) a decline in the organizational life and mobilization capacity of the neighbourhood;

(d) deteriorating business conditions; (e) the importation and domestic production of delinquency and deviance; and (f) further dramatic changes in the composition of the population. So, if people shun their neighbours and withdraw from their community, there will be fewer opportunities to form friendship networks that may help provide appropriate adult supervision of youth group activity (Sampson and Lauritsen 1993).

IMPLICATIONS FOR ADOLESCENT DEVELOPMENT

During adolescence, multiple developmental tasks converge to make this an important time for gang activity and involvement. Gangs can be an attractive alternative to an at-risk youth struggling to fulfill unmet needs and resolve emerging developmental issues. Gang membership jeopardizes adolescent psychosocial development in general and particularly threatens the adequate resolution of primary adolescent developmental tasks, including achieving effective relations with peers of both genders, achieving a masculine or feminine social role, achieving an appropriate body image and becoming competent in using the body, achieving emotional autonomy, preparation for marriage and family life, preparing for an economic career, developing a value-based ideology, and aspiring to participate responsibly in the community (Straus 1994). Gang membership, which may substitute for an adolescent's desire to be a member of an accepting and supportive social network, cannot replace the support and adequate supervision that a parent can provide. Furthermore, membership in a social network that tolerates and approves of violence is a strong predictor of violent behaviour (Callahan and Rivara 1992; Webster, Gainer, and Champion 1994). This is a particular irony for those youth who initially join a gang for protection. Females who join a gang for protection from abusive parents have, in most cases, simply placed themselves at greater risk (although perhaps different) for sexual and physical victimization (Portillas and Zatz 1995). Because victimization leads to an increased risk for perpetrating violence, the attainment of any "normative" developmental tasks in adolescence is problematic at best.

Gang membership places young people at risk for a variety of negative outcomes. Gang membership is highly associated with earlier onset of delinquency and victimization from violence (Widom 1989). For both genders, gang involvement has been associated with an earlier onset of sexual intercourse, unsafe sex, and early pregnancy or the fathering of a child (Morris et al. 1996). Gang members also more frequently report suicidal ideation and suicide attempts, often involving heavy substance abuse.

Recently, researchers have begun to specifically examine outcomes for gang-involved females. Moore and Hagedorn (1996) assert that no matter what the cultural context, and no matter what the economic opportunity structure, there appears to be one constant in the later life of women in gangs. Most of them have children, and children have more effect on women's lives than on men's. For women, but rarely for men, the new responsibilities associated with child rearing may speed up the process of maturing out of the gang. As Chesney-Lind and Brown (1999) point out, in an environment of extreme poverty and deprivation, developmental tasks are subordinate to the imperatives of short-term survival on the streets. There is little hope for the future, especially for females in this environment. Recent data suggest that the future awaiting gang girls is bleak indeed: 94 percent will go on to have children, and 84 percent will raise them without spouses. One-third of them will be arrested, and the vast majority will be dependent on welfare (Campbell 1990).

PREVENTION AND INTERVENTION

As the developmental and criminological literature illustrates, child aggressive, antisocial behaviour is highly predictive of adolescent delinquency, violence, and gang involvement. To systematically prevent adolescent gang activity, we endorse a primary prevention approach with the goal of reducing child aggressive and antisocial behaviour (Tolan, Guerra, and Kendall 1995). By the early elementary school years, aggression is predictive of later aggressive and antisocial behaviour. This suggests that interventions should begin by the first grade, especially given the significant increase in aggression between the first and second grades (Tremblay et al. 1995). It is important to note, however, that postintervention aggression scores are typically lower than developmentally expected increases and not lower than preintervention scores. Similar results were found for high-risk K through 5 children in Tucson (Flannery et al. 1996). These findings for aggression highlight the need to use normative developmental information as a measuring stick for intervention effectiveness (Kendall and Grove 1988).

Tolan, Guerra, and Kendall (1995) point out that even among aggressive children, less than half continue to engage in high rates of aggressive behaviour, and relatively few go on to escalate their involvement in serious antisocial behaviour. We need to identify multiple-risk pathways that may contain different combinations of risk factors or may be differentiated by the relative influence of risk factors common to pathways. Especially needed are studies of how intervention components affect the risk of children who differ by gender, ethnicity, socioeconomic status, and other major demographic markers. Evidence also exists for the significant influence of social-cognitive factors on delinquency and violence and their legitimacy as a focus of intervention efforts. The work of Dodge (Crick and Dodge 1994) and of Guerra and her colleagues (Guerra, Huesmann, and Hanish 1994; Guerra et al. 1995) demonstrates the link between attributional bias, social information-processing skills, and individual beliefs with aggressive and antisocial behaviour. Each of these is a potentially modifiable skill through preventive interventions. For example, Guerra et al. (1995) reported that normative beliefs supporting the legitimacy of aggression predict aggression during elementary school, and O'Donnell, Hawkins, and Abbott (1995) showed that attitudes toward substance use and aggression predicted involvement in both behaviours for adolescents. Family variables, particularly communication skills and management practices, are also increasingly the focus of both prevention efforts with young children and interventions with adolescents (Dishion and Andrews 1995).

The influence of peers has been a major focus of this chapter. Given the impact of association with antisocial peers, peer rejection, and the support network provided by peers in a gang, peer relations has become a major focus of prevention and intervention efforts. Successful interventions are not merely exercises in teaching youth to cope with peer pressure to engage in antisocial acts. Lack of effective social skills and social problem solving are critical elements in the escalation of minor conflicts into serious altercations (Dodge 1993). The tendency of delinquent youth to interpret ambiguous or neutral events as reflective of hostile intent is problematic in the classroom, at home, and on the streets. Many gang-involved youth speak about the necessity of retaliation for being "disrespected" or "dissed" because of how someone else looked at them or their girlfriend, for example.

One of the dangers of peer-focused interventions is attempting to conduct group therapy with all antisocial youth. A social network effect was described by O'Donnell, Manos, and Chesney-Lind (1987) in programs such as the Juvenile Awareness Project at Rahway State Prison in New Jersey and the Group Guidance Project (Klein 1971). These programs were associated with an increase in delinquency, gang membership, and cohesiveness of gangs because they brought fringe members into contact with active gang members who recruited them. Activities of programs that promote prosocial affiliation or disrupt existing affiliations do so by creating opportunities for youth to participate meaningfully within different networks. The Ladino Hills Project (Klein 1971), for example, offered employment as an alternative to gang membership. Although the number of offences per gang member did not change, follow-up data indicated decreases in gang membership, gang cohesiveness, and in the total number of gang offences. In a sense, interventions with a focus on social networks emphasize forming more gangs. But these gangs are of a different nature. Developing prosocial networks that bring youth into contact with others who can provide what the gang provides holds promise for prevention efforts and takes advantage of a developmental task that is a powerful influence in the lives of children and youth. It is imperative that prosocial peers be included in group settings for long-term gain (Tremblay et al. 1995). Moreover, Goldstein and Glick (1994) report some success in implementing aggression replacement training with New York City gangs.

But even programs that alter social networks are likely to be ineffective if they do no more than attempt to control behaviour or translate competitive entrepreneurial initiative (e.g., drug trafficking) into low-level job opportunities (Jankowski 1991). A pervasive sense of hopelessness about the future in a prosocial world drives many youth to seek the power and opportunity that gang membership affords. A young person with low bonding to school and family, with unlikely access to higher education, with fewer opportunities to enter the legal labour market, and with little likelihood of being socioeconomically mobile will tend to continue gang involvement into adulthood (Wilson 1987). For some youth, economic, political, and social forces compel gang membership. Although it is beyond the scope of this chapter to pursue such issues, until these forces are successfully redirected, the developmental tasks confronted by some youth will require that gangs persist.

Clearly, many demographic variables, including gender, ethnicity, family composition, and neighbourhood disorganization, affect entrance into a gang, how long a youth stays in a gang, and how and why he or she leaves a gang. Most research to date on aggressive and delinquent behaviour has focused on white, middle-class youth, whereas research on gang-involved youth has focused on ethnic minority youth. There is little work that spans the developmental literature on aggression and delinquent behaviour and the sociological/criminological work on gangs. Huff's (1995; 1996) recent studies directly comparing gang-involved and at-risk youth highlight the need to begin examining the continuum of aggressive behaviour, delinquency, gang involvement, and antisocial behaviour for both groups of adolescents. Factors that predict which youth will go from being at risk to being involved in a gang are not yet well understood beyond a descriptive level. The relative influence of normative beliefs, stress, poverty, exposure to violence and victimization, and ethnicity may all contribute differentially to this process. The relative effectiveness of any preventive intervention also may vary tremendously depending on which factors are pertinent for a particular adolescent or group.

Finally, all of the research to date on youth at risk for engaging in aggressive, delinquent behaviour and gang activity points to the need for multicomponent, multicontext interventions. To date, those that have shown the most promise include a focus on the individual (e.g., attitudes about aggression), the influence of close interpersonal relations (e.g., problem solving, peer pressure, family conflict), and the contexts within which development takes place (e.g., home, school, peer group). Promising programs include aggression replacement training with delinquent youth (Goldstein and Glick 1994), multisystemic family therapy (Henggeler, Melton, and Smith 1992), the Seattle Social Development Project (Hawkins et al. 1992), and the PeaceBuilders youth violence prevention project (Embry et al. 1996; Flannery et al. 1996). Each of these approaches takes into account a combination of intrapersonal, interpersonal, and contextual factors in attempting to reduce delinquency, violent behaviour, or gang involvement. Certainly, the relative importance of environmental risk factors, compared with individual risk factors, may vary with age and by context. This has been demonstrated quite well by Finkelhor in his model of "developmental victimology" for children exposed to and victimized by violence (Finkelhor 1995). Young children may be more affected by context (e.g., persistent family violence) than adolescents, who may have more resources to avoid becoming victims of violence.

MACROSOCIAL ISSUES THAT DELIMIT INTERVENTION

Gang activity and violence are likely to be fostered by the same macrostructural factors at the community level that have been linked to other forms of deviance and negative child and adolescent outcomes (Huff 1993). For example, highly mobile communities have been shown to have lower density of acquaintanceships, which limits their ability to control crime, socialize their youth, and care for members with special needs (Freudenburg 1986). There exists considerable evidence that the density of friendship networks, parental control over teen peer groups, and participation in voluntary organizations — all aspects of community organization — are good predictors of rates of crime and delinquency within a community (Figueira-McDonough 1991). Rates of delinquency are related to the community instability that develops in neighbourhoods that experience significant population turnover (Bursik and Webb 1982). Durkin et al. (1994) found that high census tract proportions of low-income households, single-parent families, non–high school graduates, and unemployment were significant predictors of violence and delinquency among children younger than 17 years of age. These findings are consistent with those of Coulton et al. (1995), who showed that impoverishment, population instability, child-care burden (e.g., ratio of children to adults), and geographic/economic isolation (i.e., whether a neighbourhood had a contiguous census tract with at least 40 percent poor residents) were all related to increased risk of child victimization and delinquency.

In a recently completed study, the RAND Corporation examined the cost-effectiveness of several crime-prevention strategies that involve early intervention in the lives of people at risk of pursuing a criminal career (Greenwood et al. 1996). Focusing on California, RAND contrasted California's "three-strikes" policy, which guarantees extended sentences for repeat offenders, with four different approaches: (a) home visits by child care professionals, beginning before birth and extending through the first two years of childhood, followed by four years of daycare; (b) parent training for families with aggressive or acting-out children; (c) four years of cash and other graduation incentives for disadvantaged high school students; and (d) monitoring and supervision of high school–age youth who have already exhibited delinquent behaviour. All of the examined programs, with the exception of home visits and daycare, were appreciably more effective at reducing serious crimes than was the three-strikes policy. Graduation incentives for disadvantaged youth proved the most cost-effective approach, averting nearly $260 million from serious crimes compared to about $60 million for the three-strikes option. These findings have serious implications for policymakers who believe that increased incarceration time for juvenile offenders will systematically and over time reduce the youth crime rate.

CONCLUSION

In this chapter, we have provided an overview of youth gangs from a developmental perspective and presented social and criminological literature integrated with research on development and risk to underscore the importance of including multiple disciplines in our prevention and intervention strategies. Gang membership increases in adolescence because adolescence is a developmental transition period in which peers take on a significant support and influence role, and this is done often at the expense of parents and families. The gang can provide a vehicle for identity formation and a setting where an at-risk youth can find acceptance and reinforcement for rejecting social norms and engaging in deviant, delinquent, and sometimes violent behaviour. Adolescence is a transitional period when the need to meet multiple developmental tasks makes the gang an attractive alternative to at-risk youth.

Although the challenges are complex and long-term systematic change difficult to achieve, the cost of doing nothing is too high. We know that if we start early and identify at-risk youth in the early elementary years, we can promote prosocial competence and reduce the incidence of aggressive, antisocial behaviour. Gang violence is not an insurmountable social malady. Youth seek out gang involvement typically to meet normal developmental tasks and to fulfill needs that all adolescents and all individuals have. Prothrow-Stith is fond of saying that children will eventually get our time, our money, our attention, and our resources. It is up to us, as parents, researchers, educators and advocates, to decide when that will be. Will it be when children are young, eager to learn, and perhaps not yet exposed to high levels of violence and victimization? Or will it be later, after our children reach adolescence, have failed at school, and have chosen to meet their needs through gangs? Before systems can change, individuals must take action and make their choices.

STUDY QUESTIONS

1. *Why do Flannery, Huff, and Manos endorse a primary prevention approach as a way of decreasing youth gang involvement?*
2. *According to the research findings reviewed in this chapter, what are the most significant individual-level risk factors associated with youth gang involvement? What crime prevention measures and programs could one put into place to counter these individual-level risk factors?*
3. *What macrostructural factors do Flannery, Huff, and Manos identify as possible obstacles to the success of interventions aimed at decreasing youth gang involvement?*

REFERENCES

Bell, C., and E. Jenkins. 1991. "Traumatic Stress and Children." *Journal of Health Care for the Poor and Underserved* 2: 175–85.

Block, C.R., and R. Block. 1994. *Street Gang Crime in Chicago* [Research in brief]. Washington, DC: U.S. Department of Justice, Office of Justice Programs, National Institute of Justice.

Blumstein, A. 1995. "Violence by Young People: Why the Deadly Nexus?" *National Institute of Justice Journal 229*(August): 2–9.

Bursik, R.J., and J. Web. 1982. "Community Change and Patterns of Delinquency." *American Journal of Sociology 88*: 24–41.

Cairns, R.B., and B.D. Cairns. 1991. "Social Cognition and Social Networks: A Developmental Perspective." In D.J. Pepler and K.H. Rubin, eds., *The Development and Treatment of Childhood Aggression*, 249–74. Hillsdale, NJ: Lawrence Erlbaum.

Callahan, C.M., and F.P. Rivara. 1992. "Urban High School Youth and Hand-Guns." *Journal of the American Medical Association 267*(22): 3038–42.

Campbell, A. 1990. "Female Participation in Gangs." In C.R. Huff, ed., *Gangs in America*, 163–83. Newbury Park, CA: Sage.

Chesney-Lind, M., and M. Brown. 1999. "Girls and Violence: An Overview." In D. Flannery and R. Huff, eds., *Youth Violence: Prevention, Intervention, and Social Policy*, 171–99. Washington, DC: American Psychiatric Press.

Chesney-Lind, M., M. Brown, M.B. Leisen, P. Perrone, D. Kwasck, N. Marker, and D. Kato. 1996. *Perspectives on Juvenile Delinquency and Gangs: An Interim Report to Hawaii's State Legislature*. Honolulu: University of Hawaii at Manoa, Center for Youth Research, Social Science Research Institute.

Chesney-Lind, M., and R.G. Shelden. 1992. *Girls, Delinquency and Juvenile Justice*. Pacific Grove, CA: Brooks/Cole.

Chesney-Lind, M., R. Shelden, and L.K. Joe. 1996. "Girls, Delinquency and Gang Membership." In C.R. Huff, ed., *Gangs in America*, 185–204. Thousand Oaks, CA: Sage.

Cicchetti, D., and M. Lynch. 1993. "Toward an Ecological/Transactional Model of Community Violence and Child Maltreatment: Consequences for Children's Development." *Psychiatry 56*(1): 96–118.

Coulton, C., J. Korbin, and M. Su. 1996. "Measuring Neighborhood Context for Young Children in an Urban Area." *American Journal of Community Psychology 24*(1): 5–32.

Coulton, C., J. Korbin, M. Su, and J. Chow. 1995. "Community Level Factors and Child Maltreatment Rates." *Child Development 66*(5): 1262–76.

Crick, N.R., and K.A. Dodge. 1994. "A Review and Reformulation of Social Information-Processing Mechanisms in Children's Social Adjustment." *Psychological Bulletin 115*: 74–101.

Curry, G.D., R.A. Ball, and R.J. Fox. 1994. *Gang Crimes and Law Enforcement Recordkeeping* [Research in brief]. Washington, DC: U.S. Department of Justice, National Institute of Justice, Office of Justice Programs.

Curry, G.D., R.J. Fox., R.A. Ball, and D. Stone. 1992. *National Assessment of Law Enforcement Anti-Gang Information Resources* [Draft 1992 Final Report]. Morgantown: West Virginia University, National Assessment Survey.

Dishion, T.J., and D.W. Andrews. 1995. "Preventing Escalation in Problem Behaviors with High-Risk Young Adolescents: Immediate and 1-Year Outcomes." *Journal of Consulting and Clinical Psychology 63*(4): 538–48.

Dodge, K.A. 1993. "Social-Cognitive Mechanisms in the Development of Conduct Disorder and Depression." *Annual Review of Psychology 44*: 559–84.

DuRant, R., C. Cadenhead, R. Pendergrast, G. Slaven, and C.W. Linder. 1994. "Factors Associated with the Use of Violence among Urban Black Adolescents." *American Journal of Public Health 84*(4): 612–17.

Durkin, M., L. Davidson, L. Kuhn, P. O'Connor, and B. Barlow. 1994. "Low-Income Neighborhoods and the Risk of Severe Pediatric Injury: A Small Area Analysis in Northern Manhattan." *American Journal of Public Health 84*(4): 587–92.

Earls, F.J. 1994. "Violence and Today's Youth." *Critical Issues for Children and Youth 4*: 4–23.

Elliott, D.E. 1994. "Serious Violent Offenders: Onset, Developmental Course, and Termination." *Criminology 32*(1): 1–21.

Embry, D., D. Flannery, A. Vazsonyi, K. Powell, and H. Atha. 1996. "Peace-Builders: A Theoretically Driven, School-Based Model for Early Violence Prevention." *American Journal of Preventive Medicine 12*(5): 91–100.

Eron, L.D., and R. Huesmann. 1990. "The Stability of Aggressive Behavior — Even unto the Third Generation." In M. Lewis and S.M. Miller, eds., *Handbook of Developmental Psychopathology*, 147–56. New York: Plenum.

Esbensen, F.A., and D. Huizinga. 1993. "Gangs, Drugs, and Delinquency in a Survey of Urban Youth." *Criminology 31*: 565–89.

Fagan, J. 1990. "Social Processes of Delinquency and Drug Use among Urban Gangs." In C.R. Huff, ed., *Gangs in America*, 1st ed., 183–223. Newbury Park, CA: Sage.

———. 1996. "Gangs, Drugs and Neighborhood Change." In C.R. Huff, ed., *Gangs in America*, 2nd ed., 39–74. Thousand Oaks, CA: Sage.

Farrington, D.P. 1991. "Antisocial Personality from Childhood to Adulthood." *The Psychologist 4*: 389–94.

Farrington, D.P., R. Loeber, D.S. Elliot, J.D. Hawkins, D.B. Kandel, M.W. Lein, J. McCord, D.C. Rowe, and R.E. Tremblay. 1993. "Advancing Knowledge about the Onset of Delinquency and Crime." In B.B. Lahey and A.E. Kazdin, eds., *Advances in Clinical Child Psychology*, vol. 12, 283–342. New York: Plenum.

Federal Bureau of Investigation. 1994. *Crime in the United States — 1993.* Washington, DC: U.S. Department of Justice.

———. 1995. *Crime in the United States.* Washington, DC: U.S. Department of Justice.

Figueira-McDonough, J. 1991. "Community Structure and Delinquency: A Typology." *Social Service Review 65*(1): 69–91.

Finkelhor, D. 1995. "The Victimization of Children: A Developmental Perspective." *American Journal of Orthopsychiatry 65*(2): 177–93.

Finkelhor, D., and J. Dziuba-Leatherman. 1994. "Victimization of Children." *American Psychologist 49*(3): 173–83.

Fitzpatrick, K., and J. Boldizar. 1993. "The Prevalence and Consequences of Exposure to Violence among African-American Youth." *Journal of the American Academy of Child and Adolescent Psychiatry 32*(2): 424–30.

Flannery, D.J., A. Vazsonyi, D. Embry, and H. Atha. 1996. *Longitudinal Follow-Up of PeaceBuilders Violence Prevention Program* (Centers for Disease Control and Prevention, Cooperative Agreement #U81/CCU513508-01).

Fraser, M.W. 1996. "Aggressive Behavior in Childhood and Early Adolescence: An Ecological-Developmental Perspective on Youth Violence." *Social Work 41*(4): 347–61.

Freudenburg, W.R. 1986. "The Density of Acquaintanceship: An Overlooked Variable in Community Research." *American Journal of Sociology 92*: 27–63.

Garbarino, J., N. Durbrow, K. Kostelny, and C. Pardo. 1992. *Children in Danger: Coping with the Consequences of Community Violence.* San Francisco: Jossey-Bass.

Goldstein, A.P. 1991. *Delinquent Gangs: A Psychological Perspective.* Champaign, IL: Research Press.

Goldstein, A.P., and B. Glick. 1994. *The Prosocial Gang: Implementing Aggression Replacement Training.* Thousand Oaks, CA: Sage.

Gottfredson, M., and T. Hirschi. 1990. *A General Theory of Crime.* Stanford, CA: Stanford University Press.

Greenwood, P.W., K.E. Model, P. Rydell, and J. Chiesa. 1996. *Diverting Children from a Life of Crime: Measuring Costs and Benefits.* Santa Monica, CA: RAND.

Guerra, N.G., L.R. Huesmann, and L. Hanish. 1994. "The Role of Normative Beliefs in Children's Social Behavior." In N. Eisenberg, ed., *Social Development,* 140–58. Thousand Oaks, CA: Sage.

Guerra, N.G., L.R. Huesmann, P.H. Tolan, R. Acker, and L.F. Eron. 1995. "Stressful Events and Individual Beliefs as Correlates of Economic Disadvantage and Aggression among Urban Children." *Journal of Consulting and Clinical Psychology 63*(4): 518–28.

Hawkins, J.D., R.F. Catalano, D.M. Morrison, J. O'Donnell, R.D. Abbott, and L.E. Day. 1992. "The Seattle Social Development Project: Effects of the First Four Years on Protective Factors and Problem Behaviors." In J. McCord and R. Tremblay, eds., *The Prevention of Antisocial Behavior in Children,* 139–61. New York: Guilford.

Henggeler, S.W., and C.M. Borduin. 1990. *Family Therapy and Beyond: A Multi-Systemic Approach to Treating the Behavior Problems of Children and Adolescents.* Pacific Grove, CA: Brooks/Cole.

Henggeler, S.W., G.B. Melton, and L.A. Smith. 1992. "Family Preservation Using Multisystemic Therapy: An Effective Alternative to Incarcerating Serious Juvenile Offenders." *Journal of Consulting and Clinical Psychology 60*(6): 953–61.

Howell, J.C. 1994. "Recent Gang Research: Program and Policy Implications." *Crime & Delinquency 40*(4): 495–515.

Huesmann, L.R., L.D. Eron, M.M. Leftkowitz, and L.O. Walder. 1984. "Stability of Aggression over Time and Generations." *Developmental Psychology 20*: 1120–34.

Huff, C.R. 1993. "Gangs and Public Policy: Macrolevel Interventions." In A.P. Goldstein and C.R. Huff, eds., *The Gang Intervention Handbook*, 463–75. Champaign, IL: Research Press.

———. 1995. *Final Report to the National Institute of Justice Regarding the Criminal Behavior of Gang Members.* Columbus: Ohio State University Press.

———. 1996. "The Criminal Behavior of Gang Members and Nongang At-Risk Youth." In C.R. Huff, ed., *Gangs in America*, 2nd ed., 75–102. Thousand Oaks, CA: Sage

Jankowski, M.S. 1991. *Islands in the Street: Gangs and American Urban Society.* Berkeley: University of California Press.

Joe, K.A., and M. Chesney-Lind. 1995. "Just Every Mother's Angel: An Analysis of Gender and Ethnic Variations in Youth Gang Membership." *Gender & Society 9*(4): 408–30.

Kandel, E., and S.A. Mednick. 1991. "Perinatal Complications Predict Violent Offending." *Criminology 29*: 519–29.

Kellam, S.G., and G.W. Rebok. 1992. "Building Developmental and Etiological Theory through Epidemiologically Based Preventive Intervention Trials." In J. McCord and R.E. Tremblay, eds., *Preventing Antisocial Behavior: Interventions from Birth through Adolescence*, 62–195. New York: Guilford.

Kendall, P.C., and W. Grove. 1988. "Normative Comparisons in Therapy Outcome." *Behavioral Assessment 10*: 147–58.

Kendall, P.C., and S.D. Hollon. 1979. *Cognitive-Behavioral Interventions: Theory, Research, and Procedures.* New York: Academic Press.

Klein, M. 1971. *Street Gangs and Street Workers.* Englewood Cliffs, NJ: Prentice Hall.

———. 1995. *The American Street Gang: Its Nature, Prevalence, and Control.* New York: Oxford University Press.

Klein, M.W., C.L. Maxson, and L.C. Cunningham. 1991. " 'Crack,' Street Gangs, and Violence." *Criminology 29*: 623–50.

Kupersmidt, J.B., and J.D. Coie. 1990. "Preadolescent Peer Status, Aggression, and School Adjustment as Predictors of Externalizing Problems in Adolescence." *Child Development 61*: 1350–62.

Larson, R., and M.H. Richards, eds. 1989. "The Changing Life Space of Early Adolescence." [Special issue]. *Journal of Youth and Adolescence 18*(6): 501–10.

Loeber, R. 1982. "The Stability of Antisocial and Delinquent Child Behavior: A Review." *Child Development 53*: 1431–46.

Loeber, R., and D.F. Hay. 1994. "Developmental Approaches to Aggression and Conduct Problems." In M. Rutter and D.F. Hay, eds., *Development through Life: A Handbook for Clinicians*, 288–316. Boston: Blackwell Scientific.

Martinez, P., and J.E. Richters. 1993. "The NIMH Community Violence Project: II. Children's Distress Symptoms Associated with Violence Exposure." *Psychiatry 56*(1): 22–35.

Maxson, C.L., and M.W. Klein. 1996. "Defining Gang Homicide: An Updated Look at Member and Motive Approaches." In C.R. Huff, ed., *Gangs in America*, 2nd ed., 3–20. Thousand Oaks, CA: Sage.

Miller, W.B. 1982. *Crime by Youth Gangs and Groups in the United States.* Washington, DC: U.S. Department of Justice, Office of Juvenile Justice and Delinquency Prevention.

Montemayor, R., and D. Flannery. 1990. "Making the Transition from Childhood to Early Adolescence." In R. Montemayor, G. Adams, and T. Gullotta, eds., *Advances in Adolescence Development*, vol. 2: *From Childhood to Adolescence: A Transitional Period?* 291–301. Newbury Park, CA: Sage.

Moore, J.W., and J.M. Hagedorn. 1996. "What Happens to Girls in the Gang?" In C.R. Huff, ed., *Gangs in America*, 2nd ed., 205–20. Thousand Oaks, CA: Sage.

Morris, R.E., E.A. Harrison, G.W. Knox, E. Romanjhauser, D.K. Marques, and L.L. Watts. 1996. "Health Risk Behavioral Survey from 39 Juvenile Correctional Facilities in the United States." *Journal of Adolescent Health 17*(6): 334–75.

O'Donnell, C., M. Manos, and M. Chesney-Lind. 1987. "Diversion and Neighborhood Delinquency Programs in Open Settings: A Social Network Interpretation." In E. Morris and C. Braukman, eds., *Behavioral Approaches to Crime and Delinquency: Application, Research and Theory*, 251–71. New York: Plenum.

O'Donnell, J., J.D. Hawkins, and R.D. Abbott. 1995. "Predicting Serious Delinquency and Substance Use among Aggressive Boys." *Journal of Consulting and Clinical Psychology 63*(4): 529–37.

Paikoff, R.L., and J. Brooks-Gunn. 1991. "Do Parent–Child Interactions Change During Puberty?" *Psychological Bulletin 110*: 47–66.

Patterson, G., B. DeBaryshe, and B. Ramsey. 1989. "A Developmental Perspective on Antisocial Behavior." *American Psychologist 44*: 329–35.

Patterson, G.R., and L. Bank. 1989. "Some Amplifying Mechanisms for Pathologic Process in Families. In M.R. Gunner and E. Thelem, eds., *Systems and Development: The Minnesota Symposia on Child Psychology*, vol. 22, 167–210. Hillsdale, NJ: Lawrence Erlbaum.

Patterson, G.R., J.B. Reid, and T.J. Dishion. 1992. *A Social Learning Approach: IV. Antisocial Boys.* Eugene, OR: Castalia.

Patterson, G.R., and K. Yoerger. 1993. "Developmental Models for Delinquent Behavior." In S. Hodgins, ed., *Mental Disorders and Crime*, 140–72. Newbury Park, CA: Sage.

Portillas, E., and M.S. Zatz. 1995. *Not to Die For: Positive and Negative Aspects of Chicano Youth Gangs.* Paper presented at the annual meeting of the American Society of Criminology, Boston, November.

Reiss, A.J., Jr., and J. Roth. 1993. *Understanding and Preventing Violence*. Washington, DC: National Academy Press.

Richters, J., and P. Martinez. 1993. "The NIMH Community Violence Project: I. Children as Victims of, and Witnesses to Violence." *Psychiatry 56*(1): 7–21.

Ropp, L., P. Visintainer, J. Uman, and D. Treloar. 1992. "Death in the City: An American Childhood Tragedy." *Journal of the American Medical Association 267*(21): 2905–10.

Sampson, R.J., and W.B. Groves. 1989. "Testing Social-Disorganization Theory." *American Journal of Sociology 94*: 774–802.

Sampson, R.J., and J. Lauritsen. 1993. "Violent Victimization and Offending: Individual, Situational, and Community-Level Risk Factors." In A.J. Reiss, Jr., and J.A. Roth, eds., *Understanding and Preventing Violence*, vol. 3: *Social Influences,* 1–114. Washington, DC: National Academy Press.

Sheley, J.F., and J.D. Wright. 1993. *Gun Acquisition and Possession in Selected Juvenile Samples*. Washington, DC: U.S. Department of Justice, National Institute of Justice, Office of Juvenile Justice and Delinquency Prevention.

Singer, M., T. Anglin, L. Song, and L. Lunghofer. 1995. "Adolescents' Exposure to Violence and Associated Symptoms of Psychological Trauma." *Journal of the American Medical Association 273*(6): 477–82.

Skogan, W. 1986. "Fear of Crime and Neighborhood Change." In A.J. Reiss and M. Tonry, eds., *Communities and Crime*, 203–29. Chicago: University of Chicago Press.

Spergel, I.A. 1991. *Youth Gangs: Problem and Response*. Washington, DC: U.S. Department of Justice, Office of Juvenile Justice and Delinquency Prevention.

———. 1995. *The Youth Gang Problem: A Community Approach*. New York: Oxford University Press.

Steinberg, L. 1987. "Familial Factors in Delinquency: A Developmental Perspective." *Journal of Adolescent Research 2*: 255–68.

———. 1989. "Pubertal Maturation and Family Relations: Evidence for the Distancing Hypothesis." In G. Adams, R. Montemayor, and T. Gullotta, eds., *Advances in Adolescent Development*, vol. 1, 71–97. Newbury Park, CA: Sage.

Straus, M. 1994. *Violence in the Lives of Adolescents*. New York: Norton.

Tolan, P., and N. Guerra. 1994. *What Works in Reducing Adolescent Violence: An Empirical Review of the Field*. Boulder, CO: Center for the Study and Prevention of Violence.

Tolan, P.H., N.G. Guerra, and P.C. Kendall. 1995. "A Developmental-Ecological Perspective on Antisocial Behavior in Children and Adolescents: Toward a Unified Risk and Intervention Framework." *Journal of Consulting and Clinical Psychology 63*(4): 579–84.

Tolan, P.J., and R. Loeber. 1993. "Antisocial Behavior." In P.H. Tolan and B.J. Cohler, eds., *Handbook of Clinical Research and Practice with Adolescents*, 307–31. New York: John Wiley.

Tremblay, R., B. Masse, M. Leblanc, A.E. Schwartzman, and J.E. Ledingham. 1992. "Early Disruptive Behavior, Poor School Achievement, Delinquent Behavior, and Delinquent Personality: Longitudinal Analyses." *Journal of Consulting and Clinical Psychology 60*(1): 64–72.

Tremblay, R.E., L. Kurtz, L.C. Masse, F. Vitaro, and R.O. Phil. 1995. "A Bimodal Preventive Intervention for Disruptive Kindergarten Boys: Its Impact through Mid-Adolescence." *Journal of Consulting and Clinical Psychology 63*(4): 560–68.

Webster, D.W., P.S. Gainer, and H.R. Champion. 1994. "Weapon Carrying among Inner-City Junior High School Students: Defensive Behavior vs. Aggressive Delinquency." *American Journal of Public Health 83*(11): 1604–8.

Widom, C.S. 1989. "The Cycle of Violence." *Science 244*: 160–66.

Wilkinson, D.L., and J. Fagan. 1996. "The Role of Firearm Violence: The Dynamics of Gun Events among Adolescent Males." *Law and Contemporary Problems 59*(1): 55–90.

Wilson, W.J. 1987. *The Truly Disadvantaged: The Inner City, the Underclass and Public Policy.* Chicago: University of Chicago Press.

Yoshikawa, H. 1994. "Prevention as Cumulative Protection: Effects of Early Family Support and Education on Chronic Delinquency and Its Risks." *Psychological Bulletin 115*: 28–54.

CHAPTER ELEVEN

Female Gang Involvement

G. DAVID CURRY
University of Missouri, St. Louis

Female participation in gang-related crime (Candamil 1992; Cosmos 1993; Felkenes and Becker 1995; Howell 1994), although apparently less prevalent than that of males (Curry, Ball, and Fox 1994; Miller 1975; 1982; Spergel 1990), has attracted much attention from policymakers, the public, and scholars. Here I review the literature on female gang involvement and set forth a research agenda that, I hope, will bring us a better understanding of male as well as female gang behaviour.

THEMES IN RESEARCH ON FEMALE GANG INVOLVEMENT

Three questions have emerged from the literature on female gang involvement: (1) Is a feminist perspective required for understanding female gang involvement?; (2) Is female gang involvement increasing?; (3) Is female gang involvement "liberating"?

Is a Feminist Perspective Required for Understanding Female Gang Involvement?

Over time, the research on female gang involvement has moved closer to a feminist approach that involves understanding female gang participation from the point of view of the females themselves rather than from an externally imposed male perspective. A feminist perspective is one "in which women's experiences and ways of knowing are brought to the fore, not sup-

Source: G. David Curry, "Female Gang Involvement," *Journal of Research in Crime and Delinquency* 35(1) (February 1998): 100–19. Reprinted by permission of Sage Publications, Inc.

pressed" (Daly and Chesney-Lind 1988: 498). Those who pursue a feminist perspective in developing theories of criminal behaviour do so under the assumption that heretofore criminological theory has been "unable to explain adequately the phenomenon of women and crime." There is also the assumption that "unwittingly" focusing on "the activities, interests, and values of men, while ignoring a comparable analysis of women" results in a perspective that is inevitably "sexist" (Leonard 1982: 182). One of the strongest arguments for a feminist perspective is the comparatively narrow range of behaviours attributed to females under the male-centred perspective. From the male-centred perspective, participation in gangs is by nature a male behaviour, and females can be either tools to serve the interests of male gang members or the instrument of other social institutions antithetical to male participation in the gang.

Thrasher ([1927] 1963) in his study of Chicago gangs has been praised for his appreciation of the diversity and dynamic vitality of gang life (Hagedorn 1988: 84) and as "an activist, a person committed to putting what he learned into practice so that the lives of others might be improved" (Monti 1993: 17). For Thrasher gang involvement was male behaviour. The female gang involvement he reported (Thrasher [1927] 1963: 151) was by the young female "tomboy" and more transient than that of men, soon giving way to a concern with "hair" and "long skirts." Thrasher's reasons for why females did not participate in gangs both have counterparts in contemporary feminist theories of female delinquency. That "the social patterns for behaviour of girls, powerfully backed by the great weight of tradition and custom, are contrary to the gang and its activities" (Thrasher [1927] 1963: 161) could be interpreted as an early presentation of gender-based subcultural theory (Brownfield 1996), and his observation that "girls even in urban disorganized areas, are much more closely supervised and guarded than boys" (Thrasher [1927] 1963: 161) is in keeping with power control theory as an explanation of lower levels of female participation in delinquency in patriarchal families (Hagan, Gillis, and Simpson 1987).

Still, when it came to the relationship of females to gangs, Thrasher produced a male-centred perspective that was to dominate the literature for decades. Thrasher described females as either the instruments of male gang members or the instrument of the social forces that undermine male participation. As instruments of the gang, females were portrayed by Thrasher ([1927] 1963) in terms of sexuality: "Certain girls may be taken under its protection or in other cases may become members of the gang in their sexual capacity" (Thrasher [1927] 1963: 155). His examples ranged from female participation in "orgiastic" or "immoral" gangs, "the stag party" usually involving female nude dancers (Thrasher [1927] 1963: 164–65), and the "gang shag" in which multiple gang members engaged in sex with the same female (Thrasher [1927] 1963: 166). The specific way in which girls received "protection" by these activities was not made explicit. As external to the gang, females were identified by Thrasher as "the chief disintegrating force in the gang."

> For the gang boy, marriage usually means reincorporation into family groups and other social structures of work, play, and religion which family life as a rule brings with it. The gang which once supplanted the home, now succumbs to it. (Thrasher [1927] 1963: 170)

Thrasher's male-centred view of gang life was reflected in other classic studies of gangs. Two examples serve to make the point. In Whyte's (1943) study of the Norton Street Gang, his vivid images of the "corner boys" can be contrasted to his description of the Aphrodite Club. For a period of time during Whyte's observation, the Nortons entered into an alliance with the Aphrodite Club. As a result of their association with this nondelinquent female group, relations within the structure of the male group experienced strains and, in some cases, permanent rearrangements. In a comparable way, Spergel (1964) in his study of male gangs and delinquent groups in New York City neighbourhoods described the females who associated with his gang members in terms of utility associated with their gender or sexuality or as a threat to the integrity of the gang through marriage. Females "played various roles, contributing highly to the maintenance of the gang-fighting system. She was the carrier of tales — the magnifier, the distorter, and fabricator of derogatory remarks which served to instigate conflict among the various clubs" (Spergel 1964: 88–89). More direct participation in conflict as "weapon-bearer" or "spy" was described. As in Thrasher, women still retained a role as gang destroyers. For Spergel, "Marriage and employment, in particular, compel the patterns of orientation and behaviour previously developed during the stage of adolescent delinquency to change" (Spergel 1964: 148).

The research of Whyte and Spergel had as a central focus male participation in gang activity, but comparable views were generated by other studies with female gang involvement as the primary concern. Two studies of female involvement in gangs were Rice's (1963) "A Reporter at Large" and Hanson's (1964) *Rebels in the Streets*. Each elaborated on the theme that female gangs and their members are "marginal and parasitic" (Campbell 1991: 17) to the greater social world of male gangs.

The shortsightedness of androcentric perspectives of female participation in gangs was revealed as research that transcended the male-centred stereotypes became available. The work of three male researchers is generally cited as beginning to transcend the male-centred stereotypes dating from Thrasher. Miller (1973) reported the results of his study of two female gangs, Brown (1977) recorded the gang-related activity of African American female gang members in Philadelphia, and Quicker (1983) studied Chicana involvement in gangs in southern California. One of Miller's gangs, the Molls, a gang of White Catholic girls, and the Holly Ho's, a gang of African American girls studied by Brown, were described as autonomous female gangs with their own female leadership and gang-based patterns of criminal involvement. The other gang studied by Miller, an African American gang, the Queens, and the Latina girl gangs reported by Quicker were affiliates or auxiliaries of male gangs, but sexual availability to male gang members was by no means a condition of membership as recorded by these researchers.

The argument that understanding female gang involvement required a feminist perspective was first enunciated in Campbell's (1984; 1991) *The Girls in the Gang*. Her research was presented as a set of social biographies of three women involved in three separate female gangs in New York City from 1979 into the early 1980s. Two were Puerto Rican and the other African American. All were mothers at the time of the study. Two were involved in female auxiliaries to male gangs. One had been a member of an autonomous female gang, but she had subsequently joined a mixed-sex gang with rules supporting a hegemonic gender structure of men over women. From her research, Campbell (1991: 32) arrived at two major conclusions about female gang involvement in the early 1980s: (1) "It is still the male gang that paves the way for the female affiliate and opens the door into many illegitimate opportunities and into areas that serve as proving grounds." With some exceptions, females become involved in gang activity through male relatives or boyfriends; (2) Once involved in gangs, however, "a more visible solidarity or 'sisterhood' within the gang appears. A girl's status depends to a larger extent on her female peers." "Worth" within the gang was not a matter of relationships with males or "simple sexual attractiveness."

Campbell's findings were themes that had not been absent from prior work, such as that of Miller, Brown, and Quicker reviewed above. The perspectives of females, however, had never been emphasized as being so strikingly different from the perspectives of male gang members, nor had the method of taking a female-based perspective been characterized as explicitly feminist in orientation. It could be argued that as an issue or theme in research on female gang involvement, the question of the need for a feminist perspective has historically only been an issue insofar as earlier generations of male scholars ignored the issue, and, as a result of that earlier neglect, a more recent generation of scholars feels compelled to emphasize it. Whether a feminist perspective has any meaning for theory and future research on female gang involvement other than as a manifestation of generational differences will be examined below. First, though, the other themes that have characterized research on female gang involvement will be reviewed.

Is Female Gang Involvement Increasing?

A second theme in research on female gang involvement has been the issue of whether female gang involvement is increasing. This should not be confused with the more interesting theoretical question of what the correlates of changes in levels of female gang participation might be. Likewise, this question cannot be disentangled from the question of whether gang-involvement rates for females are changing proportionally to rate changes for males (Klein 1995: 111). The idea that female involvement in gangs is increasing has often been taken for granted by researchers in the face of media and law enforcement declarations (Chesney-Lind 1993), but the idea's popularity has led Chesney-Lind, Shelden, and Joe (1996) to critique its validity.

Three national surveys of law enforcement agencies spanning two decades have gathered information on female gang involvement. Relying on data from six cities, Miller (1975) provided an estimate of the gang crime problem by gender that is still cited and used as a rule of thumb, when he noted, "A general estimate that gang members are 90 percent or more male probably obtains for all gang cities" (Miller 1975: 23). Miller's 10 percent estimate was greater than his reported statistics for any of the cities included in his study. For example, in New York City, where half of the gangs identified by police were reported to have had female auxiliaries, only 6 percent of gang membership was estimated to be females. Computations from data gathered by a 1988 survey sponsored by the Office of Juvenile Justice and Delinquency Prevention (OJJDP) (Inter-University Consortium for Political and Social Research 1993; Spergel and Curry 1993) produced an estimate of 4803 female gang members reported for 34 jurisdictions. This was 3.98 percent of all gang members reported for these jurisdictions. The 1992 National Institute of Justice survey (Curry, Ball, and Fox 1994) of law enforcement agencies requested available information on female gang members from agencies in the nation's 79 largest cities and smaller cities that had been included in the 1988 OJJDP survey. For 61 law enforcement jurisdictions reporting statistics for female gang members, a total of 9092 female gang members was reported. As a percentage of the total number of gang members reported to the study for the nation, this came to only 3.65 percent. If, in an effort to control for law enforcement policies that officially excluded female gang members, gang members are only counted from cities reporting some number of both male and female gang members, the percentage increased to only 5.7 percent, still well below Miller's 10 percent estimate.

Another statistic that is used as a measure of increased female gang involvement is greater reported numbers of autonomous female gangs. Miller (1975: 23) classified female gangs into three types: (1) female auxiliary gangs affiliated with male gangs; (2) mixed-sex gangs with both male and female members; and (3) independent or autonomous female gangs. His results indicated that by far the most common of these was the female auxiliary. Without doubt, the rarest of gangs involving females were independent, autonomous female gangs. Miller found only one in 1975. As he extended his study, Miller (1982: 74) reported six autonomous female gangs in the Bronx and Queens, but few more in other locations. The 1988 OJJDP compiled reports of the existence of 22 "independent" female gangs. The 1992 National Institute of Justice national survey (Curry, Ball, and Fox 1994) received reports of 99 independent female gangs spread over 35 law enforcement jurisdictions in 1991. There are, however, several problems with treating these survey results from law enforcement agencies as indicative of increasing female gang involvement.

First, the data from national surveys were not derived by using comparable methodology. Miller used official data. The OJJDP survey used estimates.

The National Institute of Justice survey returned to official records statistics only. Each study emphasized differences in definitions of what constituted a gang or a gang-related crime across jurisdictions and time. Only 23 of the 34 law enforcement agencies offering 1987 percentage estimates to the 1988 OJJDP survey provided official statistics on the number of female gang members in their jurisdictions to the 1992 NIJ survey. The increase for these 23 jurisdictions, over a four-year period, was from an estimated 4803 female gang members in 1987 to a tabulation of 4971 female gang members in 1991. Given the time lapse, the increase was not a particularly radical one. The apparent increases in the number of "autonomous" female gangs is also subject to skepticism. Klein (1995: 66) has questioned the ability of police or researchers to distinguish with any accuracy differences between Miller's typology of female gangs by gender mixture. Given the absence of uniform definitions and limited law enforcement ability to get accurate internal information on gangs, it would be unwise to place too much emphasis on the increased numbers of autonomous female gangs reported by studies of local law enforcement data. A related point is that these observed increases in statistics on female gang involvement occur within a context of even greater increases in similar statistics on male gang members. Within the context of these perceived increases in male gang participation, it might even be possible to argue that female gang participation as a proportion of male gang membership is declining.

It has also been argued that law enforcement agencies and researchers who have relied on law enforcement data have greatly underestimated the number of females in gangs. In a longitudinal survey of Denver respondents, Esbensen and Huizinga (1993) found that about 25 percent of youth self-reporting gang membership were females. This finding led Esbensen and Huizinga to suggest that the participation of females in gangs may be greatly underestimated. From her fieldwork with gangs, Moore (1991) estimated that females accounted for one third of all gang members. The difference between these survey estimates and the analyses of official records may be a methodological one. Not all delinquency is detected and not all gang members are identified by law enforcement. Given the lower levels of offending by females in comparison to males, even among gang members (addressed below), it may be that female gang members are less likely than are males to be identified as such by law enforcement agencies. Still, Curry, Ball, and Fox (1994: 8) noted that "in a number of cities females as a matter of policy were never classified as gang members." In an argument linked to the first theme about the need for a feminist perspective, Chesney-Lind, Brown, and Kwack (1996: 194) have cautioned that given the "gendered habits" of many gang researchers, gang involvement by females could easily have been undercounted in the past.

Is Female Gang Involvement "Liberating"?

The third theme that has arisen from the research on female gang involvement concerns the impact of female gang involvement on the young women participating. Is female gang involvement becoming more independent and autonomous of males? Is it in some way liberating for the females involved? Of the three themes in female gang involvement identified here, this is the only one around which a debate in the literature has arisen. From the research literature that has explicitly focused on the role of females in gangs, two divergent hypotheses have emerged. Chesney-Lind (1993) has characterized the first position as the "liberation hypothesis." The second is here labelled the "social injury hypothesis."

Campbell's (1991: 31) conclusion that there exists among female gang members "a more visible solidarity and 'sisterhood' " is reached through her emphasis on how much this female independence and solidarity are reached through the diminished importance of their relationships with males. Harris (1988), who conducted in-depth structured interviews with 21 Chicana girls aged 13 to 18 who were involved in gangs in southern California, found that female members governed their own cliques and gained status through their own behaviour within their cliques (Harris 1988: 125–26, 130). It is important to note that Campbell in her account of Sun-Africa and the Five Percent Nation detailed the paternalistic and sexist structure of that particular gang, and she concluded her book by emphasizing the limits of the liberation that was to be obtained through gang involvement. Harris, likewise, observed that the independence of the Chicana gang members she studied was achieved through continued resistance to recurring male gang member efforts to control and exploit them. For other research, however, the liberation hypothesis is presented with less qualification.

The two most extreme statements of the liberation theme are found in separate accounts of female gang member involvement in drug sales. Lauderback, Hansen, and Waldorf (1992) studied the Potrero Hill Posse, "a strictly independent group of young African-American women" (Lauderback, Hansen, and Waldorf 1992: 57). Ten members of the Posse were interviewed as part of a larger study of 65 gang-involved females. The evolution of the Posse paralleled Campbell's two propositions. The five Posse founders learned drug selling from their boyfriends during the proliferation of crack sales in San Francisco in the late 1980s. Reportedly, the posse founders broke off on their own because they perceived the distribution of drug profits in the operation they were involved in to be unfair. At the time of the study, the Potrero Hill Posse included 22 to 23 members. Initiation into membership required having grown up in the community and proof of criminal skill through shoplifting or crack-selling ability. The major profit-making activity of the gang was a systematic and well-organized crack cocaine dealing operation.

A similar image of female involvement in gangs and drug sales was offered by Taylor (1993) from his series of case studies of female gang members in Detroit. From his analysis of gang types and infrastructure based on "structure, function, and motivation," he concluded, "Women are participating in gangs in crime as never before in urban America. And, this is not exclusive to Detroit" (Taylor 1993: 10). For Taylor, "A new attitude of female criminal independence is emerging. The male–female gang relationship is also being altered" (Taylor 1993: 23). Crucial to this change had been the involvement of female gang members in the drug trade. According to Taylor, "The dope business has empowered young and old, female and male, in many major cities" (Taylor 1993: 9).

The "social injury hypothesis" holds that any benefit in personal liberation that girls may gain from gang involvement is outweighed by the social costs of such affiliation. The strongest proponent of the social injury hypothesis has been Moore (1991). Moore grounded her position in her interviews with a random sample of 156 male and female gang members from a population of members from two barrio gangs in two Los Angeles Mexican American communities. To some extent, Moore's results were in line with those of Campbell and Harris, with females having some level of autonomy within their cliques, but Moore based her conclusions about the greater impact in terms of social injury on the cumulative influence of gang involvement as female members made the transition into adulthood and the perspectives of male gang members toward female members.

Moore (1991) concluded that the damage that gang involvement did to the immediate and long-term social future of gang girls far surpassed that experienced by males in the same context. The stigma associated with gang involvement was particularly injurious to the social reputations of Chicana females. Few managed to escape drug addiction or gang life, and most of those required the assistance of marriage to a "reasonably square man with a reasonably stable job" (Moore 1991: 129). Long-term harm on children was also a concern. While a majority of the male and female gang members studied by Moore ultimately had children (82 percent of the men and 94 percent of the women), the women (85 percent) were significantly more likely than the men (43 percent) to rear their children (Moore 1991: 113). The women (22 percent) were more likely to report that their children had joined gangs than the men (only 5 percent) (Moore 1991: 114).

Moore chastised Campbell for suggesting "that girl gangs have outgrown their sexist image" (Moore 1991: 55). Moore herself found sexist attitudes prevalent among a majority of the male gang members and many of the female gang members whom she interviewed. Male gang members displayed one or more of three attitudes toward female gang members (Moore 1991: 54): (1) females were not considered worthy of gang membership; (2) males should always be dominant over females in gangs; (3) females were regarded as sexual objects for male "gang warriors." Moore even recorded several instances in which gang females supported or assisted in the rape of other female members. Moore's emphasis on social injury has received support from other researchers. In her study of female gang members in Ohio, Miller (1996) described sexist attitudes among female gang members and incidents of sexual exploitation in mixed-sex gangs. From their study of female gang members in Hawaii, Joe and Chesney-Lind (1995) explicitly rejected the liberation hypothesis. For them, gang involvement was not an act of rebellion but an attempt of "young women to cope with a bleak and harsh present as well as a dismal future" (Joe and Chesney-Lind 1995: 28).

Although the disagreement between the supporters of the liberation hypothesis and the social injury hypothesis has been spirited, there is evidence for both views, and, with some reservations, there are essential elements of each from which an understanding of female, and male, gang involvement can be enhanced. The option of gang involvement for at-risk females is indeed one that may offer an opportunity for some level of "solidarity" and even limited individual liberation, while, at the same time, increasing risk of exposure to violence, loss of legitimate opportunities, and victimization by male and female gang members. From a dialectical perspective, there is really no theoretical problem in the same social activity being simultaneously rewarding and destructive. The same thing can be said about a wife in a paternalistic family structure, the worker in a capitalist economy, or the volunteer to military service (Foucault 1979). Similarly for male gang members, it may be possible that the "defiant individualist" (Sánchez Jankowski 1991) can simultaneously be the individual alienated from the community with no employment future (Hagedorn 1988).

The dialectical and contradictory nature of female gang involvement can be found even in some research supporting the liberation hypothesis. Despite the observation of Lauderback, Hansen, and Waldorf (1992) that the Potrero Hill Posse was similar in nature to a family, the gang's practice was far from being a generalized "sisterhood." The ties that bound the Posse together were business oriented and instrumental. A social by-product of the crack operation as administered by the Posse was the recurring exploitation of nonposse females as "toss-ups," women used for sex in crack houses, and as heads of household in residences used as temporary crack houses.

The dialectical interplay of liberation and social injury was especially clear in Fishman's ([1988] 1995) observations of a Chicago female gang called the Vice Queens from her perspective as a fieldworker for the Short and Strodtbeck project from 1960 to 1963. The Vice Queens were the African-American female auxiliary to the male Vice Kings. In congruence with the more male-centred views of female gang participation, the Vice Queens were described in sexually instrumental roles to their male counterparts that included being available for sex — and even bearing children and working as prostitutes. They were pictured as instigating conflicts between the Vice Kings and other male gangs and serving as weapons bearers and lookouts when conflicts were most intense. At the same time, a number of Vice Queen activities were reported that do not fit stereotypic restrictions. They engaged in property crime activities independently of the Vice Kings and participated in fighting with members of other female gangs that were independent of male conflicts. Despite, or perhaps as a result of, their sexual exploitation by the Vice Kings, a number of the Vice Queens expressed a preference for homosexual relationships with each other. Although the debate over liberation versus social injury has probably been the most spirited in the literature on female gang involvement to date, its extension, if not resolution, is discussed below as one amenable to measurement and empirical testing.

AN AGENDA FOR RESEARCH ON FEMALE GANG INVOLVEMENT

An agenda for research on female gang involvement must overcome shortcomings of past research while building on the themes that have been central to that research. It should also be linked to major themes in the larger research literature on male gangs. Space prevents more than the simplest outline for such an agenda here.

Building on Prior Research

When reviews of the literature on gangs (female or male) are organized chronologically, the cyclical nature of the history of gang research is quite apparent. Nothing has characterized research on gangs more than a tendency to emphasize the degree to which each piece of research is a new "discovery" that more or less invalidates earlier efforts. Thanks to a contemporary revival of research on gangs, more is known about gangs and there is more ongoing research on gangs than ever before. Where links with earlier gang research have been made, there has been a preference to reach back to Thrasher, sometimes without a very careful reading of the original. The problems of invoking Thrasher in the case of studying female gang involvement have been noted above by emphasizing the narrowness associated with his male-centred approach.

It is important that the central themes of prior research neither be dismissed out of hand nor accepted without reservation. In particular, popular media presentations have taken for granted propositions such as increased female gang involvement, the growing violence of female gang members, and that gangs play a major role in the organized distribution of drugs. Scrutiny of the available research literature reveals the intellectual riskiness of generalizing from such reports.

Linking Research to Theory

As noted above, gang research on males and females has been characterized by a tendency to "invent" rather than expand or integrate existing theories of gang involvement and delinquency. In too much gang research, the facts have just been too exciting to bend to the mundane demands of more rigorous theory. An effective research agenda on female, or male, gang involvement must make the transition from simply describing gang behaviour to developing and testing theories about gang behaviour. In so doing, it must also move toward integrating research on gangs into the mainstream of research on delinquency and crime in general. Three theoretical themes strike me as being particularly worth pursuing.

GANGS AND THE THEORY OF THE URBAN UNDERCLASS

The growth of the urban underclass (Wilson 1987) has been linked to the emergence of gang problems in Milwaukee (Hagedorn 1988) and St. Louis (Decker and Van Winkle 1996), the entrenchment of gangs in Los Angeles (Moore 1988; 1989), and the proliferation of gangs nationwide (Klein 1995: 194–95). Wilson has postulated that unlike socially disadvantaged minority populations of the past, contemporary inner-city minority residents are irrevocably segregated and isolated from existing avenues of economic opportunity. The value of Wilson's theory to understanding gangs was enhanced by Bursik and Grasmick's (1993) reconstruction of Shaw and McKay's social disorganization theory. By integrating Hunter's levels of social control into social disorganization theory, Bursik and Grasmick were able to incorporate Wilson's conceptualization of the urban underclass into a community-level theory of gang problems.

A research effort that indicated the importance of macro-level social factors such as those posited by Wilson on female gang involvement was conducted by Bowker and Klein (1983). Bowker and Klein studied gang and nongang girls inside and outside the juvenile justice system. Survey results from 78 girls identified within the juvenile justice system were supplemented with official records information. Survey data were also collected from a comparison group of girls residing in the neighbourhoods in which gangs were active. This second population had no record of contact with the juvenile justice system. In all, the study compared 122 gang girls and 100 nongang girls. The survey data included the results of several batteries of psychological tests. Because they found no significant differences in keeping with psychological explanations of the etiology of female gang membership, Bowker and Klein (1983) suggested that

> the overwhelming impact of racism, sexism, poverty and limited opportunity structures is likely to be so important in determining the gang membership and juvenile delinquency of women and girls in urban ghettos that personality variables, relations with parents, and problems associated with heterosexual behaviour play a relatively minor role. (Bowker and Klein 1983: 750–51)

Wilson (1987: 90–91) in his construction of the urban underclass theory devoted special attention to the differential impact of the social structural changes inherent in the theory on men and women. Campbell (1991: 35–36) provided a good foundation for this kind of approach in her description of the way gender provided different kinds of access to the mainstream culture and economy for Puerto Rican women and men. As research efforts emerge to test the hypothetical importance of the emergence of the urban underclass on the emergence and proliferation of gang problems, it is important that this research encompass the measures of the differential impact of these social forces on males and females.

CULTURAL FACTORS AND GANGS

The influence of cultural context was stressed by Moore in her studies of Chicano gangs in Los Angeles, and its importance has not been overlooked in other research on female gang involvement in Mexican American communities. Female participation in gangs was not the primary focus of Horowitz's (1983) study of "coming of age" in a Chicago Chicano community, but her work illustrated how interpreting gang involvement for males or females required an appreciation of the cultural context of the community setting. Horowitz observed female gangs that were both affiliated with male gangs and autonomous, but in every case, female participation emerged as a form of (largely unsuccessful) struggle against male control (Horowitz 1983: 133). Whereas male gang involvement was pictured by Horowitz as a central component of personal identity, the role of gang involvement for females was a peripheral concern subordinate to other dilemmas facing young women.

The Chicana female gangs studied by Quicker (1983) in East Los Angeles were all affiliates of male gangs with in most cases names that were feminized versions (in Spanish) of the male gang affiliate. For the "homegirls" studied by Quicker, their role as full participants in the social life of their barrios was as important as their gang membership. The importance of cultural factors for the gang girls studied by Harris (1988) was reflected in their self-identification as Cholas, the female plural form of Cholo, a term used by Americans and more established Mexican American residents of southern California for "the poorest of the poor, marginalized immigrants" (Vigil 1990: 116).

Klein (1995) has argued that a major element in the proliferation of gang problems in the United States has been the development and diffusion of a "gang culture" (Klein 1995: 205). This gang culture has become integrated into a broader popular youth culture. Future research on gangs should examine ways in which such gang culture structures the relationships between, and the roles of, men and women. The research of Horowitz, Quicker, and Hams showing how gang behaviour is influenced by community cultural context makes it essential that studies that focus on gender relations within gangs also be sensitive to the influences of broader cultural settings on these relationships.

GANGS AND DELINQUENCY

A recurrent finding in gang research has been higher levels of delinquency associated with gang membership. Using the Denver Youth Survey, Esbensen and Huizinga (1993) found two to three times as much delinquency for gang members as nongang members. From longitudinal survey results on a representative sample of Rochester youth, Thornberry et al. (1993) also concluded that gang-involved youth were significantly more likely to report involvement in violence and other delinquency. By following youth over time, their analysis showed gang involvement to be a transitional process with delinquent activity increasing during gang involvement and declining afterward.

Differences in levels of delinquency between gang members and nongang members has held up when gender is controlled. Relying on samples of high school students and dropouts from three cities, Fagan (1990) found that both male and female gang members had higher levels of self-reported delinquent behaviour than their nongang counterparts. Although male gang members exhibited higher levels of delinquent behaviour than female gang members, female gang members had higher levels of delinquent behaviour than nongang males. Using the Thornberry data from Rochester, Bjerregaard, and Smith (1993) systematically examined gender differences in gang involvement. Increased involvement in delinquency and substance abuse were observed for both male and female gang members in comparison to nongang members, but they found surprisingly little difference in the factors that explained male and female gang involvement. The only major difference observed was that failure in school was a stronger explanatory variable for females than males.

Although research has demonstrated differences between gang members and other youth regardless of gender, it has also been shown that male gang members engage in more delinquency than female gang members and especially more violent delinquency. In a series of studies that have combined analysis of official records and interviews with gang members, Joe and Chesney-Lind (1995; Chesney-Lind, Shelden, and Joe 1996) found that male gang members offended more and engaged in more violence than female gang members. From the limited available law enforcement data on gang offences by gender, Curry, Ball, and Fox (1994) concluded that female gang offenders were proportionally more likely to have been involved in property offences and less likely to have been involved in violent offences. Both Klein (1995) and Spergel (1995) have emphasized these differences in levels of violence by gang member gender by drawing attention to the extremely small portions of gang-related homicides that have been attributed to female offenders respectively in Los Angeles and Chicago in recent years. For Spergel (1995), "the youth gang problem in its violent character is essentially a male problem" (Spergel 1995: 58).

Two papers presented at the 1996 annual meetings of the American Society of Criminology contained empirical evidence linking gender-specific attitudes toward violence and differences in violent behaviour. Chesney-Lind, Brown, and Kwack (1996), using data from their Hawaii research, argued that females regardless of gang membership status are more likely than are males to consider specific behaviours as violent in nature. Deschenes et al. (1996) analyzed survey data on 5935 eighth-grade students from 42 schools in eleven cities. They found significant differences between females and males in the neutralization of violence. Males were more likely than were females to accept physical violence and feel that violence was justified. Gang members regardless of gender were more likely to accept violence than were nongang members. Among gang members, differences between males and females, although not as pronounced, were still observed. In multivariate logistic regression analysis, these attitudinal differences were shown to be statistically significant predictors of levels of violent offending for the total population, for males, and for females.

A GENDER-CONSCIOUS PERSPECTIVE

Of the three themes central to female gang involvement identified in the first section of this article, the recognition of the need for a feminist perspective may be most important as a prelude to developing more useful theories of criminal behaviour. A review by Leonard (1982) of the major theoretical approaches to crime and delinquency, including those that had been developed from studies of male gang involvement, found anomie theory and subcultural theory (among others) inadequate to explain female criminality. Subsequent and comparable reviews reached the same conclusion (Chesney-Lind and Shelden 1992; Daly and Chesney-Lind 1988; Mann 1984). Campbell's (1984) conclusions from her review of the gang literature was a comparable revelation. This review of the literature reaches a similar conclusion that an androcentric perspective can result only in narrow interpretations that cannot encompass the empirical results of available research. A comparable example of improving the breadth of theory by the addition of a feminist perspective was suggested by Tittle (1995: 22) for the study of rape. The feminist perspective defined rape as a crime of violence, an abstraction that moved rape into the same theoretical category as other forms of violent assault. Adding a feminist perspective to the study of gang involvement has resulted in similar changes in how concepts and propositions are developed that will make it possible to incorporate a greater range of themes into the research agenda on female gang involvement.

A feminist perspective brings its demands as well as its rewards. Daly and Chesney-Lind (1988) suggest that a feminist approach must deal with two theoretical problems: the "generalizability problem" and the "gender-ratio problem" (Daly and Chesney-Lind 1988: 517). The generalizability problem concerns the degree to which findings about male gang members can be applied to understanding and responding to female gang involvement. The gender-ratio problem concerns the differences between males and females in participating in delinquency and crime. In addition, much of what has been described as male gang involvement (Horowitz 1983; Moore 1991) can be described as "doing gender" (West and Zimmerman 1987). The degree to which female gang involvement reflects "doing gender" from a female perspective and what this means are questions that must be part of the future research agenda.

As Short (1996) noted, "Gangs probably have always been more diverse than they have been portrayed in either our limited studies or in the media" (Short 1996: xi). For Moore (1991: 136–37), stereotypes that emerge from the traditional view of the gang are important tools of those who would isolate and separate gang-involved youth from the rest of society. Picturing gang members as non-white minorities is one element of creating a "social cleavage" that separates them from white, middle-class America. In the same way, picturing gangs as quintessentially male through an act of cognitive purification is likewise part of the process of social cleavage. As all-male, violent social entities, gangs can be perceived as fundamentally different from the dual-gendered society in which they exist. Attention to gender as a variable requires "the understanding that in any community or location, men and women assume different social roles" (Weiss 1993: 2). The gender-based analysis demanded by a feminist perspective, with its focus on the social roles of men and women as different, complementary, and intersecting, offers an especially useful tool for understanding the gang-related activities of females by studying the behaviour of both men and women in gang-related roles.

STUDY QUESTIONS

1. *According to Curry, to what extent has female gang involvement increased in recent years in the United States? What are some of the data collection problems associated with trying to determine whether female gang involvement has increased?*
2. *What evidence is there to support the "liberation hypothesis" versus the "social injury hypothesis" of female gang involvement?*
3. *According to Curry, why is a feminist perspective needed in the study of gang involvement?*

REFERENCES

Bjerregaard, Beth, and Carolyn C. Smith. 1993. "Gender Differences in Gang Participation, Delinquency, and Substance Use." *Journal of Quantitative Criminology* 9(4): 329–55.

Bowker, Lee H., and Malcolm W. Klein. 1983. "The Etiology of Female Juvenile Delinquency and Gang Membership: A Test of Psychological and Social Structural Explanations." *Adolescence 18*: 739–51.

Brown, Waln K. 1977. "Black Female Gang Members in Philadelphia." *International Journal of Offender Therapy and Comparative Criminology 21*: 221–28.

Brownfield, David. 1996. "Subcultural Theories of Crime and Delinquency." In John Hagan, A.R. Gillis, and David Brownfield, eds., *Criminological Controversies: A Methodological Primer*, 99–123. Boulder, CO: Westview.

Bursik, Robert J., and Harold G. Grasmick. 1993. *Neighborhoods and Crime: The Dimensions of Effective Community Control*. New York: Lexington Books.

Campbell, Anne. 1984. *The Girls in the Gang*. Cambridge, MA: Basil Blackwell.

———. 1991. *The Girls in the Gang*, 2nd ed. Cambridge, MA: Basil Blackwell.

Candamil, Maria T. 1992. "Female Gangs: The Forgotten Ones." Washington, DC: U.S. Department of Health and Human Services; Administration for Children, Youth, and Families.

Chesney-Lind, Meda. 1993. "Girls, Gangs, and Violence: Reinventing the Liberated Female Crook." *Humanity and Society 17*(3): 321–44.

Chesney-Lind, Meda, Marilyn Brown, and Dae-Gyung Kwack. 1996. "Gender, Gangs, and Violence in a Multi-Ethnic Community." Presented at the annual meeting of the American Society of Criminology, November 21, Chicago, IL.

Chesney-Lind, Meda, and Randall G. Shelden. 1992. *Girls: Delinquency and Juvenile Justice*. Pacific Grove, CA: Brooks/Cole.

Chesney-Lind, Meda, Randall G. Shelden, and Karen A. Joe. 1996. "Girls, Delinquency, and Gang Membership." In C. Ronald Huff, ed., *Gangs in America*, 2nd ed., 185–204. Thousand Oaks, CA: Sage

Cosmos Corporation. 1993. *Forum on the Prevention of Adolescent Female Gang Involvement*. Washington, DC: ACE-Federal Reporters.

Curry, G. David, Richard A. Ball, and Robert J. Fox. 1994. *Gang Crime and Law Enforcement Recordkeeping*. Washington, DC: U.S. Department of Justice, National Institute of Justice Research in Brief.

Daly, Kathleen, and Meda Chesney-Lind. 1988. "Feminism and Criminology" *Justice Quarterly 5*: 497–538.

Decker, Scott H., and Barrik Van Winkle. 1996. *Life in the Gang: Family, Friends, and Violence*. New York: Cambridge University Press.

Deschenes, Elizabeth, Fran Bernat, Finn Esbensen, and D. Wayne Osgood. 1996. "Gangs and School Violence: Gender Differences in Perceptions and Experiences." Presented at the annual meeting of the American Society of Criminology, November 20, Chicago, IL.

Esbensen, Finn-Aage, and David Huizinga. 1993. "Gangs, Drugs, and Delinquency in a Survey of Urban Youth." *Criminology 31*: 565–87.

Fagan, Jeffrey. 1990. "Social Processes of Delinquency and Drug Use among Urban Gangs." In C. Ronald Huff, ed., *Gangs in America*, 183–219. Newbury Park, CA: Sage.

Felkenes, George T., and Harold K. Becker. 1995. "Female Gang Members: A Growing Issue for Policy Makers." *Journal of Gang Research 2*: 1–10.

Fishman, Laura T. [1988] 1995. "The Vice Queens: An Ethnographic Study of Black Female Gang Behavior." Presented at the annual meeting of the American Society of Criminology, November, Chicago, IL. Reprinted in Malcolm W. Klein, Cheryl L. Maxson, and Jody Miller, eds., *The Modern Gang Reader*, 83–92. Los Angeles: Roxbury.

Foucault, Michel. 1979. *Discipline and Punish: The Birth of the Prison*. New York: Vintage.

Hagan, John, A.R. Gillis, and John Simpson. 1987 "Class in the Household: A Power Control Theory of Gender and Delinquency." *American Journal of Sociology 92*: 788–816.

Hagedorn, John M. 1988. *People and Folks: Gangs, Crime and the Underclass in a Rustbelt City*. Chicago: Lake View.

Hanson, Kitty. 1964. *Rebels in the Streets: The Story of New York's Girl Gangs*. Englewood Cliffs, NJ: Prentice Hall.

Harris, Mary G. 1988. *Cholas: Latino Girls and Gangs*. New York: AMS.

Horowitz, Ruth. 1983. *Honor and the American Dream: Culture and Identity in a Chicano Community*. New Brunswick, NJ: Rutgers University Press.

Howell, James C. 1994. "Recent Gang Research: Program and Policy Implications." *Crime and Delinquency 40*(4): 495–515.

Inter-University Consortium for Political and Social Research. 1993. National Archive of Criminal Justice Data. Ann Arbor: University of Michigan and Bureau of Justice Statistics.

Joe, Karen, and Meda Chesney-Lind. 1995. " 'Just Every Mother's Angel': An Analysis of Gender and Ethnic Variations in Youth Gang Membership." *Gender and Society 9*(4): 408–30.

Klein, Malcolm W. 1995. *The American Street Gang*. New York: Oxford University Press.

Lauderback, David, Joy Hansen, and Dan Waldorf. 1992. " 'Sisters Are Doin' It for Themselves': A Black Female Gang in San Francisco." *The Gang Journal 1*: 57–72.

Leonard, Eileen B. 1982. *Women, Crime, and Society: A Critique of Theoretical Criminology*. New York: Longman.

Mann, Coramae R. 1984. *Female Crime and Delinquency*. University, AL: University of Alabama Press.

Miller, Jody. 1996. "Gender and Victimization Risk among Young Women in Gangs." Presented at the annual meeting of the American Society of Criminology, November 21, Chicago, IL.

Miller, Walter B. 1973. "The Molls." *Society 11*: 32–35.

———. 1975. *Violence by Youth Gangs and Youth Groups as a Crime Problem in Major American Cities*. Washington, DC: Government Printing Office.

———. 1982. *Crime by Youth Gangs and Groups in the United States*. Washington, DC: U.S. Department of Justice, Office of Juvenile Justice and Delinquency Prevention.

Monti, Daniel J. 1993. "Origins and Problems of Gang Research in the United States." In Scott Cummings and Daniel J. Monti, eds., *Gangs: The Origins and Impact of Contemporary Youth Gangs in the United States*, 3–25. Albany: State University of New York Press.

Moore, Joan W. 1988. "Introduction." In John M. Hagedorn, *People and Folks: Gangs, Crime and the Underclass in a Rustbelt City*, 3–17. Chicago: Lake View.

———. 1989. "Is There an Hispanic Underclass?" *Social Science Quarterly 70*: 265–83.

———. 1991. *Going Down to the Barrio: Homeboys and Homegirls in Change.* Philadelphia: Temple University Press.

Quicker, John C. 1983. *Homegirls: Characterizing Female Gangs*. San Pedro, CA: International University Press.

Rice, Robert. 1963. "A Reporter at Large: The Persian Queens." *The New Yorker 39*(35): 153–89.

Sánchez Jankowski, Martin. 1991. *Islands in the Street: Gangs and American Urban Society*. Berkeley: University of California Press.

Short, James E., Jr. 1996. "Forward: Diversity and Change in U.S. Gangs." In C. Ronald Huff, ed., *Gangs in America*, 2nd ed., vii–xviii. Thousand Oaks, CA: Sage.

Spergel, Irving A. 1964. *Racketville, Slumtown, Haulburg*. Chicago: University of Chicago Press.

———. 1990. "Youth Gangs: Continuity and Change." In Norval Morris and Michael Tonry, eds., *Crime and Justice: An Annual Review of Research*, 171–275. Chicago: University of Chicago Press.

———. 1995. *The Youth Gang Problem*. New York: Oxford University Press.

Spergel, Irving A., and G. David Curry. 1993. "The National Youth Gang Survey: A Research and Development Process." In Arnold Goldstein and C. Ronald Huff, eds., *Gang Intervention Handbook*, 359–400. Champaign-Urbana, IL: Research Press.

Taylor, Carl S. 1993. *Girls, Gangs, Women and Drugs*. East Lansing: Michigan State University Press.

Thornberry, Terrence, Marvin D. Krohn, Alan J. Lizotte, and Deborah Chard-Wierschem. 1993. "The Role of Juvenile Gangs in Facilitating Delinquent Behavior." *Journal of Research in Crime and Delinquency 30*(1): 55–87.

Thrasher, Frederic M. [1927] 1963. *The Gang: A Study of 1,313 Gangs in Chicago*. Chicago: University of Chicago Press.

Tittle, Charles R. 1995. *Control Balance: Toward a General Theory of Deviance*. Boulder, CO: Westview.

Vigil, James Diego. 1990. "Cholos and Gangs: Culture Change and Street Youth in Los Angeles." In C. Ronald Huff, ed., *Gangs in America*, 116–28. Newbury Park, CA: Sage.

Weiss, Carolyn. 1993. "Gender Research of Economic Development Planning." Presented at the Regional Research Institute, West Virginia University, November, Morgantown, WV.

West, Candace, and Don H. Zimmerman. 1987. "Doing Gender." *Gender & Society 1*: 125–51.

Whyte, William F. 1943. *Street Corner Society: The Social Structure of an Italian Slum*. Chicago: University of Chicago Press.

Wilson, William J. 1987. *The Truly Disadvantaged*. Chicago: University of Chicago Press.

CHAPTER TWELVE

Street Gangs and Criminal Business Organizations: A Canadian Perspective

ROBERT M. GORDON
Simon Fraser University, British Columbia

It is only in the past few years that Canadian social scientists have taken a significant interest in the issue of criminal gangs, groups, and organizations. As students of the field continually discover, there is very little research addressing the topic of gangs from a Canadian perspective, despite emerging evidence that street gangs, criminal business organizations, and other similar groupings have been active in Canadian cities since well before the Second World War (Rogers 1945; Dubro 1992; Young 1993).

The apparent lack of interest on the part of Canadian social scientists is, to some extent, a product of Canada's proximity to the American criminological machine. Until a few years ago, American research tended to dominate Canadian academic and public discussions of gangs as well as both federal and provincial policymaking and the development of programs in the area. There was little incentive to move beyond the importation of explanations, policies, and programs, in part because the most visible and potentially troublesome form of gang — the street gang — tended to be an episodic, and therefore less critical, social phenomenon. As Young (1993) has pointed out, for example, street gang activity in Vancouver since 1945 has tended to follow a wave-like pattern, and it is only the most recent wave (covering the period from 1985 to approximately 1994) that has stimulated a serious interest in the development of indigenous solutions.

A kindling of interest in the gang phenomenon may also be a function of the appearance of a more confident and better equipped Canadian crimi-

Source: Robert M. Gordon, "Street Gangs and Criminal Business Organizations: A Canadian Perspective." In K. Hazlehurst and C. Hazlehurst, eds., *Gangs and Youth Subcultures: International Explorations* (New Brunswick, NJ: Transaction Books, 1998): 165–87. Reprinted by permission of Transaction Publishers.

nology. Some of the responsibility for the lack of indigenous research rests at the door of past Canadian social scientists (especially criminologists) who, understandably, tended to focus on more easily researched topics. Unless a researcher has contacts within bona fide gangs or criminal groups, gang research requires special access privileges, for example, to government file data, incarcerated gang members, or gang members who are on probation and known, primarily, to corrections systems. Such privileges are usually only granted when a social phenomenon becomes a significant social problem requiring a rapid solution. The emergence of street gangs as a social problem in Canadian cities (or, at least, their *definition* as a social problem), accounts for both the research that has been conducted in the last few years (Fasilio and Leckie 1993; Mathews 1993; Gordon 1993; 1995; Gordon and Nelson 1996), and the research projects that are in progress. Some of this recent work, and in particular the Greater Vancouver Gang Study I undertook, starting in 1993, will be examined in the discussion that follows.

CANADIAN GANG RESEARCH

The choice of the year 1993 for the release of several pieces of Canadian gang research was purely coincidental. Three reports, each written for either the federal or the provincial levels of government (Fasilio and Leckie 1993; Gordon 1993; Mathews 1993), and an unpublished M.A. thesis (Young 1993) examined different aspects of the gang phenomenon and provided not only the answers to some pressing policy-related questions (e.g., to what extent are Canadian gangs dominated by the members of visible ethnic minorities?) but also the building blocks for more comprehensive research that is currently in progress.

A study by Fasilio and Leckie (1993) of the Canadian media's coverage of gangs and gang activity undertaken for the federal Solicitor-General made an extremely valuable contribution to what was then an emerging debate over the role of the news media in amplifying the street gang "problem" and in creating a moral panic. The authors analyzed the media's focus on, and characterization of, gangs and attempted to determine if variations existed within and between the different regions of Canada (e.g., whether the coverage in Atlantic Canada was different from that in British Columbia). To this end, they undertook a content analysis of major national news magazines (e.g., *Maclean's*) and the major daily newspapers published in selected urban centres over a four-month period (July–October 1992). These centres included Winnipeg, Edmonton, Vancouver, Ottawa, Toronto, and Montreal — the cities generating the largest number of stories. The sample was, therefore, not representative of the full range of media (television and radio were excluded) and did not capture every Canadian urban centre. The selection process yielded a total of 120 gang-related news stories for analysis, out of a universe of approximately 6000 stories (2 percent of all stories).

Perhaps predictably, Fasilio and Leckie found that the media characterized gangs and gang activity as widespread, a significant threat to society, and a relatively new phenomenon. Subsequent research (discussed below) and more recent events demonstrate that this characterization was wrong in most respects. Gangs were depicted as a subject of "growing social concern" and the product of an ailing society, themes that, according to Young (1993), have been trumpeted by Canadian newspapers during every wave of urban street gang activity since at least 1945. The analysts noted the absence of any historical reference or perspective in the stories, and a focus that accentuated polarization along ethnic lines: "Asian gangs" were a particular menace. One consequence, the authors argued, was an unjustified increase in the fear of gangs and gang activity and a similarly unwarranted concern over the extent to which immigrants (especially those who were members of visible ethnic minorities) were responsible for gang-related crimes. Journalists depended heavily on law enforcement officials for commentaries on gang violence, the locations of gang crime, and the extent to which gangs constituted a threat to society. The reasons why gangs emerged were largely ignored apart from some vague references to the consequences of immigration policies and practices. Generally, in the authors' view, the media were unintentionally contributing to the creation of a moral panic.

Some regional variations in coverage were noted. The volume of gang-related news in Western Canada, and particularly the Prairie provinces, was probably over-represented (22.5 percent of stories), while Atlantic Canada was under-represented. Nevertheless, the way in which gangs were characterized was fairly consistent across all regions with one exception. In Quebec, news stories tended to be less concerned with "Asian gangs" in favour of a more diverse coverage, one that focused on the problem of "youth gangs," the Mafia, and Jamaican gangs. This, the authors argued, probably reflected the ethnic composition of Quebec's population and, therefore, both the membership of gangs and the perceptions of such membership. For example, according to 1991 census, only 1.2 percent of Montreal's population was of Chinese ethnic origin compared with nearly 8 percent in Toronto and over 16 percent in Vancouver.

To some extent, Gordon's research on gang members in British Columbia correctional centres provided a counterfoil to the news media's preoccupation with "Asian gangs" and "youth gangs" (Gordon 1993). Interestingly, the research, which was conducted for the provincial Attorney-General as part of a census of all prisoners in correctional centres in the province (see Gordon and Nelson 1993), attracted absolutely no media interest, despite the public release of the report and the currency of the topic.

The research was only intended to be a preliminary study. The correctional centre files of 41 male inmates (adult and youth) who were identified as active gang members by the police and by corrections personnel (e.g., probation officers) were examined, in depth, by a team of researchers. No female gang members were identified. The inmates were also asked to participate in an interview and, somewhat surprisingly, 34 agreed to take part in this component of the research (10 adults and 24 young offenders). The goal was to obtain information about the organization, activities, and membership of gangs in the province (especially in the Greater Vancouver area), and the reasons why young people in particular became involved with gangs. A secondary objective was to design and test some research definitions and instruments for use in a later study.

The mean age of the gang members in the research sample was 19 years, and over 92 percent of the subjects were 25 years of age or younger. The majority of incarcerated gang members were young adult males, rather than young offenders (i.e., young people between the ages of 12 and 17 who commit crimes), and this finding was of importance to combating both the false perceptions created by the news media's use of the term "young gangs" and the acrimonious criticism of the federal Young Offenders Act, which, at the time, was emanating from both victims' rights groups and their conservative political allies who were clamouring for harsher punishments for young offenders. Also of importance was the finding that, with respect to issues of ethnicity and immigration, the largest single group of incarcerated gang members were those of Caucasian ethnic origin who were born in Canada (40 percent). The next largest group were of Asian ethnic origin (34 percent), the majority having been born in Canada. There were very few gang members of East Indian, Aboriginal, and Hispanic origin, and only one Black gang member in the sample. Overall, 32 percent of incarcerated gang members were not born in Canada, a proportion considerably higher than the immigrant inmate population as a whole — 11 percent on the day of the corrections census. The proportion was also higher than the proportion of immigrants in the provincial population and, therefore, the expected percentage (22 percent). This finding lent support to a hypothesized relationship between immigration and gang membership although, as Gordon and Nelson (1996: 14) have pointed out, any apparent relationship must be viewed with extreme caution because the actual numbers of gang members in the study who were not born in Canada is extremely small especially when compared with the size of the immigrant population in the province as a whole (approximately 750 000 people).

The gang members who were interviewed were surprisingly forthcoming with confirmed information about their lives and the reasons why they became involved in gangs. The subjects felt that they were not coerced or otherwise pressured into joining gangs and the process of becoming involved happened gradually, rather than abruptly. There was a slow drift toward involvement which was often initiated by a close relative or a friend who was already a member of a gang or who knew a gang member. A prospective member would spend time on the periphery of the group but might eventually be drawn in, undergo an initiation ceremony, and then become a full member. As Gordon (1993; 1995) points out, the process was neither strange nor surprising and was akin to the process that is followed when a young person joins a legitimate "gang" such as the boy scouts, a hockey or baseball team, or a marching band.

A key to understanding involvement in gangs, especially a young person's involvement, is the availability of choices: if an individual has no access to a "legitimate" gang, or is not encouraged to join such a mainstream group, an "illegitimate" gang may be selected instead (Cloward and Ohlin 1960). With this hypothesis in mind, the researchers analyzed, in particular, the file data of all 41 subjects. Nearly one-half of the subjects had backgrounds of both family and school problems including drug, alcohol, and physical abuse in the family coupled with school records characterized by truancy, fighting, suspensions, and expulsions. The picture was one of troubled individuals from troubled backgrounds and when these problems were related to the professed reasons why the subjects became involved with gangs (as gleaned from the interview data) it became clear that the choice of an illegitimate, rather than legitimate, group was a function of the lack of alternatives. The subjects reported a desire to find a secure and nurturing surrogate family. For over one-third of the subjects the gang was a haven in an otherwise heartless world.

The reasons why the rest of the sample (just under two-thirds of the subjects) became involved with gangs were more difficult to explain. Approximately one-third appeared to have joined a gang, not because of severe problems at home (although the files of some subjects indicated family and school problems), but primarily in order to continue associations with friends, to make money, and for the relief of boredom: considerations that were not likely to be satisfied through membership of a legitimate "gang." The reasons why the remaining gang members (eight subjects) became involved with gangs could not be determined from the information available to the researchers. Contrary to the researchers' expectations, over 75 percent of subjects stated that there were no barriers to leaving a gang. Gang members remained with their gangs, not out of fear of reprisal, but because they found membership to be rewarding. They were with their friends — their "family" —and leaving the gang would involve a major life adjustment.

Research conducted in Toronto by Mathews (1993), for the federal Solicitor-General, also involved interviews with gang members: specifically, youth gang members. The study, which was intended to be a preliminary examination of the youth gang issue, was undertaken to provide young people with an opportunity to add their voices to the emerging discourse on gangs and groups, to broaden the discussion of the issues, and to have an impact on both problem definition and the development of an effective, comprehensive response.

Youth who were known to be involved in gang activity were approached by experienced social services and law enforcement personnel and asked to participate in the study. Twelve youths ranging in age from 14 to 21 years agreed and were interviewed. Additional interviews were conducted with police officers, school officials, and social workers, as well as the parents of gang members and some victims of gang activity. The number of research subjects was extremely small, especially given the size of the population of the Toronto Metropolitan Area, and this weakness undermines the study's usefulness.

Some of the results were, nevertheless, helpful. As Mathews points out, the term "gang" can be a misleading way of describing different kinds of gatherings of young people. The term "gang/group" is preferred as a better way of capturing the phenomenon; and analysts and policymakers should be thinking in terms of a continuum ranging from groups of friends who spend time together and occasionally get into trouble to more serious, organized criminal groups or gangs. This problem of definition was also recognized by Gordon (1993), who used the results of the British Columbia study to develop a typology and a set of definitions that have been used subsequently in major studies of gangs in Winnipeg and Vancouver.

Mathews also found that a reliance on official discourse and documented rates of violence did not capture the nature of the fear experienced by victims, or the climate of unrest and violence in schools. Research participants stated that youth gang and youth group violence was significantly underreported and that physically smaller, weaker, younger, isolated, and friendless youth were most often the victims of gang/group violence and extortion. The research suggested that the institutional practices of schools contributed to the perpetuation of such violence. Some teachers and administrators vying for promotion were unwilling to admit to the presence of gangs in their schools. Large class sizes, a lack of teaching resources, and poor facility management and design each contributed to the increasing violence of gangs/groups in Toronto's schools.

The fourth study to be released in 1993 was conducted by a graduate student in the School of Criminology at Simon Fraser University; namely, Young's (1993) work on the history of (youth) gangs in Vancouver. The study filled a significant gap in Canadian gang research by providing the first socio-historical analysis of youth gang activity in a large Canadian city, in this case, Vancouver from 1900 to 1985.

The primary sources of data were the main provincial newspapers and this constituted both a strength and a weakness of the research. On the one hand, the research had to proceed with the assumption that the patterns of reporting reflected more than just the patterns of news media interest: that they accurately reflected the gang phenomenon. Since there is evidence of media amplification (see, Fasilio and Leckie 1993), this assumption may be wrong. On the other hand, there were no other accessible sources (e.g., government archival materials) with the same amount of rich information stretching back to the turn of the century.

Young manually and electronically scrutinized each daily edition of a major newspaper, *The Province*, to locate, read, and analyze any and all gang-related articles during the 85-year period and, when articles were found, these were cross-checked against stories in other newspapers. These data indicated that Vancouver had experienced waves of youth gang activity that clustered into three distinct periods: the period of the "corner lounger gangs," which apparently lasted from 1924 to 1931; the zoot suit and hoodlum gang period from 1944 to 1959; and the period of the "park gangs" from 1969 to 1975, a time when youth gangs were named after the city parks where they gathered. The most recent wave of street gang activity began in 1985; and although the wave appears, at the time of writing, to be virtually spent, it was in full swing at the time Young conducted his research.

Having identified the periods of gang activity, Young then attempted to explain the wave-like pattern during the post-1945 period by focusing on two independent variables: inward migration and unemployment rates. A preliminary analysis of these variables indicated a slight positive relationship between inward migration rates and reported fluctuations in gang activity. Unemployment rates and fluctuations in gang activity were inversely related, but Young cautions against the use of these results for purposes other than the construction of hypotheses for future research.

LOS DIABLOS: A CANADIAN STREET GANG

A reasonable understanding of gangs and gang activity in Canada can be gleaned from an account of the rise and fall of the quintessential Vancouver street gang of the 1980s and 1990s: Los Diablos. Although there may be some variation in gang activity and gang membership in the cities currently most affected by the gang phenomenon (Vancouver, Winnipeg, and Toronto), an example drawn from Vancouver research is instructive.

Los Diablos and other Vancouver street gangs associated with the most recent period of gang activity are in some ways similar to both the "hoodlum gangs" of the 1950s (e.g., the Alma Dukes, and the Vic Gang) and the "park gangs" of the early 1970s (e.g., the Riley Park Gang and the Clark Park Gang) (Young 1993). Los Diablos came from and generally concentrated its activities within a particular area, eventually adopted "colours" and rituals, and seemed to be as interested in conflict with rival gangs as it was in profitable criminal activity. Like both its predecessors and other, more recently active, gangs, Los Diablos was comprised primarily of older adolescent and young adult males. Although young women have been occasionally involved with Vancouver street gangs, usually as associates or "employees," the so-called "girl gangs" that purportedly exist in other Canadian cities have not appeared in Vancouver.

Los Diablos was formed in the mid-1980s (probably in 1986) in the Killarney area of southeast Vancouver. The exact origins of the gang are unclear but it seems to have started with a small group of youth who called themselves Towa. The reasons for the creation of Towa are unknown but 1985/86 was a year when other street gangs and "wannabe" groups began to appear in larger numbers in the Greater Vancouver area (Girrard 1992; Gordon 1995). It was a year that marked the beginning of the most recent wave of street gang activity in the city (Young 1993).

The Killarney area is (and was) a quiet, middle-class, residential neighbourhood consisting of modest, single-family homes. It is a far cry from the kind of disintegrating and socially disorganized inner-city neighbourhoods commonly associated with street gang activity in North America. It is, however, an area in transition as immigrants, particularly from non-European countries, begin to make their homes there. Both Towa and, later, Los Diablos reflected the emerging ethnic composition of the neighbourhood and both gangs were comprised of young people of East Indian, European, Fijian, African, Chinese, and Iranian descent.

Towa members concentrated primarily on property crime (thefts and break and enters), assaults, and some extortion, but their activities took a more serious turn in 1986 when the gang became allied with a criminal business organization known as Lotus. This alliance coincided with a change in the demographic composition of Towa; principally, an infusion of individuals of Hispanic ethnic origin following the arrival in Vancouver of refugees from the political turmoil in Central America. Many of these new members had lived previously in Los Angeles and had been connected with street gangs in that city. It was these new members, with their recently acquired skills and knowledge of American street gangs, who began to alter the face of Towa. The name of the gang was changed, to Los Diablos ("The Devils"). The gang's activities became more organized and sophisticated and expanded beyond the immediate confines of the Killarney neighbourhood to the rest of southeast Vancouver.

By 1987, the gang enjoyed considerable recognition and notoriety, and a high status among many adolescents. The gang was probably at its peak at this time, with an active membership of between 60 and 75 young adult and adolescent males. It was also around this time that the gang came into conflict with a rival street gang known as Gum Wah, which was closely associated with a criminal business organization, the Red Eagles. There then ensued a period of violent exchange between Los Diablos and the Red Eagles/Gum Wah that included the occasional execution-style murder, fire-bombings, stabbings and, in the summer of 1988, a gun battle that became known as the Woodland Bridge shooting and that apparently established the gang as a force to be reckoned with.

Although Los Diablos was a group that had to be taken seriously, there was an amateurish element to its activities. This is reflected in a police account of the Woodland Bridge shooting in which the demise of one gang member was reported, with barely concealed mirth. Despite a significant exchange of gunfire, only three individuals were injured, two with minor wounds. The third casualty, and the source of much amusement, was a gang member who accidentally shot himself in the testicles while drawing a handgun from the waistband of his pants.

It was in the wake of the Woodland Bridge incident that Los Diablos began to copy the more obvious mannerisms of American street gangs, especially those in the Los Angeles area. Members began to wear colours (red, white, and black clothing), to use hand signals and street (territory) markings, and to initiate new members by requiring one of two possibilities: a short beating at the hands of other gang members (taking five, or the beats), or the commission of specific crimes to prove their worth. Similar practices were used by other Vancouver street gangs at the time (Gordon 1993). The reasons for these developments are unclear but the changes came in the wake of the release of the movie *Colours*. Gang members were heard copying the dialogue and the terms used in the film (especially the term "homes" or "homeboy") and territorial graffiti (notably wall markings) began to proliferate throughout the Vancouver area.

The "gang war" between Los Diablos and Gum Wah continued throughout 1987 and 1988, with running street fights, battles in shopping malls, and the occasional mobile gun battle. Some Los Diablos members also began to take a serious interest in cocaine trafficking and operated as "cells" led by particular individuals and known by that person's last name (e.g., "Doe's cell"). Indeed, by this time, Los Diablos was best described as an amalgam of groups or cells that operated in alliance with each other and that could be mustered quickly by using pagers or cellular telephones. Some cells also formed into allied street gangs, concentrated in particular suburban areas, for example, Los Panchos (in the suburb of Burnaby); the Sparrows (in the suburb of Coquitlam); and Bario Latinos (in the Kingsway-Joyce area of Vancouver).

A further complication emerged in the fall of 1988 when a dormant street gang more commonly associated with Vancouver gang activity in the 1970s, re-emerged. The East Vancouver Saints began to engage Los Diablos, which promptly responded, and by the spring of 1989 Los Diablos and its allies (including a gang known as Mara Latinos) were involved in conflicts with both Gum Wah and the East Vancouver Saints and its allies (two additional street gangs — Patook and Viet Ching). These conflicts involved drive-by shootings, molotov cocktail bombings of the homes of rival gang members, and both gang fights and beatings of individual gang members.

By the end of June 1990, the demographic profile of Los Diablos changed again, from a predominantly Hispanic group, to a predominantly Indo-Canadian (East Indian) group. It was estimated that 80 percent of the gang's members were of Fijian East Indian origin and the gang was led by a high-profile Fijian individual. There was evidence of the friendly movement of gang members from one gang to another, one goal being to form several ethnically homogeneous gangs, an enterprise that ultimately failed. By August of that year several senior members of Los Diablos had been released from prison and attempted to wrest control of the gang away from the newer Fijian membership. What followed — a major, internal fight involving the competing factions — was a defining moment for the gang. It signalled the beginning of the gang's disintegration as a significant and cohesive force. There is evidence that attempts were made by some gang members to mitigate the effects of the internal conflicts and rivalry but, by the summer of 1992, the gang was in steep decline. The coup de grace came with the arrest of the gang's high-profile leader and his conviction for murder, followed by the murder of some remaining key members of the gang who were involved in drug trafficking.

THE LESSONS OF LOS DIABLOS

What can be learned about Canadian street gangs from the account of Los Diablos? First, several key characteristics are evident, each of which points to the reasons such gangs form and are maintained but then eventually fade away. The periodic appearance, disappearance, and reappearance of street gangs in cities such as Vancouver is an interesting feature of Canadian street gang activity but the reasons for these cycles remain unclear. Second, the account casts light on the relationships among street gangs and other groups, notably criminal business organizations. It also helps to explain the formation and maintenance of gangs, and reinforces the distinctions between gangs, groups, and organizations that are critical for effective anti-gang policymaking and program development.

One of the most obvious characteristics of street gangs such as Los Diablos is their transient quality and relative instability, especially when compared with criminal business organizations. A brief case study of such an organization, Lotus, is provided below. The history of Los Diablos, for example, indicates continuous change and instability across a number of key areas. There were changes in the ethnic composition of the gang, in the leadership and core membership, in the alliances the gang formed and ended with other gangs and organizations, and in the kinds of criminal activities that were preferred by the gang, the gang's different "cells," and by individual members. The gang was riven with dissent and rivalry, and seemed to flourish more as a result of fear and myth than consistent concrete accomplishments. Los Diablos was certainly a constant presence in the Vancouver area during the late 1980s and early 1990s but, contrary to public (i.e., media-created) impressions, it was not a finely tuned and highly organized criminal machine.

Instability and transience were the hallmarks of other Vancouver street gangs and "wannabe" groups during the period. Gangs and groups appeared and disappeared with breathtaking speed, some disbanding almost as quickly as they were formed. Those that did not disband completely often amalgamated with other gangs or groups, frequently creating new gangs with new names (Gordon 1995). Indeed, attempting any analysis of the field during the peak activity period (the late 1980s and early 1990s) was virtually impossible and comparable to trying to herd cats.

In the spring of 1991, for example, there were about nine street gangs in the Greater Vancouver area, in addition to Los Diablos, including the Bacada Boys, Patook, and Persian Pride. By the fall of 1993, most of these gangs had disappeared or were in rapid decline but new street gangs had appeared, often formed by the members of disbanded or disintegrating gangs. The short-lived suburban gang known as Los Cholos, for example, was purportedly created by disenchanted members of Los Diablos. By 1995, only a handful of active street gangs could be identified in the Greater Vancouver area (e.g., CTB, or the Chinatown Boys, and the New Dragons). Some members of now defunct street gangs continued as criminal groups but the numbers of street gangs and street gang members, and the amount of street gang activity, had fallen dramatically when compared with the situation in 1991.

The example of Los Diablos helps to illuminate the relationships among street gangs and criminal business organizations. Where links existed, as they often did, organizations used gangs for such things as extralegal dispute resolution ("enforcement") and the distribution of goods and services (e.g., retailing drugs). The example is also particularly useful in identifying where some gangs came from and why they were created. Clearly, large street gangs can be the seedbed of new gangs, not only when the "parent" gang dies and the remaining members disperse (as in the case of Los Diablos) but also when the members of a flourishing gang decide to expand into other parts of a metropolitan area. Los Diablos was the parent of at least three allied street gangs (Los Panchos, the Sparrows, and Bario Latinos) and probably influenced the creation of numerous, although happily short-lived, "wannabe" groups throughout the Greater Vancouver area. New street gangs may also appear in response to threats posed by existing gangs, and a new wave of gang activity may be a product of a vicious circle of threat or perceived threat, reaction, reinforced threat, further reaction, and so on. The emergence of the East Vancouver Saints in the fall of 1988 provides a good example of this phenomenon because the gang appears to have been resurrected as a mutual protection society solely in response to a localized fear of Los Diablos and its allies. This claim is supported by the fact that the Saints disbanded shortly after Los Diablos began to disintegrate. Additionally, groups of allied gangs and organizations appear as the fear of another gang or group of gangs and organizations spreads and as the warring factions step up the conflict. As the Los Diablos example indicates, at least two groups of gangs and organizations were active in the Greater Vancouver area during the late 1980s and early 1990s. Los Diablos, Lotus, and their allies, were in conflict with Gum Wah, the Red Eagles, the East Vancouver Saints, and their allies, and were probably collectively responsible for a great deal of the gang-related criminal activity in the city at that time as well as the formation of other gangs and groups.

Germane to the issues of instability and transience among street gangs is the age of the members of gangs. Preliminary results from the Greater Vancouver Gang Study, for example, indicate that just under one-half of the members of gangs, groups, and organizations involved in the study were youth (those 12 to 17 years of age inclusively) and that those identified as members of street gangs were, on average, 19 years of age. Perhaps more importantly, 84 percent of the subjects were males between the ages of 14 and 26: the group at greatest risk of involvement in all kinds of predatory street crime but a group comprised of individuals who usually discontinue such activity as they grow older. The evidence is not yet fully confirmed, but there is some support for the conventional "maturation hypothesis" as a partial explanation for the periodic disappearance of Canadian street gangs. Gang members may simply grow older and lose interest in street gang life as more sedate and rewarding options present themselves. This sentiment was expressed by some gang members in British Columbia correctional centres who were interviewed in a study conducted in 1993 (Gordon 1993). The reasons why gangs reappear after a ten-year hiatus — a pattern that has characterized street gang activity in Vancouver since 1945 — remain unclear.

Another key characteristic reflected in the account of Los Diablos is the ethnic composition of such gangs. Preliminary results from the Greater Vancouver Study indicate considerable ethnic diversity among gangs and gang members, very few gangs being comprised predominantly of a particular ethnic group, and despite the frequent use of ethnically specific gang names (see also Gordon 1993; 1995). For example, the North Vancouver street gang known as Persian Pride, which was extremely active in the late 1980s and early 1990s, consisted of young adult males from several ethnic groups even though the name suggested a street gang dominated by individuals of Iranian ethnic origin. Los Diablos passed through a period when young males of Hispanic ethnic origin dominated the gang (and gave it its name) but these individuals were later displaced by East Indian gang members of Fijian ethnic origin. Even gangs and criminal business organizations with Chinese or Vietnamese sounding names such as Gum Wah and Lotus had (and continue to have) an ethnically diverse membership and include individuals of European ethnic origin (Caucasians) who were born in Canada.

The clear evidence of ethnic diversity found among the membership of Vancouver's street gangs is important for a number of reasons. It is of value with respect to the politics of gangs insofar as evidence of diversity helps to combat inaccurate, and sometimes vindictive, commentary about particular ethnic minorities. The evidence is especially useful when responding to the cavalier and extremely misleading use of terms such as "Asian gangs" so popular in the Canadian news media. Evidence of diversity helps to normalize the membership of street gangs: if a metropolitan area is ethnically heterogeneous one would expect to find that diversity mirrored, qualitatively and quantitatively, in a wide variety of organizations, institutions, and groupings, including street gangs and criminal business organizations.

There is, however, some evidence that street gangs in Vancouver and other Canadian cities may have memberships that are comprised disproportionately of individuals from particular ethnic minorities, albeit in relatively small numbers. In the Greater Vancouver Gang Study, for example, more than three-quarters of the research subjects were members of visible ethnic minorities. Eighty-three of these subjects (65.6 percent) were members of non-Aboriginal visible ethnic minorities compared with an estimated 13.5 percent in the general population of the province (Gordon and Nelson 1996). The largest single ethnic group was comprised of those of Asian ethnic origin (45 percent) and, of these, nearly one-half were Vietnamese. In each case, the ethnic groups were disproportionately represented although the actual numbers were small, relative to the size of the groups in the general provincial population (Gordon and Nelson 1993; 1996).

Similar disproportionate representations along ethnic lines have been noted in the case of street gangs in both Winnipeg and Toronto. In Winnipeg's two principal street gangs, the Indian Posse and the Manitoba Warriors — members of which were involved in a 1996 riot in the provincial correctional centre at Headingly, Manitoba — are comprised predominantly of young Aboriginal males. Other street gangs in the city reflect other visible ethnic minorities — Filipino and Chinese/Vietnamese in particular — but it is the Aboriginal gangs that appear to pose the greatest problem for criminal justice agencies. Similar reports of street gang activity in the Toronto metropolitan area suggest a disproportionate number of gang members of Caribbean, Hispanic, and Portuguese ethnic origins.

Ethnicity is clearly a relevant factor in understanding the Canadian street gang phenomenon but not, alone, sufficient to explain the creation and maintenance of gangs, or their eventual demise. It is only when ethnicity is combined with variables such as immigrant status and socioeconomic status that a more useful picture emerges. Preliminary results from the Greater Vancouver Gang Study indicate that just over one-half of the subjects in the study were immigrants to Canada: a significant overrepresentation given that about 22 percent of people in the general provincial population were not born in the country (Gordon and Nelson 1993; 1996). Sixty-five of the subjects in the study (50.7 percent were immigrants who were members of visible ethnic minorities and the largest single group of immigrants was from Vietnam (19.5 percent of the research population). In both cases, there is a significant overrepresentation when compared with the general population of the province although it is important to note that the actual numbers of people involved is extremely small.

As many analysts of the street gang phenomenon have pointed out, ethnicity, immigrant status, and socioeconomic status are of relevance where these variables combine with limited language competency and a lack of marketable skills to produce a variety of social and economic vulnerabilities: poverty, family disintegration, a lack of supportive community networks, and the lack of rewarding employment, to name the main concerns (Huff 1990; Mathews 1993; Spergel 1995; Gordon and Nelson 1996). In Vancouver, for example, while the socioeconomic status of the subjects in the gang study ranged from "upper middle class" to "economically disadvantaged," the largest single group (36 percent) were economically disadvantaged and the majority of these individuals were from visible ethnic minorities. A similar picture — one of cultural disenfranchisement, economic impoverishment, and a lack of legitimate opportunities — has been recognized as significant for an understanding of gangs and groups in other Canadian cities (Mathews 1993).

Ethnicity, immigrant status, economic disadvantage, and the lack of legitimate and rewarding opportunities are possibly more important in understanding involvement in, and the maintenance of, criminal business organizations than street gangs. In the Vancouver gang study, for example, 22 of the 24 subjects who were identified as members of organizations were not born in Canada and were almost invariably of Chinese or Vietnamese ethnic origin. Unlike street gangs, criminal business organizations are more stable, more constant, and as the following brief case study illustrates, involved in more serious and organized forms of criminal activity.

LOTUS: A CANADIAN CRIMINAL BUSINESS ORGANIZATION

Unlike Los Diablos, Lotus is an active Vancouver-based criminal business organization. It is generally thought that the organization first appeared in the late 1960s but its origins are murky. Likewise, little is known about the organization's early activities although it may have started as a street gang with a predominantly Chinese Canadian membership. It is clear that the organization was in conflict with the members of other Chinese gangs and groups in the late 1970s and it is believed to have been actively involved in armed robberies in British Columbia and Alberta at that time. It was also involved in extortion and targeted mainly Chinese businesses (Joe and Robinson 1980).

In the mid-1980s, the organization amalgamated with another criminal business organization, Jung Ching, to form an organization comprised primarily of individuals of Chinese ethnic origin, including Chinese members who were from Vietnam and who spoke only Vietnamese. In the main, the organization's more visible activities — occasional shootings and assaults — were extensions of its general business activities: operating social clubs, gambling, drug distribution, prostitution, restaurant extortion, and credit card frauds. Occasionally, however, the business activity entered the public domain, the best, but most tragic, example of such activity being the organization's involvement in the high-profile kidnapping and eventual murder of a Vancouver restaurant owner and his wife (the "Ming slayings"). The organization's members were also vulnerable to attack by rival gangs and organizations and these exchanges spilled over into the public domain, often in spectacular ways. For example, in January 1987 a member of Lotus was shot and killed while watching a film in a Chinese movie theatre in Vancouver by an individual working for a rival organization. This incident (the so-called "Golden Princess Theatre shooting") proved irresistible to the media and led to considerable public alarm about "gang" activity in the city.

By December 1989, there was considerable evidence that Lotus was operating a major, commercial, break and enter scheme in the Vancouver area, using young people to hit predetermined and directed targets. In addition, the organization was engaged with an allied street gang, Los Diablos, in an increasingly violent war with the street gang known as Gum Wah, a rival criminal business organization, the Red Eagles, and their allies. This took the form of frequent drive-by shootings, as well as beatings and stabbings in restaurants, bars and, in the case of the younger members of the organization, in high schools.

The following summer, Lotus began to diversify by organizing a variety of criminal activities in addition to its regular itinerary. Different groups, or cells, within Lotus were assigned to commit robberies aimed at different types of targets: one group was assigned to fast-food restaurants, another to high-profile jewellery stores, and yet another to hotels. Some groups were slow in starting but this hallmark activity was to continue for more than a year. One cell within Lotus also kidnapped the daughter of a local millionaire but were quickly identified and arrested. By the early 1990s, Lotus was deeply involved in the distribution of drugs, for resale, the primary "retail" outlet being members of the allied street gang, Los Diablos. Drug distribution through a set of interconnected cells continues to be the primary business activity for Lotus.

Although allied to Los Diablos over a long period of time, Lotus stands out as a significantly different entity. It has proved to be a more permanent and more stable form of organization having successfully survived numerous conflicts with rival organizations and gangs, primarily over market share in the field of drug distribution. This is not to suggest that all Canadian criminal business organizations, unlike street gangs, are permanent. Some merge with each other (e.g., Lotus and Jung Ching amalgamated in the mid-1980s), and some go out of business. One of Lotus's rival organizations, the Red Eagles, have disbanded.

Criminal business organizations exhibit greater ethnic homogeneity than street gangs but their membership is not solely Chinese or Vietnamese; Lotus, for example, had (and has) several Euro-Canadian members. The members also tend to be older — in the Vancouver gang study the average age was 28 years — although the membership can include adolescents. Also, a criminal business organization's activities can be city-wide and even national in scope; they tend not to be tied to particular neighbourhoods or operate in set areas of cities, as was the case with Los Diablos and other Vancouver street gangs.

Although organizations like Lotus tend to be dominated by individuals from visible ethnic minorities, many of whom were not born in Canada, analysis of the data gathered for the Greater Vancouver Gang Study indicates that organization members are less likely to be economically disadvantaged than the members of street gangs. The reasons for this are perhaps self-evident: the members of criminal business organizations are usually employed in extremely rewarding, although illegitimate, fields of work that exhibit growth rather than decline (e.g., drug trafficking). Generally speaking, given language and cultural difficulties as well as a lack of marketable skills, the members of criminal business organizations would not be able to compete successfully in the legitimate labour market for employment that was equally rewarding. Given a choice between menial work for minimum wages in the kitchen of a restaurant and an exciting and highly lucrative position working within a criminal business organization, it is doubtful whether many young adult males would forgo the latter occupation in favour of the former.

CONCLUSION

The extent to which the situation in the Greater Vancouver area, as reflected in the findings of the Greater Vancouver Gang Study, are mirrored in other Canadian cities remains unclear at this time. It is expected that the work in progress, for example, at the University of Manitoba in Winnipeg, will provide some interesting comparative data and important new information particularly with respect to Aboriginal street gangs. Additional work on the Greater Vancouver Gang Study should also provide further insight into the relationships among ethnicity, immigrant status, and membership of street gangs, criminal groups, and criminal business organizations. The results of this research should help the federal and provincial governments to identify the resources, services, and strategies that are necessary to address key issues and problems associated with immigration.

In the meantime, the results of the limited number of research projects that have recently been completed in Canada, and that have been identified and briefly canvassed in this discussion, provide partial answers to some of the questions posed by Canadian gang analysts, researchers, and policymakers. There is, for example, a better understanding of why street gangs in Canadian cities appear and then disappear in a wave-like fashion, although a comprehensive, comparative historical analysis has yet to be attempted. There is a better understanding of the relationships among gangs, groups and organizations and of the key demographic and other differences among their memberships that point to some of the reasons individuals become involved in this area of criminal activity.

The distinctions that must be made between gangs, groups, and organizations are also better understood and this bodes well for the development of effective, indigenous, anti-gang policy and programs. Clearly, the best strategy for combating entrenched and highly effective criminal business organizations (notably, vigorous and targeted enforcement and prosecution by specialist units) is unlikely to be of tremendous value when dealing with occasional suburban irritations. Noisy but transient groups of adolescent "wannabe" gang members require a different approach.

Although there is a great deal about Canadian street gangs and criminal business organizations that remains murky, it is clear that Canadian policymakers and program developers occupy a happier position than their counterparts in the United States. Street gangs and "wannabe" group activity is not yet an entrenched feature of the Canadian urban landscape and there is still enough time, energy, and commitment to develop sound ways of addressing gangs and gang-related issues. It is highly unlikely that any form of government policy or programming will prevent a resurgence of street gang and related activity. In Vancouver, and on the basis of the pattern of gang activity since 1945, this renewed activity is predicted to begin around the year 2005. It may, however, be possible to develop ways of responding more confidently and cost-effectively when the next wave arrives.

At a minimum, some important features of the Canadian social welfare and criminal justice systems should be preserved, if not strengthened. One explanation for the impermanence of street gangs and "wannabe" groups in Canadian cities (despite the nation's proximity to the United States) is the array of social safety nets that keep these cities reasonably healthy. Although inner-city areas have their share of problems, they are not home to large populations of disenfranchised, dissolute, and desperate youth and young adults living with no hope of positive change. Canadian cities have a reasonably effective education, health, and social service apparatus staffed by generally optimistic personnel who are interested in building communities and community services and who are concerned to address the various issues and problems that seem to be related to the entrenchment of street gangs: urban decay, family disintegration, cultural and language barriers, impoverishment, and unemployment.

On the criminal justice side, Canada has relatively strict firearms control and, at present, the federal government seems to be prepared to make such control even stricter, with considerable popular support. Some provincial governments also seem willing to regulate the supply and use of firearms to the extent they are able within their constitutional mandate. Criminal business organizations may not be touched by the effectiveness or otherwise of the social safety net but they will be affected by initiatives such as restricted access to firearms and ammunition and by fully staffed and supported enforcement and prosecution units working in collaboration with the communities most affected by organized criminal activity (e.g., restaurateurs who are subjected to extortion). Utilitarian theories of deterrence may not be popular explanatory or policy tools at this time but they should not be dismissed in situations where criminal activity is organized along business lines and undertaken primarily for profit.

STUDY QUESTIONS

1. *How does Gordon explain the relative absence of Canadian research on street gangs before the 1990s?*
2. *What are the different general types of gang research that have been carried out in Canada since the early 1990s?*
3. *According to Gordon's research findings, what are the main reasons youth give for deciding to join street gangs? What do Gordon's research findings reveal about the process involved in leading a young person from being a "wannabe" gang member to becoming a full-fledged gang member?*

REFERENCES

Cloward, Richard A., and Lloyd E. Ohlin. 1960. *Delinquency and Opportunity: A Theory of Delinquent Gangs*. New York: Free Press.

Dubro, J. 1992. *The Dragons of Crime: Inside the Asian Underworld*. Toronto: Octopus Publishing.

Fasilio, R., and S. Leckie. 1993. *Canadian Media Coverage of Gangs: A Content Analysis*. Ottawa: Solicitor-General Canada.

Girrard, M. 1992. *The Print Media's Portrayal of the Youth Gang Phenomenon in British Columbia.* Unpublished B.A. (Hons.) thesis, Vancouver: School of Criminology, Simon Fraser University.

Gordon, R.M. 1993. *Incarcerated Gang Members in British Columbia: A Preliminary Study.* Victoria: Ministry of Attorney-General.

———. 1995. "Street Gangs in Vancouver." In J. Creechan and R. Silverman, eds., *Canadian Delinquency*, 311–20. Scarborough: Prentice Hall.

Gordon, R.M., and J. Nelson. 1993. *Census '93: The Report of the 1993 Census of Provincial Correctional Centres in British Columbia.* Victoria: Ministry of Attorney-General.

———. 1996. "Crime, Ethnicity and Immigration." In R. Silverman, J. Teevan, and V. Sacco, eds., *Crime in Canadian Society*, 5th ed., 234–44. Toronto: Harcourt Brace.

Huff, C. Ronald, ed. 1990. *Gangs in America.* Newbury Park, CA: Sage Publications.

Joe, D., and N. Robinson. 1980. "Chinatown's Immigrant Gangs." *Criminology 18*: 337–45.

Mathews, F. 1993. *Youth Gangs on Youth Gangs*. Ottawa: Solicitor-General Canada.

Rogers, K. 1945. *Street Gangs in Toronto: A Study of the Forgotten.* Toronto: Ryerson Press.

Spergel, Irving A. 1995. *The Youth Gang Problem: A Community Approach.* New York: Oxford University Press.

Young, M. 1993. *The History of Vancouver Youth Gangs: 1900–1985.* Unpublished M.A. thesis. Vancouver: School of Criminology, Simon Fraser University.

PART FIVE
Youth Crime Prevention: Implementation and Evaluation

INTRODUCTION

In recent years there has been a proliferation of published work concerned with describing and evaluating primary, secondary, and tertiary youth crime prevention programs and alternatives. Whereas primary and secondary youth crime prevention efforts focus either on children and youth in general (primary) or on youth who are identified as being particularly "at-risk" (secondary prevention), tertiary measures involve attempting to reduce the recidivism of youth who have already become involved in the youth justice system (Lab 1997). Consequently, the topic of youth crime prevention arises when one looks at either research on youth crime, which is the focus of this book, or research on the operation of youth justice systems, which is dealt with more directly in other books (cf. Smandych, 2001).*

The three chapters included in Part Five provide information on the implementation and evaluation of different primary, secondary, and tertiary youth crime prevention efforts that have received considerable attention in recent years. Specifically, the chapters examine the findings of evaluation research on early childhood intervention programs, offender treatment programs, mentoring programs, and boot camps for young offenders. Although these chapters deal with only a few examples of currently popular youth crime prevention approaches, they nonetheless provide a good starting point for considering issues involved in the development and implementation of effective youth crime prevention programs. More specifically, the chapters in

* Russell C. Smandych also addresses current questions of youth crime prevention in the reader *Youth Justice: History, Legislation and Reform* (Harcourt Canada, 2001, in press).

Part Five will help provide a knowledge base for beginning to address questions about youth crime prevention, such as: What is the range of available youth crime prevention options? What works and what doesn't work? What are the options worth trying? It is important to recall that a number of earlier chapters — including Farrington (Chapter One), Laub and Sampson (Chapter Four), Agnew (Chapter Five), Schissel and Fedec (Chapter Nine), and Flannery, Huff, and Manos (Chapter Ten) — also deal either directly or indirectly with questions surrounding youth crime prevention. Additional insight on the topic can be gained from re-reading these chapters.

In Chapter Thirteen, Dewey Cornell, a psychologist and director of the widely cited Virginia Youth Violence Project, reviews the findings of evaluation research on a range of different primary, secondary, and tertiary youth crime prevention efforts. According to Cornell, carefully implemented primary prevention efforts, which focus on trying to keep problems that lead to criminal activity from arising in the first place, offer a great deal of promise in helping to reduce youth crime. Significantly, this view is shared by the President's Crime Prevention Council (1995) in the United States and the National Council on Crime Prevention (1996) in Canada (see also Sherman et al. 1997; Howell and Hawkins 1998). Cornell highlights several examples of community-wide, family-focused, and school-based prevention strategies that have been demonstrated to be effective early childhood interventions. He also examines evaluation research that has been done on secondary and tertiary (or offender treatment-based) prevention programs; however his assessment of these options is more cautious. For example, although in recent years a great deal of attention has been given to police-sponsored drug awareness resistance programs (like DARE in the United States), Cornell cites recent evaluations of the DARE program that seriously question its effectiveness in deterring youth from illegal drug use. Similarly, Cornell points to the limited success of both institution- and non-institution-based tertiary treatment programs that do not include well-planned treatment interventions that involve extensive individual counselling and interpersonal skills training. From his review of evaluation research, Cornell concludes that many effective programs are available for reducing violent youth crime, but that all of these programs require careful implementation by competent staff in order to be successful.

In Chapter Fourteen, Delores Jones-Brown and Zelma Weston Henriques examine the promises and pitfalls of mentoring as a youth crime prevention strategy. Mentoring, defined as "a form of intervention in which an adult volunteer is paired with a youth in need of adult support" (Anderson 1994: 60), can be viewed as either a primary or secondary youth crime prevention strategy, depending on the number of crime-related "risk factors" that are considered to be present in the life of a particular child. Mentoring is one type of crime prevention strategy directed at youth that has received considerable attention in recent years. Other comparable strategies include community and police-sponsored youth recreation programs (President's Council on

Crime Prevention 1995; Thurman et al. 1996), high school graduation incentive programs (Greenwood et al. 1996), gang resistance (Esbensen and Osgood 1997), drug awareness education programs (Hansen and Graham 1991), and the enforcement of juvenile curfew laws (Fritsch, Caeti, and Taylor 1999; Ruefle and Reynolds 1996). Jones-Brown and Henriques discuss the results of evaluation research on mentoring programs in the United States, specifically Big Brothers/Big Sisters (BB/BS) programs and the U.S. federal government–sponsored Juvenile Mentoring Program (JUMP). Jones-Brown and Henriques conclude that, unlike the findings of evaluation research on more punitive crime prevention approaches like boot camps and waiving youth crime cases to adult court, mentoring programs have been shown to have a significant effect in reducing youth crime. The authors also draw on their own experience with designing and implementing a community-based youth mentoring program to provide recommendations on how to overcome some of the problems associated with some current mentoring programs directed at "high-risk" visible minority youth. The authors' positive assessment of mentoring programs is similar to those in other recent studies of both general adult–youth mentoring programs (cf. Guetzloe 1997; Grossman and Garry 1997) and police–youth mentoring programs (Giacomazzi and Thurman 1994) carried out in the United States. Unfortunately, very little evaluation research has been done on either type of mentoring program in Canada (Dowrich Management Services 1993).

The same situation applies to the state of evaluation research on the effectiveness of boot camps for young offenders. Although the 1990s saw several Canadian provincial departments of corrections move toward implementing juvenile boot camps, no evaluations of their effectiveness have been published to date. At the same time, however, numerous studies of boot camps for juvenile and adult offenders have been completed in the United States, and research is now being undertaken in other countries, such as Australia and New Zealand, where boot camps are also being debated. While in recent years the idea of boot camps for young offenders has attracted a huge amount of attention in Canada, the United States, and other countries, views of the efficacy of boot camps tend to be polarized on a continuum, ranging from those who offer vigorous support to those who argue that "boot camps" and "youth justice" are a contradiction in terms (cf. Atkinson 1995; Henggeler and Schoenwald 1994).

In Chapter Fifteen, Sheldon Zhang presents a comprehensive review of research strategies that have been used to evaluate the effectiveness of boot camps for juvenile and adult offenders. Zhang describes and critiques the research methodology of more than twenty juvenile and adult boot camp studies published in the United States in the 1990s. In doing so, the author provides both a good summary of the current state of knowledge on the effectiveness of juvenile and adult boot camps and an insightful discussion of some of the major problems and issues associated with carrying out evaluation research in the correctional system. Zhang recognizes that it is probably impossible to answer the "blanket question" of "Do boot camps work?" first, because the findings of existing boot camp studies are complicated and difficult to interpret, and second, because the question assumes that the boot camp experience will have the same effect on all offenders. According to Zhang, trying to answer this over-simplistic question "increases the chances of drawing misleading and simplistic conclusions, which in turn lead either to summarily dismissing or to unduly extolling boot camps as a treatment option." Zhang concludes that, based on the findings of current evaluation research, the only reliable general statement one can make is that boot camps have not been shown to have any consistent effect, either positive or negative. Although most of the boot camps that have been evaluated in the United States have been designed for young adult offenders, Zhang gives specific attention to discussing the findings of the major government-funded studies that have been done on boot camps for juvenile offenders (Bourque et al. 1996).

Perhaps because they spark so much public controversy, juvenile boot camps have received more attention than other current tertiary youth crime prevention measures in recent years. Such other tertiary approaches include: social skills training with young offenders, which can be done in either community-based or institutional settings (Cunliffe 1992); various diversion programs such as alternative measures and family group conferencing (Adler and Wunderstiz 1994; Hudson et al. 1996); alternative outdoor wilderness challenge programs (Deschenes and Greenwood 1998); and residential treatment programs, which include group homes and other supervised alternative living arrangements for young offenders (Stanton and Meyer 1998). In addition, there are many other kinds of treatment programs for incarcerated youth (Becker and Rickel 1998; Howell and Hawkins 1998). Learning about these other tertiary crime prevention approaches is needed in order to develop a detailed understanding of the field of youth crime prevention.

In the end, a knowledge of each of the topics covered in this book, including patterns and theories of youth crime, the causes and consequences of youth street life and gang involvement, and the field of youth crime prevention, is important for developing more adequate community-level and national strategies aimed at reducing youth crime.

REFERENCES

Adler, C., and J. Wunderstiz, eds. 1994. *Family Conferencing and Juvenile Justice: The Way Forward or Misplaced Optimism?* Australian Studies in Law, Crime and Justice. Canberra: Australian Institute of Criminology.

Anderson, M. 1994. "The High Juvenile Crime Rate: A Look at Mentoring as a Preventive Strategy." *Criminal Law Bulletin 30*: 54–75.

Atkinson, L. 1995. "Boot Camps and Justice: A Contradiction in Terms?" *Trends and Issues in Crime and Criminal Justice 46*. Canberra: Australian Institute of Criminology.

Becker, E., and A. Rickel. 1998. "Incarcerated Juvenile Offenders: Integrating Trauma-Oriented Treatment with State-of-the-Art Delinquency Interventions." In T. Gullotta, G. Adams, and R. Montemayor, eds., *Delinquent Violent Youth: Theory and Interventions*, 230–55. Thousand Oaks, CA: Sage.

Bourque, B., R. Cronin, F. Pearson, D. Felker, M. Han, and S. Hill. 1996. "Boot Camps for Juvenile Offenders: An Implementation Evaluation of Three Demonstration Programs." *National Institute of Justice Research in Brief.* Washington, DC: U.S. Department of Justice.

Cunliffe, T. 1992. "Arresting Youth Crime: A Review of Social Skills Training with Young Offenders." *Adolescence 227*(108): 892–900.

Deschenes, E., and P. Greenwood. 1998. "Alternative Placements for Juvenile Offenders: Results from the Evaluation of the Nokomis Challenge Program." *Journal of Research in Crime and Delinquency 35*(3): 267–94.

Dowrich Management Services. 1993. "Police and Youth: Looking to the Future: Executive Summary of the Final Report of Pilot Project Police/Youth Mentoring Program." Co-funded by Ontario Ministry of the Solicitor General and Correctional Services and the Solicitor General of Canada.

Esbensen, R., and D. Osgood. 1997. "National Evaluation of G.R.E.A.T. (Gang Resistance and Education Training)." Research in Brief. Washington, DC: U.S. Department of Justice, National Institute of Justice.

Fritsch, E., T. Caeti, and R. Taylor. 1999. "Gang Suppression through Saturation Patrol, Aggressive Curfew, and Truancy Enforcement: A Quasi-Experimental Test of the Dallas Anti-Gang Initiative." *Crime and Delinquency 45*(1): 122–39.

Giacomazzi A., and Q. Thurman. 1994. "Cops and Kids Revisited: A Second-Year Assessment of a Community Policing and Delinquency Prevention Innovation." *Police Studies 4*: 1–20.

Greenwood, P., K. Model., C. Rydell, and J. Chiesa. 1996. *Diverting Children from a Life of Crime: Measuring Costs and Benefits.* Santa Monica: Rand Corporation.

Grossman, J., and E. Garry. 1997. "Mentoring–A Proven Delinquency Prevention Strategy." *Juvenile Justice Bulletin* (April). Washington, DC: U.S. Department of Justice, Office of Juvenile Justice and Delinquency Prevention.

Guetzloe, E. 1997. "The Power of Positive Relationships: Mentoring Programs in the School and Community." *Preventing School Failure 41*(3): 100–4.

Hansen, W., and J. Graham. 1991. "Preventing Alcohol, Marijuana, and Cigarette Use among Adolescents: Peer Pressure Resistance Training versus Establishing Conservative Norms." *Preventive Medicine 20*(3): 414–30.

Henggeler, S. and S. Schoenwald. 1994. "Boot Camps for Juvenile Offenders: Just Say No." *Journal of Child and Family Studies 3*(3): 243–48.

Howell, J., and J.D. Hawkins. 1998. "Prevention of Youth Violence." In M. Tonry and M. Moore, eds., *Youth Violence. Crime and Justice: A Review of Research*, vol. 24, 263–315. Chicago: University of Chicago Press.

Hudson, J., A. Morris, G. Maxwell, and B. Galaway, eds. 1996. *Family Group Conferences: Perspectives on Policy and Practice.* Monsey, NY: Criminal Justice Press.

Lab, S. 1997. *Crime Prevention: Approaches, Practices and Evaluations,* 3rd ed. Cincinnati: Anderson Publishing.

National Council on Crime Prevention. 1996. *Preventing Crime by Investing in Families: An Integrated Approach to Promote Positive Outcomes in Children.* Ottawa: National Council on Crime Prevention.

President's Crime Prevention Council. 1995. *Preventing Crime and Promoting Responsibility: 50 Programs That Help Communities Help Their Youth.* Washington, DC: President's Crime Prevention Council.

Ruefle, W., and K. Reynolds. 1996. "Keep Them at Home: Juvenile Curfew Ordinances in 200 American Cities." *American Journal of Police 15*(1): 63–84.

Sherman, L., D. Gottfredson, D. MacKenzie, J. Eck, P. Reuter, and S. Bushway. 1997. "Preventing Crime: What Works, What Doesn't, What's Promising." Research in Brief. Washington, DC: U.S. Department of Justice, National Institute of Justice.

Stanton, C., and A. Meyer. 1998. "A Comprehensive Review of Community-Based Approaches for the Treatment of Juvenile Offenders." In. T. Gullotta, G. Adams, and R. Montemayor, eds., *Delinquent Violent Youth: Theory and Interventions,* 205–29. Thousand Oaks, CA: Sage.

Thurman, Q., A. Giacomazzi, M. Reisig, and D. Mueller. 1996. "Community-Based Gang Prevention and Intervention: An Evaluation of the Neutral Zone." *Crime and Delinquency 42*(2): 279–95.

CHAPTER THIRTEEN

What Works in Youth Violence Prevention

DEWEY G. CORNELL
University of Virginia

For many years violence prevention strategies have been based largely on theoretical or ideological assumptions about "what works," in the absence of objective, scientific evidence. Indeed, so many ill-conceived strategies were so often found to be ineffective that many delinquency prevention critics popularized the cynical view that "nothing works." Such a pessimistic view is no longer tenable. Juvenile violence can be prevented and juvenile offenders can be rehabilitated. One goal of this chapter is to bring attention to the existence of a substantial and growing body of scientifically credible evidence that can be used to implement sound and cost-effective prevention programs.

This chapter will present a selective overview of prevention strategies found to reduce juvenile violence and associated problems such as substance abuse, property crime, and disruptive behaviour. Readers interested in the scientific evidence can turn to several extensive, quantitative evaluations of literature (Lipsey and Wilson 1997).

Some caveats: No strategy is effective for all youth or all settings. Every prevention program will have youth who fail, and unfortunately, failure inevitably receives more attention than success and can distort perceptions of program effectiveness. All programs are vulnerable to these misperceptions if they fail to routinely and rigorously document overall success rates. Programs that can reduce violent crime by even 10-20 percent are likely to be cost-effective in light of the high cost of juvenile crime for victims, communities, and the criminal justice system.

Source: Dewey G. Cornell, "Effective Practices in Youth Violence Prevention," from a chapter of the same title in D.G. Cornell, A. Loper, A. Atkinson, and P. Sheras, eds., *Youth Violence Prevention in Virginia: A Needs Assessment* (Virginia Department of Health, 1999): 29–42.

Finally, even the best-validated program will not succeed if it is not adequately funded and faithfully implemented by competent staff. A new treatment program must be sufficiently well specified in training manuals and guides so that it may be replicated in a new setting. More generally, programs must demonstrate adequate treatment fidelity — that is, they must faithfully implement the actual treatment program as it was designed. All too often program developers have rushed to implement new treatment programs without adequate training and preparation, so that treatment failure is a result of poor implementation, not an inadequate treatment model (for example, see Henggeler et al. 1997). Staff training and general quality control have often been neglected in prevention settings. Table 13.1 highlights the specific types of prevention strategies discussed in this chapter.

COMMUNITY-WIDE STRATEGIES

Mentoring

Mentoring is a relatively inexpensive program in which adult volunteers spend time each week with children or adolescents, typically engaged in recreational or educational activities. A controlled experiment with 959 youth in eight cities found that the Big Brothers/Big Sisters program resulted in a 46 percent reduction in drug use, a 32 percent reduction in hitting people, and a 52 percent reduction in truancy (Grossman and Garry 1997).

The Office of Juvenile Justice and Delinquency Prevention (OJJDP) supported the expansion of mentoring efforts through its Juvenile Mentoring Program (JUMP) (OJJDP 1998). JUMP has funded 93 mentoring projects as well as six SafeFutures community grants that include mentoring programs. Mentoring is also supported through the State Formula Grants program of the Juvenile Justice and Delinquency Prevention Act.

Despite the widespread popularity of mentoring, there has been relatively little research on the characteristics of successful mentors or successful mentoring relationships. What criteria should be used in selecting mentors and matching them to youth? How should mentors proceed to establish positive relationships with at-risk youth? These are important questions since some studies report that approximately half of mentor pair-

TABLE 13.1 *Effective Prevention Strategies*

Community-Wide	Family-Focused	School-Based
Mentoring	Parent education	Conflict resolution training
Supervised recreation	Family therapy	Violence prevention counselling
Community policing	Preschool programs	Bully reduction
		Social competence development
		Drug education

ings fail to develop into ongoing relationships (Freedman 1993; Morrow and Styles 1995).

A descriptive study by Morrow and Styles (1995) offered some hypotheses and directions for future research. The authors distinguished between "developmental" and "prescriptive" styles of mentoring. Developmental mentors were more flexible and relationship-focused in their approach to their youth, while prescriptive mentors were more directive and tended to prescribe activities and topics of discussion. At follow-up nine months later, developmental mentors were more likely to still be working with their little brothers/sisters while most prescriptive relationships had terminated.

Supervised Recreational Programs

The peak times for juvenile crime occur during the hours immediately after school (Snyder, Sickmund, and Poe-Yamagata 1997). The level of juvenile offending at 3 P.M. on school days is over three times greater than it is at noon or midnight. Many youth are unsupervised after school because their parents are at work. The lack of coordination between school and work in our society is an underlying structural problem in controlling juvenile crime. For this reason, after-school programs are of great potential value and deserve serious consideration in prevention planning for any community.

Most recreational programs have not been adequately tested. For example, there is little hard evidence concerning midnight basketball. However, several controlled studies have found that well-supervised after-school recreational programs substantially reduce juvenile crime, drug use, and vandalism. The Boys and Girls Club recreation and drug prevention program (Schinke, Orlandi, and Cole 1992) was effective in two studies conducted in a series of public housing projects. A Canadian study (Jones and Offord 1989) of another intensive after-school program (using sports, music, dancing, and scouting) demonstrated a 75 percent reduction in juvenile arrests, while arrests at a comparison site rose 67 percent.

The Boys and Girls Clubs of America have over 1700 affiliated clubs serving over 2.2 million children (Bureau of Justice Assistance 1995). Clubs provide a wide range of educational and counselling recreational services in addition to recreational programs. The mission of the Boys and Girls Clubs is to provide supervised recreational and educational programs to at-risk youth. Specific programs vary from club to club depending on what is needed in the community. A study of ten Boys and Girls Clubs by the U.S. Office of Substance Abuse Prevention reported 22 percent lower levels of drug activity and increased levels of parent involvement (Schinke, Orlandi, and Cole 1992). A rigorously designed three-year longitudinal study of 16 clubs in eight states (St. Pierre et al. 1997) also found reductions in alcohol and drug use, particularly in clubs that included active parent involvement. Clubs typically are open five to six days a week for four to five hours each day and are staffed by full-time youth workers as well as volunteers.

Community Policing

Community policing is a broad term and some programs labelled as community policing are not effective (Sherman et al. 1997). The most effective community policing programs seemed to have strong community participation in priority setting and a problem-oriented focus. Also noteworthy is the new research emphasis on the importance of strengthening police credibility and legitimacy with the general public, which suggests that it is important from a prevention perspective for police officers to maintain trust and respect through the quality of their everyday interactions with citizens, including youth (Tyler 1990).

FAMILY-FOCUSED STRATEGIES

Parent Education

Parents can be taught to be effective in managing their children's behaviour, but a brief course is not sufficient. Effective programs involve parents in ongoing relationships and training sessions that last from six months to several years. This investment pays off in reduced delinquency and better school adjustment for many years afterwards.

There is good research evidence that parent management training is effective with aggressive and disobedient children (Brestan and Eyberg 1998; Cedar and Levant 1990; Kazdin 1997). Parent training for families with aggressive young children is a verifiably cost-effective strategy for preventing future crime. Here are some of the more well-validated approaches to parent education:

- Parent Management Training for Conduct Disordered Children is the most influential parent training model for antisocial children. Developed by Patterson, Reid, and Dishion (1992) at the University of Oregon Social Learning Center, the program teaches parents more effective methods of disciplining and managing their children.
- The Barkley Parent Training Program provides an explicit manual used widely to train parents of children with severe behaviour problems (Barkley 1997). The program teaches a ten-step model supported by regular consultation with a therapist.
- The Parenting Program for Young Children developed by Carolyn Webster-Stratton (Webster-Stratton 1982; 1998) is a well-validated psychosocial intervention program. This 24-week program is delivered to groups of parents in two-hour weekly meetings using video vignettes to demonstrate positive parenting techniques.
- Family and Schools Together (FAST) is a more comprehensive program that incorporates parent training and home visits along with school-based efforts to improve the social skills and academic performance of elemen-

tary school children. FAST has been implemented in more than 26 states. Notably, the program has a high retention rate; 88 percent of the families who attend one multifamily session go on to complete the program (Conduct Problems Prevention Research Group 1992; McDonald et al. 1997).

As part of parent education, parents should also be encouraged to limit their children's exposure to violent television shows, movies, and video games. Despite mixed public opinion, and objections by the media industry, there is extensive, conclusive research establishing that television violence has a detrimental effect on children (Donnerstein, Slaby, and Eron 1994; Hughes and Hasbrouck 1996). Numerous formal experiments in clinical settings and schools, as well as long-term prospective field studies following young children into adulthood, demonstrate conclusively that exposure to media violence increases aggressive behaviour. Among the effects of media violence are that children learn to expect and anticipate violence in their daily life, are desensitized to violence and may even develop positive attitudes toward the use of violence, may fail to fully appreciate the negative consequences of violence, and in some cases engage in violence because they believe it to be a source of social status or an effective way to solve problems.

Few social influences are more pervasive than entertainment media violence, yet it has been difficult to convince parents to make greater efforts to supervise their children's viewing habits. In some respects, this represents a public health problem comparable to other public health challenges, such as reducing smoking, increasing exercise, and improving diet. Like smoking, the adverse effects may develop slowly over a long period of time, and only a small proportion of the population may experience the worst outcomes. Moreover, well-ingrained habits — whether it be smoking, overeating, or watching too much television — are difficult to change in part because they are so commonplace and socially acceptable. Sustained, widespread public educational efforts undoubtedly have made a difference in such areas as smoking and diet, so it is reasonable to assume that comparable efforts also might be effective.

Family Therapy

Family therapy refers to a host of different treatment approaches linked by their common emphasis on treating the whole family rather than individuals. The literature on family therapy is too extensive to summarize here. Functional family therapy (Alexander and Parsons 1982) is one form of family therapy that has been especially effective with delinquent youth. Treatment makes use of cognitive and behavioural methods to improve family relationships and increase reciprocity and co-operation among family members. Outcome studies demonstrated that functional family therapy improved family relationships and reduced recidivism among adolescents referred by juvenile court for offences such as truancy, theft, and unmanageable behaviour (Klein, Alexander, and Parsons 1977).

Multisystemic therapy (MST) (Family Services Research Center 1995; Henggeler 1991) is one of the most cost-effective and demonstrably effective treatments for high-risk or delinquent children and their families. In controlled outcome studies, multisystemic therapy has proven to be superior to standard treatments for chronic juvenile offenders, inner-city at-risk youth, child-abusive families, and other traditionally difficult populations. Multisystemic therapy is a relatively short-term (one to six months) but intensive form of therapy that is aimed at strengthening family functioning.

A hallmark of the multisystemic approach is the therapist's role as a problem solver who works closely with parents to identify and remedy problems in a wide variety of areas, ranging from a child's school attendance to marital discord. Typically, therapists begin treatment by visiting the family several times a week for sessions ranging from 15 to 90 minutes, and later gradually reduce contacts prior to termination. Therapists make flexible use of family therapy, parent education, and cognitive-behavioural techniques to improve family relationships, strengthen parental authority and effectiveness, and modify children's behaviour. This approach is carefully described in a treatment manual (Henggeler 1991; see also Henggeler and Bourduin 1990). It is important that therapists faithfully adhere to MST principles and procedures for this treatment to be effective; a recent study (Henggeler et al. 1997) found that MST effectiveness declined when therapists failed to follow the treatment model.

Preschool Programs

There is extensive evidence that some preschool programs, especially when combined with weekly home visits over a period of years, can have substantial, long-term impact on families and the quality of a child's adjustment (Tremblay and Craig 1995; Yoshikawa 1994). Some programs like the Perry Preschool Project found that children randomly assigned to the preschool and home visit program not only did better in school than control children, but had fewer arrests as juveniles and adults (Berreuta-Clement et al. 1985). A strength of the Perry Preschool Project was its emphasis on facilitating parent involvement in children's academic and social development. Another early childhood program that has received similar positive evaluations is Project Head Start, which is designed to provide a positive preschool learning environment and support for disadvantaged children and their families (Sherman et al 1997; Webster-Stratton 1998).

SCHOOL-BASED PROGRAMS

Conflict Resolution and Peer Mediation

The heart of conflict resolution is teaching students to listen carefully and respectfully to another person's point of view, accept that there are meaningful differences, and develop creative, mutually satisfactory solutions. Furthermore, students can be taught to mediate disputes between peers by facilitating a dialogue through which disputants find their own solution. The National Institute for Dispute Resolution estimates that there are over 8500 conflict mediation programs nation-wide. Although stand-alone peer mediation programs have not been examined in rigorous, controlled outcome studies (Sherman et al. 1997), there is more convincing evidence in support of comprehensive programs incorporating peer mediation and other forms of conflict resolution. For example, Johnson and Johnson (1995a) conducted extensive research in support of the "peacemaker" approach, using whole-school or cadre methods, with programs for all grade levels. Their controlled outcome studies (Johnson and Johnson 1995b) demonstrated that students can learn and retain conflict resolution skills, and subsequently apply their skills to actual conflicts in both school and family settings. Their program reduced overall school problems and facilitated academic achievement.

Violence Prevention Counselling

Violence prevention counselling can help aggressive youth cope with their frustration and hostility, and resolve conflicts without fighting. For example, the Duke University "Coping Power" program developed by Lochman (1992) to teach aggressive youth to cope with their anger has been shown to help children correct distortions in their perceptions of social interactions and choose nonviolent alternative courses of action. Hammond and colleagues have developed the Positive Adolescents Choices Training (PACT) program for work specifically with African American youth (Hammond 1991; Hammond and Yung 1993). PACT uses culturally sensitive videotapes to teach youth social skills such as strategies for expressing and responding to criticism and negotiating solutions to disputes.

The Violence Prevention Curriculum for adolescents is part of the Teenage Health Teaching Modules (THTM) program. Developed by Deborah Prothrow-Stith, the curriculum lends itself to working in schools with anger management, family violence, media violence, and dating violence. Teachers use handouts and videos to teach the program. Evidence of program effectiveness is available (Grossman et al. 1997).

Overall, there is considerable research in support of cognitive-behavioural approaches that not only reduce aggressive behaviour, but in some studies also improve school attendance and grades, and reduce substance abuse (Bry 1982; Izzo and Ross 1990; Lochman 1992; Rotheram 1982). Unfortunately, some briefer, but more popular approaches to violence prevention have not been well supported.

Bullying Reduction

Bullying is a pervasive problem that is often overlooked or minimized in schools. Because bullying is so pervasive, it is sometimes regarded as a normal or inevitable part of growing up. On the contrary, research (Craig 1998; Crick, and Bigbee 1998) indicates that school victimization has substantial and lasting effects on children's social and emotional adjustment. In one study, approximately three-quarters of Midwestern school children reported some episodes of bullying, with about 14 percent experiencing severe reactions to abuse (Hoover, Oliver, and Hazler 1992). Repeatedly victimized children often experience a variety of mental health problems including depression, anxiety, and low self-esteem. Victims tend to feel unsafe at school and are more likely to have school attendance problems than other students. Victims of chronic bullying continue to exhibit social adjustment problems in adulthood. Young bullies develop attitudes and values that lead to more serious aggressive behaviour in adolescence. Adult tolerance for bullying sends the wrong message to children and promotes acceptance of coercion, harassment, derogation, and violence as means of controlling others.

School-wide campaigns that condemn bullying and encourage more appropriate behaviour can dramatically reduce bullying, and in turn lower the likelihood of later aggression and delinquency that often follows. Dan Olweus developed and tested a highly successful program used first in Norway and later in the United States and other countries. Olweus (1997a; 1997b) evaluated the effectiveness of this program in 42 primary and secondary schools in Norway. He found a 50 percent reduction in bully/victim problems, as well as marked reductions in vandalism, truancy, and fighting.

There are numerous programs and guides for schools to conduct bullying reduction campaigns (National School Safety Center 1999). For example, *Bully-Proofing Your School* (Garrity et al. 1994) is a prevention program designed to make the school environment physically and psychologically safer. Through staff training, student instruction, intervention with bullies, and collaboration with victims and parents, the program uses role-playing, modelling, and class discussions to teach anger control and empathy, and strategies for victims.

Social Competence Development

Children as young as age 4 can be taught to solve interpersonal problems in an empathic and considerate manner. Social competence generally refers to the ability to get along with others and cope with problems effectively. There are several well-designed and rigorously evaluated programs that teach social competence. One of the best-known programs, Interpersonal Cognitive Problem Solving (ICPS, also known as "I Can Problem Solve") was developed by Myrna Shure and colleagues over the course of 35 years of research. This approach teaches children to identify problems, recognize the feelings and perspectives of others, consider the consequences of alternative solutions, and then choose the best course of action (Shure 1992; 1996). Numerous evaluations, including multi-year follow-up studies, document that training improves children's behaviour and generalizes across classroom, home, and peer situations (Shure 1997). Children are less impulsive and disruptive, and more cooperative and pro-social with peers and adults.

The Primary Mental Health Prevention (PMHP) project is one of the oldest and most respected school-based programs for identifying and treating children at risk for emotional and behavioural problems (Cowen et al. 1996). PMHP has changed and evolved over the course of nearly 40 years, with a basic model involving carefully supervised, paraprofessional counselling for children with emotional or behavioural problems. There are specialized components to teach social problem solving, assist children with divorced parents, facilitate peer relationships, and encourage cooperative learning (the "Study Buddy" program). A variety of large-scale, multi-year program evaluations involving thousands of students documented positive changes in the emotional and behavioural adjustment of PMHP children.

Drug Education

Drug education programs typically involve school-based instruction about the negative effects of alcohol and drug use, accompanied by efforts to encourage responsible decision making. No prevention program is more popular, or more controversial, than Drug Abuse Resistance Education (DARE). DARE began in 1983 as a collaborative effort between the Los Angeles Police Department and the Los Angeles Unified School District and has been adopted in over 70 percent of the nation's school districts, as well as 44 foreign countries (*Law Enforcement News,* 1996). The original core curriculum was designed for uniformed police officers to teach a specific drug prevention curriculum to students in their last (fifth or sixth) grade of elementary school. The core curriculum has been the subject of extensive research, although there are DARE programs for other grade levels that have received much less attention.

In 1994, Ringwalt and colleagues (Ringwalt et al. 1994) released an evaluation of the DARE program based on a meta-analysis of eight methodologically rigorous studies. All eight studies assessed students before and after completion of the core DARE curriculum and included control groups of students not receiving DARE. Overall, the studies involved more than 9300 students and 215 schools. The results indicated that DARE was most effective at increasing knowledge about drug use and in improving social skills. There was a small improvement in attitudes toward police, attitudes about drug use, and self-esteem. Unfortunately, however, the effect size for reported drug and alcohol use was not statistically significant. These results helped generate a storm of criticism and often contentious debate concerning the merits of DARE. Some researchers and reporters who presented unfavourable findings about DARE effectiveness were the recipients of harsh criticism and even harassment (Glass 1998; Rosenbaum and Hanson 1998).

In defense of DARE, one limitation of most outcomes studies was that they examined drug and alcohol use shortly after completion of DARE, when students are 11 or 12 years old and the baseline rates of drug use are so low that the effects of DARE might not be evident. To overcome this limitation, Rosenbaum and Hanson (1998) reported results of a six-year longitudinal study of 1798 students from 36 schools. This methodologically rigorous study employed randomized control groups and corrected for many statistical and methodological problems of previous studies. It was expected that this study would salvage DARE's reputation and demonstrate conclusively that it was effective. Unfortunately, this study again found that DARE did not reduce drug use, and in suburban schools, DARE was associated with a 3–5 percent increase in drug use.

DARE is an appealing, popular program that has fostered cooperation between education and law enforcement. It has many benefits for students, including increased knowledge about drugs and improved attitudes toward law enforcement. Nevertheless, the research evidence about DARE's effectiveness in reducing drug use has been weak and cannot be discounted (Sherman et al. 1997). To its credit, DARE has made changes to its curriculum and focused more efforts on older students, who are most likely to use drugs. Recently, DARE advocates and critics have met to discuss constructive methods of improving DARE and resolving some of the controversial questions about DARE's effectiveness (Modzeleski 1999).

Educators are well advised not to fashion their own alternatives to DARE, since many non-DARE drug education programs are either ineffective or, worse, have the unintended effect of increasing drug use (Rosenbaum and Hanson 1998). There is, however, evidence that some drug education programs are effective. Interactive programs that emphasize interpersonal skills to counter peer pressure and use a participatory teaching approach are more effective than programs that rely on moral exhortation, fear arousal, or self-esteem building (Ringwalt et al. 1994).

TREATMENT OF JUVENILE OFFENDERS

In addition to the prevention programs described above, treatment of juvenile offenders constitutes one of the most cost-effective forms of prevention. Table 13.2 highlights the juvenile offender treatment interventions discussed in the rest of this chapter.

TABLE 13.2 *Juvenile Offender Treatment Strategies*

Institutional Treatment	Noninstitutional Treatment
Treatment programs	Counselling
Wilderness/challenge programs	Intensive community supervision
Boot camps	
Group homes	

INSTITUTIONAL TREATMENT

Treatment Programs

Lipsey and Wilson (1997) examined 83 studies of institutional treatment for serious juvenile offenders and identified the kinds of treatment approaches that were most successful in reducing recidivism. How effective is institutional treatment? The average treatment program reduced re-offence rates by about 12 percent beyond the baseline re-offence rate for the institution as a whole (baseline rates vary by institution). This is probably sufficient to be a cost-effective and worthwhile reduction, when the expense and social impact of juvenile crime is considered. However, the most effective treatment programs reduced recidivism by 30 to 40 percent, which clearly represents a substantial benefit.

Using the statistical methods of meta-analysis, Lipsey, and Wilson (1997) were able to identify the characteristics of the most effective programs. The most effective programs made extensive use of individual counselling and interpersonal skills training. Youth reviewed difficult social situations or past experiences, learned more skillful responses, and practised their skills using methods such as role-playing, videotape feedback, and homework tasks. Young offenders also improved their ability to identify and cope with angry feelings. Examples of effective programs are Aggression Replacement Training (Glick and Goldstein 1983), the Social Interactional Skills Program (Shivrattan 1988), and social-cognitive training (Guerra and Slaby 1990).

Wilderness/Challenge Programs and Boot Camps

Notably, some popular programs were not effective. There is little evidence to support the use of wilderness/challenge programs (Lipsey and Wilson 1997). Boot camps (also called shock incarceration) are another popular program that has had disappointing results. Although offenders sent to boot camps tend to develop less antisocial attitudes while at the camp, camps have little or no effect on recidivism after return to the community.

It is important to recognize that programs with novel or appealing qualities — such as wilderness programs and boot camps — often have little or no lasting impact on juvenile crime, and may prevent the implementation of more effective programs. Despite their political popularity and seemingly down-to-earth emphasis on self-discipline and personal responsibility, wilderness programs and boot camps do not deliver what they promise. However, some boot camps do have lower recidivism than others. The most effective boot camps are not the camps with the greatest emphasis on military discipline or physical training; instead, effectiveness is associated with intensity of aftercare and community supervision.

Group Homes

Lipsey and Wilson (1997) reported that effective community residential programs provide an array of services including group and individual counselling, educational support, and vocational training. The most effective programs utilized a family home approach in which adult supervisors served as "teaching parents" working closely with a small number of youth. For example, Achievement Place (Kirigin et al. 1982) places six to eight youth with a couple who serve as surrogate parents and child advocates while administering a behaviourally oriented program. Youth can return to their own homes on weekends and remain in their local schools. Critical to the success of group homes is the training and experience of treatment personnel and their faithful adherence to effective treatment procedures.

NONINSTITUTIONAL TREATMENT

Counselling

Lipsey and Wilson (1997) synthesized the results of 117 studies of juvenile offenders treated outside of institutional settings. In general, noninstitutional treatments reduce recidivism to about half the rate that it would have been without treatment (Lipsey and Wilson 1997). A wide variety of treatment approaches were effective, with individual counselling the most effective. Several types of counselling were beneficial, including reality therapy (Bean 1988) and multisystemic therapy (Henggeler and Borduin 1990). Training programs emphasizing interpersonal skills, parent training, and behavioural contracts were also effective (see also Guerra, Tolan, and Hammond 1994).

Despite some differences in treatment methods, the most effective programs had some common characteristics: greater length of treatment (generally more than the median of 25 weeks for all treatments), greater attention to treatment integrity (i.e., checks to make sure the therapists followed the treatment procedure), and use of mental health personnel rather than juvenile justice personnel to administer treatment.

Intensive Community Supervision

Intensive community supervision, also called Intensive Supervised Probation (ISP) is a widely used but controversial approach. ISP programs use a variety of methods to monitor offenders and increase their level of direct contact with probation officers. Early enthusiasm for ISP programs waned when careful research uncovered limitations and problems with the claims of ISP advocates. A scientifically rigorous, controlled study of fourteen ISP programs in nine states (Petersilia and Turner 1995) found that ISP participants overall had a re-arrest rate no different from nonparticipants. Moreover, the average ISP probation violation rate was 65 percent compared with 38 percent for controls. The primary virtue of ISP appeared to be that increased monitoring led to increased detection of probation violations. Other studies have found mixed results for ISP, but the general consensus is that the increased monitoring of ISP does not reduce recidivism (Sherman et al. 1997). However, there is evidence that ISP does reduce recidivism if the program includes treatment services beyond simple monitoring (Sherman et al. 1997; Petersilia and Turner 1995). A recurrent theme apparent in the evaluation of many programs is that effective treatment is often linked to the delivery of high-quality services designed to improve social competencies, prevent substance abuse, and facilitate employment.

AN INTEGRATIVE MODEL: COMMUNITIES THAT CARE

Communities That Care (Hawkins, Catalano, and Associates 1992) is a systematic, theoretically grounded approach to helping communities create conditions and relationships that protect youth against drug and alcohol abuse. The Communities That Care model describes how communities can plan, undertake, monitor, and evaluate a series of programs and strategies to reduce risk factors and strengthen protective factors in individual children, their families, schools, and neighbourhoods. In addition to a core emphasis on substance abuse, this ambitious model is designed to improve family functioning, increase school achievement, and generally reduce antisocial and delinquent behaviour. The evolving Communities That Care model is both comprehensive and flexible, and can be adapted to individual community needs and goals. There is considerable outcome research in support of various components of the approach — for example, parent education, teacher training, substance abuse prevention, social skills counselling, and others (Hawkins et al. 1992; Hawkins et al. 1991).

WHAT'S NEXT?

We have made considerable progress in identifying what works in reducing youth violence. Nevertheless, there is substantial work to be done. Even the most effective programs can be improved. A 50 percent reduction in juvenile crime is a remarkable accomplishment, but not an ultimate goal.

Moreover, we need better means of assuring that programs are accurately disseminated and faithfully implemented in order for them to be effective. The best-validated, proven programs will fail if staff are not ready and able to carry them out according to their established procedures. Workshops and conferences make good introductions, but they are not sufficient training to assure programs function as intended.

Next, it is important to recognize that youth at-risk to engage in violent behaviour are not a homogeneous group. We need better means of matching youth to the programs that are most effective in addressing their problems and concerns. This means improved identification and assessment methods, as well as a better understanding of the differential effects of different programs.

Finally, the criteria for program success or effectiveness require careful consideration and ongoing evaluation. The most obvious sign of program success is a reduction in juvenile crime, but there are other important goals as well, for example, educational achievement and gainful employment. There are many ways to define and measure desirable outcomes for individuals, institutions, and communities as a whole. The complex relationship among these outcomes remains to specified. Ultimately, it will be most useful to identify those outcomes or goals for young children and their families that best facilitate and make possible the attainment of future success —however defined — as those children pass through adolescence to adulthood.

STUDY QUESTIONS

1. *According to Cornell, why do supervised recreational programs have a great deal of potential as a strategy for reducing youth crime? Discuss examples of supervised recreational programs that exist in your community or that could be implemented in your community as part of a youth crime prevention strategy.*
2. *What does the research reviewed by Cornell indicate about the effectiveness of primary youth crime prevention strategies involving families and schools?*
3. *What concerns does Cornell raise about the effectiveness of existing institutional and noninstitutional tertiary or treatment-based approaches to youth crime prevention? What key qualities does a treatment-based youth crime prevention strategy need in order to be effective?*

REFERENCES

Alexander, J.F., and B.V. Parsons. 1982. *Functional Family Therapy*. Monterey, CA: Brooks/Cole.

Barkley, R.A. 1997. *Defiant Children: A Clinician's Manual for Assessment and Parent Training*. New York: The Guilford Press.

Bean, J.S. 1988. "The Effect of Individualized Reality Therapy on the Recidivism Rates and Locus of Control Orientation of Male Juvenile Offenders." Unpublished Ph.D. dissertation, University of Mississippi.

Berreuta-Clement, J.R., L.J. Schweinhart, W.S. Barnett, A.S. Epstein, and D.P. Weikart. 1985. *Changed Lives: The Effects of the Perry Preschool Program on Youths through Age 19*. Ypsilanti, MI: High Scope Press.

Brestan, E.V., and S.M. Eyberg. 1998. "Effective Psychosocial Treatments of Conduct-Disordered Children and Adolescents: 29 Years, 82 Studies, and 5,272 Kids." *Journal of Clinical Child Psychology 27*(2): 180–89.

Bry, B.H. 1982. "Reducing the Incidence of Adolescent Problems through Preventive Intervention: One- and Five-Year Follow-Up." *American Journal of Community Psychology 10*: 265–76.

Bureau of Justice Assistance. 1995. *Boys and Girls (B and G) Clubs of America. Bureau of Justice Assistance Fact Sheet.* Washington, DC: U.S. Department of Justice.

Cedar, B., and R.F. Levant. 1990. "A Meta-Analysis of the Effects of Parent Effectiveness Training." *The American Journal of Family Therapy 18*(4): 373–83.

Conduct Problems Prevention Research Group. 1992. "A Developmental and Clinical Mode for the Prevention of Conduct Disorder: The FAST Track Program." *Development and Psychopathology 4*: 509–27.

Cowen, E.L., A.D. Hightower, J.L. Pedro-Carroll, W.C. Work, P.A. Wyman, with W.G. Haffey. 1996. *School-Based Prevention for Children at Risk: The Primary Mental Health Project.* Washington, DC: American Psychological Association.

Craig, W.M. 1998. "The Relationship among Bullying, Victimization, Depression, Anxiety and Aggression in Elementary School Children." *Personality and Individual Differences 24*(1): 123–30.

Crick, N.R., and M.A. Bigbee. 1998. "Relational and Overt Forms of Peer Victimization: A Multi-Informant Approach." *Journal of Consulting and Clinical Psychology 66*(2): 337–47.

Donnerstein, E., R. Slaby, and L. Eron. 1994. "The Mass Media and Youth Aggression." In L.D. Eron and J.H. Gentry, eds., *Reason to Hope: A Psychosocial Perspective on Violence and Youth*, 219–50. Washington, DC: American Psychological Association.

Family Services Research Center. 1995. *Multisystemic Therapy Using Home-Based Services: A Clinically Effective and Cost Effective Strategy for Treating Serious Clinical Problems in Youth.* Charleston, SC: Author.

Freedman, M. 1993. *The Kindness of Strangers.* San Fransisco, CA: Josey-Bass.

Garrity, C., K. Jens, W. Parter, N. Sager, and C. Short-Camilli. 1994. *Bully-Proofing Your School: A Comprehensive Approach for Elementary Schools.* Longmont, CO: Sopris Press.

Glass, S. 1998. "Truth and DARE: The Nation's Most Prestigious Drug Prevention Program for Kids is a Failure. Why Don't You Know This?" *Rolling Stone* (March 5): 42–43, 81.

Glick B., and A.P. Goldstein. 1983. "Aggression Replacement Training." *Journal of Counseling and Development 65*: 356–62.

Grossman, J.B., and E.M. Garry. 1997. "Mentoring — A Proven Delinquency Prevention Strategy." *Juvenile Justice Bulletin* (April). Washington, DC: U.S. Department of Justice, Office of Juvenile Justice and Delinquency Prevention.

Grossman, D.C., H.J. Neckerman, T.D. Koepsell, P.Y. Liu, K.N. Asher, K. Belandia, K. Frey, and F.P. Rivara. 1997. "Effectiveness of a Violence Prevention Curriculum among Children in Elementary School: A Randomized Controlled Trial." *Journal of the American Medical Association 277*(20): 1605–11.

Guerra, N.G., and R.G. Slaby. 1990. "Cognitive Mediators of Aggression in Adolescent Offenders: 2. Intervention." *Developmental Psychology 26*(2): 269–77.

Guerra, N.G., P.H. Tolan, and W.R. Hammond. 1994. "Prevention and Treatment of Adolescent Violence." In L.D. Eron, J.H. Gentry, and P. Schlegel, eds., *Reason to Hope: A Psychosocial Perspective on Violence and Youth,* 383–403. Washington, DC: American Psychological Association.

Hammond, R. 1991. *Dealing with Anger: Givin' It, Takin' It. Workin' It Out.* Champaign, IL: Research Press.

Hammond, R., and B. Yung. 1993. *Evaluation and Activity Report: Positive Adolescent Choices Training*. Unpublished grant report. U.S. Maternal and Child Health Bureau, Washington, DC.

Hawkins, J.D., R.F. Catalano, and Associates. 1992. *Communities That Care: Action for Drug Abuse Prevention*. San Francisco: Jossey-Bass.

Hawkins, J.D., R.F. Catalano, D.M. Morrison, J. O'Donnell, R.D. Abbott, and L.E. Day. 1992. "The Seattle Social Development Project: Effects of the First Four Years on Protective Factors and Problem Behaviors." In J. McCord and R.E. Tremblay, eds., *Preventing Antisocial Behavior: Interventions from Birth Through Adolescence,* 139–61. New York: Guilford.

Hawkins, J.D., J.M. Jenson, R.F. Catalano, and E.A. Wells. 1991. "Effects of a Skills Training Intervention with Juvenile Delinquents." *Research on Social Work Practice 1*: 107–21.

Henggeler, S.W. 1991. *Treating Conduct Problems in Children and Adolescents (Treatment Manual).* Columbia, SC: S.C. Dept. of Mental Health.

Henggeler, S.W., and C.M. Borduin. 1990. *Family Therapy and Beyond: A Multisystemic Approach to Treating Behavior Problems of Children and Adolescents*. Pacific Grove, CA: Brooks/Cole.

Henggeler, S.W., G.B. Melton, M.J. Brondino, D.G. Scherer, and J.H. Hanley. 1997. "Multisystemic Therapy with Violent and Chronic Juvenile Offenders and Their Families: The Role of Treatment Fidelity in Successful Dissemination." *Journal of Consulting and Clinical Psychology 65*: 821–33.

Hoover, J., R. Oliver, and R.J. Hazler. 1992. "Bullying: Perceptions of Adolescent Victims in the Midwestern U.S.A." *School Psychology International 13*: 5–16.

Hughes, J.N., and J.E. Hasbrouck. 1996. "Television Violence: Implications for Violence Prevention." *School Psychology Review 25*(2): 134–51.

Izzo, R.L., and R.R. Ross. 1990. "Meta-Analysis of Rehabilitation Programs for Juvenile Delinquents." *Criminal Justice and Behavior 17*(1): 134–42.

Johnson, D.W., and R.T. Johnson. 1995a. *Teaching Students to Be Peacemakers,* 3rd ed. Edina, MN: Interaction Book.

———. 1995b. "Teaching Students to be Peacemakers: Results of Five Years of Research." *Peace and Conflict: Journal of Peace Psychology 4*: 417–38.

Jones, M.B., and D.R. Offord. 1989. "Reduction of Anti-Social Behavior in Poor Children by Nonschool Skill Development." *Journal of Child Psychology and Psychiatry and Allied Disciplines 30:* 737–50.

Kazdin, A. 1997. "Parent Management Training: Evidence, Outcomes, and Issues." *Journal of the American Academy of Child and Adolescent Psychiatry 36*(10): 1349 – 58.

Kirigin, K.A., C.J. Braukmann, J.D. Atwater, and M.M. Worl. 1982. "An Evaluation of Teaching-Family (Achievement Place) Group Homes for Juvenile Offenders." *Journal of Applied Behavior Analysis 15*: 1 – 16.

Klein, N.C., J.F. Alexander, and B.V. Parsons. 1977. "Impact of Family Systems Intervention on Recidivism and Sibling Delinquency: A Model of Primary Prevention and Program Evaluation." *Journal of Consulting and Clinical Psychology 45*: 469 – 74.

Law Enforcement News editorial. 1996. "When It Comes to the Young, Anti-Drug Efforts are Going to Pot." *Law Enforcement News 22*: 441 – 47.

Lipsey, M.W., and D.B. Wilson. 1997. *Effective Intervention for Serious Juvenile Offenders: A Synthesis of Research*. Vanderbilt Institute for Public Policy Studies. Nashville, TN.

Lochman, J.E. 1992. "Cognitive-Behavioral Intervention with Aggressive Boys: Three-Year Follow-Up and Preventive Effects." *Journal of Consulting and Clinical Psychology 60*(3): 426 – 32.

McDonald, L., S. Billingham, T. Conrad, A. Morgan, N. Oo, and E. Payton. (1997). "Families and Schools Together (FAST)." *Families in Society 78*(2): 140 – 55.

Modzeleski, W. 1999. Personal communication, February 26.

Morrow, K.V., and M.B Styles. 1995. *Building Relationships with Youth in Program Settings: A Study of Big Brothers/Big Sisters*. Philadelphia: Public/Private Ventures

National School Safety Center. 1999. "Bullying: Peer Abuse in Schools." *School Safety Update* (March): 1 – 7.

Office of Juvenile Justice and Delinquency Prevention. 1998. *Juvenile Mentoring Program (JUMP): 1998 Report to Congress*. Washington: U.S. Department of Justice, Office of Justice Programs.

Olweus, D. 1997a. "Bully/Victim Problems in School: Knowledge Base and an Effective Intervention Program." *The Irish Journal of Psychology 18*(2): 170 – 90.

———. 1997b. "Tackling Peer Victimization with a School-Based Intervention Program." In D. Fry and K. Bjoerkqvist, eds., *Cultural Variation in Conflict Resolution: Alternatives to Violence*, 215 – 31. Mahwah, NJ: Lawrence Erlbaum Associates, Inc.

Patterson, G.R., J.B. Reid, and T.J. Dishion. 1992. *Antisocial Boys: A Social Interactional Approach*. Eugene, OR: Castalia.

Petersilia, J., and S. Turner. 1995. "Evaluating Intensive Supervision Probation/Parole: Results of a Nation-Wide Experiment." In K.C. Haas and G.P. Alpert, eds., *Dilemmas of Corrections*, 3rd ed, 489 – 511. Prospect Heights, IL: Waveland Press.

Ringwalt, C., J. Greene, S. Ennett, R. Iachan, R.R. Clayton, and C.G. Leukefeld. 1994. *Past and Future Directions of the DARE Program: An Evaluation Review: Draft Final Report.* Washington, DC: National Institute of Justice.

Rosenbaum, D., and G. Hanson. 1998. *Assessing the Effects of School-Based Drug Education: A Six-Year Multi-Level Analysis of Project DARE.* Unpublished manuscript. Department of Criminal Justice and Center for Research in Law and Justice, University of Illinois at Chicago.

Rotheram, M.J. 1982. "Social Skills Training with Underachievers, Disruptive, and Exceptional Children." *Psychology in the Schools 19*: 532–39.

St. Pierre, T.L., M.M. Mark, D.L. Kaltreider, and K.J. Aikin. 1997. "Involving Parents of High-Risk Youth in Drug Prevention: A Three-Year Longitudinal Study in Boys and Girls Clubs." *Journal of Early Adolescence 17*(1): 21–50.

Schinke, S.P., M.A. Orlandi, and K.C. Cole. 1992. "Boys and Girls Clubs in Public Housing Developments: Prevention Services for Youth at Risk." *Journal of Community Psychology* (OSAP Special Issue): 118–28.

Sherman, L.W., D. Gottfredson, D. MacKenzie, J. Eck, P. Reuter, and S. Bushway. 1997. *Preventing Crime: What Works, What Doesn't, What's Promising: A Report to the United States Congress.* Washington, DC: National Institute of Justice.

Shivrattan, J.L. 1988. "Social Interactional Training and Incarcerated Juvenile Delinquents." *Canadian Journal of Criminology 30*: 145–63.

Shure, M.B. 1992. *I Can Problem Solve (ICPS): An Interpersonal Cognitive Problem Solving Program.* Champaign, IL: Research Press.

———. 1996. *Raising a Thinking Child: Help Your Young Child to Resolve Everyday Conflicts and Get Along with Others.* New York: Pocket Books.

———. 1997. "Interpersonal Cognitive Problem Solving: Primary Prevention of Early High-Risk Behaviors in the Preschool and Primary Years." In G.W. Albee and T.P. Gullota, eds., *Primary Prevention Works*, 167–88. Thousand Oaks, CA: Sage.

Snyder, H.N., M. Sickmund, and E. Poe-Yamagata. 1997. *Juvenile Offenders and Victims: 1997 Update on Violence.* Washington, DC: Office of Juvenile Justice and Delinquency Prevention.

Tremblay, R., and W. Craig. 1995. "Developmental Crime Prevention." In Michael Tonry and David P. Farrington, eds., *Building a Safer Society. Crime and Justice*, vol. 19, 151–236. Chicago: University of Chicago Press.

Tyler, T. 1990. "Justice, Self-Interest, and the Legitimacy of Legal and Political Authority." In J. Mansbridge, ed., *Beyond Self-Interest.* Chicago: University of Chicago Press.

Webster-Stratton, C. 1982. "The Long-Term Effects of a Videotape Modeling Parent-Training Program: Comparison of Immediate and 1-Year Follow-Up Results." *Behavior Therapy 13*: 702–14.

———. 1998. "Preventing Conduct Problems in Head Start Children: Strengthening Parenting Competencies." *Journal of Consulting and Clinical Psychology 66*: 715–30.

Yoshikawa, H. 1994. "Prevention as Cumulative Protection: Effects of Early Family Support and Education on Chronic Delinquency and Its Risks." *Psychological Bulletin 115*: 28–54.

CHAPTER FOURTEEN
Promises and Pitfalls of Mentoring as a Juvenile Justice Strategy

DELORES D. JONES-BROWN
ZELMA WESTON HENRIQUES
City University of New York

Poor timing may be the benchmark of a bureaucratic system. In 1993, the Office of Juvenile Justice and Delinquency Prevention (OJJDP) proposed a "Comprehensive Strategy" for addressing the problem of juvenile crime. Under this comprehensive strategy, it was recognized that the family and community, with support from other "core" social institutions (such as schools, churches, and local organizations) have primary responsibility for meeting the basic socializing needs of American children (Wilson and Howell 1993: 10). It was also recognized that failure to meet these basic needs is a primary contributor to juvenile crime.

A vote by the federal legislature in 1997, however, evidenced an abandonment of the wisdom underlying the comprehensive strategy and converted juvenile "justice" to a mirror image of the arguably ineffective system of adult "justice" — a system based upon notions of retribution and deterrence only, without regard for the context in which law-violating behaviour develops.

Just as statistics were beginning to indicate a drop in juvenile crime (under the comprehensive strategy), the House of Representatives voted 286 to 132 in favour of a bill that would establish a new program of "juvenile accountability block grants." The "accountability" grants program made $1.5 billion available to states over the next three years. The block grants, however, are only available to those "states that require juveniles charged with serious violent crimes to be charged as adults, make juvenile criminal records public, and otherwise impose tough[er] sanctions on serious juvenile offenders." Interestingly, this $1.5 billion is in contrast to the mere one million dollars in grants that the President's Crime Prevention Council and OJJDP have announced for drug

Source: Delores D. Jones-Brown and Zelma Weston Henriques, "Promises and Pitfalls of Mentoring as a Juvenile Justice Strategy," *Social Justice 24*(4) (1997): 212–33.

abuse prevention programs targeted at juveniles. Even that figure is to be divided into approximately ten grants of merely $100 000 each.

The shift in focus for juvenile justice, from prevention and rehabilitation to retribution, deterrence, and perhaps incapacitation, is indicative of a surrender of sorts. The government, having failed to help the nation's children and families, is willing to settle for the easier task of meting out punishment to those who offend.

The tragedy of this approach is that it comes at a time when the tide of juvenile crime had begun to turn by using holistic, less punitive measures than those approved by the House. The shift also comes at a time when evidence of community intervention (rather than governmental intervention) was beginning to emerge as a viable means of preventing and/or reducing juvenile crime.

Given the equivocal nature of research findings regarding the effectiveness of harsh punishment as a means of deterring criminal behaviour, two major questions face the justice system for the 21st century. Does a societal need for revenge outweigh the obligation to protect would-be youthful offenders from elements that have been demonstrated to lead to offending? Once youth have offended, should they be treated as if they have crossed some threshold from which there is no redemption?

Drawing upon the available literature and the experiences of a program designed and implemented by one of the authors, this article argues that mentor programs represent a viable strategy for delinquency prevention and reduction, even for youth who have been adjudicated for serious offences. However, we caution that the promise of such programs can only be achieved through careful design and implementation that takes into account the special needs and circumstances of the population to be mentored.

We first outline the sociopolitical context in which community self-help began to develop as a necessary means of delinquency prevention and reduction coterminous with more punitive means of attempting to achieve the same goals. Next, mentor programs, a community intervention approach, are distinguished from the (more intrusive) governmental approaches of boot camps and waiver. Then, results from the Big Brothers/Big Sisters Project (BB/BS) and the federal Juvenile Mentoring Programs (JUMP) are presented as showing the promise of mentoring as an effective means of delinquency prevention and reduction. Finally, from one of the author's experiences creating a mentor program for adjudicated youth, the article identifies critical areas that must be effectively addressed to design and implement successful mentor programs to service minority youth, a group most "at-risk" for criminal involvement.

BACKGROUND

The 1980s and early 1990s saw the convergence of two events, a reduction in the availability of government funds for addressing social problems (such as crime) and an increase in the juvenile crime rate. The unfortunate timing of these two events has led to a divergent view on how best to address the juvenile crime problem.

There are those who believe that the limited governmental resources should be spent on more punitive crime control measures such as boot camps and on waiving juveniles to adult court. Others believe that delinquency prevention and reduction can be achieved through self-help — i.e., volunteerism in the form of "mentoring" (Freedman 1992). For this discussion, juvenile justice mentoring involves the one-to-one interaction of law-abiding members of a community with delinquents or juveniles "at-risk" of becoming delinquent, with the aim being to prevent or reduce the juveniles' involvement in law-violating behaviour.

THE CARROT OR THE STICK APPROACH: MENTOR PROGRAMS VERSUS BOOT CAMPS, WAIVER, AND OTHER PUNITIVE MEASURES

In June 1996, House Republicans proposed legislation that would end federal mandates requiring states to segregate juveniles from adults in jails and prisons. DiIulio (1996), among others, acknowledges that the proposal is a "step in the wrong direction." Several points DiIulio makes dictate against mixing juvenile offenders and adult inmates in correctional facilities and favour greater support for community-based mentor programs, preferably early in a youth's delinquency history. He notes that:

> [H]ousing juvenile criminals with adult felons will not help decrease the rate of violent crime. . . . Most juvenile offenders are not guilty of repeated or random acts of serious violence. Most kids who get into serious trouble with the law need adult guidance. And they won't find suitable role models in prison. Jailing youths with adult felons under Spartan conditions will merely produce more street gladiators. (1996: 15)

DiIulio notes further that:

> [T]he evidence shows that children are less likely to commit violent crime if they have responsible adults in their lives. Even impoverished kids living in crime-ravaged neighbourhoods tend to make it if they have an adult — parent, teacher, coach, or clergy — to protect and guide them. (1996)

Public/Private Ventures' (P/PV of Philadelphia, Pennsylvania) study of the impact of Big Brothers/Big Sisters (Tierney, Grossman, and Resch 1995) tends to confirm DiIulio's claims. Referring to the study, the Office of Juvenile Justice and Delinquency Prevention (OJJDP) noted that the research "presented clear and encouraging evidence that caring relationships between adults and youth, resulting in a wide range of tangible benefits, can be created and supported by mentoring programs" (OJJDP 1994: 2). Details of the promise stemming from that study are provided below. However, the promise of mentor programs is not limited to pre-adjudicated or nonviolent, nonserious juvenile offenders.

According to DiIulio (1996: 15), "most teenage predators begin as severely at-risk children." A National Institute of Justice (NIJ) study, he notes, found that part of the notion of being "at-risk" includes the fact that a child who suffers from abuse and neglect is 40 percent more likely to become delinquent. Roughly half of jailed youngsters have at least one immediate family member who was incarcerated. Moreover, many juveniles who commit violent crimes have witnessed or experienced serious violence at an early age. Hence, treating such juveniles harshly via the juvenile justice system may only serve to increase the risk that they may become, or continue to be, serious felony offenders. The continuation of harsh treatment, with its potential for exacerbating rather than reducing delinquency, is a shortcoming of both boot camps and waiver as methods of handling juvenile offenders.

Boot Camps

Although not as restrictive as confinement in a secure facility, boot camps are known for their rigid militaristic style. Juvenile participants are commonly organized into platoons and required to wear uniforms and to participate in daily regimens of drill exercises and physical training. Daily routines may extend from 5:30 or 6:00 A.M. to lights out at 9:00 or 10:00 P.M. Beyond attempting to change attitudes and behaviour through discipline, boot camp programs also typically offer traditional rehabilitative activities, including remedial education, life skills education, and counselling and substance abuse education (Bourque et al. 1996). Striking a balance between the militaristic and rehabilitative aspects of the programs has been difficult. As a NIJ evaluation report states, "the effects of discipline, an important motivating tool when youth can be closely monitored, may quickly dissipate once offenders leave the boot camp environment" (Bourque et al. 1996: 7).

Recently, Arizona and Maryland closed their boot camps after evaluations revealed that they were costly and had a questionable impact on recidivism rates. Arizona specifically found that the cost of running its military-style boot camp was higher than its potential costs for incarceration in a secure facility. During an OJJDP teleconference, three other states indicated that their boot camp programs had shown a high dropout rate for participants during the aftercare portion of the programs (National Criminal Justice Association 1996: 1).

Waiver

Another popularly cited means of achieving delinquency prevention or reduction has been waiver of juvenile offenders to adult court. Waiver is most often advocated for violent juvenile offenders, but Department of Justice statistics indicate that a significant proportion of those waived are property offenders or other less serious repeat offenders (Snyder and Sickmund 1995). By waiving juveniles to adult court, there is an increased chance that they will come into contact with adult felony offenders. Among the risks associated with this contact is that the juvenile will "learn" to be a better or more aggressive criminal (DiIulio 1996). Also, to avoid victimization the juvenile may need to become a better "street gladiator." Failure to do so is likely to mean that he will become the victim of sexual and other forms of abuse.

Though greater use of waiver may result in increased antisocial behaviour and victimization of juveniles, jurisdictional technicalities may also lead to more lenient treatment of juvenile offenders who appear in adult court for the first time. For example, in New Jersey, a juvenile appearing in adult court for the first time for an offence of the third degree or less is entitled to a presumption of nonincarceration. This is true no matter how often he may have been confined as a juvenile and regardless of the number and seriousness of his juvenile offences. The prospect of a more lenient sentence and the guarantee of all the constitutional rights afforded adults encourages the attorneys of some juveniles to seek waiver.

Such use of waiver has at least two downsides. First, the perception that juveniles will receive more lenient treatment when waived than they would have in the juvenile court undermines any deterrent effect that the procedure is expected to have. Second, particularly for poor and minority youth, the future consequences of waiver may not be clearly understood.

In most jurisdictions, juvenile records and court proceedings are still closed to the public. Juveniles who are adjudicated delinquent, even for serious offences, are confined in juvenile correctional facilities with the possibility of being recalled from confinement based on good behaviour. However, once the juvenile has begun his first adult sentence, whether probationary or not, his life becomes a matter of public record that will follow him through future efforts to vote, enter a school, or obtain a job. In addition, the presumption of nonincarceration exists only once. Subsequent convictions for the waived juvenile are presumed to result in incarceration in an adult correctional facility. Thus, though the juvenile justice system in many ways is designed to avoid negative labelling, the adult system is not. Once a decision is made for a juvenile to enter that system, whether by consent or adjudication, he carries the label of "convict" and the attendant negative social consequences.

There is no clear indication that such punitive methods do a better job of protecting the public than do other less or nonpunitive measures. Yet they are certainly costly in terms of dollars required to implement and sustain them and of the human capital that is damaged or lost through their use. In the words of President Clinton, "there isn't a single victim of crime who wouldn't trade the toughest sentence in the world for some way to have prevented the crime from happening in the first place." Mentoring as a juvenile justice strategy represents a humane approach to delinquency prevention and reduction.

The Carrot: Mentor Programs

Unlike boot camps and waiver, mentor programs involve a helping, modelling strategy. Their most attractive feature is that rather than removing the youth from his or her environment, they take place in the community where the youth must learn to cope with daily situations that significantly affect their lives. The mentoring relationship takes place in a dynamic setting that greatly increases the likelihood of success or failure.

Most programs involve volunteer staff who see themselves as giving something to or sharing something with the youth who are being mentored. Mentor programs are less costly than other approaches to delinquency prevention because often the mentors are volunteers who may or may not receive reimbursement for out-of-pocket expenses related to mentoring activities.

In an ideal society concerned with the well-being of children, Cullen (1994) provides perhaps the best analytical framework for choosing the carrot (mentor programs) over the sticks (boot camps and waiver). He suggests that social *support* rather than social *control* should be the primary focus for reducing rates of criminal involvement by youth in "high-risk neighbourhoods."

Citing Sampson (1986a; 1986b) and Sampson and Groves (1989), Cullen notes that research reveals that crime rates are higher in communities characterized by family disruption, weak friendship networks, and low participation in local voluntary organizations. Though these characteristics have been interpreted as affecting a community's ability to exert informal social control over residents, Cullen suggests that these variables could as easily be viewed as factors that contribute to a community's inability to provide needed support networks.

He cites Zuravin's (1989) research as providing preliminary data that child maltreatment — often a predecessor to delinquency — is inversely related to the ecology of support. According to Zuravin (1989: 102), "high-risk neighbourhoods are characterized by demographic, social, and physical characteristics that negatively impact on family and individual stress levels by decreasing the availability as well as the adequacy of support systems."

As a juvenile justice strategy, mentoring is an opportunity to provide support where it is missing and to supplement it when it is weak. Particularly in instances of high rates of family disruption, mentoring makes alternate adult support networks available to youth and provides alternate opportunities for developing intimate relations (Cullen 1994). However, the development and acceptance of these alternatives present the greatest challenge to the large-scale, long-term, successful use of mentoring as a delinquency intervention tool.

EVIDENCE OF PROMISE

Unlike the problems associated with boot camps and waiver, evaluations of volunteer mentor programs indicate that they may work effectively to prevent the onset of various kinds of antisocial behaviour. They may also work to arrest the behaviour once it has begun. The results from formal evaluations of Big Brothers/Big Sisters of America and informal feedback from federally funded programs have been particularly encouraging.

Big Brothers/Big Sisters

Big Brothers/Big Sisters of America (BB/BS) is a federation of agencies that have been providing volunteer mentors to children, especially those in single-parent households, for over 90 years. The BB/BS mentoring relationship is not specifically designed to prevent delinquency. Instead, it is designed to "provide support to all aspects of young people's lives" (Grossman and Garry 1997: 2). As broad as this function may sound, when BB/BS was evaluated for its ability to affect the lives of young people in seven areas, the results were overwhelmingly positive. These areas were: antisocial activities, academic performance, attitudes and behaviours, relationships with families, relationships with friends, self-concept, and social and cultural enrichment.

Among other things, the Public/Private Ventures (P/PV) study of Big Brothers/Big Sisters found that:

- Mentored youth were 46 percent less likely than the control group to initiate drug use during the study period. The finding was even stronger for minority youth: they were 70 percent less likely to initiate drug use when in a positive mentoring relationship.
- Mentored youth were 27 percent less likely than the control group to initiate alcohol use.
- Mentored youth were less assaultive, skipped fewer days of school, and had much better relationships with their parents (OJJDP 1994: 2).

The findings regarding drug and alcohol use are very important given the abundance of research that links delinquency and criminality, particularly in the form of aggressive or assaultive behaviour, to the consumption of such substances (Gropper 1985).

The Juvenile Mentoring Program (JUMP)

Federal recognition of the potential for mentoring as a way to prevent or reduce juvenile delinquency became evident in 1992. In that year, "Mentoring" was included as Part G of the Reauthorization of the Juvenile Justice and Delinquency Prevention Act of 1974. Since then, Congress has made more than $19 million available to fund such programs (Grossman and Garry 1997: 2).

OJJDP describes the role of JUMP as:

> [T]o reduce juvenile delinquency and gang participation, improve academic performance, and reduce school dropout rates. . . . To achieve these purposes, JUMP brings together caring, responsible adults and at-risk young people in need of positive role models. (Grossman and Garry 1997: 2)

During fiscal year 1995 alone, JUMP attempted to service more than 2000 "at-risk" youth in 25 states. Though the formal evaluation of such programs has not yet been conducted, preliminary informal feedback indicates that JUMP-funded mentoring programs are "making a difference in the lives of many young people." Highlights from one JUMP-sponsored mentor program are listed below:

- 30 percent of the youth who participated in the program showed improvement in their school attendance;
- 30 percent showed academic improvement;
- 35 percent showed improvement in their general behaviour; and,
- 48 percent increased the frequency of appropriate interactions with peers (Grossman and Garry 1997: 5).

Programs have also shown initial signs of delaying or preventing teen pregnancy and alcohol or drug abuse, at least during program involvement. Regardless of long-term outcomes, virtually all the JUMP-funded mentor programs provided the youth involved with opportunities they may not have otherwise had, including a chance to engage in activities (such as being a panelist on a cable news show) and to meet people (such as legal professionals, members of the military, and corporate executives) that would have been unlikely without the program.

The positive impact of mentoring for minority youth strongly suggests that such programs may represent one mechanism for attempting to reduce the overrepresentation of minority youth in secure detention facilities or at other points within the juvenile justice system (Tierney, Grossman, and Resch 1995). If, as Cullen (1994) suggests, criminal justice authorities are willing to turn their focus from social control to social support, the findings from BB/BS and JUMP indicate that through mentorship, communities can play a significant role in shaping and perhaps reshaping the lives of their youth.

The task of reshaping the lives of older youth who have been adjudicated delinquent, and particularly those who have been adjudicated for felony offences, presents a special challenge. However, that does not mean that the effort is not worthwhile. It is no more challenging than trying to maintain control of young people in artificial environments marked by fear and boredom, often located far from their families or other outside support.

COMMUNITIES ORGANIZED TO REGAIN THEIR ENVIRONMENT

In 1993, the lead author of this article was involved in designing and implementing a community mentor component for a program called Project CORE (Communities Organized to Regain their Environments). Under the auspices of the New Jersey Department of Human Services, the New Jersey Division of Juvenile Services (DJS) entered a partnership with the state university (Rutgers 1993) to develop a comprehensive, highly structured eight-month program for adjudicated youth, ages 15 through 18, from Newark, New Jersey. The program provided a means of early release and supportive aftercare for motivated male juveniles confined to three model residential correctional facilities within the state.

The development and implementation of Project CORE represents a unique collaborative model that may warrant replication in other locations. Besides the partnership between DJS and the state university, implementation of the program brought together a variety of community-based agencies and different funding sources. For example, the Salvation Army's Division of Human Services provided the space in which the program was headquartered. The initial funding for the program was through federal drug confiscation and forfeiture monies, supplemented by state educational funds.

As part of its mission, Project CORE was designed to address the root causes of crime, which the program summary identified as "poverty, joblessness, the breakdown of the family unit, and the disintegration of shared community structure and values." The inclusion of a community mentoring component, along with other comprehensive services, was viewed as a viable means of combating some of these "root causes" during the aftercare portion of the program.

It was also desirable that, via appropriate matching of educational or vocational interests, mentors might be able to assist the program in its goal "to prepare, place, and monitor the youths in jobs or appropriate educational [settings]" (Rutgers 1993: 1). Goals of matching also included finding mentors in the youth's proximate community and of the same sex, ethnicity, and similar socioeconomic background (Jones 1995).

The effectiveness of same-sex versus cross-sex matches has not been systematically studied, and there is no clear evidence that matches along racial or ethnic lines are indeed more successful than unmatched pairs (Anderson 1994; Mecartney, Styles, and Morrow 1994; Grossman and Garry 1997). However, the mentor component of Project CORE, which then served only minority males, was designed with the assumption that pairing males of similar circumstances would:

1. Maximize the potential for identity formation, thereby allowing the mentor to be seen as a realistic role model;
2. Foster a sense of trust both interpersonally and in the accuracy of practical information provided by mentors;

3. Help the mentees develop various male competencies within and despite the limitations of socio-structural factors (such as racism); and,
4. By using mentors who had achieved various goals despite their ethnic or socioeconomic background, provide the students with a desire to set higher goals for themselves.

The main goal of the matching criteria was to maximize the potential for effective sustained matches.

During the approximately 14 months that the mentor component of the program was in operation, a total of 40 different males served as mentors for 51 youths. Mentors were recruited locally from five college and university campuses, through professional organizations, churches, and other community organizations.

To assist Project CORE "students," as they were referred to, in making decisions about careers or vocational choices, it was possible to pair them with mentors who were working at a job compatible with their career interests in about 20 percent of cases (Jones 1995: 15).

All mentors worked or lived in Newark or the surrounding area. However, in only about 10 percent of cases did the mentor actually live in, or very near, the assigned student's neighbourhood (Jones 1995: 15). Failure to meet this criterion for a more substantial number of the mentored youth reduced their access to the mentors after standard business hours. Once the relationships were underway, more than one student was heard to comment, "I wish I could spend more time and do more with my mentor."

Several mentors in professional jobs did have pagers. Access to mentors at any time via the pagers helped give the mentees a true sense of having a supplemental support system. In one instance, a Project CORE student became distraught when his father died and there was no way to transport his family to the funeral and burial site. When he paged his mentor, the mentor called back immediately, left work, and used his personal vehicle to drive the family approximately 60 miles round-trip.

The same young man had been doing quite well in all aspects of the CORE program, but began to show signs of depression and withdrawal following the death of his father. The mentor shared his story of losing his own father at age 11. He explained that the mentee was lucky since his father had died after a substantial period of illness. The mentor described his own bitterness after the sudden death of his father, who was murdered during a robbery attempt. The mentor described his pain at not having had an opportunity to say good-bye to his father. He then shared with the mentee his strategies for coping with and overcoming the bitterness and pain. The mentee went on to successfully complete aftercare and had not been rearrested within a year following release from the residential facility.

In another instance, a Project CORE student who had recently become a father lacked the financial resources to obtain a car seat in which to take the new baby home. Without the car seat, the hospital would not release the child. The young man contacted his mentor hoping to borrow a car seat from someone the mentor knew. The mentor bought a car seat as a gift for the baby and arranged for the transportation home.

The extent to which these and other positive interactions with previous strangers will work to produce long-term change in the lives of the youth involved in Project CORE is unknown. Because Project CORE consisted of numerous components, it is not possible to attribute any one student's success or failure solely to the mentoring component.

However, mentors did help find employment and vocational and alternative educational placements for mentees. Often, if a mentor became aware of a need and knew how to address it, he would provide helpful information for placing a student, even if that student was not in a one-on-one relationship with him. On a mentor component questionnaire, one student wrote that the mentor program provided "good connections and opportunities." Verbal comments from mentees indicated that mentors were valuable as listeners, as sources of information for problem solving, and as someone positive to spend time with. Mentors who were ex-offenders were particularly effective because the CORE students felt that those mentors really could understand where they "were coming from."

The following list of activities engaged in by CORE students and their mentors is not exhaustive and is similar to activities reported by other programs (Anderson 1994; Grossman and Garry 1997). Like the mentor relationships in Big Brothers/Big Sisters and JUMP, the CORE mentor component provided the youth involved with a host of new and not-so-new experiences. The mentoring also provided the youth with opportunities to receive support in areas where existing familial and friendship networks were unwilling or incapable of providing such supports. The activities included:

- Exploration through visits to the mentor's workplace or visits to other workplaces arranged by the mentor;
- Trips to the movies and to live theatre;
- Recreational activities such as bowling, skating, playing pool, basketball, baseball, and gym workouts, as well as visits to video arcades, attending cookouts, going shopping, and going out to eat;
- Attending various professional, college, and local sporting events;
- Participating together in community service projects;
- Assistance with employment readiness, job hunting, and informal educational tutoring;
- Emergency transportation to work, home, community service sites, or other locations; and
- Attending to personal needs such as haircuts and other matters related to health and hygiene.

Given that many of the CORE youth had at one time or another been arrested for selling drugs, there was also an aspect of the program that focused on legitimate entrepreneurships, in which several of the self-employed mentors participated as speakers.

A promising aspect of mentoring was that all of this was done relatively cheaply and safely. Mentors were all volunteers who took on the expense of planning and executing the various activities and almost never requested reimbursement for out-of-pocket costs. Out of the 51 mentor/mentee matches, there were no known incidents of exploitation, abuse, or other criminal victimization among the matched pairs. As for general public safety, during the program only one of the 51 mentored youth was rearrested for a serious personal crime. This was particularly impressive given that the offences for which the mentees had been confined ranged from drug dealing and car theft to robbery, gun possession, and manslaughter.

Juvenile crime in a particular area may be affected by local and regional differences in factors such as the prevalence of gangs, family mobility, opportunities for youth recreation and employment, and other socio-structural limitations. However, the authors believe that the experiences with youth in Project CORE strongly suggest that mentoring represents a community-oriented, cost-efficient, and safe means of handling and helping some delinquent youth.

Despite evidence that mentoring holds promise for preventing delinquency in "at-risk" youth who have not been processed through the criminal justice system and can have an impact on the lives of adjudicated youth, the design and implementation of mentor programs is not without potential pitfalls. The first step in avoiding these pitfalls is recognizing their existence. Below we summarize potential pitfalls that may be encountered in attempts to institute mentoring as a large-scale, long-term juvenile justice strategy. Given the often severe socio-structural limitations confronted by minority and urban youth, if these pitfalls are not recognized and addressed, they hold great potential for derailing mentoring efforts. We therefore also recommend ways to avoid these pitfalls.

POTENTIAL PITFALLS OF MENTORING AS A JUVENILE JUSTICE STRATEGY

Lack of information can be a major flaw in designing any program. Therefore, before developing the proposal for Project CORE's Community Mentor Component, several individuals who had been involved in the design or implementation of other mentor programs were contacted for advice. Final reports and replication manuals of other programs were also reviewed. This preliminary research keyed the designer into many of the problems that could be expected in attempting to implement and sustain a volunteer mentoring program for youthful mentees.

Although efforts were made to exclude through design as many of these problems as possible, the Project CORE mentoring program still encountered nearly all of them at one time or another. The primary problems included:

unavailability of suitable mentors, the limited time desirable mentors had for mentoring, maintenance of relationships over time, resistance of youth to being mentored, holding mentors accountable to mentoring requirements and necessary documentation, ensuring that youth responded to the relationship as a "two-way street" rather than as a "give me," holding youth accountable to mentoring requirements, and having the necessary personnel to monitor the relationships.

Our recommendations for avoiding these potential problems include:

1. Hire full-time rather than part-time staff to run the program.
2. Provide comprehensive services.
3. Allow adequate lead time for recruitment, screening (of both mentors and mentees), and matching.
4. Include a "mentoring readiness" component to familiarize youth with the concept of mentoring.
5. Receive input from those to be mentored.
6. Consistently make information about the program public.
7. Recruit and train mentors in an ongoing process.
8. Make adjustments in the program design as necessary.

Comments

The National Research Council's Panel on High-Risk Youth (1993: 213) writes, "perhaps the most serious risk facing adolescents in high-risk settings is isolation from the nurturance, safety, and guidance that comes from sustained relationships with adults." The panel notes further that:

> The empirical foundation for mentoring programs stems from the literature on resiliency, which indicates that a key factor in successful adolescent development is the presence of a sustained and nurturing relationship with adults. (National Research Council 1993: 213)

One of the major pitfalls to the effective establishment and maintenance of useful programs is the notion of a sustained relationship. High-risk youth need a level of consistency in mentoring relationships that, despite good intentions, individuals who may have the most to offer, as mentors, are sometimes unable to provide. Though Masten, Best, and Garmezy (1990) suggest that older youth are likely to benefit the most from mentoring as a means of compensating for family inadequacies, experience has taught that older youth also come with entrenched attitudes and behaviour patterns that are more resistant to change (than those of younger youth).

Since most of the work in mentor programs is carried out by volunteers, safely bringing together a suitable, capable, and dependable volunteer with an appropriate young person in need of support is an awesome task. Insuring that a healthy, dependable, helping relationship is maintained between the pair adds to the challenge. The task requires skills beyond those of the average person. To be done properly, it requires round-the-clock dedication. Only through constant recruitment efforts can the necessary number of desirable mentors be obtained as needed. However, a desirable role model is not necessarily an available role model. Making positive information about the program available to the public serves the dual purpose of reducing the public's resistance to using community correction with juvenile felony offenders and quieting any fear of victimization among potential qualified mentors. Continuous recruiting in private and public forums is necessary for maintaining a reserve pool of mentors (with available time and energy) to be matched to the needs and special interests of individual youth as they come into the program. This is possible only if there is adequate time for program staff to accurately assess the needs of each youth and attempt to match them to the interests and competencies of a suitable volunteer.

Because the need for support among "at-risk" youth is great and varied, mentor programs that are part of a larger network of comprehensive social services show greater promise than stand-alone programs. The needs of "at-risk" youth may encompass economic issues and issues related to family, peers, mental health, recreation, and education. Some of these areas require special attention that may be beyond the competency of the volunteer.

Simply because a young person is in need of help does not mean that he or she is amenable to it, particularly when the aid is coming from a stranger. In fact, nearly every Project CORE student who responded to a post-program questionnaire indicated that they were not initially motivated about the idea of having a mentor.

Like job readiness programs that precede employment, our suggestion for a "mentor readiness" component gets the mentees ready to be mentored. Unlike mentor training, which exists in virtually every mentoring program, the "mentor readiness" component is designed to directly assist the mentees rather than the mentors. The component presents an opportunity for program staff to explain, in detail, the supportive function of mentors and to address any questions or concerns that potential mentees may have. The indirect benefit to mentors is that, in theory at least, the mentees will be less resistant to the notion of being mentored by a stranger.

If program staff and mentors are trained to develop ways in which family members can be included in the mentoring process, this may serve to quiet fears about mentors attempting to replace family members and intruding upon the personal autonomy of mentees, thus also reducing resistance. Another effective tool for reducing resistance to mentoring is to allow mentees to have a say in what their needs are, and then using that information in their program plan. Though middle-class America and social scientists believe that they know what is best for urban, minority, and otherwise "at-risk" youth, that belief may not be accurate. Psychological research supports the notion that youth are more engaged by programs that they have had a role in developing. Use of mentee input may also serve as a powerful esteem-building tool.

Matching across gender, race, ethnicity, and socioeconomic background may also be helpful in sustaining mentoring relationships. However, research by Styles and Morrow (1992) found that the ways in which the adult and youth related to each other, rather than their identity or activities, were the distinguishing factors between satisfied and dissatisfied mentor pairs (Styles and Morrow 1992: 57; Anderson 1994: 69). Among the traits identified by mentees and mentors as producing satisfying relationships were factors such as:

1. The mentor understood the youth's reluctance to trust.
2. The mentor understood that at least initially, the relationship would be one-directional.
3. The mentor identified the youth's interests and took them seriously. (The adult did not criticize or preach to the youth.)
4. The mentor attempted to relate to the youth's experience (but did not pry into private matters).
5. The mentor attempted to understand the youth's family. (Styles and Morrow 1992: 57–59)

It does everyone a disservice to hold onto aspects of a program that have proved to be unworkable. For example, many people are wedded to the idea that mentors should be volunteers. However, to better motivate mentors to adhere to mentoring requirements (such as the duration and frequency of contacts) and to keep accurate records of mentoring activities, monetary stipends may be useful.

Under all circumstances, program staff, mentors, and mentees must be encouraged to ask questions and even make complaints when they are warranted. Staff must be willing and prepared to act on those requests and complaints, or be able to explain why change may not be possible or necessary. Working through the rough spots is an essential element of mentor program survival and "success."

Measuring Outcomes

Too often the success or failure of an intervention program is measured in terms of recidivism. Beyond the difficulties of defining recidivism (i.e., rearrest versus readjudication or reconfinement) is the notion that outcome measures that only account for one type of negative event miss other positive changes that may have taken place for the youth during the program.

Given that the youth involved in this program had already been adjudicated delinquent, the authors use the terms "delinquency prevention" or "reduction" to represent two possible outcomes for these youth. Delinquency prevention represents that ideal situation where program involvement or other factors result in the mentee's long-term desistance from delinquency. Delinquency reduction represents an incremental curtailment of delinquent behaviour (i.e., the mentee engages in delinquent acts less frequently or de-escalates the level of offences committed).

Incremental change is an important measure of success (rather than simple recidivism) for the mentees in this group, since almost none of them were first-time offenders. Further, the acts they were confined for before involvement in the mentor program were real crimes, not status offences. The prevention of even one such offence is significant.

Finally, like BB/BS and JUMP programs, there was clear evidence of improved behaviour and attitudes among youth involved in the Project CORE mentor program. Some mentees who were permitted to return to mainstream schools (rather than alternative schools) showed significant improvement in attendance and academic performance. Many family members reported better relationships with the mentored youth and credited the mentors with the change. Mentors also assisted mentees with finding employment (often for the first time) and introduced them to various new career possibilities.

It is nearly impossible to assess how these events will play out in the long term. For some mentees, other risk factors contributed to why they absconded or were reconfined. However, to ignore incremental changes in favour of an absolute, "all or nothing" measure of recidivism does the mentoring relationship a disservice and belittles the efforts of concerned volunteers. Recidivism as the sole measure of success also makes it easier to claim that "nothing works" if program participants are rearrested, even if the charges are not sustained or even if the new charges are status or relatively minor offences, or technical program violations.

CONCLUSION

Although mentoring is not a panacea or a magic bullet, there is evidence to suggest that mentor programs can effectively make a difference in the lives of "at-risk," even "high-risk" youth. Society at large can reap the benefits of that difference if we are willing to let go of our retributive mindset.

Despite the challenges involved in designing and implementing mentor programs as a community-based correctional alternative for adjudicated youth, evidence suggests that such programs can be developed safely. Safe implementation does require a host of comprehensive services that meet a variety of needs that, if left unattended, are potentially criminogenic.

Shifting the focus of juvenile justice from social control to social support can result in significant gains in the areas of delinquency prevention or reduction, academic performance, personal development, and peer and family relations. The key, however, is to cultivate the promise and avoid the pitfalls. Designing, implementing, and sustaining effective mentor programs takes time. There is no one scientific formula. However, hastily designed and implemented programs run the risk of failure. The risk of repeat program failure is that policymakers will continue to resort to the "quick fix" of punitive measures as the preferred mode of handling "the juvenile crime problem."

STUDY QUESTIONS

1. *How do mentoring programs work and what are they designed to achieve?*
2. *According to Jones-Brown and Henriques, why are mentoring programs a promising juvenile justice strategy (compared with other measures like boot camps and the waiver of juvenile offenders to adult courts)?*
3. *What are the potential pitfalls of mentoring as a juvenile justice strategy, and how do Jones-Brown and Henriques recommend avoiding these pitfalls?*

REFERENCES

Anderson, Michelle. 1994. "The High Juvenile Crime Rate: A Look at Mentoring as Preventive Strategy." *Criminal Law Bulletin 30*: 54–75.

Bourque, Blair, Roberta Cronin, Daniel Felker, Frank Pearson, Mei Han, and Sarah Hill. 1996. "Boot Camps for Juvenile Offenders: An Implementation Evaluation of Three Demonstration Programs." *National Institute of Justice Research in Brief.* Washington, DC: U.S. Department of Justice.

Cullen, Francis. 1994. "Social Support as an Organizing Concept for Criminology: Presidential Address to the Academy of Criminal Justice Sciences." *Justice Quarterly 11*; 527–59.

DiIulio, John, Jr. 1996. "Stop Crime Where It Starts." *The New York Times* (Tuesday, July 31): A15.

Freedman, Marc. 1992. *The Kindness of Strangers: Reflections on the Mentoring Movement.* Philadelphia, PA: Public/Private Ventures.

Gropper, Bernard. 1985. "Probing the Links between Drugs and Crime." Washington, DC: National Institute of Justice Research in Brief.

Grossman, Jean, and Eileen Garry. 1997. "Mentoring — A Proven Delinquency Prevention Strategy." *Juvenile Justice Bulletin* (April). Washington, DC: U.S. Department of Justice, Office of Juvenile Justice and Delinquency Prevention.

Jones, Delores. 1995. *Project C.O.R.E. Mentor Program: Final Report.* Rutgers University, Office of Continuing Professional Education. New Brunswick, NJ: Cook College.

Masten, Ann, Karin Best, and Norman Garmezy. 1990. "Resilience and Development: Contributions from the Study of Children Who Overcome Adversity." *Development and Psychopathology 2*: 425, 429.

Mecartney, Crystal, Melanie Styles, and Kristine Morrow. 1994. *Mentoring in the Juvenile Justice System: Findings from Two Pilot Programs*. Philadelphia, PA: Public/Private Ventures.

National Criminal Justice Association. 1996. "Arizona, Maryland Close Boot Camps, Citing Questionable Impact, Costs." *Justice Bulletin 16*: 1, 17–18.

National Research Council Panel on High-Risk Youth. 1993. *Losing Generations: Adolescents in High-Risk Settings*. Washington, DC: National Academy Press.

Office of Juvenile Justice and Delinquency Prevention. 1994. "Juvenile Mentor Program (JUMP) Guidelines Notice." *Federal Register 59* (July 28): 144, Washington, DC.

Rutgers University, Office of Continuing Professional Education. 1993. *Project C.O.R.E. Program Summary*. New Brunswick, NJ: Cook College.

Sampson, Robert. 1986a. "Neighborhood Family Structure and the Risk of Personal Victimization." In J. Byrne and R. Sampson, eds., *The Social Ecology of Crime*, 25–46. New York: Springer-Verlag.

———. 1986b. "Crimes and Cities: The Effects of Formal and Informal Social Control." In Albert Reiss, Jr., and Michael Tonry, eds., *Communities and Crime*, 271–311. Chicago: University of Chicago Press.

Sampson, Robert, and W. Byron Groves. 1989. "Community Structure and Crime: Testing Social-Disorganization Theory." *American Journal of Sociology 94*: 774–802.

Snyder, Howard, and Melissa Sickmund. 1995. *Juvenile Offenders and Victims: A National Report*. Washington, DC: Office of Juvenile Justice and Delinquency Prevention.

Styles, Melanie, and Kristine Morrow. 1992. *Understanding How Youth and Elders Form Relationships: A Study of Four Linking Lifetimes Programs*. Philadelphia, PA: Public/Private Ventures.

Tierney, Joseph, Jean Grossman, and Nancy Resch. 1995. *Making a Difference: An Impact Study of Big Brothers/Big Sisters*. Philadelphia, PA: Public/Private Ventures.

Wilson, John, and James Howell. 1993. *A Comprehensive Strategy for Serious Violent and Chronic Juvenile Offenders, Program Summary*, U.S. Department of Justice. Washington, DC: Office of Juvenile Justice and Delinquency Prevention.

Zuravin, Susan. 1989. "The Ecology of Child Abuse and Neglect: Review of the Literature and Presentation of Data." *Violence and Victims 4*: 101–20.

CHAPTER FIFTEEN

In Search of Hopeful Glimpses: A Critique of Research Strategies in Current Boot Camp Evaluations

SHELDON X. ZHANG
California State University, San Marcos

The rapid growth of boot camps in recent years, together with other forms of intermediate sanctions, is largely the result of overcrowding in correctional agencies (Byrne, Lurigio, and Petersilia 1992). As early as 1983, criminal justice administrators identified prison and jail crowding as the most important issue facing them (Gettinger 1983). From 1970 to 1990, jail and prison populations in the United States increased by nearly four times their original populations (National Council on Crime and Delinquency 1992). By 1995, there were 1.6 million offenders in jails and prisons, or 600 inmates per 100 000 residents (U.S. Bureau of Justice Statistics 1996). Many state prisons are under court order to reduce their inmate populations (Cronin 1994).

Since its appearance in Georgia and Oklahoma in 1983 (Parent 1989), the idea of "shocking" criminal offenders into conformity through activities resembling those of military basic training has been embraced by an increasing number of both politicians and criminal justice practitioners across the nation (Cronin 1994; MacKenzie et al. 1995; Morash and Rucker 1990; Hunter et al. 1992). Despite the disappointing findings from most evaluations, the number of boot camps continues to grow (for detailed overviews of the development of boot camps nation-wide, see Cronin 1994; MacKenzie 1993; Bourque et al. 1996).

Most boot camps appear to share similar system-level goals, such as rehabilitating offenders, providing alternatives to long-term incarceration, and reducing prison/jail crowding. In a survey of boot camp administrators (MacKenzie and Souryal 1991), rehabilitation, recidivism reduction, and drug

Source: Sheldon X. Zhang, "In Search of Hopeful Glimpses: A Critique of Research Strategies in Current Boot Camp Evaluations," *Crime and Delinquency* 44(2) (1998): 314 – 34. Reprinted by permission of Sage Publications, Inc.

education were ranked most highly as program goals, followed by reduction of crowding, development of work skills, and provision of a safe prison environment. The goals of deterrence, education (GED), and drug treatments were judged as somewhat less important, whereas the least important were punishment and vocational training.

Despite these ambitious goals, the results have not been promising. Although some have found positive changes in participants' attitudes (MacKenzie and Shaw 1990; MacKenzie and Souryal 1995; Ransom and Mastrorilli 1993; Hunter et al. 1992), few program evaluations have provided "hard" evidence of the effectiveness of these camps in terms of rehabilitation or reducing recidivism. According to the most comprehensive study to date (MacKenzie et al. 1995), based on a comparative analysis of programs in eight states, no clear-cut statements can be made about the effectiveness of boot camps. In general, boot camp graduates do not fare better or worse after release than their counterparts in the conventional correctional system. Boot camp programs have to be examined individually in terms of specific program components and characteristics to look for possible explanations for their different outcomes (MacKenzie et al. 1995). Empirical efforts have also failed to produce consistent findings on other program effectiveness indicators such as increased prosocial behaviour, reduction of technical violations, or reduced drug involvement of camp graduates (MacKenzie and Shaw 1993; MacKenzie and Brame 1995; Shaw and MacKenzie 1992). At present, the only summarizing statement one can make about boot camps is the lack of any consistent effect, either positive or negative.

However, it may be premature to declare boot camps useless as designed and implemented thus far, in that these findings, however mixed or disappointing, have largely been generated by studies using a limited range of techniques and methods. Cronin (1994) pointed out in her overview that it is unlikely that researchers will learn much more about the impact of boot camps on recidivism without better measures and research designs to ascertain the meaning and effects of the camp experience on subsequent behaviour. As a first step in this effort, it seems appropriate to carry out a systematic overview of current boot camp research to assess critically what has been learned.

METHODS AND PROCEDURES

To accomplish this goal, a comprehensive literature review of current boot camp evaluations was conducted. However, the review was by no means exhaustive. The numerous internal studies conducted by boot camp administering agencies were not included here because it would be difficult to select a representative range of these publications. Therefore, readers need to take into account the limited scope of this literature search, which focused on published studies involving primary data collections.

A mapping scheme was developed, as shown in Table 15.1, to identify four major areas of boot camp evaluations. This scheme included (1) program types (i.e., boot camp administering agency); (2) evaluation strategies; (3) data gathering methods; and (4) outcome measures.

This study identified the governmental agency responsible for operating the boot camp, and the identification of boot camp administering agencies was fairly straightforward. This review also identified the primary methodological approaches employed among the various evaluation design strategies. Although boot camps vary significantly in program designs and camp characteristics, in general they share similar goals at both the system and the individual levels. The outcome measures were selected on the basis of the extensive survey work done by MacKenzie and her colleagues (MacKenzie 1993; Souryal and MacKenzie 1995).

PATTERNS AND ISSUES IN CURRENT BOOT CAMP EVALUATIONS

There are several clear patterns in current boot camp research efforts, as shown in Table 15.1. First, most of the studies examine programs that are operated by state agencies and designed for adults. Second, most studies are quantitative with designs involving eligible subjects or a pre- and post-design. Third, most evaluations rely on official records only and, finally, most studies have only examined individual outcomes (e.g., recidivism and prosocial attitudes), rather than system impacts (e.g., reduction in overcrowding and cost-effectiveness).

BOOT CAMPS OPERATED BY FEDERAL/STATE AGENCIES VERSUS LOCAL JURISDICTIONS

Although the Federal Bureau of Prisons also operates boot camps (MacKenzie 1993), no studies on any of its programs were located. This review found only four studies on two county-operated adult boot camps. A study by Freeman (1993) failed to find any significant change in the moral and maturational development among participants in a boot camp in Travis County, Texas, whereas the other three studies, all on the same program in Harris County, Texas, produced mixed findings (Hunter et al. 1992; Jones 1996; Anderson and Dyson 1996).

Because most of our knowledge on boot camps comes from state-operated programs, which presumably deal with different criminal populations from those of local jurisdictions, we know little about how county-level programs affect the local correctional population. An increasing number of counties have become interested in boot camps and for much the same reasons as the states. However, these local programs tend to be more financially precarious and often short-lived, which makes them less feasible for systematic evaluation. For instance, before the National Council on Crime and

Delinquency could complete its evaluation, the Los Angeles County Sheriff's adult boot camp was forced to shut down prematurely because of funding problems (Austin, Jones, and Bolyard 1993).

Still, because jails house significant numbers of prison-bound offenders and serving time in them is often used in lieu of a prison sentence, boot camps could be a preferable option for local criminal justice jurisdictions (Austin, Jones, and Bolyard 1993). Additionally, evaluating boot camps in the local correctional environment with different populations will add to our understanding of the functions of this intermediate sanction.

Most boot camps have been designed for young adults convicted of non-violent crimes (MacKenzie and Souryal 1994). However, many local jurisdictions have also started boot camps for juvenile delinquents (Bourque et al. 1996). After all, the juvenile justice system also faces crowding problems as the number of delinquents in custody increased by 35 percent from 1978 to 1989, even though the nation's youth population actually declined by 11 percent (Office of Juvenile Justice and Delinquency Prevention 1992).

The most visible juvenile boot camps were the three demonstration projects funded in 1991 by the Office of Juvenile Justice and Delinquency Prevention (OJJDP) in Mobile, Alabama; Cleveland, Ohio; and Denver, Colorado. All published studies on juvenile boot camps identified in this review were on these three projects. Two of them found positive changes in participants' attitudes and behaviour during the program (Bourque et al. 1996; Polsky and Fast 1993). But the positive changes were only observed among those who completed the program and stayed in the aftercare. Had these studies included those who dropped out of either the boot camps or the aftercare programs, the positive changes might have been less pronounced. Attrition rates were high in all three locations, ranging from 41 to 76 percent (Bourque et al. 1996), and were attributed to new arrests for criminal offences, going AWOL, and failure to comply.

In the recently published interim reports, serious operational and organizational problems were noted in all three demonstration projects, including high staff turnover, lack of understanding of the project among participating staff, unclear division of roles and responsibilities, reduction in funding, and extensive program changes at all levels in both the residential and aftercare phases. In fact, all three boot camp programs were considered only partially implemented (for details, see Peters 1996a; 1996b; Thomas and Peters 1996). As for recidivism, boot camp participants did not differ much from their control group counterparts, or worse, as in the case of Cleveland, youngsters in the experimental group recidivated at a higher rate than that of the control subjects. In Denver and Cleveland, it cost less to operate the boot camp programs than the traditional institutions, whereas in Mobile, the boot camp was more expensive than the control setting.

These studies have provided valuable information on how well boot camps can be adapted to the needs of juvenile correction systems, particularly those operated by local jurisdictions. One obvious question for the three

TABLE 15.1 *Boot Camp Evaluation Component Assessment*

	1 MacKenzie and Shaw 1990	2 MacKenzie and Parent 1991	3 Hunter, Burton, Marquart, and Cuvelier 1992	4 MacKenzie, Shaw, and Souryal 1992	5 Shaw and MacKenzie 1992	6 MacKenzie and Shaw 1993	7 Polsky and Fast 1993	8 Ransom and Mastrorilli 1993	9 Freeman 1993	10 Christenberry, Burns, and Dickinson 1994	11 MacKenzie and Piquero 1994	12 MacKenzie and Brame 1995	13 MacKenzie, Brame, McDowall, and Souryal 1995	14 MacKenzie and Souryal 1995	15 MacKenzie and Donaldson 1996	16 Benda, Toombs, and Whileside 1996	17 Bourque, Cronin, Pearson, Felker, Han, and Hill 1996	18 Peters 1996a (OJJDP-Mobile)	19 Peters 1996b (OJJDP-Denver)	20 Thomas and Peters 1996 (OJJDP-Cleveland)	21 Jones 1996	22 Anderson and Dyson 1996
Program type																						
Federal							×										×	×	×	×		
State	×	×		×	×	×		×		×	×	×	×	×	×	×						
County			×						×												×	×
Adult	×	×	×	×	×	×		×	×	×	×	×	×	×	×	×					×	×
Juvenile							×										×	×	×	×		

	1	2	3	4	5	6	7	8	9	10	11	12	13	14	15	16	17	18	19	20	21	22
Evaluation strategies																						
Quantitative																						
Random assignment																		×	×	×		
Eligible subjects	×			×	×	×						×	×								×	
Pre/post test			×						×	×							×					
Other		×									×					×						×
Qualitative							×	×							×							
Data gathering method																						
Official records	×	×	×	×	×	×			×	×	×	×	×	×	×	×	×	×	×	×	×	×
Field observations							×															
Self-reports														×	×							
Case study								×														
Outcome measures																						
Individual level																						
Rehabilitation																						
Attitude change	×		×					×	×					×	×		×					
Positive behaviour				×			×	×				×			×		×	×	×	×		
Recidivism					×	×							×			×		×	×	×	×	×
Drug education					×																	
Education										×							×	×	×	×		
System level																						
Reducing crowding		×									×											
Cost saving																		×	×	×		

counties is, Will these boot camps, some of which have produced promising results, continue in operation once the federal money runs out? This has been a problem for many treatment programs that have been launched by federal or state agencies and then terminated before enough information about their effectiveness could be accumulated. Even with these problems, the three OJJDP demonstration projects represent the only published evaluations of the efficacy of boot camps employing experimental designs.

SELECTION OF "ELIGIBLE" SUBJECTS FOR COMPARISON

True experimental designs are rarely employed in criminal justice research, where judicial officers usually oppose the "randomized administration of justice." Evaluation strategies often must be modified to accommodate the target program or be restricted because of inadequate funding. But the most serious threat to a research project is the inability of the administering agency to implement the program as originally designed or planned, thus compromising the integrity of the research design and opening the results to alternative interpretations. The three OJJDP demonstration boot camp evaluations offer apt examples of these problems.

Most of the evaluations in this review employed quasi-experimental designs involving the use of comparison subjects in lieu of control groups or statistical techniques to control for possible confounding variables. A large number of these studies, especially those by MacKenzie and her colleagues, typically used so-called eligible candidates (defined by the researchers) for comparison purposes. In a study on the characteristics associated with successful adjustment to supervision after boot camp treatment, MacKenzie, Shaw, and Souryal (1992) used three groups of offenders who were compared to the boot camp graduates: (1) parolees who had served time in a regular prison, (2) probationers, and (3) dropouts from the boot camp program. The justification for the inclusion of the first two types of offenders was that they met legal eligibility, suitability, and acceptability criteria set up by the correctional agency. An obvious question is, Why then were these "eligible" candidates not selected for the boot camp? A possible explanation is the discrepancy between the official criteria and the actual screening process, which was not examined in their study. The very fact that these individuals had not been selected implies that they were considered less eligible than those who had been, irrespective of the "official criteria." Not surprisingly, MacKenzie, Shaw, and Souryal (1992) reported major discrepancies between the boot camp participants and their comparison subjects in terms of age, age at first arrest, and criminal history. These same factors were later found to be associated with higher levels of recidivism and poorer behaviour during community supervision; thus the true effect of the boot camp experience remains unclear.

The inclusion of boot camp dropouts for comparison purposes (see MacKenzie, Shaw, and Souryal 1992; MacKenzie et al. 1995) is particularly troublesome. In most cases (except for medical reasons), these dropouts either terminated their participation due to personal objections to the militaristic structure and chose to serve their sentences in prison or were dismissed for disciplinary problems and therefore can hardly be considered comparable to those who finished the boot camp program.

INDIVIDUAL OUTCOME MEASURES — OFFICIAL DATA VERSUS SELF-REPORTS

Nearly all evaluations reviewed here relied solely on official records or information gathered by correctional agencies to measure recidivism, the most commonly used indicator of program effectiveness. With the exception of a few ethnographic studies, not a single study was found in which program participants were interviewed by independent researchers using self-report instruments. MacKenzie and Brame (1995: 114) acknowledged the limitation of relying exclusively on official records in current boot camp research and the importance of including self-report measures. However, it is not the case that boot camp participants have never responded to questions pertaining to their postprogram activities or attitudes. Several studies employed testing instruments administered by program officials to gather information on attitude changes and educational attainment during and/or after boot camp (Bourque et al. 1996; Shaw and MacKenzie 1992).

Self-report instruments to measure program effectiveness were used by MacKenzie, Shaw, and Souryal (1992) in their study of characteristics associated with successful adjustment to supervision in a Louisiana boot camp, and by MacKenzie and Brame (1995) in their analysis of community adjustment by boot camp participants in five states. In both studies, adjustment scales were constructed to measure employment, education, residential and financial stability, participation in treatment programs for drug abuse, and compliance with probation/parole conditions. However, rather than asking the offenders the questions directly, the researchers went to the community supervision (probation or parole) officers for the answers. In other words, the supervising officers were asked to report on their clients' performance. Although some measures were built into the instrument to assess the supervising officers' knowledge of the offenders' activities, these "self-reports" were in reality an extension of official records.

In short, our current knowledge of the impact of boot camps on recidivism comes from official sources. It is widely recognized that most criminal activities are neither detected nor acted upon by anyone in authority. The small fraction of crimes ever recorded may well contribute to the lack of significant findings about shock incarceration. Additionally, most evaluations track offenders for no longer than one year after the boot camp. Given the lag between the time of arrest and the time it is registered in the computer database, the actual observation period of these studies could be even shorter.

The point here is not to discredit the use of official data, but to illustrate the importance of including self-report measures to complement official statistics. Official data are easily accessible and inexpensive to compile, but they mainly reflect police activities. Self-report data, on the other hand, can provide much richer information on the issues of prevalence and incidence of criminal behaviour. Although not as systematic as official records, self-reports have been found to be a reliable source of information with a remarkable degree of consistency between self-reported answers and official data (Erickson and Empey 1963; Gibson, Morrison, and West 1970; Blackmore 1974; Reuter, MacCoun, and Murphy 1990).

Many useful self-report instruments are readily available. The International Self-Report Delinquency questionnaire (ISRD) is one example. This instrument, originally created by criminologists from fifteen Western countries, has gone through a series of empirical tests and is now considered methodologically sound (for a detailed discussion of it, see Junger-Tas, Terlouw, and Klein 1994). In addition, it has been used in Los Angeles and Omaha, where its validity and applicability to U.S. populations was demonstrated (Junger-Tas, Klein, and Zhang 1992). The instrument contains well-constructed items to measure (1) the types of delinquent acts committed during a specified time frame; (2) the frequency of these acts; (3) the onset of admitted offences; (4) the circumstances of the incidents; and (5) sociodemographic variables, including attitudes toward school and work, living arrangements, and circle of friends. Data uncovered by instruments such as this would be a valuable addition to official records.

System Impact and Individual Measures

Very few evaluations have examined the system goals that boot camp programs set out to accomplish. Shock incarceration emerged primarily as a response to prison crowding; but most published evaluations thus far have focused only on individual outcomes (i.e., recidivism, attitude, and behaviour change). Although recidivism patterns invariably may affect prison crowding, the effect is usually indirect and requires long-term evaluation (MacKenzie and Parent 1991).

Part of the methodological problem here may be due to the small size of most programs. To ease current prison crowding, boot camps must be large enough to have institutional impact. Except for the boot camps in New York state with a total average camp population of about 1500, few states operate programs that can be considered influential. In addition, many other factors also affect the impact of a boot camp on prison crowding: (1) the probability that participants would otherwise have been imprisoned; (2) the rate of program completion; (3) the difference between actual time served in prison and in boot camp; and (4) the rate of return to prison among inmates released from each type of program (Cronin 1994). Needless to say, collection of relevant data on these factors is a formidable task in program evaluation.

According to the U.S. General Accounting Office (1993), 11 out of 26 states operating boot camps in 1992 considered their programs helpful in reducing prison crowding. Although the cost of running boot camps rivalled that of traditional prisons in most states, New York, Georgia, Florida, and Louisiana reported significant savings from the use of boot camps. It is difficult to make meaningful comparisons among these agencies because of their different ways of accounting for savings and estimating prison crowding (Cronin 1994).

Due to the lack of computerized prison data from the past for comparison purposes, few independent studies have examined the direct impact on the correctional system of boot camps as currently designed and implemented. MacKenzie and Parent (1991) used a mathematical model to estimate the impact of the boot camp program on the Louisiana prison system and found modest bed-space savings. The same method was later repeated in a five-state evaluation (MacKenzie and Piquero 1994). Both studies affirmed that if boot camps were to reduce prison crowding, they must be carefully designed and administered with that purpose in mind. Furthermore, both studies raised the troublesome issue of "net widening" — extending shock incarceration to offenders who would otherwise have received a lesser punitive sentence, depending on who has the authority over placement (i.e., the sentencing judge or the correctional agency), boot camp programs vary significantly from state to state in the process of entry and exit decision making. Sentencing judges tend to use intermediate sanctions as an alternative to regular probation, but where correctional agencies control placement, more prison-bound offenders are likely to enter the program (Morris and Tonry 1990; MacKenzie and Souryal 1991). If program administrators cannot address the issue of enrolling participants who are truly prison-bound, then whatever system impact they claim is open to question.

Besides alleviating prison crowding and reducing costs, boot camps have also been established to offer safe but punitive alternatives to long-term incarceration. Currently all boot camps have mechanisms to discharge participants deemed unsuitable or to allow for voluntary exit (back to prison); thus they are safe to the extent that they are not releasing offenders into the community. However, the safety of program participants is a less clearly defined issue. Although physical dangers have not been reported in any study, some researchers have criticized the military drills as a potential source of abuse and as possibly detrimental to the offender's psychological well-being (Mathlas and Mathews 1991; Henggeler and Schoenwald 1994; MacKenzie and Donaldson 1996). Others have accused current boot camps of promoting misplaced masculinity and misogynistic attitudes (Morash and Rucker 1990). However, this critical rhetoric has not been supported by hard data. Obviously, more research attention should be directed at these system-level practices and goals in future studies.

MEASURING FAILURE OR SUCCESS

Definitive findings of success or failure as a result of shock incarceration are not likely to be produced. Mixed results often frustrate practitioners and policymakers who tend to discard equivocal findings as meaningless or irrelevant and retreat to their "gut feelings" or ideological convictions. To bridge the distance between researchers and practitioners, future studies should provide concrete guidance as to what can be reasonably expected from boot camps and what can be improved in the current intake and selection criteria, based on the characteristics associated with successful (not failed) program participants. In other words, instead of simply telling justice practitioners whether a boot camp works as a whole, researchers should produce specific suggestions as to where improvements can be made and what type of candidates are most likely to benefit from the program.

To identify these characteristics requires the use of both official records and self-report data. In each program, there are always participants who do not recidivate and who move on to become productive members of society. Few efforts have been made to examine the characteristics of these individuals or to provide profile information about the types of persons who are likely to succeed in a boot camp. Research focusing on such characteristics can generate far more useful information to practitioners to guide future program implementation. Such information would enable correctional officials to develop realistic expectations about their programs and their screening processes.

Program "effectiveness" should mean more than merely reducing recidivism, measured by most studies as arrests or parole revocations. Most current studies do not examine prosocial activities such as employment, schooling, drug treatment, or vocational training, thus leaving readers with the impression that the success or failure of a program is solely a matter of how many offenders continue to commit crimes. Also, little information is available about how varied use of one's social support network may lead to different levels of community reintegration. The involvement of offenders' family members in their correctional activities may prove to be more influential to their postprogram behaviour than any official intervention. This possibility is particularly likely in that most program participants are young adults. No studies thus far have included measures on the involvement of family members in boot camp treatment.

There are many factors to consider in the search for characteristics associated with successful graduates. They include the offender's sociodemographic background (e.g., age, race, education, living arrangement, education, general attitudes toward school and work, social network, employment, and income), prior criminal history (e.g., the number of prior arrests, the nature of the incident offence, prior contacts with welfare agencies for dependent or neglect status), and correctional history (e.g., the number of prior probation terms, jail/prison sentences, lengths, and any violations). These factors can provide far more specific profile characteristics of program participants than the current reliance on loosely conceived eligibility criteria, in which offenders are mainly distinguished from each other in terms of risk level (nature of incident offence and prior criminal history). These factors may enable us to better understand the type of youth for whom the boot camp structure is likely to be effective.

TREATMENT COMPONENTS AND NONPROGRAMMATIC FACTORS

Closely related to the task of identifying characteristics associated with successful and unsuccessful camp graduates is the delineation of the impact of different programmatic and nonprogrammatic components of boot camps on the outcomes. Many correctional intervention programs appear to share identical or similar treatment strategies; however, few researchers have been able to explain why some programs were effective while others were not (Palmer 1995). No one generic intervention approach is likely to be found to be very successful or unsuccessful because confounding factors external to the treatment usually have a significant impact on the outcome. In other words, the effect of any treatment program is determined by the interaction of programmatic elements such as behavioural modification, education/counselling, and life skills with nonprogrammatic factors such as staff/client interactions, setting, and flexible programming (Palmer 1995: 104).

Thus far, few studies have attempted to sketch out the connections between different components of a boot camp program and their outcomes, and even fewer have considered the relevance of nonprogrammatic factors. Most boot camp programs contain components that are not much different from traditional interventions — group/individual counselling, education, and vocational training. Successful examples of these traditional treatment models do exist. For instance, in his literature review covering more than 400 experimental studies from 1975 to 1989, Palmer (1991) found that, using a $p < .05$ criterion, experimental programs outperformed control programs in 25 to 35 percent of all studies, whereas control programs led in less than 10 percent. Clearly, some interventions under some circumstances have worked; the central question in evaluation research is *which* ones have produced positive effects (Palmer 1995).

It is also important to conduct systematic examination of nonprogrammatic factors and conditions that are capable of influencing program outcomes irrespective of the particular generic treatment approach (Palmer 1995). For example, using the same self-report index developed by MacKenzie and Shaw (1990), McCorkle (1995) found that both boot camp participants and their prison comparison inmates became more prosocial, raising doubts about the necessity of the military atmosphere to improve behaviour and suggesting that the attitudinal improvement was likely due to factors extraneous to the boot camp program (e.g., staff competence and commitment, program integrity, and the timing of intervention).

External factors may help explain why some programs had a positive influence on certain offenders whereas others did not. Palmer (1995) classified these factors into four categories: (1) staff characteristics (e.g., personal styles, volunteers/professionals, commitment, and competence); (2) quality of staff/client interactions (e.g., surveillance, control, and self-expression); (3) individual differences among offenders (personalities and maturity levels); and (4) program settings (e.g., institutional, noninstitutional, and direct parole). For instance, Jesness (1975) found that positive changes occurred more often when the delinquents felt positive toward staff, whereas Kelly and Baer (1971) found that delinquents reacting to situational stress associated with their developmental stage (e.g., identity crisis) were more responsive to a wilderness program than those who were immature and/or emotionally disturbed.

Clearly, it is not enough to study program components alone and examine how they might produce certain outcomes. Palmer's review (1995) offered an excellent guide for future studies on specific programmatic and nonprogrammatic factors to be included in a systematic manner. The task of identifying effective combinations of treatment components and nonprogrammatic factors may appear formidable. Aside from the many treatment strategies, the four areas of nonprogrammatic factors each consist of numerous features or variables. The complexities involved in the search for successful combinations require researchers to develop clear and precise conceptual frameworks on which systematic data items and assessment strategies can be plotted.

This review suggests a conceptual framework that views a boot camp program as a multifaceted intervention process composed of operational goals and treatments that are implemented by a staff with varying personalities and professional qualifications. The program goals and strategies, as well as nonprogrammatic factors, all interact with the characteristics of the delinquents. In this conceptual framework, the effectiveness of boot camp treatment is mediated by two main variables — individual differences and nonprogrammatic factors. On one hand, it is likely that boot camp programs are more likely to produce successful outcomes when there is a high level of program integrity (consistency in treatment activities) and when involved staff are well trained and motivated, and when the staff–client interactions are positive. The nonprogrammatic factors are further divided into two phases — in-camp and aftercare. The aftercare phase involves nonprogrammatic factors that are slightly different from the in-camp ones, in which family interactions, social support network, and community environment may play an important role in treatment effectiveness. On the other hand, individual factors such as prior history, substance abuse, and the age of onset may combine to influence the effectiveness of boot camp treatment. However, neither set of variables (individual and nonprogrammatic) functions independently of the other; instead, they are expected to have interactive effects on program outcomes.

CONCLUSION

Findings of current boot camp studies are complicated and difficult to interpret. Much more research needs to be undertaken with greater use of different methodological approaches and analytical strategies to firm up our understanding of boot camps as compared to traditional incarceration. These approaches and strategies include the use of both official records and self-reports that can examine both programmatic and nonprogrammatic factors as related to different aspects of the boot camps. The search for information to explicate the functions of different program components and explain why some offenders succeed whereas others fail requires researchers to resist the temptation to address the simple question: "Do boot camps work?" Such a blanket question increases the chances of drawing misleading and simplistic conclusions, which will in turn lead either to summarily dismissing or to unduly extolling boot camps as a treatment option.

It is hoped that future studies can generate a set of guidelines for administrators as to what type of participants to look for and what can be reasonably accomplished. To this end, they will not only contribute to our currently scarce knowledge on boot camps in general but also provide practical and policy-relevant information to correctional agencies.

This chapter has focused mainly on methodological issues in current boot camp research but has *not* claimed that boot camp outcomes will somehow drastically change if we include the alternative strategies as discussed earlier; nor has it suggested that the current lack of consistent findings results solely from inadequate research designs. It is possible that the lack of clear findings (positive or negative) may result from the fact that boot camps, as currently designed and implemented, are indeed not consistently effective. The discussion here only called attention to the aspects and strategies that have largely been neglected thus far in boot camp research, and claimed that informed conclusions about the effectiveness of boot camp programs should only be made by taking a more holistic approach in evaluation research designs.

Another issue, which is beyond the scope of this study but which deserves serious attention from researchers, is the relative absence of theoretical guidance behind most current boot camp research. None of the studies reviewed here set out to measure any theory-based outcomes. The question is not why boot camps, as evaluated thus far, have failed to produce successful outcomes, but rather why we should expect them to be effective in the first place. Lacking a clear conceptualization of what effects different components of boot camp programs are supposed to produce and how they are supposed to produce them, most evaluation studies thus far have relied on "commonsense" criteria for outcome measures.

Theory-guided research that illuminates the logical connection between the deployment of certain treatment strategies and their expected outcomes is required. All criminological theories have some implications for criminal justice policy, and conversely, most correctional practices are based on, either explicitly or implicitly, some understanding of human behaviour. Unfortunately, as Ronald Akers poignantly pointed out (1996: 11), "in most public discourse about criminal justice policy, the underlying theoretical notions are ill-stated and vaguely understood. A policy may be adopted for political, economic, or bureaucratic reasons, then a theoretical rationale is formulated or adopted to justify the policy." As a consequence, a program may be driven by no single coherent theory but instead by an admixture of several or even conflicting theoretical positions.

All of the boot camp programs surveyed by MacKenzie and Souryal (1991) had multiple goals at both system and individual levels. Obviously it would require a very comprehensive theory to accommodate or explain goal compatibility across the system and individual levels. For instance, the top three goals in these surveyed boot camp programs were rehabilitation, recidivism reduction, and drug education, which were not much different from the goals of most correctional efforts in the past few decades, the only difference being in the delivery mechanism — the paramilitary environment. Without theory-guided evaluations, our understanding of boot camps as a treatment model will probably remain limited and our conclusions questionable, because we cannot divine why the many components of the program are placed together and how they interact to produce the results we have found.

At a philosophical level, boot camps as now operated run counter to the current climate of opinion about criminal justice practices. Because politicians advocate "tough" treatment for criminals, and correctional officials want to "straighten out" offenders in a regimented environment, one would expect the deterrence doctrine to be the theoretical pillar of current boot camp treatment. In reality, the deterrent effect, if any, must be minimal in that most programs allow voluntary exit for participants and the rest simply expel problematic participants. If politicians and practitioners expect boot camps to be effective, then the experience of a boot camp must be unpleasant so that offenders will not want to recidivate.

On the other hand, most descriptions of boot camp programs suggest that they are driven by one or both of two criminological theories: (1) control theory (Gottfredson and Hirschi 1990), which centres on weak self-control over deviant impulses as a result of inadequate or poor training in early childhood; and (2) social learning theory, which focuses on differential identification and reinforcement, which fosters conformity (Akers 1996). Most program administrators would agree that the military environment and its regimented activities are designed to instill discipline and respect for authority in offenders and reinforce self-control over criminal impulses and that the social learning process, with its drills and emphasis on group success over individual needs, prepares participants for the transition toward a more prosocial lifestyle after graduation.

The argument for theory-guided research may not resonate with practitioners, in that utility and pragmatism, not theoretical relevancy, are their focal concerns. There may also be practical or ethical obstacles against carrying out the actions that testing a theory may require (Akers 1996). There may be political or economic factors that come into play to enhance or retard the efforts needed to change criminal behaviour, reduce recidivism, or make the system operate better. Still, these issues should not reduce the importance of applying theoretical guidance to the designs of boot camp research, and a holistic approach in assessing boot camps should also include theoretical constructs. As Palmer (1995) pointed out, a holistic approach in an evaluation strategy would require long-term, multistudy research projects focusing on nonprogrammatic as well as programmatic factors in an effort to determine the specific combinations of treatment modalities that lead to the most successful outcomes.

STUDY QUESTIONS

1. *What have studies carried out in the United States found about the effects of boot camps on young offenders?*
2. *What are the different evaluation strategies and data-gathering methods that researchers have used in their attempt to evaluate the effectiveness of boot camps?*
3. *Why has the research carried out on boot camps so far been unable to draw any clear conclusions about their effectiveness in preventing youth crime? What type of research would need to be carried out in order to more adequately evaluate the effectiveness of boot camps in preventing youth crime?*

REFERENCES

Akers, Ronald L. 1996. *Criminological Theories: Introduction and Evaluation.* Los Angeles: Roxbury.

Anderson, James F., and Laronistine Dyson. 1996. "A Tracking Investigation to Determine Boot Camp Success and Offender Risk Assessment for CRIPP Participants." *Journal of Crime and Justice 19*: 170–90.

Austin, James, Michael Jones, and Melissa Bolyard. 1993. "The Growing Use of Jail Boot Camps: The Current State of the Art." *National Institute of Justice Research in Brief* (October). Washington, DC: U.S. Department of Justice.

Benda, Brent B., Nancy J. Toombs, and Leanne Whiteside. 1996. "Recidivism among Boot Camp Graduates: A Comparison of Drug Offenders to Other Offenders." *Journal of Criminal Justice 24*(3): 241–53.

Blackmore, John. 1974. "The Relationship between Self-Reported Delinquency and Official Convictions amongst Adolescent Boys." *British Journal of Criminology 14*: 172–76.

Bourque, Blair B., Roberta C. Cronin, Frank R. Pearson, Daniel B. Felker, Mei Han, and Sarah M. Hill. 1996. "Boot Camps for Juvenile Offenders: An Implementation Evaluation of Three Demonstration Programs." *National Institute of Justice Research in Brief.* Washington, DC: U.S. Department of Justice.

Byrne, James M., Arthur J. Lurigio, and Joan Petersilia, eds. 1992. *Smart Sentencing: The Emergence of Intermediate Sanctions.* Newbury Park, CA: Sage.

Christenberry, Nola J., John L. Burns, and Gerald B. Dickinson. 1994. "Gains in Educational Achievement by Inmates during the Arkansas Prison Boot Camp Program." *Journal of Correctional Education* 45(3): 128–32.

Cronin, Roberta C. 1994. *Boot Camps for Adult and Juvenile Offenders: Overview and Update*. Washington, DC: U.S. National Institute of Justice.

Erickson, Maynard L., and LaMar T. Empey. 1963. "Court Records, Undetected Delinquency, and Decision-Making." *Journal of Criminal Law, Criminology and Police Science 54*: 456–69.

Freeman, Loyal W. 1993. "Boot Camp and Inmate Moral Development: No Significant Effect." *Journal of Offender Rehabilitation 19*: 123–27.

Gettinger, Stephen. 1983. "Assessing Criminal Justice Needs." *National Institute of Justice — Research in Brief*. Rockville, MD: National Criminal Justice Reference Service.

Gibson, H.B., Sylvia Morrison, and D.J. West. 1970. "The Confession of Known Offenses in Response to a Self-Reported Delinquency Schedule." *British Journal of Criminology 10*: 277–80.

Gotttredson, Michael R., and Travis Hirschi. 1990. *A General Theory of Crime*. Palo Alto, CA: Stanford University Press.

Henggeler, Scott W., and Songja K. Schoenwald. 1994. "Boot Camps for Juvenile Offenders: Just Say No." *Journal of Child and Family Studies 3*: 243–48.

Hunter, Robert J., Velmer S. Burton, James W. Marquart, and Steven J. Cuvelier. 1992. "Measuring Attitudinal Change of Boot Camp Participants." *Journal of Contemporary Criminal Justice 8*: 283–98.

Jesness, Carl F. 1975. "Comparative Effectiveness of Behavior Modification and Transactional Analysis Programs for Delinquents." *Journal of Consulting and Clinical Psychology 43*: 758–79.

Jones, Mark. 1996. "Do Boot Camp Graduates Make Better Probationers?" *Journal of Crime and Justice 19*: 1–14.

Junger-Tas, Josine, Malcolm W. Klein, and Xiaodong Zhang. 1992. "Problems and Dilemmas in Comparative Self-Report Delinquency Research." In D.P. Farrington and S. Walklate, eds., *Offenders and Victims: Theory and Policy*, 83–103. London: British Society of Criminology and the Institute for the Study and Treatment of Delinquency.

Junger-Tas, Josine, Gert-Jan Terlouw, and Malcolm W. Klein. 1994. *Delinquent Behavior among Youngsters in the Western World*. Amsterdam: Kugler.

Kelly, Francis J., and Daniel J. Baer. 1971. "Physical Challenge as a Treatment for Delinquency." *Crime & Delinquency 17*: 437–47.

MacKenzie, Doris Layton. 1993. "Boot Camp Prisons in 1993." *National Institute of Justice Journal* (November): 21–28.

MacKenzie, Doris Layton, and Robert Brame. 1995. "Shock Incarceration and Positive Adjustment During Community Supervision." *Journal of Quantitative Criminology 11*(2): 111–41.

MacKenzie, Doris Layton, Robert Brame, David McDowall, and Claire Souryal. 1995. "Boot Camp Prisons and Recidivism in Eight States." *Criminology 33*(3): 327–57.

MacKenzie, Doris Layton, and Heidi Donaldson. 1996. "Boot Camp for Women Offenders." *Criminal Justice Review 21*(1): 21–43.

MacKenzie, Doris Layton, and Dale Parent. 1991. "Shock Incarceration and Prison Crowding in Louisiana." *Journal of Criminal Justice 19*: 225–37.

MacKenzie, Doris Layton, and Alex Piquero. 1994. "The Impact of Shock Incarceration Programs on Prison Crowding." *Crime & Delinquency 40*(2): 222–49.

MacKenzie, Doris Layton, and James W. Shaw. 1990. "Inmate Adjustment and Change During Shock Incarceration: The Impact of Correctional Boot Camp Programs." *Justice Quarterly 7*: 125–49.

———. 1993. "The Impact of Shock Incarceration on Technical Violations and New Criminal Activities." *Justice Quarterly 10*(3): 463–87.

MacKenzie, Doris Layton, James W. Shaw, and Claire Souryal. 1992. "Characteristics Associated with Successful Adjustment to Supervision — A Comparison of Parolees, Probationers, Shock Participants, and Shock Dropouts." *Criminal Justice and Behavior 19*: 437–54.

MacKenzie, Doris Layton, and Claire Souryal. 1991. "National Survey — An Overview of Boot Camp Goals." *Corrections Today 53*(6): 90–96.

———. 1994. *Multisite Evaluation of Shock Incarceration.* Washington, DC: U.S. National Institute of Justice.

———. 1995. "Inmates' Attitude Change during Incarceration: A Comparison of Boot Camp with Traditional Prison." *Justice Quarterly 12*: 325–53.

Mathlas, Rudolf E.S., and James W. Mathews. 1991. "The Boot Camp Program for Offenders: Does the Shoe Fit?" *International Journal of Offender Therapy and Comparative Criminology 35*(4): 322–26.

McCorkle, Richard C. 1995. "Correctional Boot Camps and Attitudinal Change: Is All This Shouting Necessary? A Research Note." *Justice Quarterly 12*(2): 365–75.

Morash, Merry, and Lila Rucker. 1990. "A Critical Look at the Idea of Boot Camp as a Correctional Reform." *Crime & Delinquency 36*: 204–22.

Morris, Norval, and Michael Tonry. 1990. *Between Prison and Probation — Intermediate Punishments in a Rational Sentencing System.* New York: Oxford University Press.

National Council on Crime and Delinquency. 1992. *Criminal Justice Sentencing Policy Statement.* San Francisco: Author.

Office of Juvenile Justice and Delinquency Prevention. 1992. *National Juvenile Custody Trends, 1978–1989.* Washington, DC: U.S. Department of Justice.

Palmer, Ted. 1991. "The Effectiveness of Intervention: Recent Trends and Current Issues." *Crime & Delinquency 37*: 330–46.

———. 1995. "Programmatic and Nonprogrammatic Aspects of Successful Intervention: New Directions for Research." *Crime & Delinquency 41*(1): 100–31.

Parent, Dale. 1989. *Shock Incarceration: An Overview of Existing Programs.* Washington, DC: U.S. Department of Justice.

Peters, Michael. 1996a. *Evaluation of the Impact of Boot Camps for Juvenile Offenders — Mobile Interim Report.* Washington, DC: U.S. Department of Justice, Office of Juvenile Justice and Delinquency Prevention.

———. 1996b. *Evaluation of the Impact of Boot Camps for Juvenile Offenders — Denver Interim Report.* Washington, DC: U.S. Department of Justice, Office of Juvenile Justice and Delinquency Prevention.

Polsky, Howard, and Jonathan Fast. 1993. "Boot Camps, Juvenile Offenders, and Culture Shock." *Child and Youth Care Forum 22*: 403–15.

Ransom, George, and Mary Ellen Mastrorilli. 1993. "The Massachusetts Boot Camp: Inmate Anecdotes." *The Prison Journal 73*: 307–18.

Reuter, Peter, Robert MacCoun, and Patrick Murphy. 1990. *Money From Crime: A Study of the Economics of Drug Dealing in Washington, D.C.* Santa Monica, CA: RAND.

Shaw, James W., and Doris Layton MacKenzie. 1992. "The One-Year Community Supervision Performance of Drug Offenders and Louisiana DOC-Identified Substance Abusers Graduating from Shock Incarceration." *Journal of Criminal Justice 20*(6): 501–16.

Souryal, Claire, and Doris Layton MacKenzie. 1995. "Shock Incarceration and Recidivism: An Examination of Boot Camp Programs in Four States." In J. Smykla and W. Selke, eds., *Intermediate Sanctions: Sentencing in the 1990s*, 57–87. Cincinnati: Anderson.

Thomas, David, and Michael Peters. 1996. *Evaluation of the Impact of Boot Camps for Juvenile Offenders — Cleveland Interim Report.* Washington, DC: U.S. Department of Justice, Office of Juvenile Justice and Delinquency Prevention.

U.S. Bureau of Justice Statistics. 1996. *Prison and Jail Inmates, 1995.* Washington, DC: U.S. Government Printing Office.

U.S. General Accounting Office. 1993. Prison Boot Camps: Short-Term Prison Costs Reduced, But Long-Term Impact Uncertain. Washington, DC: Author.

READER REPLY CARD

We are interested in your reaction to *Youth Crime: Varieties, Theories, and Prevention*, by Russell C. Smandych. You can help us to improve this book in future editions by completing this questionnaire.

1. What was your reason for using this book?

☐ university course ☐ college course ☐ continuing education course
☐ professional development ☐ personal interest ☐ other____________________
____

2. If you are a student, please identify your school and the course in which you used this book.

3. Which chapters or parts of this book did you use? Which did you omit?

4. What did you like best about this book? What did you like least?

5. Please identify any topics you think should be added to future editions.

6. Please add any comments or suggestions.

7. May we contact you for further information?

Name: ____

Address: ____

____

Phone: ____

E-mail: ____

(fold here and tape shut)

MAIL POSTE

Canada Post Corporation / Société canadienne des postes

Postage paid If mailed in Canada

Port payé si posté au Canada

Business Reply

Réponse d'affaires

0116870399 01

0116870399-M8Z4X6-BR01

Larry Gillevet
Director of Product Development
HARCOURT CANADA
55 HORNER AVENUE
TORONTO, ONTARIO
M8Z 9Z9